D0761162

The Art of Democracy

The Art of Democracy

A Concise History
of Popular Culture
in the United States

Jim Cullen

Monthly Review Press
New York

Grateful acknowledgment is made to the following for permission to use photographs and artwork: p. 11, William Claxton; p. 19, American Antiquarian Society; p. 35, Houghton Library, Harvard University; p. 41, Harvard Theatre Collection; p. 56, Harry T. Peters Collection, Museum of the City of New York, originally published by N. Currier, 1849; p. 78, photograph by Gurney & Son, New York, Sophia Smith Collection, Smith College; p. 91, Harvard Theatre Collection; p. 122, Harvard Theatre Collection;   p. 129, photograph by Adolph Witteman, Leonard Hassam Bogart Collection, Museum of the City of New York; p. 135, Photofest; p. 149, Film Stills, Museum of Modern Art; p. 184, Frank Driggs Collection; p. 195, Photofest; p. 209, Photofest; p. 246, photo by Fredrik Nilsen, Slash/Warner Brothers Records; p. 257, Discovery Channel Multimedia; p. 262, MTV Networks, a division of Viacom International, Inc., © 1982 MTV Networks.

Library of Congress Cataloging-in-Publication Data
Cullen, Jim, 1962-
    The art of democracy : a concise history of popular culture in
the United States / Jim Cullen.
            p.   cm.
    Includes bibliographical references and index.
    ISBN 0-85345-919-3 (cloth). — ISBN 0-85345-920-7 (paper)
    1. Popular culture—United States—History. I. Title.
E161.C85 1995
306'.0973—dc20   95-12965
                                                            CIP

Monthly Review Press
122 West 27th Street
New York, NY 10001

Manufactured in the United States of America
10 9 8 7 6 5 4 3 2 1

For
MARI JO and **PAUL BUHLE,**
mentors

Contents

Acknowledgments

A few words of thanks:

Jack Thomas and Susan Smulyan of Brown University discussed and read drafts of this book, and encouraged many of the ideas in it. John Ameer, formerly of the Harvard Graduate School of Education, invited me to discuss my arguments with students there, which helped refine my thinking. Nancy Sizer took time out from her manifold projects to give me a careful layperson's reading and numerous useful suggestions.

At Monthly Review Press, Susan Lowes exhibited acute intelligence and heartening enthusiasm throughout the writing process, while Akiko Ichikawa did a marvelous job of assembling the photos and Renee Pendergrass did the elegant design of the cover and text.

My wife, Lyde Cullen Sizer, remained my faithful editor and companion. My son, James Faust Cullen, showed me on a daily basis that popular culture is only one of life's pleasures.

This book is dedicated to Mari Jo and Paul Buhle, whose scholarship, teaching, and almost palpable sense of decency embody some of the most noble traditions in U.S. history. I am indebted to them in ways that can only be repaid to others.

Introduction

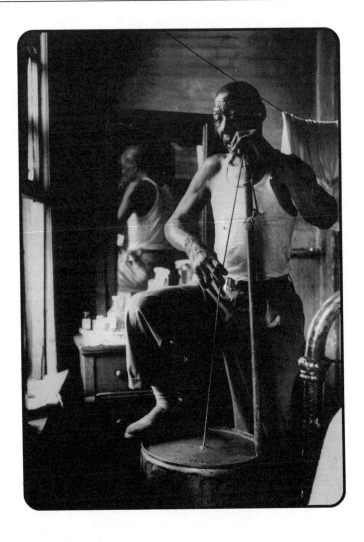

THE ART OF DEMOCRACY was written as an introductory history of the U.S. experience with popular culture, an experience that shares important parallels with other societies, but one that has had a unique trajectory and global influence. There has long been a need for this kind of book for the scholar, student, and general reader.

One reason for this need is that popular culture has only recently been considered a subject for serious scholarly inquiry. For most of this century, it has been denigrated by intellectuals of all ideological stripes as either meaningless escapism or a dangerous narcotic.[1] While such views are not altogether lacking in validity—one need not defend popular culture by arguing for its universal excellence—they seriously underestimate the complexity and relevance of those arts most passionately embraced by ordinary working people and their families. The escapist argument, for example, begs questions of where people escape *from,* where they escape *to,* the varied *choices* they make in their means of escape, and what those choices reveal about them and the world in which they live. The narcotic argument, by contrast, overlooks the often desperate uncertainty that marks the products peddled by corporate culture lords to a presumably gullible public, as reports of any recent box-office flop will attest. But if the study of popular culture is surrounded by a great deal of uncertainty, even mystery, it also affords valuable clues—about collective fears, hopes, and debates.

Indeed, even if one assumes the worst about popular culture, the attention and affection it receives merit explanation, which is why labor historians were among the first to explore the popular arts in any detail. So were more theoretically minded writers keenly attuned to the gaps in the visions of preceding generations of intellectuals. At its best, such work testified to the democratic spirit that has animated U.S. scholarship since the 1960s.

This book grew out my own first-hand experiences with popular culture and my frustration with the burgeoning literature I read to enhance my understanding of it (if the problem had once been scarcity, it now seems to be one of dizzying abundance). My irritation was not so much that this literature was boring or lacked insight; often the opposite was true. But much of it was fragmented into discrete media or time periods, riddled with obscure jargon, or governed by theoretical concerns that overshadowed the materials being analyzed. Again, much of this literature was—and remains—valuable,

---

Reverse page: "Will Shade with His Tub Bass, Memphis, 1960," one of jazz photographer William Claxton's photographs of the jazz scene in the 1950s and 1960s.

and this is especially true of professional scholarship since the 1980s. My goal here has been to synthesize that scholarship and put a simple analytical frame around it.

The book was written to proceed in a loosely chronological fashion, although it need not be read that way. Actually, my hope is that in addition to providing a coherent narrative, it will serve as a reference that can be consulted after (or instead of) being read from cover to cover. To facilitate additional study, I have included brief bibliographic essays for each chapter. Some of these sources, of course, were used in more than one chapter, and when appropriate are cited in each. More specific sources are cited in the notes, which I have tried to streamline for the sake of brevity and readability.

The focus of the book will be on mass-produced texts (a term that encompasses novels and periodicals, as well as plays, films, television shows, and other media) intended for large audiences to enjoy in their spare time. This textual approach allows me to narrow an otherwise unmanageably large field of study. At the same time, I know—as should any reader—that popular culture can be defined more broadly to include festivals, rituals, handicrafts, and other cultural practices. (I consider these to fall within the realm of folk culture, which will be discussed in Chapter 1.) Perhaps the most obvious omission from the book is sports, a highly visible aspect of everyday life notable for its ability to cross class and racial lines. But sports is a world unto itself, divided by particular games and amateur, professional, and scholastic sectors that would be too unwieldy to survey. And so while I may not cover all areas of popular culture, I invite the reader to draw parallels between what I do discuss here and what I do not. Indeed, the patterns I describe and their implications may ultimately be more important than any specific material covered.

Even those media discussed here are treated in an abbreviated way. To deal with them comprehensively would lead to progressively larger and more unwieldy chapters as new forms are introduced and older ones diversify, defeating my overriding goal of writing a streamlined one-volume history. Instead, I have chosen to focus on those forms (and genres, or distinct styles within forms, like jazz in music or Westerns in literature or film) that are crucial to a particular period. In the late eighteenth and early nineteenth centuries, for example, literary forms, especially the novel, were of decisive importance. In the middle of the nineteenth century, theater and minstrel shows reflected important changes in popular culture specifically and in U.S. society generally. Movies transformed virtually all the popular arts at the turn of this century; computer technology is doing the same in the transition to the next. Such stories—and the commonalities between them—are the building blocks for the chapters that follow.

Another organizational (and ideological) strategy is demographic. Although this is an elusive and imprecise matter, I tried to keep my attention on working-class people and the issues, artists, and documents that have mattered most to them. So, for example, I have done relatively little with magazines (a largely middle-class affair), except in the case of those (like dime novels) whose working-class orientation was clear.

A bottom-up approach to cultural history also has important racial ramifications. Despite their status as members of an oppressed minority, African Americans have invented, elaborated, or inspired more popular culture than any other racial or ethnic group in the nation's history. Their achievements figure prominently in the stories that follow.

A question that often looms over assessments of cultural phenomena in a society is whether those phenomena reflect or shape historical forces. Was the emergence of rock & roll a spur to the nascent Civil Rights movement or a sign that a movement with roots in the 1940s (or earlier) was having a discernible effect? Empirically, the question is impossible to answer. I'm inclined to think, however, that ideas do have consequences, and that popular culture has at least potential power to change hearts, minds, and behavior. Here, then, is one more reason to explore it. Indeed, even if one concludes that ideas are not the engine of history, the study of popular culture can be usefully employed as a pulse-taking measure.

Four recurrent ideas provide the thematic glue for the book. The first is this: that new forms of popular culture are almost always resisted by elites. From the proliferation of novels read by white women in the late eighteenth century to the proliferation of rap songs listened to by black men in the late twentieth century, there have been consistent—and strikingly similar—criticisms of those who make and use such forms. The argument that popular culture expresses the brazen excesses of urban life, seduces and corrupts young people who need to be quarantined from it, and functions as an enervating substitute for more "serious" forms of culture is made again and again in a variety of contexts (most recently in presidential elections). The repetition is unwitting but suggests class, racial, gender, and other ideological interests that are often a smokescreen for the more frankly political interests in some way threatened by popular culture. Such concerns should not be dismissed out of hand; to say that popular culture cannot have potentially negative effects also denies its potentially positive effects and thus negates its power altogether. Of course, some popular culture *is* repellent and even dangerous, and I will note it as such as this history unfolds. At the same time, it seems to me that far too much energy has been expended on moralistic judgments at the expense of an attempt to understand why particular works and forms command the allegiances they do.

The second theme of the book is that new cultural forms often move up the cultural ladder over time. That novels went from being the most despised form of western culture to the most exalted in the space of a century—a transformation often overlooked by readers, writers, and critics alike—suggests a kind of collective amnesia that can be dispelled only by looking to history. In the twentieth century alone, immigrant-oriented "movies" became intensively studied "films"; jazz changed from a mass cultural phenomenon to a modernist avocation of aficionados; and the perception of television shifted from a wasteland to a fertile field of social meanings. Such developments can be explained as an elite co-optation of working-class forms, as a belated recognition of the artistic power of culture rooted in working-class concerns, or both. In any case, a historical perspective helps remind us that no form of culture is the sole province of any group of people, and that signs of migration from one constituency to another can provide valuable indications of other shifts taking place within U.S. society. These shifts also demonstrate that aesthetic values are rooted more in historical circumstances than in transcendent objective values, and that cultural hierarchies are never pure or invulnerable to change.

A third theme relates to a particularistic/universal dialectic in popular culture. As the succeeding chapters will suggest, different forms and texts originated in highly specific milieux: white working-class politics in the Jacksonian era, African-American communities in the aftermath of slavery, leisure practices in rural communities on the cusp of industrialization, and so on. These settings gave each new kind of popular culture a very distinctive flavor. At the same time, almost by definition, the most resonant popular culture becomes emblematic of the society as a whole, connecting disparate and even hostile constituencies. Perhaps the best example of this is the minstrel show, a hugely popular white cultural form that grew out of a peculiar fascination with pre-Civil War slave life. In the twentieth century, U.S. movies, which have been the product of a singular array of social, political, and economic conditions, are often nevertheless seen as having universal appeal—which in some narrow sense they probably do. But the passage of time (and the waning of U.S. imperial power) will also no doubt make increasingly clear how historically rooted—and limited—they have been.

The last and perhaps most important theme I wish to present to readers is what I call the "hardware/software" metaphor, a term that evokes the crucial role of technology in popular culture in general and the centrality of computers in contemporary U.S. society in particular. Repeatedly, I have found, new cultural forms are generated and changed by elites with access to capital and technical know-how, resources quickly funneled into commercial purposes. Printing presses, movie projectors, recording equipment, and other forms of "hardware" are usually introduced at the top of the U.S. economic structure and diffuse downward as part of an often mad scramble for private profit. But after an initial melee, it becomes increasingly apparent that the economic—and, especially, cultural—viability of these forms actually depends on content, or "software": the particular books, movies, and records that win large audiences. This is important because ordinary working people are the key to those large audiences—they are what makes *popular* culture truly popular. Perhaps even more important is that unlike the labor market, residential patterns, local government, and other sites of everyday life, popular culture affords a unique degree of economic, social, and even political access for those otherwise marginalized in U.S. society. The success of "damned female scribblers" (as an envious Nathaniel Hawthorne called popular women novelists), African-American musicians, and ethnic stage and screen performers testifies to an unusual degree of diversity, mobility, and ferment in a divided populace.

This, ultimately, is why I decided to title the book "The Art of Democracy." Certainly, there is plenty about U.S. culture that is less than altogether democratic (its ruthlessly exploitative commercial structure, its tendency to dominate cultural discourse abroad) and plenty that illustrates the worst aspects of democracy (mindless pandering, compromise to the point of diluting real change). For these reasons, a title like "The Art of Democracy" can be read as bitterly ironic, and such a reading is one whose partial legitimacy I cannot deny.

In the final analysis, however, I find myself focusing on how full the bottle is, not how empty. In terms of enriching everyday life, opening windows on alternative ways of life, and providing intellectual and emotional experiences that offer incalculable surplus value beyond a material plane, popular culture has enriched countless lives. It has also been an exceptionally effective means of describing what one scholar has called the "hurts of history."[2] Despite disenfranchisement, discrimination, and the most basic denials of the pursuit of happiness, popular culture has given a voice to the oppressed and generated dialogues that have been heard all around the world. This book seeks to preserve its best aspects and to furnish a truly usable past for the popular culture of the future.

1

Novel Approaches:
The Rise
of Popular Culture

PERHAPS THE SIMPLEST, though not the most precise, way to begin telling the story of popular culture in the United States is to state that it did not exist until the nineteenth century. That is because (as I will be defining it in the next few pages) popular culture depends on the existence of a modern working class to use it, as well as to play a pivotal role in creating it. The phenomena we think of as "modern"—urbanization, mass migration, technological innovation, and other elements of the Industrial Revolution—reached a kind of critical mass in the three decades after 1800. The cultural explosion that resulted will be explored in some detail in the next chapter.

But popular culture was not the result of spontaneous combustion. It had clear lines of origin, and in retrospect we can see the various elements converging, and even taking a recognizable form, well before 1800. These converging lines will be the focus of this introductory chapter.

The cultural landscape of any civilization at any time is lush with artistic forms. For all this diversity, however, it is possible—at least in the West before the eighteenth century—to divide these cultures into two categories: elite and folk. Elite culture is official culture. It is the art produced for (and often by) the rich and powerful. Elite culture usually draws on the most valuable material resources available at any given time, as well as on the talents of individuals deemed most successful at producing artifacts for the enjoyment of the privileged. Elite culture is also often designed to demonstrate the authority of those who support it, authority not only to determine what beauty is but also to project political power—as in monumental sculptures to a ruler. In earlier times this was the art of the palace, the court, and its administrative apparatus. Elite culture is still a part of contemporary societies, often supported by corporations and the national state.

Folk culture, by contrast, is the culture of ordinary working people. It is intensely local, and it relies on readily available materials and on techniques that, in theory at least, can be practiced by almost anyone. Folk art is not concerned with projecting the power of the state. In some cases, it seems to acquiesce to the authority of a ruling class; in others, it subtly subverts that authority. Occasionally, folk art even challenges authority directly. In any case, folk culture derives from a different set of social, economic, and political interests than elite culture, interests that often conflict with it.

Reverse page: Frontispiece, Amelia: or the Faithless Briton. An Original American Novel *(1798). A typical novel of the period,* Amelia *depicts an innocent woman who, seduced and abandoned by a British soldier who fathers her child, is finally redeemed by her father's forgiveness.*

This is not to say that there is no interaction between the two, or that any particular artistic form is *inherently* either elite or folk. Indeed, some art—Italian opera, for example—migrates over a period of time from one camp to the other as works or forms lose their cachet and diffuse to the masses, or as elites develop an interest in folk arts and appropriate them for their own use. The blurring of such lines might well lead one to question the value of the distinction at all. I make it, however, to highlight the very real differences in the creation, use, and meaning of art that are the result of people living in different material circumstances.

Essentially, popular culture is a modern offshoot of folk culture. Like folk culture—which continues to exist to this day in rich traditions of handicrafts and communal rituals that range from ethnic cuisines to community parades—popular culture relies on plentiful materials and common techniques and values. The difference is that popular culture is refracted (and magnified) through the prism of mass production. One historian more elegantly defined popular culture as the "folklore of industrial society."[1] "Industrial society" is used here as shorthand for a series of social changes that began appearing in Europe during the eighteenth century. Among other things, those changes include the processes I mentioned above: urbanization, mass migration, and the acceleration of technological change, no one of which is wholly extricable from any other, and all of which are central to the formation of popular culture (and make it different from folk culture). It is useful to artificially compartmentalize these processes for the sake of clarity.

Cities are a prerequisite for popular culture. This does not mean that popular culture is simply urban culture. In fact, popular culture represents a symbiosis between city and country, as rural people pour into cities, they bring their backgrounds with them, and as popular culture emerges from cities and diffuses into the countryside, where the whole process begins again. What cities have historically provided is a common ground where disparate groups of people can meet, and where there is sufficient population and capital for the creation of relatively complex organizations to produce and distribute popular cultural products. Such organizations can be found at least as far back the Middle Ages, when the growth of towns led to the formation of an urban artisan milieu. Most historians agree, however, that the Industrial Revolution represented a perceptible intensification of this process.

Immigration has also provided a seed bed for the creation of popular culture, especially in the United States. As world trade increased, some people began moving more freely across national borders, while slaves and impoverished rural folk were forced to move against their will. As with native-born populations moving from country to city, these people also brought their cultures with them. Yet close contact with other groups inevitably meant that their original cultures lost their "purity" (if they ever had it) as they combined with other cultures and created altogether new ones. In the United States, the general impact of these developments has been dramatic from the very beginning, and has played a decisive role in the history of U.S. popular culture.

Finally, there is the role of technological innovation. Until well into the nineteenth century, the innovation crucial for the development of popular culture was the refinement and proliferation of the printing press. The introduction of movable type, which allowed many copies of a single work to be reproduced mechanically, dates back to the fifteenth century, and one could plausibly date the birth of popular culture there. Yet the quantitative differences between the fifteenth and eighteenth centuries in terms of the scale of the publishing industry, the relative freedom of the press from religious or state control, and the pace of modernization—which in the United States underwent a quantum leap over the space of a generation in the early nineteenth century—are so great as to be qualitative as well.[2]

But whatever its origins, popular culture emerged most clearly in England during the eighteenth century, triggering a "long revolution" whose effects are with us still.[3] This revolution, which included developments ranging from the growth of a large reading public to the destruction of the medieval craft system in printing, was replicated elsewhere in the centuries that followed. The first traces of it began to appear in England's American colonies toward the end of that century—that is to say, right around the time those colonies declared their political, if not quite cultural, independence.

Getting the Word:
The Origins of a Popular Audience

In some respects, the constitutionally ratified United States of 1789 was not very different from the thirteen still-loyal colonies of 1776—or, for that matter, those of 1676 (the year of a civil war in Virginia over the rights of Indians). Compared to the Europe of those same years, the United States exhibited a good deal less class stratification, though racial tensions with

Native Americans were sharp and immediate. Compared to the United States of the late twentieth century, the colonies were overwhelmingly rural—and Founding Fathers like Thomas Jefferson hoped and expected that they would stay that way.

For most people on the Eastern seaboard between the settlement of Jamestown in 1607 and the ratification of the Constitution, cultural life was rooted in folkways. For sure, there was a cultural elite, personified by Jefferson himself. People like him experienced the official culture of Europe, and brought it here via imported books, paintings, and ideas. For the rest of the country, however, artistic production was vernacular and localized.

One good example of this is music. Both Anglo-Celtic and African arrivals brought their songs with them, singing and playing them as an accompaniment to work, leisure, and religious rituals. Virtually none of this music was written down; it was transmitted orally and in the process mutated gradually into something new. Only oral tradition, combined with careful sleuthing by scholars and the serendipitous discoveries of folklorists such as John Lomax, who occasionally stumbled onto isolated rural folk still performing music in traditional ways, give us an idea of what this music sounded like. Fortunately, the far-sighted New England publisher Isaiah Thomas published a collection of broadside song sheets "to show what articles of this kind are in vogue with the vulgar at this time, 1814," leaving us an invaluable historical record.[4] Later, greater mobility, along with the advent of recording and broadcast technology, would lay the foundations for an American popular music.

The first step in the creation of popular culture on these shores, however, was the establishment of printing presses. The future growth of this industry was important not only for reading materials, but also for products like sheet music, lithography, and photography, which would allow the unprecedented diffusion of artistic production across geographic, racial, and class lines. In general, the dissemination of these materials did not become widespread until well into the nineteenth century. I mention them here so that they can be kept in mind as I discuss the literary dimensions of popular culture.

The first printing press in the colonies was established in Cambridge, Massachusetts, in 1638.[5] Given the religious imperatives of radical Protestantism, where individual effort might at least signal future salvation, it is not surprising to learn that Cambridge-Boston was the publishing capital of the colonies in the seventeenth and eighteenth centuries, and that New England's literary output outstripped that of the mid-Atlantic states and the South. (Georgia was apparently the last state in the colonies to establish a press, in 1763, suggesting just how long it took for publishing to diffuse throughout the colonies.[6])

Nor is it surprising to learn that one of the most popular works in the colonial era had a religious orientation. In 1640, the Cambridge press published a quarto, or sheets of paper cut four ways and bound into a booklet, of 148 pages. Originally called *The Whole Book of Psalms*---and later to be known as the *Bay Psalm Book*—the volume was a collection of translations from Hebrew to English with some commentary by Richard Mather (forefather of the famous Boston family that included Cotton and Increase). The first printing of 1,700 copies sold out. Since there were only about 3,500 white families in northern New England at the time, many of whom disliked the pieties of the Puritans in Boston, it seems likely that many were sold abroad. Wherever they went, by the end of the eighteenth century there were fifty-one editions of the *Bay Psalm Book* available in New England and Great Britain. For these reasons, it seems plausible to call it the first American bestseller.[7]

Despite its creation in an urban setting, the role of immigration in dictating the need for it, and the use of modern technology for its production, however, there are two reasons why we might have reservations about calling early versions of the *Bay Psalm Book* popular culture. Both are class-related. First, books were very costly commodities in the colonies, widely available only to the wealthy. Second, they had little value to poor and working people who could not read, which included most non-white males (and maybe even the majority of white men as well) in the colonies before the Revolution.[8]

By 1750, the first of these issues had been partially overcome by journalism: almanacs, newspapers, and magazines. While religious life remained a powerful cultural force throughout the Western world in the seventeenth century—nowhere was this more true than in New England—an early demand for practical, secular knowledge was evident. In fact, the Cambridge press had published *An Almanack for the Year 1639* before the *Bay Psalm Book*. Almanacs, which included data on the weather and other information of use to farmers, were peppered with jokes, sayings, and political opinions. The most famous of these was *Poor Richard's Almanack*, published in Philadelphia by Benjamin Franklin from 1733 to 1757. By the time he died in 1790, Franklin had completed a transformation from a poor boy in Boston to one of the most cosmopolitan men in the world, and the last edition of the almanac, which reflects his more genteel side, was published to widespread acclaim in France in 1776; it has decisively shaped popular perceptions of his persona ever since. The earlier editions, spiced with pungently colloquialized versions of dated epigrams (in the 1736 Almanac the English proverb "God restoreth health and the physician hath the thanks" became "God heals and the doctor takes the fee"), have a more democratic, class-conscious edge. Cheaper than most imported or domestically published books, *Poor Richard* sold 10,000 copies a year—or one copy for every one hundred people in the colonies—making it the most popular reading material other than the Bible. As one of Franklin's more recent biographers notes, "*Poor Richard* had special flavor and was the foundation of a popular American culture."[9]

One might expect newspaper publishing in the colonies to have preceded either books or almanacs, but in fact newspapers did not appear until a half-century later, leaving news-hungry colonists to rely on the English press or widely circulated personal correspondence. Besides the absence of an obvious market, the primary reason was political: printers could not risk the loss of property, or worse, should they publish material that offended local or English officials. The fate of the first newspaper is highly revealing in this regard. Published on September 25, 1690, Boston's presumably monthly *Publick Occurrences Both Forreign and Domestick* was suppressed four days later by the colonial government, which issued a statement saying the paper did not have permission to operate. It was not until 1704 that the more cautious *Boston Gazette* became the first paper to survive more than one issue. Its price was sufficiently high that the famed Judge Samuel Sewall would give copies as gifts to the women he visited. Although newspapers were almost certainly passed around and read by those who could not afford subscriptions, it was not until the next century that it became possible to speak of a mass press that catered to working-class interests.[10]

Then there were magazines. An even more difficult proposition than newspapers, magazines were not indigenously produced until 1741, when Franklin published *American Magazine* and his rival Andrew Bradford launched *A Monthly View of the Political State of the British Plantations of America,* both in Philadelphia. A steady magazine industry did not take off until after the Revolution, and not until the mid-nineteenth century was there a flourishing periodical culture. Yet like newspapers, magazines reached far beyond urban elites. One study of *New-York Magazine,* a moderately sized monthly that counted George Washington, John Adams, and John Jay as readers, found that a significant percentage of the 370 subscribers in 1790 were shopkeepers and artisans—members of professions that had begun (or would soon begin) to experience proletarianization as a result of industrialization. Cartmen, laborers, and mariners also sub-scribed—a subscription cost $2.25 a year, at a time when the average workingman's daily wage was $.50. Perhaps the most compelling evidence of wide readership concerns women, for while there were only seven who subscribed in their own names, there were numerous articles about or even specifically directed at women (such as "On the Choice of a Husband"), which indicated a wider readership.[11]

The most popular form of reading material for poor and working people was the chapbook. The term "chapbook" did not come into general use until the nineteenth century, and these small, inexpensive books—pam-phlets, really—at first went by a variety of names: "small books," "chapman's books," or "small histories." They were usually between sixteen and thirty-two pages, and were illustrated with simple woodcuts. Most were imported from England, and since they didn't go out of date, like almanacs, they were profitable for the publisher. Paper shortages made chapbooks difficult to manufacture in the colonies, although they were sometimes published on the backs of sheets recovered from pirated Spanish ships, or on paper made from old rags. Ironically, their very availability then makes them very rare today. They were so commonplace that few people bothered to preserve them, and so cheaply made that the vast majority were, in the words of one scholar, "read to pieces." Most evidence of their popularity comes from accounting records, advertisements, and other retailers' documents.[12]

The subjects of chapbooks ranged from religious instruction to light entertainment. The reputedly factual story of Dick Whittington, a poor English boy who moved from rags to riches in medieval London, was widely read in the colonies and was a forerunner of Horatio Alger tales. But an indigenous chapbook tradition took root very early. Captivity narratives, or accounts of experiences as prisoners of Indians, were extremely popular, and the most famous of these, Mary Rowlandson's, was published in chapbook form in 1682. "Richard Rum" tales, seriocomic stories about temperance that were published throughout the eighteenth century, were also a largely American phenomenon. Eventually chapbooks became asso-ciated with children's literature, and remained available in this form through the nineteenth century.[13]

In the seventeenth and eighteenth centuries, there were two major ways for literary products to be distributed: shops and peddlers. The former were largely based in the cities and sold printed matter alongside a variety of other products; the latter carved out a marginal existence by visiting inland settlements. In early Massachusetts, such people were stigmatized and even barred from bookselling, but by the late eighteenth century hawkers had become an important source of gossip, political discussion, and reading material. Occasionally all three would intertwine. The astounding success of Thomas Paine's revolutionary manifesto *Common Sense*—which sold 100,000 copies between January and March 1776, or one copy for every twenty-five people in the colonies—was at least partially the result of the peddlers' distribution network. Peddlers also knew their market. In 1799, the itinerant Mason Locke (or "Parson") Weems had enjoyed success selling a variety of books, mostly in the mid-Atlantic states. But it was not until he got the idea of writing a biography of George Washington—and convincing Philadelphia publisher Matthew Carey to back it—that he really hit the jackpot. *The Life and Memorable Actions of George Washington,* published immediately after the president's death in 1799 (the fifth edition of which included his apocryphal cherry tree story) became a huge hit and had gone through at least eighty-four printings by 1829. Weems also wrote successful biographies of Ben Franklin, William Penn, and Chief Justice John Marshall, although none could compare with the Washington biography.[14]

Beginning in the mid-eighteenth century, there arose another form of literary distribution that had powerfully democratic ramifications: the lending library. Once again, Benjamin Franklin was at the vanguard, when he established a subscription library in Philadelphia in 1731. This was a private affair that required participants to put up a large sum of money in order to gain lending privileges. But before long the elitist subscription library was supplemented by the institutional library, which lent books to members (such as schools) and, more importantly, by the circulating library, which rented books at rates affordable to a common laborer. This contributed dramatically to an expansion of literary culture: as more books became available, growing numbers of people read them, and publishers then increased production. Wealthy merchants referred to lending libraries as "slop-shops of literature."[15]

Yet there remains the larger question of exactly who could read by 1800. Certainly, the mere proliferation of books contributed to the growth of literacy in colonial America by giving more people access to reading materials. But other factors were also at work, factors that need to be taken into account for a fuller understanding of the creation of a large reading audience by the early nineteenth century.

The question of literacy in colonial New England has been strenuously explored by literary scholars, but no one has been able to come up with decisive figures. In part this is because there is no widely shared definition of the term. Do we measure literacy by the ability to read a legal contract, a personal letter, or a spelling book? And even if we have a clear definition, not all historical subjects were willing to be counted—slaves and some white women, for example, surely concealed what they (often illegally) knew. Finally, there is the matter of what means we use to count literacy, and how reliable they are. One modern study, for example, uses New Englanders' ability to sign wills with their initials as an index of the ability to read. Even by this standard, literacy was low: barely one-half of white men and less than one-third of white women could read in 1660. Some studies contend that using a broader range of documents would yield higher rates, while one argues that reading and writing were separate skills and that women were far more likely to be able to perform the former than the latter. All of this demonstrates the ongoing resistance of history to empirical quantification.[16]

Nevertheless, some plausible generalizations can be made. Whatever we consider the baseline of literacy, it is clear that New England led the colonies (and perhaps even the world). As early as 1642, Massachusetts passed a law requiring reading instruction for all children. Connecticut followed in 1650, New York in 1665, and Pennsylvania in 1683. Many of the instructors hired to fulfill this task were women. Nevertheless, for quite some time "all children" only included a fraction of young people, and usually meant boys. Even when girls were taught, their training was not taken as seriously as that of boys. Massachusetts added a writing requirement for boys in 1703, but it was not until 1771 that a similar provision was made for writing instruction for girls.[17]

Despite such inequities, reading instruction was greatly facilitated by the growing availability of teaching materials. At first, hornbooks (single pages tacked onto a wooden board) were used, as were psalters (books of psalms), primers, and bibles. These texts were gradually replaced by spellers, the most famous of which, Noah Webster's *American Spelling Book,* sold 24 million copies between 1783 and the author's death in 1843, making it the best selling book in U.S. history before 1850. As these and other kinds of reading matter gave students an incentive to master the skill, literacy grew in the colonies and the fledgling United States in a manner unprecedented in the Western world. It has been estimated that by 1790 over 90 percent of the nation's white population was literate.[18]

Again, the exact meaning of this statistic, if accurate, remains unclear, and also probably obscures the differential between men and women. On the other hand, some historians have noted the interest in—and official sanction of—female literacy that was part of the ideology of "Republican Motherhood" that emerged after the Revolution. According to this ideology, the success of the new nation rested on a virtuous, educated white male citizenry devoted to the common good, but the keystone for the development of such a populace was the virtuous, educated mother, who would inculcate the proper values and provide an atmosphere that would encourage the development of a leadership class (in some versions) or a more egalitarian population (in others). Thus, although Republican Motherhood fit into older patriarchal models that confined women to specific private, domestic tasks, its advocates also called for women to be provided with the opportunities and skills that would allow them to secure the future of the state.[19]

That was the theory, anyway. In practice, the constrictions on women were still considerable—women did not approach equity with men as readers or as teachers of readers until the second quarter of the nineteenth century—and U.S. education remained unequal in class and gender, not to mention racial, terms, a situation that still holds true today.[20] Yet while it would be a mistake to overestimate the possibilities afforded by these developments, it would also be a mistake to minimize their potential. "I thank God there are no free schools or printing, and I hope we shall not have these [for a] hundred years; for learning has brought disobedience, and heresy, and sects into the world, and printing has divulged them, and libels against the best government," said Virginia governor William Berkeley in 1619.[21] A century and a half later, many colonists no doubt found such sentiments unrealistic, but the anxieties they reflected had by no means disappeared. Once people could read, there was no telling what they might think—or do. And while elites wanted women and working people to read and write so that they could contribute to the national economy, it was difficult to control the uses to which people would put these skills. This was particularly the case for a new kind of culture that was beginning to generate both attention and condemnation: the novel.

Opening Chapters:
The Rise of the Novel

As its name implies, the novel is a relatively new form. Its roots can be traced back to Miguel de Cervantes's *Don Quixote,* published in 1605. It arrived in English in the work of Samuel Richardson, Henry Fielding, and Laurence Sterne. The developments that have been described in this chapter—urbanization, cultural mixing across national/class/racial lines, technological innovation, and rising literacy—were preconditions for the novel, and all were at least to some degree present in imperial Spain in the seventeenth century and industrializing England in the eighteenth. In our own day, the works of these men are seen as elite culture that reached high levels of artistry. In the eighteenth and early nineteenth centuries, however, virtually all novels were dismissed as trivial and/or looked upon with suspicion. How and why this came about reveals a good deal about the ways that, at its best, popular culture offers expressive and ideological opportunities to people shunted to society's margins.

One of the most thoughtful and provocative thinkers on this development was the Soviet literary theorist M.M. Bakhtin. According to Bakhtin, the novel was heir to the epic—grand oral or written narratives such as the *Iliad* or the Assyrian legend of Gilgamesh. Such stories usually articulated a national tradition; they described collective social experiences and were set in a distant past peopled with heroic characters. The novel, by contrast, explores ordinary life, plumbs a character's personal and even psychological dimensions, and has a strong sense of contingency: unlike epics, novels posit a world where events can unfold any number of ways, and derive interest from the very uncertainty as to how they will turn out. This sense of contingency, and the presence of a particular writer looming over the proceedings, makes novels, in Bakhtin's terms, "dialogic."[22]

Some important consequences resulted from this cultural matrix. First, unlike mature forms such as the epic, the early novel had no fixed aesthetic, no hardened hierarchic sense of what an ideal version should be like. It invigorated older forms, creating new possibilities even as it borrowed motifs and themes. Novels endowed poetry and drama with a new sense of realism, for example, even as they took old plots and rearranged them to tell different stories. A similar process appeared again later, when novels did begin to formalize and develop hierarchial values, and upstart forms like film began the process all over again.

In early modern Europe and colonial America, the novel had tremendous subversive potential. Like folklore and satire (two cultural streams Bakhtin argues contributed to its formation), novels often critiqued the social order, but their widespread availability, coupled with the privacy in which they could be read, made their reach unprecedented.

English imports exercised an exclusive monopoly before the Revolution and continued to dominate the scene for decades afterward. Daniel Defoe's *Robinson Crusoe* (1719), Henry Fielding's *Tom Jones* (1749), and Laurence Sterne's *Tristram Shandy* (1760-1767), were early favorites. With their realistic descriptions, and their occasional bawdiness, these books offended some but enthralled many.

Perhaps the most popular novelist in the colonies was Samuel Richardson. His *Pamela* (1740-1741), an upward mobility tale about a servant girl who becomes a lady, and *Clarissa Harlowe* (1747-1748), the story of a woman who falls from grace for having sex with her fiancé, affirmed traditional pieties. Indeed, *Clarissa* became a prototype for a series of seduction tales that littered the U.S. literary landscape through the late eighteenth and early nineteenth centuries. Read today, these stories seem humorously, even annoyingly, quaint. Their dogged insistence on the necessity of female virginity testifies to powerful constraints on womens' lives at the time and reveal patterns of patriarchy that continue today, from warnings about promiscuity to the economic and sexual double standards that remain facts of life for billions of women around the world.

Yet this does not fully explain the extraordinary power of these stories for their readers—many if not most of them women, and many if not most of them working women who shared the dilemmas of the novels' heroines with the emerging bourgeoisie. In an analysis of such recent horror movies as *Jaws* and such gangster movies as the *Godfather* series, one theorist noted the "utopian" undercurrents that exist alongside deeply conservative messages. In the end, such stories seem to say that you should not transgress conventional mores or that you can't fight city hall; but in the process they offer intriguing glimpses of just how to do precisely those things.[23] We can apply this insight to seduction novels as well: they may say that good girls don't, but in case you wondered, here's how.

Maybe that's why novels quickly attracted the attention of elites. From the very moment the colonists arrived on the continent, even the most egalitarian settlements sought to regulate private as well as public behavior. Exhortations against dancing and drinking were among the most obvious examples. So were invectives against drama. As early as 1716, Williamsburg, Virginia, had acquired a theater that mounted classical productions, but the Southern colonies were generally more tolerant of such diversions. Timothy Dwight, the minister, poet, and eventual president of Yale, spoke for many respectable New Englanders in the late eighteenth century when he asserted that "to indulge a taste for play-going means nothing more or less than the loss of that most invaluable pleasure, the immortal soul."[24]

Novel reading soon joined the list of activities that warranted condemnation. Late-eighteenth-century critics complained that they gave young people "false ideas of life" and rendered the "ordinary affairs of life insipid." They also led women to waste time that could be put to more practical ends. Worst of all, "a 'novel-reading female' expects attention from her husband, which the cares of business will not permit him to pay." An English article entitled "Novel Reading a Cause of Female Depravity," initially published in 1797, was reprinted in the United States several times, and Harvard decided to focus its principal commencement address in 1803 on the dangers of fiction.[25] Such criticism proved amazingly persistent. A half century later, the *Ladies' Repository,* a middle-class women's magazine from Cincinnati, was still sounding similar themes: novels "*destroy* the *power* of severe mental *application,*" made young readers unfit for "the arduous duties and stern realities of life," and, worst of all, had a tendency to "weaken the barriers of virtue" by "introducing impure scenes and ideas into pure minds."[26] As we will see, this strategy of focusing on threats to womanhood and youth would surface again and again as a means of attacking popular culture.

Such attacks led to an equally common response: that contrary to respectable opinion, popular culture was actually good for you. This approach goes back at least to the late seventeenth century, when the Puritan clergyman William Perkins specifically singled out *Scoggins Jests,* a collection of ballads and jokes, as dangerous to the moral health of his followers. Either anticipating such criticism or directly responding to it, bookseller John Usher included a foreword in the editions he sold in the 1680s, explaining that "there is nothing beside the goodnesse of God, that preserves the health so much as honest mirth." When a 1761 production of Shakespeare's *Othello* came to Rhode Island, the most tolerant of the New England colonies, the manager described it as "a moral dialogue, in five parts, depicting the evil effects of jealousy and other bad passions, and proving that happiness can only spring from the pursuit of virtue."[27] Such sentiments were used by those who sought to defend (or merely sell) novels, often accompanied by an insistence that the events about to be narrated were factual. The dedication page of Charles Brockden Brown's *The Power of Sympathy*, published in 1789, is typical in this regard. It reads as follows:

TO THE
YOUNG LADIES
OF
UNITED COLUMBIA
These VOLUMES
Intended to represent the specious CAUSES,
and to Explore the fatal CONSEQUENCES
OF
SEDUCTION;
to inspire the FEMALE MIND
With a principle of SELF COMPLACENCY
AND TO
Promote the economy of HUMAN LIFE
ARE INSCRIBED
With esteem and sincerity
by their
Friend and humble servant
THE AUTHOR

It is possible that many such attempts to uphold the practicality of popular culture in this way were sincere. And there can be little doubt that at least some people accepted these explanations. Yet, as many producers, purveyors, and consumers no doubt realized, suggestive songs, Shakespearian plays, and novels with the word "seduction" printed in bold-faced capital letters on their dedication pages simply could not be reduced to exercises in moral instruction. No one would bother with them if they were. Everyone would instead go to church and listen to what their betters had to say.

In this regard, novels and other forms of reading were not simply supplements to formal education; they were also alternatives to it. In part, this is because many girls and women did not have the opportunity to attend schools, or to do so to their satisfaction. And, as I have suggested, there may have been ideological motivations as well. Either way, the thirst for learning was evident. In her exhaustive study of novels in America before 1820, literary historian Cathy Davidson reports that she encountered a call for better female education in every single one. The emphasis was not institutional but personal: women should read to educate themselves. And the profusion of such self-help books as spellers, and the presence of books like Mary Wollstonecraft's early feminist manifesto, *A Vindication of the Rights of Women* (1792) in 30 percent of libraries surveyed in one study, suggests that women were acting on this principle.[28]

The nascent fiction industry seems to have made a concerted effort to meet this demand. Davidson notes that much early fiction operated at a relatively unsophisticated linguistic level. Many books were shortened versions of longer, more complex works, using plainer language. Moreover, many included advertisements that were specifically directed toward women, children, or uneducated men.[29] This is perhaps the clearest evidence of the diffusion of literature to a large number of people.

It may also be evidence of the growing sophistication of the early capitalist system. Yet here too there is evidence that suggests that it is simplistic to assume that mass culture is foisted on an uncritical populace. This is evident from Davidson's imaginative effort to examine many copies of the same novel to see how individual readers personalized them with notes, doodling, and other marginalia. From such work, it became clear that even the most inexpensive editions of a book could have tremendous personal value. One reader, for example, decorated the cover of a novel in an edition so crude that the author's name was spelled incorrectly. Inside she wrote poetry, and crossed out her maiden name and added a new one when she got married, suggesting that the book had become a prized keepsake. Conversely, the disgusted reader of another novel wrote that "a book more polluted with destruction and abominable sentiments cannot be put in the hands of anyone—shame to the age and country that produced it."[30]

These novels attracted male readers as well. The inscriptions studied by Davidson indicate that men read seduction novels, while it seems likely that women, by the same token, read those that were directed at men.

A closer look:
A *TEMPLE* OF THE IMAGINATION

Multiple allegiances—of sex, race, and ethnicity, among others—have been central to the American experience from the very beginning. So it seems appropriate that the first Great American Novel

THE FICTIONAL CHARLOTTE TEMPLE

was written by a woman whose nationality has been open to question. That ambiguity—along with the author's gender—has until recently led literary scholars to overlook both Susanna Rowson as the first major American fiction writer and her book *Charlotte Temple* as the first major American novel.

Rowson was born (as Susanna Haswell) in England in 1762 to a mother who died soon after her birth. Her father, an officer in the British navy, remarried and brought her to Massachusetts, where she enjoyed a happy and affluent childhood until the outbreak of the Revolutionary War. Though her father tried to remain neutral, political tensions made the Haswells' situation untenable, and he was taken as a prisoner of war in 1776. The family's property was confiscated, and the adolescent Susanna found herself tending to a makeshift home and trying to support her ill and depressed father (who was under house arrest) and stepmother. In 1778, the family was repatriated to England in a prisoner exchange. They began again in England, penniless, and dependent on Susanna's skills as a teacher of wealthy women and a writer of verse for the theater.

In 1786, Susanna married William Rowson, an actor, musician, and sometime hardware merchant who was later described as a "deadbeat" by one of his relatives. The task of supporting the family—which eventually included two adopted children and her husband's sister—fell to the young woman. (Her husband, however, assumed the rights to all her earnings under both British and U.S. law. Not that there was much involved: the prevailing wisdom was that, unlike men, women were not interested in money, and they were thus not paid very much.) Between 1786 and 1792, Susanna published a series of novels, including *Charlotte: A Tale of Truth* in 1791 (which, against prevailing custom, she authored in her own name). After her husband's hardware business went bankrupt in 1792, the couple was recruited by a theater company in Philadelphia. Susanna became a U.S. citizen when her husband was naturalized in 1802.

Susanna Rowson might have been better known as an actress—or later, as the founder of a highly successful women's academy—had it not been for Matthew Carey. Carey was an Irishman who had been imprisoned by the British for publishing an Irish nationalist newspaper. He emigrated to the United States in 1784, when he was twenty-four years old, to avoid further persecution and to begin a new publishing operation (with a loan from the Marquis de Lafayette, who aided the cause of U.S. nationalism by fighting alongside Washington in the Revolutionary War). Carey's publishing house, founded in Philadelphia, went on to become one of the most successful in early U.S. history.

In 1794, Carey published a stateside edition of *Charlotte*. It was relatively cheap and easy for him to do, since there was no international copyright law. Indeed, an excited Carey reported the book's steady sale to the Rowsons apparently without any thought of sharing the profits. Yet such a casual attitude toward what we now call intellectual property was a factor in the novel's phenomenal success. Domestic publishers soon did unto Carey what he had done unto Rowson's British publisher and the novel spread like wildfire, until there were over two hundred editions, ranging from expensive leatherbound volumes to the most ephemeral chapbooks. Gradually it became known by the title *Charlotte Temple*.

The plot of the novel can be easily summarized. When a British nobleman named Temple aids a heavily indebted army officer, he is gratefully offered the hand of the soldier's daughter. This turns out to be a match of love, not money (which Temple essentially renounces by refusing to marry the woman his father had chosen for him) and the happy couple are soon blessed with a daughter named Charlotte. They send her off to a boarding school, where she befriends an unscrupulous schoolteacher named Mademoiselle La Rue. An army lieutenant named Montraville bribes La Rue to introduce him to Charlotte, with whom he has become sexually infatuated. Montraville and his friend Belcour are bound for the colonies to fight the Americans in the Revolutionary War, but they convince La Rue—and manipulate a reluctant Charlotte—to join them. Once in New York, Montraville sets the fifteen-year-old girl up as his mistress in a house outside of Manhattan, and the two live happily until he meets an aristocratic woman whom he wants to marry. La Rue fails to be a friend to Charlotte, and the evil Belcour steals the money Montraville intends to give her. Pregnant, impoverished, and alone, Charlotte finds her way to New York City as her distraught father searches for her, hoping to reunite her with her anxious family. But despite the efforts of a poor servant of La Rue's, it is too late to save her life.

"For the perusal of the young and thoughtless of the fair sex, this Tale of Truth is designed; and I could wish my fair readers to consider it not as merely the effusion of Fancy, but as a reality," Susanna Rowson wrote in the introduction. The factual accuracy of the story (supposedly, only the names were changed to protect the innocent) seems to have been an important motive to Rowson, but it has never been independently verified. Perhaps this emphasis on reality was designed to justify writing fiction to disapproving elites; more likely, Rowson believed that underlining the factualism of the story would give it more impact (much in the same way docudramas appeal to television viewers today).

On the face of it, Rowson's message to her readers is deeply conservative. "Oh my dear girls—for to such only I am writing—listen not to the voice of love, unless sanctioned by paternal approbration," she counseled. Yet her advice that young women be wary of men, even relatively well-intentioned men like the thoughtless Montraville, was sound in the context of late-eighteenth-century America, where female sexual expression resulted in severe social censure—and, more importantly, where unplanned pregnancy could have deadly consequences, as the fate of both Charlotte and the mother of Rowson herself powerfully testifies. But if Charlotte Temple does not strike us as a feminist role model (though some of the characters in

Rowson's other novels do), her novel nonetheless suggests the defeat of, and ongoing need for, gender solidarity.

The astounding success of *Charlotte Temple* is one indication of such solidarity. By the time of Rowson's death in 1824, it had become the most famous and beloved novel in the United States, and it remained so for another generation—until it was replaced by Harriet Beecher Stowe's *Uncle Tom's Cabin.* The varied editions, prints, and versions of the story (unauthorized sequels surfaced, and Rowson's own *Charlotte's Daughter* was published posthumously) suggest the deep emotional attachment many Americans, especially the women for whom Rowson explictly wrote, and who were largely assumed to be her readers, felt for the story.

There is another striking measure of the novel's impact. In the first decade of the nineteenth century, a gravestone to the fictional Charlotte Temple was erected in lower Manhattan's Trinity Church cemetery, which housed the remains of luminaries like Alexander Hamilton and Robert Fulton. For the next hundred years, Charlotte received more visitors than anyone else in the cemetery, as tens of thousands of people left behind flowers, books, and other mementoes in her honor. "In that churchyard are the graves of heroes, philosophers, and martyrs, whose names are familiar to the youngest scholar, and whose memory is dear to the wisest and best," a lawyer who had worked in an office overlooking the cemetery for forty-seven years wrote in 1903. "Their graves, tho' marked by imposing monuments, win but a glance of curiosity, while the turf over Charlotte Temple is kept fresh by falling tears."

Most of the so-called "best and wisest" had little interest in a seduced and abandoned character from a novel about and for some of the least valued members of U.S. society. But a great number of "little people" obviously felt that *Charlotte Temple* revealed fundamental truths about life in the early United States.

One novel genre was the picaresque. Of Spanish origin (*Don Quixote* was the prototype), these books featured faraway locations, unusual characters, and deceptive appearances. In part, such stories—which had titles like *Adventures of Alonso* (1775), *The History of Constantius and Pulchera* (1794), and *The Algerine Captive* (1797)—catered to a taste for the exotic and for escapism. As noted in the introduction, however, escapism is never an adequate explanation for the appeal of any work of popular culture. It always occurs within a particular context, and the different ways people choose to escape, and the places they escape *from* and *to* reveal a good deal about them.

In the case of the picaresque, setting a tale on the geographic, social, or political margins offered an opportunity for an oblique critique that might not have been countenanced if stated forthrightly. In *The Algerine Captive,* for example, a naive doctor who agrees to work on a slave ship is himself enslaved in Africa when the ship is captured. His six years as a hostage impress upon him the evils of slavery (a position of more than casual significance for a country that had a constitutionally sanctioned slave trade until 1808) and a new appreciation for a vigorous (if also vulgar) democracy that he had considered full of avarice and cupidity before he left. The novel was written by Royall Tyler, a well-to-do lawyer and judge of Jeffersonian sympathies. As we shall see in the next chapter, he had many of the class prejudices of the ruling elite in early-nineteenth-century America. Yet the abolitionist and mass-democratic elements that suffused his narrative and helped make it popular had explosive tendencies that hit raw nerves. This was especially true in the new United States of the 1790s, when Shays' Rebellion (which, ironically, Tyler helped suppress), the Whiskey Rebellion, increasing party polarization, elite anxiety over the French Revolution, and growing demands for political equality triggered the Alien and Sedition Acts of 1798, one of the most repressive censorship and law-and-order measures ever passed in U.S. history. In the contemporary popular imagination, the early United States was a country of idyllic equality and calm rural land-scapes. But close readings of its fiction and history suggest otherwise.

Gothic novels reveal similar conflicts. These stories were often set in decaying aristocratic mansions and focused on the unprivileged men (and occasionally women) who had to overcome dangers. Threats were as much internal as external: as Davidson has suggested, gothic novels posed troubling questions about the corrupting effect of power on those previously denied it. They also expressed, as modern gothic stories do, skepticism about any serene confidence in the efficacy of Progress. The early popularity of native gothics novels like Charles Brockden Brown's *Wieland* (1798) and *Arthur Mervyn* (two parts, 1799-1800) is especially interesting in this regard, as is the persistence of a gothic sensibility that runs through the work of Brown's heir, Edgar Allan Poe, and even through to Stephen King. It is ironically appropriate that horror stories took such firm root in a land supposedly predicated on optimism and opportunity.[31]

Brown is an interesting example because he was the first U.S. author who was able, albeit with great difficulty, to eke out a living as a writer. Independently wealthy people like Royall Tyler could afford to write novels, but they did so without the expectation of making much money from them. One reason for the relative lack of financial support from publishers and readers was the sense that U.S. authors were culturally inferior to Europeans, an attitude that persisted well into the nineteenth century. This cultural factor was reinforced by an economic one: the lack of international copyright protection. U.S. publishers printed English novels without paying royalties, making them cheaper to produce than domestically written ones. Moreover, a novel written in one state was often pirated by a publisher in another colony or state, who drained the original printer of sales and bilked the writer of royalties. In 1790, Congress passed a copyright law that protected authors' rights for fourteen years, followed by similar protections for prints, music, and plays. In 1831, the term of protection was extended to twenty-eight years, with an option to renew, but an adequate, well-enforced law was not enacted until 1891. Such laws laid the foundation for more Charles Brockden Browns, and for their female counterparts, who would prove even more important in the coming century.[32]

Copyright law was only one of many changes in the United States as it entered the nineteenth century, however. A new age was dawning, and popular culture would play a pivotal role in creating, reflecting, and explaining it.

2

Democratic Vistas:
The Emergence
of Popular Culture,
1800-1860

"ALL MEN ARE CREATED EQUAL."

Rarely have five words had more revolutionary impact on a society than these did in the United States, and rarely have five words embodied more omission, ambiguity, and outright hypocrisy. This presumably "self-evident" assertion from the Declaration of Independence was intended to be a definitive statement—a "truth"—but it ultimately raised far more questions than it answered. In the secular context in which it was written, what does it mean to say that all men are created equal? Does it mean that everyone is born with equal capacities, intellectual and otherwise? That is patently untrue. Does it mean that all begin equal before the law, whatever material advantages may otherwise be inherited or accrued? It now seems amazing that such a statement could have been made in a world that included black slaves and conquered Indians, people whose "inalienable" rights were constantly violated and whose pursuit of happiness was systematically denied. And even if we exclude nonwhite peoples from the Declaration's purview, where do women fit in a society where all *men* are created equal?

None of these questions was of decisive importance to Thomas Jefferson, John Adams, or Benjamin Franklin in 1776. For them and others, the Declaration of Independence was a revolutionary manifesto designed to lay the philosophical foundations for political autonomy from Great Britain. Yet even these people were compelled to take up such overlooked issues in the years following the Revolutionary War. Adams's wife Abigail admonished him to "remember the ladies" while drafting the Declaration of Independence with Franklin and Jefferson, and Jefferson's ambivalent writings on race in his *Notes on the State of Virginia* (1784) ranged from a sunny optimism that an enlightened harmony between the races was possible to a belief that African Americans were inherently inferior human beings. His recognition of the evils of slavery—which he unsuccessfully proposed abolishing on a number of occasions, including an early draft of the Declaration—also led him to "tremble for my country when I reflect that God is just."[1]

To greater or lesser degrees, many of the Founding Fathers realized that the Revolution had unleashed powerfully egalitarian tendencies, and a number of steps, including the repression of the Shays' and Whiskey

---

Reverse page: Cover of the sheet music for "Long Time Ago," a minstrel song popularized by T.D. Rice, the premier minstrel of the Jacksonian era who prided himself on his "authentic" portrayals of slave life.

rebellions, as well as the drafting and ratification of the Constitution itself, were measures designed to check the radical possibilities inherent in the Declaration of Independence. Adams himself went to even greater lengths to suppress any challenges to governmental authority by signing the Alien and Sedition Acts of 1798, which provided for the deportation of foreign refugees and the imprisonment of anyone convicted of writing, printing, or uttering comments deemed to be false, scandalous, or malicious to the government. The acts were revoked by Jefferson when he assumed the presidency in 1801.

Given the legacy of discrimination that has marked U.S. life in the centuries since the Alien and Sedition Acts, it would be easy to conclude that such attacks on the principle of equality have largely been successful. Nonetheless, monumental political achievements, such as the Emancipation Proclamation, women's suffrage, and the revocation of legal segregation, all drew intellectual sustenance from the Declaration of Independence, and it would be difficult to imagine such victories without it. At the same time, the intense resistance to these developments, and the amount of time it took to secure them, remind us that "progress" rarely moves in a straight line. Nor can it be considered inevitable.

Long before the fuller social or economic dimensions of the Declaration of Independence were on the national agenda, however, the promises it offered loomed large on the cultural horizon. Certainly, many of the inequities common in other areas of U.S. life could be found here, as well as a viciousness toward those on society's margins. Women were second-class citizens even in the artistic realm, Native Americans were subjects rather than objects of cultural discourse, and African Americans tended to influence popular culture rather than participate directly in it. Still, even in the nineteenth century there were signs that these inequities were not monolithic. The most racist artists were often fascinated by black forms, and often drew on their expressive power. By the end of the century, African Americans were literally and figuratively beginning to take the stage on their own terms, a process that will be traced in Chapter 3.

This chapter is bound by Andrew Jackson's rise in U.S. politics in the 1820s and the end of the Civil War. At the beginning of this period, popular culture was a fairly tentative phenomenon, but a series of transformations that affected U.S. society as a whole led to its emergence as a recognizable social force. By the end of the period, popular culture had become remarkable in its dazzling diversity.

The first societal transformation was demographic. As we have seen, one element in the development of popular culture in the eighteenth century was the steady rise in literacy among the white population, which created a large market for reading materials. The expansion of that market was greatly amplified by the burgeoning of the population, which grew from 3.9 to 9.6 million between 1790 and 1820, and to 17 million by 1840, by which time the United States had the largest reading audience ever created. The nation had about 200 newspapers in 1800, 375 in 1810, and 1,200 by 1835. And between 1820 and 1829, 128 novels were published—five times the number published between 1810 and 1820, and almost forty more than in the entire period from 1770 to 1820.[2]

The distribution of these materials was facilitated by dramatic improvements in the nation's transportation system. The completion of the Erie Canal in 1825 and the beginnings of a national railway system a decade later created a vast infrastructure that laid the foundation for a national market. Philadelphia, and later New York, displaced Boston as the publishing capital, providing an intellectual and economic nexus for cultural products that could now reach people across the continent. Meanwhile, a series of interior cities (Cincinnati, St. Louis, and eventually Chicago in the West; Charleston, New Orleans, and eventually Atlanta in the South) served as regional cultural centers and points of connection with the rest of the country.

Changes in modes of production were also a factor in this larger revolution. Mirroring developments in other industries, new processes in typesetting, bookbinding, paper manufacturing, and mechanical reproduction made publishing a wide variety of materials—newspapers, magazines, sheet music, lithographs, books, and later, photographs—faster and cheaper than ever before.[3] By the middle of the nineteenth century, more people had more access to ideas and art forms outside their immediate surroundings than at any previous point in human history.

All these gains, however, inevitably brought losses. In the case of the publishing industry, these gains meant the end of a guild system that had provided class mobility to generations of workers who had been able to prosper by moving from apprentice to journeyman to master. Technological innovation greatly simplified jobs, which made them less fulfilling—and less remunerative, as employers turned to unskilled labor that could be exploited more cheaply than journeymen who had dedicated their lives to learning their craft. Nor, of course, could unskilled laborers hope for the training that might lift them out of poverty. Moreover, the great sums of money involved in acquiring the new methods of production put them out of the reach of all but the wealthy few, who grew more wealthy still. It was during this period that a pattern emerged that shapes the course of U.S. popular culture to this day: ever larger organizations controlling the production of art for common people while depending on those same people not only to buy, but often to produce, the individual works.

In its best and worst aspects, the new order emerged first in the world of journalism.

Class Operations:
The Birth of the Mass Press

For all their differences (which at some points in their fifty-year relationship led to bitter enmity), Thomas Jefferson and John Adams shared a belief that the American Revolution had been waged to replace a corrupt established aristocracy with what they called a "natural" one. In such a world, the plowman and the professor would have equal standing before the law, and there was the chance—even the hope—that any plowman could, by dint of effort, become a professor. It was always assumed, however, that the professor, whatever his origins, would lead the plowman.

Over the course of the first quarter of the nineteenth century, this last assumption became increasingly difficult to take for granted. The rapid growth of the Union through the addition of new states, many of which lacked elites comparable to the monied, privileged Federalist faction of 1789-1800, created new democratic pressures. So did increasing agitation by reformers and working people back East who were seeking to organize the growing numbers of men who lacked the vote because they did not own property. Many of these people flocked to the banner of the Jeffersonian Democratic-Republican Party, which offered a vision of an agrarian republic rooted in equality. Yet even before the last dyed-in-the-wool Jeffersonian, James Monroe, left office in 1825, many Democratic-Republicans realized that their vision of a natural aristocracy was ebbing. The increasing prominence of Andrew Jackson—a (pseudo) "plowman" with no interest in becoming a "professor"—following his victory at the Battle of New Orleans in 1815 and culminating in his election to the presidency in 1828, was taken by many as emblematic of a new breed of frank, colorful, decisive Americans ready to take destiny into their own hands. Jackson, a wealthy, authoritarian slaveholder, was in some ways an unlikely champion of the Little Man. But even if the movement he supposedly represented was far more limited than its supporters then and since have claimed, a bona fide reorganization of politics was taking place, one whose effects would subsequently ripple outward.

This political reorganization is clearly reflected in the transformation of newspaper publishing over the course of the first half of the nineteenth century. As discussed in Chapter 1, newspapers got off to an uncertain start in the colonies, and it was not until the eighteenth century that the industry had securely established itself in the cities. The Stamp Act of 1765, which required all printed documents to use a stamped paper that carried a special tax, hit newspapers especially hard, and their publishers played an important role in galvanizing opposition to British rule. There were thirty-seven papers in the colonies at the outbreak of the Revolutionary War in 1775, twenty of which survived paper shortages, difficulties in gathering information, and British occupation. One of these, the *Pennsylvania Evening Post* (published in Philadelphia), became the first daily.[4]

By the turn of the nineteenth century, U.S. newspapers had a primarily mercantile readership. In addition to carrying domestic politics and news from abroad, they featured shipping schedules and paid announcements by wholesalers seeking to sell imported goods to retailers. Indeed, their very names—Boston's *Daily Mercantile Advertiser,* Baltimore's *Daily Commercial Advertiser,* Philadelphia's *Pennsylvania Packet*—suggest their economic (and often maritime) orientation. These papers were generally sold in yearly subscriptions, and individual copies were relatively expensive.

By the early nineteenth century, however, the political functions of the press were becoming increasingly important, as politics itself became a kind of bruising competitive sport. The schism between Federalists and Democratic-Republicans in the 1790s was an unexpected and unpleasant development for a governing elite that professed antipathy toward sectarianism. As a result, many of their disputes were not played out directly but by proxy in the press. "Should the infidel Jefferson be elected to the Presidency, the *seal of death* is that moment set on our holy religion, our churches will be prostrated, and some famous prostitute, under the title of Goddess of Reason, will preside in the Sanctuaries now devoted to the Most High," claimed one Federalist organ during the campaign of 1800, using rhetoric that was typical of the time.[5] Jeffersonians, it should be added, gave as good as they got.

The growing scale of newspaper publishing, and the new prominence given editorial matter, led to the rise of an important new figure in U.S. politics and culture: the editor. Previously, newspapers had been small operations run by printers. Now, however, there was a new premium on political and entrepreneurial savvy. Party operatives with access to capital became central to the evolving direction of journalism, and parties became key funding sources and exerted tight control over editorial direction.[6]

The founding of the *New York Evening Post* by Alexander Hamilton in 1801 illustrates these patterns. The pre-eminent member of the Federalist opposition after the election of his arch-rival Jefferson, Hamilton raised $10,000 from some wealthy patrons, and established the *Post* as a counterweight to the Jeffersonian *American Citizen*. Hamilton did not actually edit the *Post* himself, but he was essentially the paper's editorial director, using it to advance the Federalist political program (and writing articles under a pseudonym) until his death in a duel with Aaron Burr in 1804. Ironically, Hamilton's hand-picked editor later turned the editorship over to William Cullen Bryant, who became a Jacksonian Democrat committed to overturning Hamilton's political and economic legacy (embodied most concretely by the Bank of the United States). Still more ironic was the *Post*'s later incarnation as a working-class tabloid that sought to sell papers with tart headlines. By the end of the twentieth century, it has become the longest running continuous daily newspaper in the United States, but has also moved a long way from Hamilton's original vision.[7]

The *Post*'s success anticipated an important newspaper tradition that emerged in full flower during Jackson's presidency: the mass-based daily catering to a working-class readership. Many of the strategies that mark contemporary tabloids—human interest stories, a fascination with crime and sex, the use of vernacular language, and a declared indifference to respectable opinion—can be traced back to the penny dailies of the 1830s. These newspapers were among the most important forms of popular culture in the nineteenth century, and a key influence on (and distributor of) such forms as dime novels, which will be discussed below.

The first successful example of this kind of journalism was the New York *Sun,* a daily founded by printer-turned-editor Benjamin Day. "The object of this paper is to lay before the public, at a price within the means of every one, ALL THE NEWS OF THE DAY, and at the same time afford an advantageous medium for advertising," he proclaimed in his inaugural issue of September 3, 1833. To achieve this end, the *Sun* sold for one cent—one sixth the price of the mercantile or political papers sold by subscription. Moreover, Day followed the British practice of selling copies at a discount to boys who in turn sold them on the street. This greatly enhanced the paper's circulation, which reached 2,000 by November 1834, 5,000 by early 1835, and 15,000 by the middle of that year.[8]

The *Sun* sold in such quantities because it defined "the news of the day" in terms that made sense to an ever growing laboring class of immigrants and rural migrants, for whom international trade and even partisan politics were largely irrelevant. Certainly, the paper catered to advertisers, much to the chagrin of readers who learned the hard way about the dangers of buying fraudulent products from the array of merchants who saw opportunities in a market that was just beginning to emerge. Still, a paper could not sell advertising unless it attracted readers, and Day did so with a mix of human interest stories, police reporting, and exposés of churches, courts, banks, and government.

Contemporary accounts make it clear that the *Sun*—as well as the Philadelphia *Public Ledger* (1836), the Boston *Daily Times* (1836), the Baltimore *Sun* (1837), and a wave of other papers that sprang up along the Eastern seaboard—created a vast new readership. As with so much else in popular culture in this period, the center of the newspaper world was New York. Surveying the scene, the *Ledger* described an environment that clearly excited the writer in its novelty:

> In the cities of New York and Brooklyn, containing a population of 300,000, the daily circulation of the penny papers is not less than 70,000. This is nearly sufficient to place a newspaper in the hand of every man in the two cities, and even every boy old enough to read. These papers are to be found in every street, lane, and alley; in every hotel, tavern, counting-house, shop, etc. Almost every porter and dray-man, while not engaged in his occupation, may be seen with a paper in his hands.[9]

The *Sun*'s success was soon matched, and then eclipsed, by the New York *Herald,* founded by James Gordon Bennett in 1835. The *Herald* borrowed many of the *Sun*'s techniques, but took them a step further, as when Bennett made the trial of a young clerk for the murder of a prostitute—two people of no social standing—into a gripping national saga.

The paper was also particularly aggressive in attacking church leaders, as well as its own rivals. Bennett's decision to raise the price of the *Herald* to two cents in its second year turned out to be a savvy investment, for it allowed him to expand and to experiment with new techniques, ranging from buying a fleet of boats to meet news-bearing vessels from Europe to developing his business reporting to the point where it was competitive with the mercantile papers.[10]

Indeed, the *Herald*'s success was so great that it inspired attacks from the elite press, which in 1840 declared a "moral war" that was joined by papers in Boston, Philadelphia, and even England. Sinking to the level they supposedly deplored, these papers excoriated the *Herald* and its editors for "reckless depravity" and "moral leprosy." Barely concealed beneath their fear of an encroaching rival was a growing concern over the direction of American journalism.[11]

Meanwhile, the expansion of penny newspapers along the Eastern seaboard—and their steady penetration westward—was greatly facilitated by technological developments. The first penny papers were printed on hand-operated presses, but mechanically powered steam and cylinder machines soon allowed for a tremendous growth in productive potential. Moreover, the relationship between newspaper culture and technology was a reciprocal one: new technologies created new markets, and new markets spurred the development of more efficient presses, paper manufacturing, and distribution methods.[12]

Probably the most important technological development in this period was the telegraph. Building on the work of other scientists and inventors, Samuel Morse, a New York professor of art and design, gave the first public demonstrations of his new device in 1838. Although many early observers were impressed, it took a while before the telegraph's tremendous potential—the opportunity to communicate instantly across space—overcame early skepticism and logistical problems. Journalistic adoption of the telegraph was pioneered by the Baltimore *Sun*, which used an experimental line between that city and Washington to report on the presidential nomination of James Polk at the Democratic National Convention in 1844. Baltimore was also strategically located on the Baltimore & Ohio railroad line, which made it a key communications center in the years that followed. The outbreak of the Mexican War in 1846 also stimulated the rapid expansion of telegraphy as a means of communication. In the first week of

1848, Bennett claimed to have spent over $12,000 for 79,000 words of telegraphic content in the *Herald*.[13]

As has so often happened in the annals of technological revolution, the telegraph opened possibilities that soon became severely constricted by commercial interests. Samuel Morse was desperate to sell his new invention to the government, which he hoped would build and operate its own lines for the public good. The government refused, failing to recognize the telegraph's potential and fearing waste and fraud. A series of companies that wanted to exploit—and control—the telegraph for profit then rushed into the vacuum. In a pattern that would be repeated throughout the next 150 years, the result was a bruising financial battle over how to organize the new communications technology and whom it should benefit. In the case of telegraphy, this at first meant the proliferation of duplicate lines, many of poor quality, and rampant speculation. By the late 1840s, however, three organized interests had emerged: those who owned the lines, those who operated them, and those who prepared the information to be sent along them. In 1849, a consortium of six New York daily papers formed the Harbor News Association, later to be called the Associated Press. AP brought telegraph operators into the organization, but it passed up the opportunity to buy telegraph lines, leaving that part of the field to others. Beginning in the 1850s, the Western Union Telegraph Company began to buy and build lines, until it eventually became a monopoly. After the Civil War, AP and WU formed a communications axis (a matter to be discussed in Chapter 3).

Unlike the political press, the penny papers generally disavowed party affiliation. Nevertheless, they did become involved in the political issues of day, and they reflected the powerful, if incomplete, egalitarian currents that suffused the Jacksonian era. Indeed, many newspaper editors participated in an artisanal radicalism (a kind of proletarian politics with a Jeffersonian spin) that marked a class order still in flux. Three years before founding the *Sun,* for example, Benjamin Day was briefly listed as one of six directors of the *Daily Sentinel,* a political arm of the Workingmen's Party. The party, which had shown surprising strength in the New York municipal elections in 1829 and which published a weekly paper for fifteen years, suggested the rich possibilities for radical politics that would resurface periodically in the decades before the Civil War.[14]

By the mid-1830s, much of this vitality had been absorbed by the new Democratic Party, which had become a broad-based coalition of Northern urban workers and wealthy Southern agrarians deeply distrustful of the nascent capitalists who would soon be known as Whigs. Men like Day, who had trimmed their radical sails in the process of starting their own businesses, nonetheless retained a deep distrust of financial elites. To some extent this reflected their personal frustrations in securing capital while upper-class newspapers could serenely count on the help of banks, especially the hated Federalist-founded Bank of the United States (which Jackson eventually destroyed by refusing to renew its charter). To some extent too, the penny press's political stance was tailored to the perceived needs of its audience. There can be little doubt, in any case, that there was an important democratic component at its core.

Unfortunately, the coalition between Northern urban workers and Southern agrarians was an unstable compound. Rhetoric notwithstanding, politicians like Jackson's successor Martin Van Buren probably had more in common with his Whig rivals than the working people he presumably represented (his power base was tellingly known as the Albany Regency). Moreover, the rich Southern planters' and poor Northern workers' shared fear of Whig domination created a powerful, and lasting, institutionalized foundation for racism. Both Whigs and Democrats realized that slavery was a bulwark against the expansion of free market, free labor capitalism, and many of them therefore saw it as a positive good. In the insecure labor market of Northern cities, white workers saw free blacks as a threat to their job security, while slavery gave them a twisted source of psychic satisfaction in their whiteness. One of the most unlikely partnerships in working-class history was the alliance between the fiercely pro-slavery theorist John Calhoun and the rabble-rousing, Bowery-based politician Mike Walsh.[15]

It was an alliance that dismayed many Democratic voters and newspaper readers, and further fractured the party into abolitionist ("Barnburner") and anti-abolitionist ("Hunker") wings. Into the breach rushed such new Whiggish papers as the New York *Tribune,* founded in 1841 by Horace Greeley, and the *New York Times,* which was launched in 1851 but whose Olympian reputation was still a half-century away. Drawing on many of the same techniques as the Democratic penny press, these political papers signalled the formation of a new political order that would finally crystallize with Abraham Lincoln's election to the presidency in 1860.

In New York, at least, resistance to the racist tendencies of the Democratic Party and its papers also came from the African-American press. The first black paper in the country was *Freedom's Journal,* founded in 1827, followed shortly thereafter by the *Colored American*. These papers were largely oriented to the free black elite of ministers, teachers, and other professionals, and focused on religious issues, opposition to black coloniza- tion of Africa, and the prevention of white mob violence. They also debated the propriety of black participation in such white celebrations as the Fourth of July, and condemned black patronage of parades and shows that drew on racist stereotypes. At times this concern for the image of the community shaded into class bias, as when forms of religious worship among poor black people, such as the highly expressive "ring shout," were criticized as undignified.[16] Yet the existence of papers like the *Colored American* suggests how, by the Jacksonian era, even relatively small constituencies were able to support their own publications.

Meanwhile, the mass press continued to proliferate. By 1860, Illinois had over 400 newspapers, with eleven dailies in Chicago alone. St. Louis had ten. And Cincinnati, an emerging cultural center, had twenty-six monthlies, semi-monthlies, and quarterlies. In addition, while penny, mercantile, and political papers remained important, other journalistic forms were emerging and blending with them. Sunday papers, which were first issued as extras during the Revolutionary War, became increasingly common in the early nineteenth century. Some were published on Saturdays for Sunday reading, such as Philadelphia's *Saturday Evening Post.* They included news along with pieces of a magazine-like tenor. Story papers, which published fiction, poetry, and essays in a newspaper format, flourished after 1840. Pictorial weeklies, which became tremendously popular before and during the Civil War, blurred the lines even further. This is not to say there were no magazines in the modern sense of the word. On the whole, however, they tended to be aimed at the emerging class of merchants, professionals, and their families.[17]

There was much to dislike about the penny press: its habits of manufac- tured outrage and sexual pandering; its aggressive support of Jacksonian Indian removal in the South and West, instead of policies of toleration (or even the less brutal National Republican policy of assimilation); its rabid enthusiasm for the Mexican War in the name of Manifest Destiny; and its often tacit—and occasionally explicit—support of slavery. All too often in U.S. history, those with the most egalitarian class politics have had the worst race politics (and vice-versa), a pattern that these newspapers amply document. Yet this connection was complicated. Important figures in the Workingmen's Party, most notably the irrepressible writer, lecturer, and reformer Frances ("Fanny") Wright, were principled abolitionists, and the realities of interracial cooperation remained alive throughout the rest of the century (particularly in the early Populist movement). If the early mass media was limited in spreading its egalitarian ethos, it nonetheless represented an important first step in the eventual development of a diverse popular culture.

The Curtain Rises:
Antebellum Performing Arts

The American stage (a term used here to describe theater, opera, and minstrel shows) also underwent a major transformation in the first half of the nineteenth century. The period was marked by the quest for a native dramatic idiom, one that had both nationalistic and class overtones, but a distinctive theatrical style did not develop until race became a central issue in American politics.

In the colonial era, theater was at the center of a religious controversy that pitted secular aristocrats against clerical authorities. Radical Protestant church leaders generally regarded the theater as subversive, which is why it tended to be more common in the South, where sacred influences were less strong. In fact, it was not until 1792 that the last official strictures on theatrical performances were finally lifted in Boston. From this point on, clerical resistance increasingly became a rear-guard action. At the same time, however, secular aristocrats became relatively less important in theater.[18]

The rapid growth of cities after the War of 1812 gave new life to the theater. Unmoored from the social and familial traditions of Europe and the U.S. countryside, a mobile urban population turned to new forms of entertainment as a release from the ravages of wage-earning labor. Playhouses were built to accommodate this new audience, and soon priced themselves to maximize profits. New York City's Park Theatre, which opened in the late eighteenth century, charged between $1 and $2 for one of its 300 seats; its replacement, finished in 1821, was over eight times larger and charged between 37½¢ and 75¢. The new Park, in turn, was expensive compared to the 4,000-seat Bowery Theatre, which opened in 1826. Theatergoers got a lot for their money: the average evening featured a full-length play punctuated by orchestral music, dances, and novelty acts, followed by a farce or short comic opera.[19]

Opera was another popular form of mass entertainment in the early nineteenth century. Nothing illustrated mass enthusiasm better than the triumphant tour of Swedish opera star Jenny Lind between 1850 and 1852 (the first part of which was managed by the famous impresario P.T. Barnum, who will be discussed below). Tens of thousands of people gathered to greet Lind's arrival in New York, and tickets for her shows were auctioned off for as much as $225. Jenny Lind clothing, including gloves, hats, shawls, and robes, became a fad.[20]

The most beloved operas tended to be Italian works performed in English. As would later be the case with Broadway plays and Hollywood movies, opera became the source of much popular music, as individual arias were performed by entertainers and published in sheet music form to be sung at home. The songs of composers like Rossini and Mozart (whose *Barber of Seville* and *Don Giovanni* were tremendous favorites) took their place beside those of Stephen Foster and other songwriters.[21]

Perhaps the most striking aspect of show business in the early nineteenth century was the diversity of the audience, which cut across racial, class, and gender lines. Within the theater itself, however, segregation prevailed. This was accomplished by dividing the house into box, pit, and gallery seats. Boxes were the most expensive and were usually reserved for the wealthy. The pit held a spectrum of theatergoers, from the swelling ranks of the middle classes to boisterous youths known as "Bowery B'hoys and G'hals": pleasure-loving working people who partook of the rich street life and entertainments of the Bowery, especially its theater.[22] The gallery was at the top of the theater and was generally understood to be the place for African Americans, and for prostitutes and their customers. The observations of a Maine farmer who visited a Boston theater in 1820 note the various lines that separated the theater audience, but also show how thin those lines could be and how much jostling took place:

It appeared that the gallery was the resort of the particolored race of Africans, descendants of Africans, and the vindicators of the abolition of the slave trade; that the tier of boxes below it in the center was occupied by single gentlewomen who had lodgings to let, and who were equally famous for their delicacy and taciturn disposition. The remainder of the boxes, I was given to understand, were visited by none but the dandies, and people of the first respectability and fashion; while the pit presented a mixed multitude of the lower orders of all sorts, sizes, ages and deportments.[23]

Given his ironic description of prostitutes as "single gentlewomen," one may wonder whether this farmer was joking when he suggested abolitionists sat in the gallery with blacks. Nevertheless, his observations indicate the fluidity of the theatergoing audience. Outside the South, blacks and whites often shared the gallery, and well-to-do free blacks were allowed to sit in boxes in northern cities (and in New Orleans, which had developed an elaborate multiracial social structure long before it became part of the United States).

An evening at the theater was a rowdier affair then than it is today. The house lights were never dimmed (this was too complicated before electricity), and people went as much to see and be seen as to watch the show. Nonetheless, as paying customers they felt entitled to comment on the entertainment by cheering or hissing at the performers, and the crowd's wishes often determined which pieces the orchestra would play. If their disapproval was particularly strong, some members of the audience would throw objects at those actors and musicians who had provoked their scorn.[24]

Eventually, this social porousness led the new bourgeoisie to leave these theaters and form a genteel culture centered around museums, concert halls, opera houses, and academies beyond the reach of ordinary citizens. But this process would not become complete for another century, and in the meantime the theater remained a remarkably democratic institution.[25]

This egalitarianism extended to the performers. With some exceptions, acting was still the largely marginal occupation it had been in Susanna Rowson's day. It required exhausting amounts of travel and a good deal of versatility, because plays turned over rapidly (one week was considered a long run). Except for a few superstars, pay was poor. In fact, one of the most important sources of income for a theater company was the "benefit night," when the profits from the performance were designated for actors, play-wrights, managers, or others.[26]

The stage life was especially hard on women. Not only did the social stigma surrounding the stage remain powerful, but women who pursued any profession were regarded as somewhat suspect. A few women thrived: Women's rights activist Fanny Wright lent her radical voice to drama by writing *Altorf* (1819), a celebration of Swiss independence. Actress Char-lotte Cushman sustained a successful acting career in the 1830s and 1840s, and novelist/playwright/actress Anna Cora Mowatt enjoyed considerable success with her hit play *The Fashion* (1844), a patriotic comedy that was successfully revived in the 1920s and again in the 1950s. Yet even these women struggled financially in order to achieve their status. More typical was the remark of an avowed friend of the theater who described one neophyte as "a young actress yet undebauched by her profession."[27]

As with fiction, the overwhelming influences on drama in the United States came from Great Britain well into the nineteenth century. England supplied not only the plays, but a large number of players who came to the United States and traveled widely. As one historian put it, "The English began to dump their surplus stars—or, more accurately, the surplus time of their stars—on the Americans."[28] Growing resentment of British performers and a belligerent sense of nationalism led to a number of conflicts, including the Astor Place riot in 1849.

A closer look:
THE ASTOR PLACE RIOT

From angry New Jersey tenant farmers in 1766 to frustrated Los Angeles residents in the aftermath of the Rodney King verdict in 1992, rioting is an American tradition. Such outbursts are usually the result of accumulating social tensions that have gone unaddressed by those in authority, and New York's Astor Place riot of 1849 was no exception. What made it unusual, however, was its immediate cause: a dispute about the correct way to perform the lead role in William Shakespeare's *Macbeth*.

THE ASTOR PLACE OPERA HOUSE ON THE NIGHT OF THE RIOT

Unlike in the twentieth century, when Shakespearian drama became a largely academic passion for the well-read few, the early nineteenth century was a time when the Bard enjoyed mass appeal. Working people were intimately familiar with many of his plays and had firm ideas about proper interpretations of them. As a result, Shakespearian actors developed large and devoted followings in both England and the United States.

In the 1820s, 1830s, and 1840s, the premier American actor was Edwin Forrest. Born in 1806 into a working-class Philadelphia family, Forrest exhibited theatrical promise as a child and apprenticed himself to the great English tragedian Edmund Kean when he toured the United States. Taking a cue from his mentor, Forrest developed an expressive style of performing Shakespeare that was very popular with U.S. audiences. Something of what we might call a method actor, Forrest built up his body, analyzed scripts, and tried to immerse himelf emotionally and intellectually in his roles. To play King Lear, for example, he visited mental institutions so as to better portray insanity. He was also an ardent nationalist, ever ready to proclaim the superiority of his country. In this regard, he may have reflected a cultural insecurity of Americans vis-à-vis Europe that persists at least to some degree to the present day.

Forrest was also well regarded in England, particularly for his performance as an Indian chief in *Metamora,* a play he commissioned to create a showcase for himself. As a Shakespearian actor, however, he had a rival in William Macready, a prominent London tragedian whose style tended to be more restrained. Like Forrest, Macready had built up a following on both sides of the Atlantic, but his more refined demeanor and elitist sympathies led to a different set of dramatic priorities. The two men were at least civil to each other until Forrest's second English tour, in 1845, where he was met with small, unenthusiastic audiences and hostile reviews, including one written by a friend of Macready. In retaliation, Forrest hissed during one of Macready's performances in Scotland. An outraged Macready denounced Forrest, who insisted he was simply exercising his right to show his feelings about the performance. Forrest then returned to the United States to a hero's welcome, denouncing the British in particular and aristocracy in general. In the events that followed, the right of an audience to express its opinion, friendly or otherwise, became a banner around which Forrest's followers would rally.

In 1848, Macready left for a U.S. tour with some trepidation (his friend Charles Dickens, who had written a critical portrayal of Americans in *Martin Chuzzlewit*, considered it too risky even to see him off). Matters went well until Macready reached Philadelphia, where Forrest opened a version of *Macbeth* opposite his own. Both attracted large audiences, but by this point the controversy had been widely reported and Macready was attacked by a barrage of rotten eggs and vegetables. He cut short his Philadelphia run and went South and West, but found a great deal of hostility there too.

Five months later Macready ended his tour playing Macbeth at the Astor Place Opera House in New York. This grand hall was a symbol of the economic disparities that would grow ever greater over the course of the nineteenth century. Forrest once again played the same role, this time at the Bowery Theatre, which was in a tough neighborhood, the turf of "Bowery B'hoys" and "Bowery G'hals" who wore flashy clothes and participated in a rich street life that included parades, horse races, and fights between gangs. The Bowery Theater was at the heart of the neighborhood's nightlife, a place where journeymen, laborers, and factory workers went to socialize and enjoy entertainment. These people formed the core of Forrest's constituency.

The two actors took the stage to play their respective Macbeths on May 7. Forrest's performance was hailed as brilliant, but Macready's was never heard: he was drowned out in a barrage of hisses and hurled objects. When chairs began to be thrown down from the gallery, almost hitting the actress playing Lady Macbeth, he stopped the play. He decided to leave the city, but a number of fellow artists, including Washington Irving, Herman Melville, and Jacksonian editor and playwright Mordecai Noah, urged him not to back down, and he gave another performance two nights later.

Forrest's partisans were waiting. They had papered the city with rabid diatribes in the press and on posted signs: "WORKING MEN, shall AMERICANS OR ENGLISH RULE in this city?" asked one, making the actors' dispute into a referendum on national autonomy. Much of the effort was orchestrated by an "American Committee" headed by E.Z.C. Judson (a.k.a. dime novelist Ned Buntline), who gathered a collection of Bowery B'hoys and planned to disrupt Macready's second show. But audience support for the actor—he was greeted with a fifteen-minute standing ovation—and arrests of troublemakers inside the theater stymied this effort, and Macready was able to finish his performance and safely leave the theater by hiding in the audience, which exited through a police cordon.

The situation was much more tense outside the opera house. There, police efforts to quiet the crowd only inflamed it. Rocks began to fly, and the officers called on the help of the local militia, which had been put on standby in case of trouble. When Macready left the opera house, the militia fired over the heads of the crowd. Believing that soldiers were shooting blanks, the crowd surged forward. The next round of firing revealed their miscalculation. Moreover, when the militia tried to avoid further confrontation by again firing over the crowd, they ended up hitting some of the bystanders. In the end, at least twenty-two people died and over 150 were wounded. Eighty-six were arrested, including butchers, carpenters, machinists, bakers, and clerks—a cross-section of the working class of New York. Attempted unrest the next night was held firmly in check by police and soldiers.

There was a good deal of commentary in the New York press in the aftermath of the riot, predictably divided between those who condemned the hooliganism of the rioters and those who condemned the deadly response of the police. Virtually everyone, though, saw class tensions and values as the underlying issue. "There is now in our country, in New York City, what every good patriot has hitherto considered it his duty to deny—a high class and a low class," a writer for the *Philadelphia Ledger* noted. In the first stages of the attacks on Macready, the New York *Tribune*, edited by future Republican presidential candidate Horace Greeley, condemned the "miscreants," but after the riots it concluded that a series of reforms was called for, including greater government action to curb inequities of wealth. Even Lydia Maria Child, appalled by the "blind rage of the mob" she saw as she tried to pass by the disturbance, acknowledged the justice of its grievances. "There are *instants,* when the sight of rags and starvation make *me* almost ready to smash thro' the plate-glass of the rich and seize their treasures of silver and gold," the pacifist writer later wrote in a letter to some friends.

The behavior of Forrest, the Bowery B'hoys, and the more irresponsible elements of the New York press suggest they share some of the blame for the Astor Place riot. It is hard to ignore the chauvinism that accompanied so much of the search for, and celebration of, a home-grown artistic tradition in the first half of the nineteenth century. Not that Macready was miscast as a snob: as early as 1826, he wrote that Forrest showed promise as an actor—*if* he stopped performing for Americans, whom he would repeatedly describe in later years as "vulgar," "coarse," "underbred," and "disagreeable." Nevertheless, he was repeatedly rebuffed in his efforts to resolve his dispute with Forrest and his Yankee enthusiasts, who thirsted for confrontation.

Riots never occur in a vacuum. The Forrest-Macready conflict reflected a growing awareness of the class divisions that the United States prided itself on having avoided. Equality of *opportunity* was increasingly rare for both white and black workers; the relatively large ranks of artisans (like Greeley himself) who managed to launch enterprises before the Civil War would not find much success after it. The United States was becoming afflicted by injustices that would create a clearly defined, self-conscious working class by the second half of the century.

This emerging polarization was reflected in the world of entertainment. In the 1820s and 1830s, theaters were a microcosm of the larger society, populated by men and women, rich and poor, white and black. By the 1840s and 1850s, performing halls like the Astor Place Opera House evidenced a segregation by wealth and race that would become a gulf by the end of the century. At the same time, the raucous audience participation that was a major aspect of the performing arts early in the century was gradually being replaced by an expectation of passivity. The Astor Place riot reflected, and intensified, movement in this direction.

In its wake, new entertainment forms would emerge and new ideological possibilities would be created. But a moment of considerable excitement, and fluidity, was now past.

———————

Whatever political or cultural differences they may have had with England, American theatergoers embraced William Shakespeare as one of their own. Fully one-fourth of all the plays mounted in Philadelphia between 1810 and 1812 were written by the Bard, and twenty-one of his thirty-seven plays were performed there between 1800 and 1835. Nor was Shakespeare's appeal solely Eastern: Chicago had only 4,000 people in 1837 when *Richard III* played. The Mississippi towns of Vicksburg and Natchez mounted at least 150 Shakespeare plays between 1814 and 1861, and by the 1830s, Shakespearean plays were being performed on riverboats in the North American interior.[29]

In the twentieth century, Shakespeare became the supreme symbol of high culture, the subject of intensive scholarly exegeses, textual reverence, and highbrow performance on stage and public television. Americans of the nineteenth century, though, knew Shakespeare on a much more chummy basis—and were not afraid to "improve" him for their own purposes. Juliet, for example, was typically older than she was in the seventeenth century, and did not kiss Romeo at their first meeting. Richard III became even more of a villain than originally written. And King Lear ended up a happy man. In general, the moral prescriptions of Shakespeare's plays were more heavily underlined, the characters more dichotomized. This made the plays more simplistic, in keeping with the popular romanticism of the time. Yet in its own way, this moralistic stance was more sophisticated than the pieties of Enlightenment drama, where characters were evil because they didn't know any better and where happy endings were simply a matter of applying the infallible logic of reason.[30]

Shakespeare aside, however, a call for plays by and about Americans was heard very early in the young republic and became ever more insistent over the course of the nineteenth century. The first major play to fulfill this prescription was Royall Tyler's *The Contrast* (1787). The title referred to the difference between sturdy American republicans and effete British degenerates, embodied in the difference between the play's protagonist, Revolutionary War hero Colonel Manly, and the duplicitous Billy Dimple, heir of a Hudson River estate. A secondary contrast was suggested through Dimple's valet Jessamy and Manly's waiter Jonathon. A simple, assertive, yet likeable yeoman, Jonathon was clearly intended to be Manly's social and intellectual inferior. But he evoked the archetypal "Brother Jonathan" who emerged in this period and reappeared in numerous reincarnations in later plays (e.g., Zachariah Dickerwell, Jediah Homebred, and Solomon Swap, made famous by U.S. actor James Hackett). For the next thirty years, the representative American was a sparsely educated but quick-witted farmer who drove a hard bargain but had a soft heart.

By the 1830s and 1840s, Brother Jonathan had become less a national figure and more one associated with New England. New archetypes emerged, among them the rustic backwoodsman Davy Crockett, the riverboat pilot Mike Fink, and Mose the fireman. In their evocation of the Southerner, Westerner, and working-class city dweller, such archetypes represented the elaboration of a sectional, as well as national, identity whose accents gave U.S. actors an advantage over their British counterparts. Not only were their voices distinctive, but a full appreciation of their foibles depended on an immersion in the American milieu.[31]

It should be noted that these vernacular characters tended to appear in comedies. By twentieth-century standards, nineteenth-century dramas and tragedies often had a melodramatic quality—although, as has already been suggested, the romanticism and moral didacticism of the early nineteenth century can be seen as a reaction to Enlightenment drama, as well as a justification for what was still a suspect form of entertainment. In comedy, however, lower artistic and moral expectations permitted a kind of social commentary that was bracing in its frankness. This was especially true with regard to representations of women. Certainly, the stage was a patriarchal institution that treated women's claims for autonomy as humorous. But such jokes could be revealing and even subversive. One can see this dynamic at work in William Dunlap's 1796 play *The Archers,* in which a young woman tells her sweetheart *not* to go to war:

> *Cecily:* I shall like you the better for it as long as I live—if you're not killed.
> *Conrad:* Why, you should like me better for dying for my country.
> *Cecily:* Should I? Well maybe I should; but somehow I shall never like a dead man as well as a live one.
> *Conrad:* Well I don't know but that your taste is as well founded as your politics.[32]

The Archers, however, is still an eighteenth-century comedy of manners. A broader humor was evident in "The Magna Charter of Heaven," a song from the 1822 play *Deed of Gift:*

> While each freeman's son
> boasts of rights a plenty
> Daughters have but one
> E'en at one and twenty.
> 'Tis the right to choose
> Tom or Dick or Harry
> Whom we will refuse
> Which we wish to marry
>
> *Chorus:*
> 'Tis our chartered right

> Nature's hand has penn'd it
> Let us then unite
> Bravely to defend it
> While our fathers fought
> For our Independence
> Patriot mothers taught
> This to their descendants:
> Daughters guard and save
> Rights too dear to barter
> Spurn the name of slave
> Freedom is our charter[33]

Such a song would only be permissible in the context of comedy—and if the charter was portrayed as of Heaven, not Earth. Nevertheless, it would not have had such vitality if it had not expressed a feeling that resonated with at least some of its audience, and a hope for this world, not the next one.

The mock-utopian injunction to "spurn the name of slave" in the "Magna Charter of Heaven" serves as an important reminder that freedom and equality in the pre-Civil War United States were predicated on whiteness. As everywhere else in the society, race was a major issue on the stage. After Europeans, the two most commonly represented racial groups were Native Americans and African Americans. Depictions of the former tended to occur in the realm of drama; the latter in comedy. The difference reveals a great deal about the relative place of each group in relation to white society.

From the very first settlement, European Americans tended to dichotomize red-white relations between nature and civilization. The rapid development of technology, coupled with progressive Indian removal westward (two processes that were, of course, intimately related), intensified this attitude, turning the Native American into something of a romantic figure—a tragic, dignified embodiment of a vanishing way of life. This portrayal usefully limited white guilt, for if the natives were doomed anyway, white incursions did not need to be seen as brutal. While in many cases portrayals of the destruction of Native Americans centered on evil white men, more often it was internecine conflict or bad Indians who were responsible.

If Indians were allowed a measure of respect, they were still not considered the white man's equal. One important index of this was the treatment of women. Unlike with African Americans, with Native Americans there was at least some toleration of interracial sex, although for the most part playwrights implicitly or explicitly upheld racial separation. Indian women who did marry white men usually converted to Christianity or took up white folkways. And while white women were only sexually propositioned by the most vile villains, red women tended to have to contend with garden-variety boors ("Bad Man! Indian girl's cheek grows redder with shame!" says one such victim).[34]

Perhaps the most well-known play about Native Americans was John Augustus Stone's *Metamora* (1828), commissioned by Edwin Forrest, the most famous actor of his day. The story of an Indian chief who perished fighting New Englanders in King Philip's War of 1675-1678, *Metamora* features the usual depiction of the noble savage who patiently endures his mistreatment by the white man. What makes this play unusual, though, is that Metamora finally strikes out against his oppressors. "Our Lands! Our nation's freedom! Or the Grave!" he cries. Finally surrounded, he kills his wife rather than have her raped by whites, then dies with her name on his lips. In his passion for freedom—which evokes Patrick Henry's famous slogan "Give me liberty or give me death!"—and in his possessive sexual anxiety about women, Metamora seems more white than red. Of course, he represents a white man's idea of what a great Indian should be, and his dramatic actions at the end of the play were probably as much calculated to show off Forrest's physique and generate standing ovations as to make a political statement. But the play was nonetheless a genuine critique of white policy toward Indians. "Let us hope, for the honor of humanity, that this applause is bestowed on Mr. Forrest, rather than the ferocious savage he impersonates," said a reviewer in the *American Quarterly Review* in 1830. In all likelihood the writer need not have worried, for the pace of aggression toward Indians did not slow in any perceptible way. Moreover, Robert Bird, who helped revise the play to suit Forrest's purposes, later became the author of *Nick of the Woods* (1837), a novel that essentially justified a policy of extermination.[35]

By the mid-nineteenth century, Native Americans were a dwindling group living outside white society. African Americans, by contrast, were part of a racially hierarchial system *within* white society, and their numbers were increasing. These facts help account for the different treatment of the two groups on the stage. A disappearing danger, Indians were often romanticized, the subject of nostalgia for a vanishing world. Black-white relations, on the other hand, were a subject of increasing conflict and uncertainty.

It must be noted that while an assumption of black inferiority has been a staple of white thinking since the first slave arrived on these shores, this attitude toward blacks has not been monolithic. "In certain places and at certain times between 1607 and 1800, the 'lower sorts' of whites appear to have been pleasantly lacking in racial consciousness," writes David R. Roediger in his study of nineteenth-century racism. Thus, he notes, white indentured servants and black (and Indian) slaves sometimes fled oppressive masters together in the colonial era, and blacks and whites socialized—and engaged in petty crime—together. Some slave revolts, notably in New York City in 1741 and Richmond in 1800, included white participants.[36]

When present at all, African Americans were generally relegated to small roles on the early American stage. Free men of color did occasionally appear, and were treated with relative respect. And there were a few plays about the plight of slaves, usually centering on the tragedy of broken families. Most of the time, however, blacks were the butt of jokes, often stemming from their unusual dialects. In this regard, they were not unlike such ethnic types as the (drunk) Irishman, also a source of humor. More specific to blacks was comedy based on a purported love of finery, which reflected a racist contempt for any effort to enjoy white economic privilege. By the time Brother Jonathan was a clearly elaborated archetype, so was his black counterpart, Sambo. Although this "happy darky" was generally not allowed to express the confidence and pride of white characters like Jonathan, he was sometimes portrayed as a person of simple integrity, although this changed as the Civil War approached.[37]

These black characters were almost always portrayed by whites in blackface—white men who covered their faces with burnt cork and used what they considered black language, mannerisms, songs, etc. By about 1820, such characters were common, especially for songs or brief *entr'acte* ("between act") performances. However, this cultural practice was placed on an entirely new basis sometime around 1828, when Thomas D. Rice, an actor who specialized in blackface performances, saw an old African-American man perform an unfamiliar dance while singing "Wheel about and turn about jus' so/Every time I wheel about, I jump Jim Crow." Rice learned the song and dance, added new verses, and began performing "Jump Jim Crow" on stage. It was a sensation across the country, and even in London when Rice took it on tour.

In the 1830s, blackface entertainment became increasingly popular but remained only one part of an evening's stage entertainment. It was not until the early 1840s that groups of blackface actors began banding together to form troupes for what became known as minstrel shows. Many went on tour through the South and West, but the demand was so heavy that some cities were able to sustain troupes for a decade or more.

Between the mid-1840s and the onset of the Civil War, the minstrel show evolved into the three-part structure that would define its course for the rest of the century. In the first part, the entire company formed a semicircle, with the star performers, called "Tambo" and "Bones" for the instruments they played, at either end. Individual minstrels sang or danced, while the rest of the company sang the choruses. Such numbers were interspersed with jokes and comic songs, presided over by a white master of ceremonies known as the interlocutor. The first part ended with a group song-and-dance number.

The second part of the show, known as the "olio," was a variety section that featured any number of novelty acts. One important element of the olio was a stump speech, usually given by an endman, who spoke in the garbled language of a pretentious black man "putting on airs." "Transcendentalism is dat spiritual cognoscence ob psychological irrefragibility," began one such speech, which simultaneously lampooned the "uppity" black man and the pieties of such intellectuals as Ralph Waldo Emerson. Indeed, class critiques were a very big part of minstrel social commentary, so much so that African Americans occasionally had a laugh at the expense of the white elite, as in this story about a black man who rides a ferry with a white one:

> When I got out a little piece from the shore, de man axed me if I knowed anyting about frenologism [phrenology, the mid-nineteenth century pseudoscience that mapped the brain]. I told him no. Ah, says he, den one quarter of your life is gone. Finally he says, does you know anyting about grammar. I told him no. Ah, says he, den one half ob you life am gone . . . He axed me if I knowed anyting about dickshionary. I told him no and he say tree quarters of your life is gone. We hit a rock and den I axed him if he knowed how to swim. He said no. Den, says I, de whole four quarters of your life am gone—shure.[38]

In this story, blacks and whites share the kind of practical knowledge and wit so often celebrated on the U.S. stage, and the "other" is the formally educated white American who is both arrogant and ignorant.

Shakespeare, incidentally, was a favorite among minstrels, both in such speeches and as a source of simple jokes. "When was Desdemona like a ship?" a comic would ask. "When she was moored," came the answer. "Get thee to a brewery!" Hamlet would tell Ophelia—a telling joke on middle-class temperance advocates who considered alcohol a major moral issue. Such comedy is an important reminder not only of Shakespeare's popularity with the mechanic's set, which formed the core of the minstrel audience, but also of the often risque and decisively male humor that characterized it.[39]

The final part of the minstrel show was a one-act skit. These generally had Southern plantation settings and featured slapstick comedy "nearly always ending in a flurry of inflated bladders, bombardments of cream pies, or fireworks explosions that literally closed the show with a bang," according to one historian of minstrelsy. Such climaxes were typical of stage entertainment in the early nineteenth century, when even the most sober Shakespearian tragedy was followed by a farce to lighten the audience's mood.[40]

Broad comedy was only one side of minstrelsy, however. The other was a kind of melancholy that took a variety of forms in the songs. Some were laments for lost family members; others expressed nostalgia for plantation life. The most famous composer of such music was Stephen Foster, who began his career as a blackface singer before selling a series of songs to minstrel troupes in the 1840s and 1850s. His "Old Folks at Home" and "Massa's in the Cold Ground" were great favorites in his time, while others ("O! Susanna," "Jeannie with the Light Brown Hair") are still familiar today. Many described dying or dead lovers, which intensified their impact. Foster drank himself to death during the Civil War.

Both the comic and the sentimental sides of the minstrel tradition were racist. With certain partial exceptions, like the ferry story quoted above, most humor in minstrel shows was at the expense of African Americans and was emphatically hostile to any hint of equality with whites. The sentimental strain in minstrel entertainment, a form that generally celebrated plantation life, implicitly or explicitly sanctioned slavery as the natural and most comfortable place for African Americans (escaped slaves were usually depicted as unhappy). In the early days of minstrelsy, there were important exceptions to this rule, among them depictions of rape, alcoholism, and broken families, as well as humorous jibes at slaveholders. For instance, "Blue Tail Fly," with its famous chorus "Jimmy crack corn and I don't care/master's gone away," expresses pleasure at the death of a slaveowner. But such sentiments became progressively less common as sectional conflict intensified and slavery became an increasingly divisive political issue.

As the controversy over slavery intensified in the 1840s and 1850s, it strained the national political system to the breaking point and polarized the parties along racial lines. The Whig Party had collapsed completely by the early 1850s, giving way to the Free Soil and Republican parties, both of which were against slavery. During the same years, pro-slavery forces got the upper hand in the Democratic Party, driving many Barnburners into Free Soil and/or Republican ranks and recruiting Southern pro-slavery Whigs. The effect was to make the Democrats more racist, and this new hard line was reflected in minstrel shows, whose cultural politics were strongly consonant with those of the Democratic Party.[41]

There were two powerful ironies in all of this. First, while minstrelsy was considered a cultural form that displayed the variety and mirth of Southern plantation life, some of the most important figures in its development—E.P. Christy, Thomas Rice, and Foster, among others—were of Northern, urban origin. So was Dan Emmett, an Ohioan whose "Dixie's Land," a paean to the plantation sung from the point of view of a slave ("I wish I war in the land ob cotton/Old times dere am not forgotten"), eventually became a Confederate anthem. In fact, there is a logic to this apparent contradiction, in part because minstrelsy was largely an urban creation for urban audiences, and in part because it embodied the Southern planter–Northern working-man alliance that had been forged in the 1840s.

The larger, more powerful irony in minstrelsy was its dependence on the very African-American culture it satirized, belittled, and feared. In fact, many minstrels prided themselves on the degree of verisimilitude in their renditions of black culture. E.P. Christy and other influential troupe leaders boasted about their immersion in African-American life and fancied themselves amateur anthropologists. While these men undoubtedly overestimated their powers of observation and recall, there can be little question that minstrel shows did tap into the immense vitality of an Afro-American folklore that had accumulated over the course of two centuries of bondage. The ferry story quoted above suggests the humorous, pragmatic thrust of secular black storytelling, while melancholy minstrel songs evoked the otherworldly quest for reassurance found in black sacred music. For all their fear of and condescension toward black people, minstrels captured the genuine beauties of pastoral life for white rural refugees who were forced to leave the Irish, German, or American countrysides for subsistence wages in large cities. If minstrelsy was a cultural form that often projected fierce hatred, it also, often despite itself, betrayed a deep admiration and affinity for the world the slaves had made under conditions of severe adversity.[42]

In terms of the future course of popular culture, what was most significant about minstrelsy was its heterogeneous character. Not only did whites alter black culture in the course of its translation and migration into the cities—many minstrel songs have a strongly Celtic flavor that draws on shared traditions of oppression—but minstrelsy also found its way back into black communities, where it underwent further refinement. For the most part, minstrel songs that became part of the slave cultural tradition were those, like "Blue Tail Fly," that retained their critical character.[43] They eventually formed part of the bedrock for blues, gospel, and other forms of African-American music. Meanwhile, minstrelsy's ideas and forms—comic skits, monologues, and a variety format—laid the foundations for burlesque, vaudeville, and eventually television. For better and worse, here was a true wellspring of U.S. culture.

Deceptive Simplicity:
Show Business in the Age of Barnum

The stage represented only one facet of the entertainment world in the decades before the Civil War. A series of separate but interrelated developments evolved in tandem with it: new forms of popular culture, new attitudes toward it, and the economic elaboration of what became known as show *business*. No one better understood these developments, or better integrated them, than P.T. Barnum, and no history of U.S. culture would be complete without him.

There was little in Phineas Taylor Barnum's early life that would indicate the breadth of his later success. He was born in rural Connecticut in 1810, the son of a man who struggled financially, as tailor, farmer, tavern-keeper, livery-stable operator, and country-store merchant. Working in the store, young Barnum learned about the false pieties of Yankee business practices. In his famous memoir *Struggles and Triumphs*, he used the example of a New England deacon and grocer who asked his clerk: "'John, have you watered the rum?' 'Yes, Sir.' 'And sanded the sugar?' 'Yes, Sir.' 'And dusted the pepper?' 'Yes, Sir.' 'Then come up to prayers.'"[44]

Barnum's father died when the boy was fifteen, leaving behind heavy debts and five children. Over the course of the next decade, Barnum worked as a grocery clerk in New York, tried unsuccessfully to sell used books in Connecticut, and founded a weekly newspaper (he was a fervent Jacksonian Democrat in a highly conservative state). He also established a store of his own, where he made a fair amount of money managing a local lottery until new regulations forced him to curtail that activity. After his marriage in 1834, he returned to New York to try the grocery business again. His prospects seemed to be narrowing.

In 1835, however, Barnum heard about a slave named Joice Heth who was reputed to be George Washington's 161-year-old wet nurse. The woman's owner claimed to have a 1727 bill of sale proving her authenticity, and her appearance—she was blind and toothless, but very spirited and convincing in her talk of "dear little George"—was dramatic. Sensing an opportunity, Barnum bought her, sold his interest in his store, and launched his career as a stage manager by advertising Heth as a traveling entertainment exhibition.

In so doing, he was participating in a long-standing traveling-show tradition that predated the American Revolution. Exhibitors would present miscellaneous, crude, and often deceiving "entertainments": animals, mechanical oddities, wax figures, peep shows, and so on. The practice continued through the nineteenth century and eventually became the featured element in the medicine show—the highly theatrical (and often tawdry) entertainment event that was used to create a crowd that could then be sold tonics, elixirs, and other products of dubious value.[45]

As Barnum himself must have realized—but never admitted—Joice Heth's claim of being Washington's nurse was highly dubious.[46] The fledgling showman recognized her potential at a time when Washington was almost universally revered and anything about him was sure to attract an audience. Moreover, in a pattern that would mark many other such enterprises in his career, he was able to base Heth's appeal less on his ability to *prove* her claims than on her and her former owner's having *made* them in the first place, allowing others to judge for themselves. He also developed a number of the techniques that he would continue to use repeatedly: careful packaging through press releases, relentless exploitation of the local press, and indignant denials of lies he himself had planted. It would not be too much to say that Barnum was the inventor of the modern publicity business.

Barnum went on to manage a number of other acts, among them a blackface dancer and a professional Italian juggler. When another juggler boasted he could do everything Barnum's performer did, Barnum publicly offered him $1,000 to try. When the juggler refused, Barnum secretly struck a deal with him to stage a rivalry, which Barnum portrayed as a test of national character, between foreign skill and native genius (foreign skill would win).

Over the course of the next few years, Barnum travelled widely, invested his earnings in a more respectable company—and lost them. He mounted a few more shows, sold pictorial bibles, and even wrote advertisement copy for the Bowery Theatre. By 1841, his fortunes were at low ebb.

That year, Scudder's American Museum, a once impressive but now run-down collection of exhibits, went up for sale in New York. Since the late eighteenth century, museums had been halls of learning for the elite, the most famous of which was Peale's Museum of Philadelphia, founded in 1784. A bastion of the U.S. Enlightenment (Benjamin Franklin and Thomas Jefferson were among its donors, and Jefferson was its first president), this and other museums were designed to collect, catalog, and exhibit artifacts of natural history. Their mission also included educating the public, but by the Jacksonian era they were facing increased competition from the theater and from other forms of entertainment that lacked the museum's didactic air. On the other hand, museums had an undeniable cachet, particularly for a growing middle class that considered theater disreputable and museums a legitimate form of self-improvement.

Sensing an opportunity to fuse these cultural sensibilities, Barnum went to great lengths to acquire Scudder's Museum. Through a series of clever machinations, he leased the site and began to reorganize the exhibits. Although many were retained, Barnum put a premium on the rapid turnover of attractions and was continually on the watch for novelty. He also orchestrated dramatic presentations, which brought to the museum people who would never have dreamed of attending even the relatively upscale Park Theatre. By blurring the line between edification and entertainment, he was able to greatly expand both the range of popular culture and the market for it.

Barnum applied many of the tricks he had learned over the previous years to attract visitors to the museum, including intense publicity, colorful displays, and staged controversies. He also played jokes on the public. As a publicity gesture, for example, he advertised that he had hired a band to play free music outside the museum. He then chose the worst band he could find. "When people expect 'something for nothing,' they are sure to be cheated, and so, no doubt, some of my out-door patrons were sorely disappointed," he later reported in *Struggles and Triumphs*. Those willing to part with a quarter and go inside would get their money's worth and more.[47]

Many did spend the quarter. For while some were offended by such tricks, others were fascinated by them. And Barnum was hardly alone in playing jokes on the public. One of the most famous examples of such trickery was the "Moon Hoax" of 1835, when the New York *Sun* ran a series of articles describing astronomical breakthroughs in South Africa that would allow a new picture of the solar system. The climax of the series was a piece describing winged men inhabiting the moon, prompting Yale University to send a delegation to investigate and Baptist preachers to lead prayer-meetings for their fellow beings. These stories were fabricated, of course, and those who considered themselves respectable, as well as the *Sun*'s ever growing cast of competitors, were indignant; most readers, however, were amused. Indeed, the paper gave itself credit for "diverting the public mind, for a while, from that bitter apple of discord, the abolition of slavery."[48]

The antebellum years were also the age of the "confidence man," a mysterious figure who took advantage of the naive and managed to hoodwink even the suspicious. Herman Melville's 1857 novel of the same name presented a character who might or might not have been what he appeared to be, which offered the novelist a way to explore his fascination with the larger ambiguities surrounding the hectic commercial life of the 1840s and 1850s. To a great extent, there was a class dimension in attitudes toward the confidence man. For the emerging middle class, he was widely seen as a deplorable figure and caused a great deal of social anxiety, perhaps because he belied the powerful myths of self-reliance, upward mobility, and moral certitude central to the legitimacy of the political system. For white workers losing hope of ever moving beyond wage-earning status, there was a kind of pleasure in figures who exposed the contradictions of U.S. life, and an interest in trying to discover the underlying logic of trickery.[49]

Although they still largely lacked a voice within popular culture, African Americans had their own folklore version of the confidence man: Brer Rabbit. A trickster who routinely exploited larger and more dangerous animals in the jungle and then escaped their subsequent rage, this allegorical character figured in countless slave tales as an example of how the weak could survive—and even defeat—the strong. The most famous tale was the story of the briar patch, where the captured rabbit used reverse psychology by begging the wolf to do anything but throw him into the briar patch, which, of course, was exactly where he wanted to be—and ended up. While Brer Rabbit was not an object of universal veneration (especially after emancipation, when there appeared at least some hope that freedpeople could gain access to, and mobility within, white society), he was nevertheless a clear-eyed realist who recognized relations of power and adopted effective, if not always moral, strategies for realizing his goals.[50]

Folk tales like those of Brer Rabbit existed in profusion in both black and white society in the early nineteenth century. As the outlines of a modern industrial society emerged, many of these tales were revised, adapted, or simply reproduced in mass-produced cultural forms, especially plays and minstrel shows. But they received their fullest elaboration in the many kinds of storytelling that came of age in the Jacksonian era.

Transgressing Lines:
Antebellum Popular Narrative

There were three major influences on popular writing between 1820 and 1860. The first was regional folklore, an often humorous form that reached large national audiences through a rapidly expanding media infrastructure. The second was cheap, often sensational, fiction emanating from Eastern cities, much of which exhibited a radical edge infused by the content and style of the reform movements that were unfolding across the antebellum United States. The third was the conventional novel, a form in which women writers played an especially large role. These elements intersected at various points in time and in the work of a number of writers, creating a dynamic literary culture.

In the 1820s, as Brother Jonathan moved from a secondary to a major figure on the stage, his comic analogue appeared in print. He went under a variety of guises, the most famous of which was Jack Downing. Downing was the creation of Portland, Maine journalist Seba Smith. Starting in 1830, Smith's fictional character wrote a series of letters on local politics for the Portland *Daily Courier,* the paper Smith edited. Jack Downing drew on what folklorists would call Down East humor: a clipped, understated sensibility that relied heavily on irony. (His spirit survives in contemporary folklore as the kind of person who, after prolonged reflection, advises lost tourists looking for help that "you can't get there from here.") Downing played the role of the country bumpkin who would visit cities like Portland or Boston and puncture urban pretensions. As his popularity grew—the Downing letters were published all over the country by the 1850s—Downing became an advisor to President Andrew Jackson and commented on the national scene.[51]

As with Brother Jonathan, Jack Downing (and Sam Slick, a similar Down East character) was a regional figure who simultaneously represented a more broadly national Yankee spirit. By the 1840s, however, it was the characters and humor of the Old Southwest, which stretched from Kentucky to Texas, that were capturing national attention. This regional sensibility, which revealed a good deal about the quest for national identity (and territory) also generated a pool of images and concepts that would later be refashioned by Northern intellectuals and urban purveyors of popular culture.

As mentioned earlier, the quintessential Southwesterner was Davy Crockett. What makes Crockett unusual is that, unlike fictional characters such as Downing or more generalized stereotypes like Sambo, he was a real person. A veteran of the War of 1812, he acquired conquered Indian lands in Tennessee and became an ardent supporter of settlers' rights against those of the Indians who were forcibly moved West and the land speculators back East. His image as a rugged frontiersman (he killed over one-hundred bears in one season alone) and his common-man demeanor (that famous coonskin cap, which later became part of his legend) made him a popular figure in state politics. Elected to Congress in 1827, the slaveholding Crockett began as a rank-and-file Jackson supporter, but a dispute over land policy led to a break with the Democrats. The party failed in its first attempt to unseat him with a rival candidate in 1829, but succeeded in 1831. Crockett then cast his lot with the Whigs, who gave him political and financial support and gained a frontiersman icon to compete against the appeal of Jackson. An avid expansionist, Crockett was executed by Mexican soldiers for his role as an insurrectionary at the Alamo in 1836.

But it was the mythic Crockett, not the real one, who won enduring fame. In 1832, just after he lost his Congressional seat, a Cincinnati newspaper published an account of Crockett's adventures. Two years later, *A Narrative of the Life of David Crockett of the State of Tennessee, Written by Himself* (actually written by a ghostwriter) became an immediate success, going through seven printings in the first year alone. Three more Crockett books had been published by 1836, the last of which claimed to be based on a diary found on his body at the Alamo. Written in homespun Southwestern dialect, these books described a series of adventures, rendered in a tone of masculine bravado that pleased male readers in city and countryside alike. "On the subject of my style, it is bad enough, in all conscience, to please critics, if that is what they are after," Crockett explained in the first book. "They are a sort of vermin, though, that I shan't even so much as stop to brush off." His widely quoted maxim, which appeared on the title page and in the books' advertising, was "I leave this rule for others, when I'm dead: Be always sure you're right—THEN GO AHEAD."[52]

In terms of the direction of popular culture, perhaps even more important than the "official" Crockett books were the approximately fifty "Crockett almanacs" published between 1835 and 1856. These capture the essence of Southwestern literary vision in two important ways. First, the humorous anecdotes show the same exaggerated, legendary quality that marked the plethora of tall tales from the region. In one such almanac, Crockett is asked by Andrew Jackson to wrestle a comet. "I was appointed by the President to stand on the Alleghany [sic] Mountains and wring the comet's tail off," he relates with deadpan surrealism. "I did so, but got my hands most shockingly burnt, and the hair singed off my head, so that I was as bald as a trencher. I div right into the Waybosh river, and thus saved my best stone blue coat and grass green small clothes."[53] In such tales of superhuman exploits, Crockett joined a pantheon of heroes that emerged in the nineteenth century, including riverboatman Mike Fink, his sidekick Sal Fink, and the black railroad worker John Henry, mightier than the machine.[54]

A second important dimension of the Southwestern narrative style was its reliance on vivid and violent imagery. When Crockett's uncle gets married, he presents his beloved with two eyes he has gouged. She dries them out, makes earrings out of them, and wears them to church. Sal Fink escapes from the stake to which she was bound by fifty Indians and then ties her captors together by their heels. Crockett, for his part, deals with a swindling squatter by forcing him to eat pig dung. Such violence and exaggeration, which crossed gender and race lines, can be understood in a number of ways: as a commentary on the real crudity and danger of frontier life; as a form of compensation for a sense of cultural insecurity; or as an assault on the niceties of respectable opinion. Whatever the case, the power and appeal of this imagery went far beyond the region of its origin (indeed, its spread depended on Eastern publishing houses). It could be seen in the horror stories of Edgar Allan Poe and the often bizarre images in some of Herman Melville's work. Even Ralph Waldo Emerson's famous depiction of the artist as a "transparent eyeball" was an adaptation of the imagery common to a Crockett almanac.[55]

Regional humor and storytelling were just two of the elements in the antebellum popular cultural matrix. A third was the blizzard of reform literature that blanketed the country in the first half of the nineteenth century.

In one sense, reform had little impact on many forms of popular culture because much of it came from the emerging middle class and was directed at working people, as a kind of social control. Efforts to stop the consumption of alcohol (the first American "Just Say No" campaign was the temperance movement of the early nineteenth century), police public morals, and enforce religious piety were often aimed at the people who went to the theater or spent time sampling the amusements of the Bowery. At the same time, however, many reforms—antislavery and women's rights, to name two examples—had at least some relevance to those outside the middle class, not least because in many cases the problems addressed by reformers were very real. For instance, one temperance group, the Washingtonians, were themselves reformed alcoholics, and one of the most popular plays of the period was William Henry Smith's *The Drunkard* (1844), in which an upright man is lured into alcoholism and his family blackmailed by an evil lawyer. This motif would recur in T.S. Arthur's Washingtonian-influenced novel *Ten Nights in a Barroom* (1854), which later became *The Drunkard* of the late nineteenth century (see Chapter 3).[56]

The wellspring of antebellum reform was a religious revival known as the Second Great Awakening. Like the First Great Awakening that surged through the colonies between 1720 and 1760, the Second Great Awakening was a powerful evangelical movement that stressed personal power and responsibility. Central to any transformation was the concept of perfectibility, whereby individuals could identify and destroy evil within themselves and thus collectively usher in a paradise on earth before, not after, the return of Christ. Rejecting the more formal and intellectual foundations of established religions, the key institution of the Awakening was the revival meeting, at which people gathered from far and wide to worship, as well as to interact in social and even commercial ways.[57]

Beginning in the South and West in the early decades of the nineteenth century, and especially affecting poor black and white communities, the Second Great Awakening fanned out across the country over the first half of the century. Along the way, it became diffused and secularized. Personal perfectibility increasingly moved into the realm of social perfectibility, and moral suasion gradually took on more aggressively political dimensions. The classic case in point is antislavery agitation, which moved from churches to secular organizations and eventually into the political parties. By the 1850s, the religious impulse remained strong, but it joined with a patchwork quilt of movements that ranged from bourgeois attempts to close working-class saloons to proto-socialist utopian communities that emphasized communitarian values in work and even sex.[58]

Such increasingly political reform projects depended on proselytizers. Some were preachers, who in African-American communities adopted a dramatic style that would have an incalculable influence on future black culture, especially music. In the emerging middle class, there arose the institution of the lecture circuit, which created opportunities for former clerics like Emerson to make a living by giving speeches and catering to the mania for self-improvement among the upwardly mobile. A third form of transmission was written: small, cheap pamphlets that exploited the same possibilities tapped by newspapers in the Jacksonian era.

The most prolific publisher of such pamphlets—or, for that matter, any printed material at the time—was the American Tract Society. Tract publications were distributed by colporteurs, or missionary salesmen, and at commercial outlets. By the 1850s, the ATS had published over 500 tracts, and its *smallest* printing was 6,000 copies. The largest, "Quench Not the Spirit," numbered almost 1 million. The ATS was only one of a number of tract publishers, and spiritually oriented material was only one component in a field that included conduct manuals, self-help books, and sociopolitical exposés.[59]

This rich world of printed matter provided the backdrop for the emergence of one of the most important popular cultural forms of the nineteenth century: the dime novel. Perhaps the best known were the Westerns that were published in the decades after the Civil War (see Chapter 3), but these cheaply made booklets, usually bound in yellow covers, first emerged in the 1840s. They represented only one of the forms this highly sensational fiction took. Another common vehicle was the story paper, which serialized novels before their publication in dime-novel format. The most famous story paper was the New York *Ledger,* which was founded by Robert Bonner, a Scotch-Irish immigrant who began as a printing apprentice and built a newspaper empire. In the early 1850s, he bought an old mercantile paper and transformed it by publishing fiction, verse, and moral essays. Bonner scored an editorial and publicity coup in 1855 when he persuaded Sara Willis Parton—a.k.a. Fanny Fern—to write a regular column for the *Ledger* (see below). At its peak, the paper had a circulation of 400,000, the largest of any periodical in the country.[60]

<u>A closer look:</u>

THE ART AND LIFE OF FANNY FERN

It was hot and humid in the dank boardinghouse, and Ruth Hall was faint with hunger. Ever since her husband had died the previous winter, leaving her with two daughters to raise, her financial straits had become increasingly desperate. There were no jobs for school-teachers, sewing did not pay enough to support the children, and there were no other leads. Time and hope were running out.

Hall's family was of little help—in fact, it was downright hostile. Since her mother's death, Ruth's father only reluctantly gave her a

pittance and urged her to give up the children. Her in-laws, who had never liked her when their son was alive, now schemed to gain custody of the girls. And former friends avoided her. When she finally turned to writing for newspapers and sought help from her brother, a promi-nent editor, he told her she lacked talent and should "seek some *unobtrusive* employ-ment." Working women, it seemed, should be neither seen *nor* heard.

SARA WILLIS PARTON, C.1868

Ruth Hall was a fictional char-acter. But her creator—Sara Willis Parton, a.k.a. Fanny Fern—was not. In many important ways, Ruth Hall's story was Fanny Fern's story, and Fanny Fern's story, one of the best known and most controversial of the mid-nineteenth century, opens a window on some of the less visible aspects of women's lives in the Victorian era.

The life of the future novelist and columnist began in relative privilege. Grata (soon changed to Sara) Payson was born in Portland, Maine, in 1811, the daughter of an anti-Federalist newspaper editor who relocated the family to Boston when Sara was a child. Given a nickname of "Sal Volatile," she impressed her classmates at Cather-ine Beecher's seminary in Hartford, Connecticut, and after graduat-ing wrote pieces for the *Youth's Companion,* a magazine founded by her father. In 1837, she married a well-to-do banker, and over the next seven years bore three daughters.

Then things began to fall apart. Her mother, eldest daughter, and husband died between 1844 and 1846, leaving her with unsympathetic relatives and without a means of supporting herself and her two remaining children. She turned to teaching and sewing, but neither earned her enough to support her family, and she was forced to relinquish one daughter to her in-laws. In 1849, she reluctantly entered a marriage of convenience to a Boston widower, but when he enlisted his children to spy on her, she left him and moved to a hotel (he then left town to avoid supporting her, and subsequently divorced her for desertion).

Widow, divorcee, and single mother, Sara was again left to her own resources, now more than ever a pariah to her relatives. In 1851, she turned to writing and succeeded in selling pieces to small Boston newspapers, adopting the pen name "Fanny Fern" (a joke on the florid style of women writers popular at the time). But when she asked one of her two brothers, poet Nathaniel P. Willis, editor of the New York *Home Journal*, to publish her work, he refused. Her brother's assistant, James Parton, then printed them without her brother's knowledge. When Willis found out, he demanded Parton stop; Parton tried to persuade Willis of the worth of his sister's work, but when he failed, he resigned. Eleven years Fern's junior, he became her third and final husband in 1856. She kept her pen name, however, and the two signed a prenuputial agreement to protect her assets for her children.

Meanwhile, Fern had an easier time with her other brother, Richard Willis, editor of the *New York Musical World and Times*. Its publisher, Oliver Dyer, sought Fern's services for his paper, unaware that she was related to his employee. Richard Willis was not as implacable as his brother, and cooperated when Dyer hired her to write a weekly piece on the issues of the day. As such, she became the first woman in the United States to work as a professional columnist.

Fanny Fern's columns, which covered a wide variety of topics, many of them personal, were pirated and reprinted in newspapers and magazines around the country; soon, she had a national reputation. Her writing had a humorous, ironic, and sometimes sarcastic edge that was considered unusual for a woman writer. In fact, there was speculation about whether she was a woman at all. While not generally considered a women's rights activist, she consistently argued that women must seek to provide for themselves financially, develop their creative talents, and take, rather than ask for, the same rights men enjoyed in marriage. "You see, you had no 'call,' Mrs. Tom Cabin, to drop your babies and darning-needle to immortalize your name," Fanny Fern wrote of Harriet Beecher Stowe amid the clamor surrounding *Uncle Tom's Cabin.* "Well, I hope your shoulders are broad enough and strong enough to bear all the abuse your presumption will call down upon you."

In 1853, an upstate New York publisher collected a series of Fern's columns into a collection called *Fern Leaves from Fanny's Portfolio,* which became an instant bestseller. A second *Fern Leaves* appeared the next year, as well as a book for children, *Little Ferns for Fanny's Little Friends.* The three books together sold over 130,000 copies in the United States and almost 50,000 abroad, finally giving her financial security.

Fern was now able to write *Ruth Hall: A Domestic Tale of the Present Time.* The novel, based closely on the events of Fern's life, appeared at the end of 1854. She assumed no one would know her true identity, but a former employer who saw himself unfavorably portrayed in the book let the cat out of the bag. This created an immediate sensation, and readers scooped up the novel, especially because of Fern's portrayal of Hyacinth Ellet, a pretentious fop who was clearly modeled on her brother Nathaniel. While some revelled in the controversy, others were appalled, for revealing reasons: "If Fanny Fern were a man, a man who believed that the gratification of revenge were a proper occupation for one who has been abused, and that those who have injured us are fair game, *Ruth Hall* would be a natural and excusable book," wrote a reviewer for the *New York Times* in December 1854. "But we confess that we cannot understand how a delicate, suffering woman can hunt down even her persecutors so remorselessly. We cannot think so highly of [such] an author's womanly gentleness."

Yet it was also clear that whatever they may have thought about the writer and the publicity surrounding her, there were those who found *Ruth Hall* a compelling piece of work. Nathaniel Hawthorne, who had little patience for the "d——d female scribblers" who were so popular in the 1850s, held the novel in high regard. "The woman writes as if the devil was in her; and that is the only condition under which a woman ever writes anything worth reading," he wrote his publisher. "Can you tell me anything about this Fanny Fern?" he concluded at the end of his letter. "If you meet her, I wish you would let her know how much I admire her."

Fern followed *Ruth Hall* with *Rose Clark* (1856), a novel loosely based on her second marriage. But her primary occupation remained that of newspaperwoman. In 1855, Robert Bonner of the New York *Ledger,* the fabulously successful story paper, sought her services for a weekly column, offering the princely sum of $25 a week. When she declined, he doubled the figure. When she declined again, he raised his offer to $75. She finally agreed to do it for $100, making her the most highly paid newspaper writer of her time. She wrote the column without fail for the next sixteen years, a champion of everything from women's suffrage to the poetry of Walt Whitman (though a financial dispute would poison her relationship with the poet). Her last piece appeared two days after her death in 1872.

Fanny Fern was an American original. At a time that saw a celebration of the working man, she lived and described the travails of the working woman. At a time that embraced the myth of the happy family, she frankly depicted the power struggles and conflicts that lay at the heart of domestic life. And at a time of often rigid gender roles, she expanded the scope of what it was possible for women to do. "I cherish the hope," she wrote in the preface to *Ruth Hall*, "that, somewhere in the land, it may fan into a flame, in some tried heart, the fading embers of hope, well-nigh extinguished by wintry fortune and summer friends." In art as in life, Fanny Fern achieved that goal for many American women.

―――――――――

While the appeal of dime fiction was broad, it seems to have been produced with an eye toward a white working-class clientele. The stories were typically written in a mode of artisan radicalism, whereby good-natured, diligent workers were preyed on by feckless, hypocritical, and exploitative owners. Good triumphs over evil, often either with the help of poor heroines who turn out to be wealthy heiresses or through the foiling of dastardly plots that are revealed in the nick of time. The class accents in dime novels invoked the ideological energy and moral outrage that animated reform literature: they claimed to perform a social mission even as they diverted and entertained.[61]

One of the most interesting of the dime novelists was George Lippard. A Philadelphia newspaper writer who turned to fiction, Lippard wrote a number of historical novels before his most famous work, *The Quaker City, or the Monks of Monk Hall* (1844). A lurid exposé of aristocratic lechery and corruption, *Quaker City* tells the story of an upright young woman tricked into marriage by a rake. He takes his bride to an old mansion called Monk Hall, where members of an evil fraternity carry on all kinds of perversions. In the end, virtue emerges victorious, but not before the reader can voyeuristically observe the villains gloating over the "snowy globes" and "voluptuous limbs" of their victims. Lippard's class-conscious stories were laced with such erotic overtones.[62]

Lippard was not alone. The stereotypical image of the Victorian American is that of a comically uptight prude who cannot tolerate even a hint of sexuality. In fact, however, pornographic popular fiction was avidly consumed by dime-novel readers. (Of course, prudery and lechery can be seen as two sides of the same sexual coin, but at the very least, the prevailing view does not suggest the dynamic element of Victorian sexual tensions.) One of the most popular erotic writers was George Thompson, author of works with titillating titles like *The Gay Girls of New York* and *Fanny Greeley: or, Confessions of a Free Love Sister* (both 1853). In these novels, as in such other works as George Foster's *New York by Gaslight* (1850) and Ned Buntline's *The G'hals of New York* (1850), homosexuality, group sex, child pornography, and sadomasochism were vividly evoked or openly described. Much of this writing catered to male fantasies, although it should be noted that Thompson and Lippard also depicted women with strong sexual drives, which made their work more textured, even if such characters can also be seen as a form of male fantasy. Many of these writers defended their work on the grounds that they were reformers trying to root out moral corruption. But like the reformers from whom they borrowed their rhetoric and imagery—the most ardent Washingtonians were those most likely to lapse back into drinking—they protested too much.[63]

Cheap fiction was not solely for, by, or about men. One of the most prolific and beloved novelists of the mid-nineteenth century was E.D.E.N. Southworth, the so-called queen of American novelists, who overcame early poverty to become an enormously successful writer for Bonner's *Ledger*. Southworth's serialized novels, later published in book form, featured strong heroines who performed daring exploits, sometimes by disguising themselves as men. For instance, in *The Hidden Hand* (1859), Southworth's most popular novel, her protagonist Capitola dons the garb of a newsboy to support herself and evade grasping men. *How He Won Her* (1868; originally serialized as *Britomarte, or The Man-Hater),* features a woman who cross-dresses as a Union soldier in order to fight alongside her lover in the Civil War and then rises through the ranks on the strength of her bravery under fire. Southworth's protagonists often settled down to conventional marriages, but not before they provided both escapism and imaginative possibilities for male and female factory workers caught in the grip of increasingly grim industrial conditions. After the Civil War, these conditions themselves became the topics of dime-novel fiction.[64]

Southworth is an important figure in antebellum literary history because her audience overlapped with that of the so-called "sentimental novelists" (as they were then known), or "domestic novelists" or "literary domestics" (as they are now known), who occupied a prominent place on the cultural landscape. These writers had a largely middle-class orientation, but their writing affected the racial and gender dynamics of the period and therefore bear examination. To do so, however, it is necessary to place them in the context of the standard literary history of the period.

As noted at the end of Chapter 1, fiction in the United States was poised for takeoff in the early nineteenth century. New forms of production and distribution, a rapidly growing population, and a rising literacy rate created large new audiences for novels and new ways for authors to provide these novels.

It should be noted, however, that there was not necessarily a direct connection between a growing number of books and a growing number of readers; nor did a national print culture evolve in a straightforward way. In the Northeast, for example, the coming of the railroads brought about a centralization of the publishing industry, which increasingly focused on New York; but in the Midwest, where the literary infrastructure was less developed, publishing became decentralized. This meant, for instance, that a novel needed to sell far fewer copies in the less-literate South to have a major regional (or even national) impact than in the North. It also meant that a novel with a large number of Northern readers would be perceived as national even when it was regional.[65]

Nationally, British novelists remained popular throughout the century. Charles Dickens was probably the most widely read, but Sir Walter Scott's medieval romances were embraced, especially among well-to-do Southern whites who fancied their plantations as latter-day Camelots. Indeed, Scott spawned a host of imitators dedicated to portraying the beneficence of the slave system, and in the process helped found the myth of the "happy darky" that would persist straight through to *Gone with the Wind* a century later. Mark Twain would later dub this tendency "Sir Walter's Disease."[66]

Beginning in about 1820, a growing number of writers were able to make a living from their art. One of the most important was Washington Irving. Irving began his career as a New York humorist, part of a circle of writers known as the "Knickerbocker Group," a name that evoked the city's Dutch origins. He became famous on the strength of *The Sketch Book of Geoffrey Crayon, Gent.* (1819-20), a collection of essays and stories that included his classic tales "Rip Van Winkle" and "The Legend of Sleepy Hollow." The former, about a man who falls asleep for twenty years, and the latter, a Gothic horror story, were both based on German sources but evince characteristically American preoccupations with country bumpkins, the decline of the republic, and the supernatural. Together with Brown, Irving paved the way for Nathaniel Hawthorne and Edgar Allan Poe. Poe, often cited as the first mystery writer, was also known for his horror tales and the supernatural: his long poem "The Raven" (1845) won him critical as well as commercial success. Poe was moody and probably mentally ill, and his melodramatic life and premature death made him something of a celebrity.[67]

The other writer who received much attention, in this period and ever since, was James Fenimore Cooper. Cooper first came to prominence with *The Spy* (1821), a novel about the American Revolution. But he was best known for what came to be called his "Leatherstocking" tales, a series of novels about an eighteenth-century frontiersman that included *The Last of the Mohicans* (1826), *The Prairie* (1827), and *The Deerslayer* (1841). Much of Cooper's work focused on relations with Indians, especially Leatherstocking's loyal sidekick Chingachgook, and were written in the tragic mode characteristic of such dramas as *Metamora*. However, his Indians were relatively textured: good *and* evil, resilient *and* vulnerable, they were handled with more sympathy than were the urban and poor whites whom he regarded with increasing condescension and contempt. Nominally a Democrat, by the end of his life Cooper was an avowed elitist.[68]

The most popular work about Native Americans, however, was Henry Wadsworth Longfellow's "Hiawatha," a long epic poem that peddled the usual stereotypes. Longfellow was considered a literary giant in his time, although his stock has dropped sharply ever since. By and large, however, formal poetry was not a major form of popular culture for working people, although comic verse was a fixture of the performing arts. But Walt Whitman, a Brooklyn journalist and author of the temperance novel *Franklin Evans* (1842), synthesized a number of strands of antebellum vernacular language into *Leaves of Grass* (1855), one of the great artistic expressions of democratic sensibility in the nineteenth century. *Leaves of Grass* went through numerous revisions before the final edition of 1892, by which time Whitman had become an American icon.[69]

For most of this century, writers like Irving, Cooper, Longfellow, and Whitman (as well as Emerson, Melville, Hawthorne, and a handful of others) were the focus of historians and critics of the literary culture of the nineteenth century. Dime novels were either ignored or treated as the dross these authors had struggled to rise above, rather than as an important source of rhetorical and thematic inspiration. And perhaps the most scorned were the women writers, even though they dominated the literary scene and wrote the most popular works. In 1855, Nathaniel Hawthorne complained to his publisher that "America is now wholly given over to a d——d mob of scribbling women, and I should have no chance of success while the public taste is preoccupied with their trash—and should be ashamed of myself if I did." Almost a century later, literary historian Frank Luther Mott asserted that it was difficult for a "modern reader to find qualities in these novels sufficient to account for their great popularity." Only since the 1970s has this work been sympathetically reassessed by women's historians and literary scholars.[70]

Women's literary culture was grounded not only in novels, but in a number of magazines that catered to specifically middle-class interests, notably *Godey's Ladies Book,* founded in the 1820s under the editorship of Sara Josepha Hale, and *Peterson's Lady's Magazine,* which began in the 1840s. Women readers were also an important constituency for *Harper's* and *The Atlantic,* both begun in the 1850s. *(Harper's*, a monthly, should not be confused with *Harper's Weekly,* a more broadly based publication with a newspaper flavor. Its illustrations and dispatches were particularly prized during the Civil War.[71]) In addition to poetry and nonfiction, these periodicals published stories and serialized novels, launching the careers of Ann S. Stephens, Rebecca Harding Davis, and Elizabeth Stuart Phelps.

These women came of age at a time of reconfigured gender relations. The ideal of Republican Motherhood that had circulated during the late eighteenth and early nineteenth centuries had gradually evolved into what historians have called "separate sphere ideology." This construct was more class-bound than Republican Motherhood because it was predicated on the formation of a proto-managerial class of men who could earn enough for their wives to raise children without engaging in wage-earning labor. For those who subscribed to separate spheres, life was divided into the aggressive, dynamic world of work (the male sphere) and the placid, nurturing world of home (the female sphere). After a day in the industrial jungle, a man would return to his pastoral refuge, where the woman spent her time raising children—who, unlike their working-class counterparts, would never work in factories.

"Separate spheres" can be a misleading phrase. Although it was widely used and understood by nineteenth-century women, the separate spheres were far more an ideal than a reality. One intriguing hint of this emerges from the circulation statistics of an elite private lending library, which showed no major distinction between the kinds of novels read by men and women.[72] On the other hand, the prevalence of the phrase gave it a kind of reality. One consequence of the growing acceptance of separate sphere ideology was a "feminization" of print culture, as women began to play a discernibly greater role in teaching, reading, and writing books.

The fiction that described this culture and reflected its values, from Hale's *Northwood* (1827) through Susan Warner's *The Wide, Wide World* (1850), has been classified by scholars under the rubric of the "domestic novel." Domestic novels have been criticized as sickly sweet, hidebound in their conservatism, and boring—*The Wide, Wide World,* stuffed with the bromides Warner acquired as a colporteur for the American Tract Society, daunts even the most committed reader of nineteenth-century women's fiction—but such a view overlooks some significant aspects of this writing. First, these books represent a notable departure from the seduction-and-abandonment tales of the late eighteenth century. Like the works of Richardson and Rowson, domestic novels place women front and center, but their protagonists are not victims but resilient people who triumph over all kinds of adversity. The heroines of Maria Cummins's *The Lamplighter* (1854) and Fanny Fern's *Ruth Hall* (1855) demonstrate a wiliness, and even sauciness, that stretched the boundaries of Victorian propriety.[73]

Indeed, a vein of subversion runs through many domestic novels. The morally powerful and assertive women who inhabit their pages were an oblique commentary on the decline of male religious authority at a time when the immoral reformer was an archetype in the sensational and reform literature.[74] And while separate spheres was a confining model of behavior, some women used it to argue for their responsibility to speak out on public issues, especially temperance and slavery, that affected their lives at home.

In fact, after a certain point the very phrase "domestic fiction" becomes inaccurate, for women writers—who in any case transgressed spheres by writing books—depicted characters who strayed far from hearth and home. Rebecca Harding Davis anticipated the rise of literary realism with her grim look at women's labor in *Life in the Iron Mills* (1861), first published in *The Atlantic*. Racial issues were also explored. Lydia Maria Child, a member of Washington Irving's Knickerbocker circle, won renown for *Hobomok* (1824), a novel about a (temporary) interracial romance between a white woman and an Indian chief. Catherine Sedgewick also explored red-white romance in *Hope Leslie* (1827), a novel that depicts a spirited black woman who rescues a white man being held captive by Indians and defeats the attacker who tries to stop her. Such feats—like Harriet Tubman's celebrated real-life rescues of slaves during the Civil War—may have been considered permissible because black women were not really "ladies" anyway. But relative to the often vicious stereotypes depicted on the stage, such characters were a step in a more liberal direction.[75]

By the 1830s, a number of domestic novelists were being drawn into the growing abolitionist movement. Child was active as a journalist throughout this period, an involvement that culminated, in the aftermath of John Brown's raid on Harper's Ferry in 1859, in the publication of an exchange of letters about the raid with the governor of Virginia.[76] She also explored black-white interracial relationships in her later fiction, notably *Waiting for the Verdict* (1867).

Both male and female abolitionists were influenced by the black writers who began to surface before the Civil War. The foundation for this African-American literary culture was the slave narrative. The first of these stories appeared in 1701, when Judge Samuel Sewall of Boston published the anonymous *The Selling of Joseph,* a description of the horrors of the slave trade and a call for the end of the institution. Beginning in the 1830s, the slave narrative grew in visibility as the abolitionist movement gained new momentum and as attention became focused on the problem of the slaveholder. The most famous work of this type was the *Narrative of Frederick Douglass, An American Slave, Written by Himself* (1845), which was revised and expanded during Douglass's long and eventful life. Recent scholars have focused on Harriet Jacobs's autobiographical *Incidents in the Life of a Slave Girl* (1861), which was edited by Child. Slave narratives, which were based on fact but necessarily rooted in unverifiable memory, were the forerunners of the first novels written by African Americans: William Wells Brown's *Clotel* (1853) and Harriet Wilson's *Our Nig* (1859). Both challenged the optimistic endings of domestic fiction and also took Northerners to task for the racism they considered a Southern problem.

While New England abolitionists showed the most interest in reading books about African Americans (and writing them on their behalf), these books reached other audiences as well. A magazine writer in the 1850s lamented that "the whole literary atmosphere has become tainted" with "literary nigritudes."[77] Perhaps even more striking, the hugely successful dime novel firm of Beadle and Adams, which published books for the soldiers at the front in the Civil War, published Metta Victor's *Maum Guinea and her Plantation "Children"; or Holiday Week on a Louisiana Estate* (1861), a novel that clearly was influenced by slave narratives.[78]

Whatever the interest in these works, none compared in impact with Harriet Beecher Stowe's *Uncle Tom's Cabin,* which was serialized in the abolitionist newspaper *The National Era* in 1851 and published in book form in 1852. The daughter, sister, and husband of clergymen (her brother Henry Ward Beecher would be ridiculed as the stereotypical immoral churchman after a marital scandal in the 1870s), Stowe was deeply immersed in the religious culture of the early nineteenth century and was a professional writer who struggled to support her husband and raise their children. *Uncle Tom's Cabin* distilled into one potent whole the swirling currents of gender and racial politics, the moral fervor of reform literature, and the graphic realism of slave narratives.[79]

Uncle Tom's Cabin gave U.S. culture a series of characters—some would say stereotypes—that became household names over the following century: Little Eva, the angelic child whose death scene was the ultimate tearjerker; Simon Legree, the slavetrader whose very name became a virtual synonym for calculating, heartless evil; Augustus St. Clare, the ineffectual intellectual who recognizes that slavery is wrong but fails to do anything about it until it is too late; and the stoic Uncle Tom, whose utter sinlessness is meant to stand as a rebuke to the slave system and as a statement that black people deserved freedom. By the twentieth century, "Uncle Tom" had taken on thoroughly pejorative connotations for blacks, and *Uncle Tom's Cabin* was more generally seen as typifying the worst sentimental excesses of nine-teenth-century women's fiction. In its own day, however, it was a powerful polemic of moral rigor and political significance. One African-American critic, comparing Stowe favorably to Alice Walker, recently noted that "Stowe pleads just as strenuously and far more effectively for the humanity and protection of women and children and for the assertion of the values of home against the values of the marketplace that have dehumanized and debased all human relationships." Far from being a dreamy idealist, "Stowe knows that conversions like the one experienced by St. Clare are rare; most people who participate in a comfortable social order will not change until they are forced to." Abraham Lincoln was joking—but only half joking—when, on meeting Stowe at the height of the Civil War, he greeted her by saying, "So you're the little woman who made this great war."[80]

It would be hard to overstate the effect that *Uncle Tom's Cabin* had on U.S. culture. The book sold 3,000 copies on the first day it was published, over 300,000 within a year, and half a million by the time of the panic of 1857—not counting pirated editions. By 1861, it had become the most popular novel ever written by an American, and a tremendous international success as well. Yet such numbers can only begin to suggest its reach. Perhaps more revealing is the fury it provoked in the South, where it was widely banned. By the standards of what followed, *Uncle Tom's Cabin* was a moderate document, at least as harsh on the North as it was on the South and notable in that the evil Simon Legree was a Northerner while the slave-owning St. Clare was portrayed somewhat sympathetically. Nevertheless, the power of Stowe's moral indictment was unmistakable, as was her point of view. The novel was rebutted in a flurry of "Anti-Tom" novels, such as *Aunt Phyllis's Cabin; or Southern Life as It Is* (1852) and *The Planter's Northern Bride* (1854). Stowe's rejoinder, *The Key to Uncle Tom's Cabin* (1853), attempted to prove that the scenes she had depicted were, if anything, too mild. "Tom" literature, pro and con, became a kind of subgenre of its own in the years preceding the Civil War, although no work came close to Stowe's in articulating a political critique that both drew on and reconfigured the conventions of domestic fiction.

"Tom" also became a staple of the stage for the rest of the nineteenth century. The first dramatic version, which opened in 1853, retained the antislavery spirit of the novel, but it was soon challenged, and then supplanted, by a pro-Southern version that ended happily and turned Tom into a comic caricature of Stowe's character. Satiric minstrel versions, with titles like "Happy Uncle Tom," also flourished. One comic song, first performed after the novelist made a trip to England, revealed the class tensions that divided Democrats from abolitionists: "When us happy darkies

you pity in your prayer/Oh don't forget de WHITE SLAVES dat's starvin'
over dar!"[81] It may be, however, that the minstrels and other critics paid
Stowe the ultimate compliment through their preoccupation with her work.
Indeed, the only works of twentieth-century popular culture that have rivaled
the impact of *Uncle Tom's Cabin* are *Birth of a Nation* and *Gone with the
Wind*—and both represent active attempts to refute the imagery, rhetoric,
and message of Stowe's novel. Long before the Civil War and long after it,
the issues and perceptions at the heart of the conflict have continued to be
fought out in U.S. popular culture.[82]

It is always a question for historians whether wars cause or simply reflect
the underlying transformations that often accompany them. The Civil War
was clearly the culmination of a long process of sectional friction that
involved industrial development, commercial competition, racial ideology,
and regional identity, all of which were amply documented in the popular
culture of the time. But the war also dramatically accelerated these trends,
and its immediate effects were so great that one can reasonably say that
certain events—from the creation of the modern banking system to the
Emancipation Proclamation—were directly attributable to the war. In any
case, the last third of the nineteenth century had a distinctly different tenor
in popular cultural terms than the first two-thirds. If the antebellum period
witnessed the emergence of many popular cultural forms, the postbellum
decades were a period when culture became an industry in the modern sense
of the word. Some of this was becoming apparent even before the war. In
the 1840s, men of humble backgrounds like P.T. Barnum and Horace
Greeley were able to found their enterprises with a little bit of credit and a
lot of pluck; a decade later, the *New York Times* was capitalized for
$100,000, half of which went for technology that had not even existed a
few years before.[83] At the same time, however, the Civil War would not mark
the end of the poor boy (or, occasionally, girl) who could make good. In fact,
for African Americans, this period was about to begin. More important still,
the late nineteenth century would not mark the end of the cultural innovation
that had characterized the antebellum period. Now, that innovation would
take place in a world that was becoming increasingly recognizably modern.

3

Stages of Development: The Segmentation and Consolidation of Popular Culture, 1860-1900

IN 1891, NEW YORK'S METROPOLITAN MUSEUM OF ART for the first time opened its doors to the public on Sunday afternoons. The museum, which had been privately funded and operated by some of the city's richest citizens since its creation in 1870, had long espoused a presumably democratic mission of enlightenment and the diffusion of "culture" to all. (In this regard, it echoed themes of similar institutions in Boston and Chicago.) But by remaining closed on Sundays—the day most working people could actually visit—access was effectively restricted to the leisured few.

Under pressure from New York's largely Democratic political leaders, the museum relented. The *New York Times,* a proponent of Sunday hours, nevertheless announced that "Kodak camera fiends" would not be allowed, and that canes and umbrellas would have to be checked "so that no chance should be given for anyone to prod a hole through a valuable painting, or to knock off any portion of a cast." Fortunately, 12,000 largely working-class patrons visited without a hitch, and the museum's director proudly reported that "Boys tagged at their mothers' heels and laughed at the queer-shaped pottery of the Egyptians. But they did no harm. A few could not help putting a hand on the piece of statuary now and then, but this is done just as much on a week day, and cannot be spoken of as an evil exclusively attending a Sunday opening." By the end of the year, roughly a third of all visitors to the museum came on Sundays. Among these was Mark Twain. When asked to check his cane in the cloakroom, he reportedly replied, "Leave my cane! Leave my cane! Then how do you expect me to poke holes through the oil paintings!"[1]

As usual, Twain's humor served a critical function, in this case as a commentary on the fussiness of high society and its bourgeois imitators, and on their anxieties about a mass society they sought both to escape and to control. These dual impulses were at their height in the United States in the late nineteenth century. As noted in Chapter 1, a division between the cultural interests of the elite and ordinary people long predates industrialization, and, for that matter, the formation of modern societies. Even if we accept this premise as a fixed truth for all times, however, there has nevertheless been a waxing and waning in the degree of *distance* between

---

Reverse page: Publicity still from an early production of The Black Crook, *first mounted in New York in 1866. A landmark in the history of American live performance and a tremendous popular success,* The Black Crook *is now widely considered the first burlesque show and a notable instance of sexual subversion in popular culture.*

elements in each society, and in the specific forms, movements, or ideological tendencies that mediate this gap. So while cultural hierarchy remained a powerful force in the early nineteenth century, reflecting the growing economic polarities of the antebellum United States, it was nevertheless a period of enormous vitality and flux: new forms arrived on the scene and new practitioners of popular culture blurred class lines—not only through their personal class mobility, but also through the audiences that gathered to absorb the new forms of culture.

The latter part of the nineteenth century saw a marked retreat from this fluid situation. We saw the origins of this process in the opening of the gilded Astor Place Opera House in 1847, and in the riot there two years later. Over the course of the next few decades, well-to-do Americans increasingly segregated themselves into "legitimate" theaters, listened to "serious" music, read "respectable" publications—and imposed new restrictions (ideological as well as spatial) on those who would participate in their cultural milieu. Although their institutions were supposedly open to all, they only welcomed those who played by the new rules of sobriety, orderliness, and respect for authority.

The supreme expression of this cultural division was the World's Columbian Exposition, which opened in Chicago in 1893. The exposition's planners, mostly businessmen and architects, intended it to be a celebration of the four hundred years of progress since the "discovery" of America, a showcase of all that was great about the United States. The main attraction was to be the White City, a collection of classically inspired temporary plaster buildings that represented the highest values of U.S. civilization. (Ironically, one emerging building form that was quintessentially American, the skyscraper, was pointedly omitted. Its aggressive modernity would have overshadowed the temples of gentility.)

Yet the White City was too sterile, too narrowly limited to represent, or attract, a large audience, and planners reluctantly made concessions to popular taste. The 1876 Philadelphia Exposition celebrating the Declaration of Independence had had the atmosphere of a fair, so the Chicago planners constructed a contained area, called the Midway Plaisance, to house entertainments and exhibits deemed unfit for the White City—which was white in more ways than one. At its worst, the Midway was a showcase for "exotic" nonwhite peoples, who were objectified for mass consumption. Frederick Douglass attended not as a U.S. citizen but as a commissioner from Haiti (he dubbed the White City "a whited sepulcher"). Still, the Midway was also responsible for much of the exposition's vitality. The suggestive dance of a woman named "Little Egypt," which went by the name of the "hootchy-kootchy," fascinated visitors and affected popular dance for years to come. A giant mechanical steel wheel designed by engineer George G.W. Ferris enchanted those who rode it, and would later be replicated in the Coney Island amusement parks (see below). If the hustle-and-bustle of the multiracial, multiethnic Midway did not embody a white businessman's ideal of America, it was closer to, if still far from, a true cultural democracy.[2]

Moreover, these and other efforts to compartmentalize, segregate, and rank culture never completely took hold. As the crowds attending the Metropolitan Museum of Art showed, many working people were interested in the art the elite liked to call its own. And classical music had an appeal that crossed class lines, especially in the case of composers like Verdi or Chopin, where issues of ethnicity or emigré nationalism were at stake.

Meanwhile, even as the elite was leaving previously shared cultural institutions, some important social segments of the population were creating or refining artistic forms that had a distinctly working-class cast. African-American music, cheap fiction, and urban stage entertainment were all avenues of innovation that appealed to men and women of varied racial and ethnic backgrounds. On the other hand, the vitality of such "lowbrow" forms as burlesque and ragtime increasingly appealed to segments of the upper classes as well. By the early twentieth century, a reconvergence of high and low was apparent, in movie theaters and jazz clubs, for example—a phenomenon that will be discussed in more detail in Chapter 4.

In addition to increasing stratification, the other distinctive characteristic of this period was a sharply intensified commodification of culture that has continued undiminished to this day. If the first half of the nineteenth century marked the birth of *show* business, the last half witnessed the rapid growth of show *business*. As discussed in Chapter 2, many of the early popular cultural entrepreneurs (especially newspaper editors) were working people who were immersed in producing cultural works as well as distributing them. But the rise of P.T. Barnum signalled the advent of a managerial class that would supplant the artisan character of the early producer/purveyors. By 1900, many areas of popular culture had become professionalized industries dominated by vertically controlled corporations. The late nineteenth century therefore marked the start of an era whose heavily commercial character continues to shape our lives.

From this time forward, the purveyors of popular culture generally allied themselves with working people against the encroachments of those "reformers" who sought to restrict popular culture and the activities (drinking, prostitution, unruliness) they associated with it. This allowed the new entrepreneurs to appear as champions of cultural freedom even as they staked out vast markets that produced huge profits. In many cases, it was their power that stopped saloons and nickelodeons from being shut down. Such maneuvers were not motivated by altruism, of course, and the entertainment industry sometimes acted ruthlessly against attempts to check its power, as the organizers of a labor union for vaudeville workers would learn at the turn of the century.

These are among the reasons that so many leftist intellectuals have viewed popular culture with suspicion. As noted in the Introduction, these scholars have emphasized popular culture's hegemonic qualities and narcotic effects. Such a point of view has considerable cogency, and provides one aspect of an understanding of this period. As I argue throughout this book, however, it is a perspective that tends to ignore those elements of a working people's worldview that survive commodification, as well as the subversive elements within it that defy control or price tags.

Nevertheless, even those most cheerful about popular culture's authenticity and revolutionary potential must confront both the banality and viciousness that characterizes much of it, and the late nineteenth century was hardly immune to these. Racial hatred and sexual subordination remained staples of popular cultural representation, either transferred to new forms or rearticulated in old ones.

The previous chapters were organized around popular cultural forms and their evolution, and this chapter will continue that practice, because it allows us to attend to structural particularities and their relation to the culture as a whole. The main sections of the chapter, however, will be divided geographically. Sectional identity, which played a major role in the coming of the Civil War, did not end with that conflict; rather, it shifted—now it was primarily between East and West, country and city, and only to a lesser extent between North and South. The art of African Americans in former slave states, the new forms that evolved in small towns and in the vast expanse west of the Mississippi, and continuing developments on the East Coast and in the nation's major cities were distinctive but also increasingly interlocking.

Sounds of Freedom:
Toward an African-American Popular Culture

To say that the Civil War represented a watershed in black life is to simultaneously state the obvious and the far from obvious. On the one hand, the destruction of slavery, subsequently codified in the thirteenth, fourteenth, and fifteenth amendments (which abolished slavery, granted civil rights to blacks, and gave black men the vote) represented the culmination of decades of effort on the part of African-American leaders and their abolitionist and (Radical) Republican allies. On the other hand, the severity of the white backlash in the South, notably in the creation of the Ku Klux Klan and *its* allies, along with government reluctance to enforce the new amendments, made life more difficult than ever for many African Americans. And the rise of tenant farming put new freedpeople at the mercy of rapacious landowners who charged high rents for land and exorbitant prices for supplies. So while freedom represented an important beginning, it was only that—a beginning.

By 1865, African Americans had been enslaved in North America for almost 250 years. Yet across many generations, a vast expanse of land, and widely varied experiences, they had retained many aspects of their original (western) African cultures and absorbed elements of white European cultures as well. The result was something altogether new—an amalgam that would decisively shape the American experience.

Nowhere was this unique matrix more evident than in music, especially vocal music. In many African cultures, singing is an important accompaniment to worship, work, and other communal activities. This practice was a fixture of slave life, and specific vocal forms—ring shouts for religious ceremonies, work songs for labor, and field hollars for personal expression—were developed to meet the varied needs of black communities. All of these song styles employed a call-and-response pattern: one person would sing a line and a group of others would reply, either by repeating the line or embellishing it.

Despite importation to North America, adoption of English as a primary language, and conversion to Christianity, some important African elements persisted in the slaves' musical culture. The first was the dense cross-rhythmic patterns largely missing from European music. The second was the use of different musical scales than those common on the European continent (although they were common in Scotch-Irish folk music, among Native Americans in North and South America, and in parts of the Far East). Finally, transplanted Africans continued to use a series of verbal techniques—guttural tones, rasps, falsettos, and melismas—that could not be directly translated into European-American terms.

Historian Lawrence Levine has summarized the African accents of black American music as follows:

> . . . slaves engaged in widespread musical exchanges and cross-culturation with the whites among whom they lived, yet throughout the centuries of slavery and long after emancipation, their song style, with its overriding antiphony, its group nature, its pervasive functionality, its improvisational character, its strong relationship in performance to dance and bodily movement and expression, remained closer to the musical styles and performances of West Africa and the Afro-American music of the West Indies and South America than to the musical style of Western Europe.[3]

Many of these qualities remain abundantly evident in African-American music today.

Another African influence on slave music was percussion. It was not as common as song, because slaveholders who tolerated singing as an aid to productivity were suspicious that drumming was a secret form of communication. Nevertheless, the dense, polyrhythmic tradition of African drumming remained alive in the United States, often surreptitiously, emerging into view during such communal celebrations as the "Pinkster" festivals that marked Pentecost. In these elaborate community events, slaves (or free blacks in the North) dressed in finery, gave speeches, and performed dances, accompanied by a variety of drums closely resembling their African counterparts. Most such festivals had been banned or modified beyond recognition by the beginning of the nineteenth century, although they were held publicly in New Orleans until 1855.[4]

Transplanted slaves also learned to play European instruments, usually through imitation and hands-on playing rather than formal training. They were often encouraged by their owners, who enjoyed their playing or could earn extra income by renting out their musical services. Instrument adoption worked the other way, too. The banjo, now widely associated with bluegrass and country music, was an African instrument (one musicologist has speculated it became popular among slaves after drums and horns were banned).[5]

By the Civil War, then, African Americans had drawn on a variety of sources and developed many ways to express themselves musically. This process remains shrouded in mystery, however, because its study relies on scattered shards of evidence and oral transmission rather than systematically collected written records. It is only after Emancipation that we can really begin to trace the evolution of black music.

One reason is that the newly freed African Americans began to move, literally and figuratively, into the purview of the larger society. Many former slaves expressed their freedom by migrating—to other farms, to other states, and in some cases to other parts of the country. Of course, crushing debt, difficult family circumstances, or the lack of economic opportunity made this difficult or impossible, and freedpeople often found their new locales as difficult as their old ones. Nevertheless, moving was one of the few things many former slaves *could* do, and it was an act of personal autonomy as much as a logistical necessity. Whatever the case, this new fluidity had important cultural consequences, as different African-American communities—urban and rural, Northern and Southern, Eastern and Western, previously free and recently emancipated—came into contact and blended the sounds of Appalachia, the Mississippi Delta, the inner-city ghetto, and so on.

African Americans also had increasing contact with white Northerners. This process began during and immediately following the Civil War, when Northern white women joined relief and education efforts in newly liberated black communities, and Northern white officers began directing black troops who enlisted during recruitment drives. Many of these men and women were deeply impressed by African-American culture, especially music. In 1867, the first book on the subject, *Slave Songs of the United States* was published. Two years later, former Union officer Thomas Wentworth Higginson included a chapter of slave spiritual lyrics in his 1869 memoir *Army Life in a Black Regiment.*[6]

Sacred black music became a national phenomenon with the success of the Jubilee Singers of Fisk University in Nashville, Tennessee, in 1871. Fisk had been founded by missionaries in 1865, and its treasurer thought he could raise money for the school by sending its singing group on tour. At first, the Jubilee Singers' repertoire consisted of the hymns, anthems, and standards that were sung by every American choir. But although the group was warmly received, the tour was not a financial success until it reached Oberlin, Ohio, and added spirituals to the program. The response was overwhelming. From that point on, the Jubilee Singers were national and international artists, generating significant income for Fisk. Their fame was further augmented with the publication of a collection of their songs in 1872. In 1873, the Hampton Institute, another black school, founded its own highly regarded group of spirituals singers, and many others followed.[7]

Ironically, while performers such as these were celebrated for their "authentic" renderings of sacred African-American music, the spirituals had been subtly altered in the process of their transmission to white audiences. Grammar was changed, voices were smoothed, and tones were "improved" in an effort to make them more like classical European music. While this did not fundamentally change the music's African-American character—and in fact contributed to a cross-cultural dialogue that excited European composers like Anton Dvorak (who asserted that the "future music of America must be founded on what is called 'Negro melodies'")—many members of the black intelligentsia responded with ambivalence. So did less educated blacks. As one former slave put it, "Dose are the same old tunes, but some way dey do'n sound right."[8]

Spirituals represented only one facet of late-nineteenth-century African-American music. Another important development, much more tied to black working people, was the rise of the blues. Again, this is not a process that can be traced with any precision, because it did not originate with any one person, record, or event. Although the first blues records were not made until early in the twentieth century—most notably by Ma Rainey, who was born in 1886—the major pieces were in place by the 1890s and drew on musical elements that had been in circulation during previous decades.

Musically speaking, the blues are not very different from antebellum African-American forms, especially work songs. What sets them apart is their ideological character: the more secular, individualistic accents in the blues reflect broad attitudinal changes that occurred in the years following Emancipation. Nevertheless, the line between the sacred and the secular was not as sharp for slaves as it was for whites—another African cultural trait that survived even after most slaves had been converted to Christianity. God and man, heaven and earth, the natural and the supernatural were intertwined and immediate. Moreover, African culture emphasized collective enterprise while Europeans emphasized individual autonomy. To some extent, then, the blues were the result of African-American acculturation into white society, even as African techniques and sensibilities were reinscribed into the black musical tradition.

Musically speaking, the blues drew on an eight-note European scale, but "flattened" fifths and sevenths to create what musicians call a "blues scale."

Most blues pieces consisted of a twelve-bar, three-line stanza structure played on a guitar, with vocal accompaniment. As with work songs or field hollars, the first line was repeated, but unlike such communal forms, the singer typically repeated it alone. As the name suggests, much of this music was at least nominally an expression of despair, but there was often a sense of catharsis associated with it—and a good deal of humor, as in this piece anthologized by the early blues collector and performer W.C. Handy that employs (and satirizes) the blues sensibility:

> Gwine lay my head right on de railroad track,
> Gwine lay my head right on de railroad track,
> 'Cause my baby, she won't take me back.
>
> Gwine lay my head right on de railroad track,
> Gwine lay my head right on de railroad track,
> If de train come 'long, I'm gwine to snatch it back.[9]

Most early blues performers went unrecognized by mainstream white America until the early twentieth century, when bluesmen like Blind Lemon Jefferson and Huddie Ledbetter (later known as "Leadbelly") attracted large and enthusiastic audiences. Yet however nameless the early architects might have been, they established a simple, sturdy, and versatile foundation for jazz, rock, and other forms of popular music.

The other musical innovation of the late nineteenth century was ragtime. Ragtime was performed on a variety of instruments, but was widely associated with the piano. It applied the African penchant for cross-rhythms and the manipulation of time signatures to create syncopation. As one jazz historian has described it, "Phrases were stretched out of their natural length; notes were jumped in early. The general effect was a lifting away of the melody from the time scheme, detaching it from the beat so that it seemed to float above it."[10]

By the 1870s, and probably earlier, itinerant ragtime players were performing on riverboats, and in saloons, clubs, and brothels, often to racially mixed audiences. It was not until the 1890s, however, that ragtime became a national sensation. Some of its appeal lay in its audience's appreciation for African-American music. Yet like so much else, this was perverted for racist purposes: a craze for "coon songs" (with titles like "He's Just a Little Nigger but He's Mine All Mine" and "Every Race Has Its Flag but the Coon") fused offensive lyrics with ragtime rhythms. On the other hand, caricature could work in complex ways. Ragtime was often the accompaniment for a turn-of-the-century dance fad called the cakewalk. Whites saw the cakewalk as a satire on black attempts to appropriate the finery of whites; little did they know that it had developed centuries before as a *black* satire of white pretensions.

The foremost ragtime performer and composer was Scott Joplin. Joplin, who had had a first-class musical education that had included study in Europe, settled in St. Louis, and sensed a building ragtime boom. In 1899 he published a collection of "rags" that sold extremely well. One piece, the "Maple Leaf Rag," became a huge hit, selling hundreds of thousands of copies within six months and making Joplin a rich man (it remains one of the best-known ragtime pieces). But he was not really interested in becoming a popular songwriter: his later rags were too complex to be played easily, and he had nothing but scorn for more popular writers like Irving Berlin, who enjoyed great success with "Alexander's Ragtime Band." Ultimately, Joplin wished to be known for his operas, especially his magnum opus *Treemonisha* (1915), which drew on many elements of African-American music. Neither black nor white audiences showed much interest in this work, and he died a frustrated man.

Joplin's St. Louis, a meeting point for the South and Midwest, may have been the birthplace of ragtime, but the capital of African-American music was New Orleans. Besides the city's being a center for spirituals, blues, ragtime, and other musical forms, its French and Spanish history, location at the gateway of the Caribbean, and role as the South's most important urban center made it a crossroads in all kinds of ways. The city also had a unique racial mix of blacks, whites, Indians, and creoles (descendants of French settlers and their black mistresses). Creoles were a kind of (light) black middle class that had developed its own economic, political, and cultural institutions even as it mixed with whites. But the end of Reconstruction in Louisiana in 1877 ushered in a severely racist regime that disenfranchised those with even a drop of African-American blood. As a result, creoles were driven into closer association with blacks, which had important musical consequences.

New Orleans supported an instrumental tradition that stemmed from the formal musical training many creoles had been able to afford and from the city's position as a military center. Black bands were very popular in the U.S. and European armies, and marches became an element in the musical mix. When the Spanish-American War ended in 1898, the army sold off a mass of band instruments in New Orleans, one of the ports nearest Cuba.[11] If

African-American music before 1900 underwent a complex process of evolution, the events of the years following 1900 can be fairly called a revolution—one that would go by the name of jazz. That story will be picked up in the next chapter.

Music was only one component of a rich African-American cultural life that included the fiction of writers like Charles Chesnutt, the poetry of Laurence Dunbar, the folklore of anonymous storytellers, and many other forms. But more than any other art, music reached across time, space, regions, and classes to become authentic popular culture, and the linchpin of a distinctive U.S. culture as a whole.

Expansive Vistas:
Popular Culture in the West

New Orleans' role as the linchpin of African-American music is one more illustration of the role of cities as greenhouses of popular culture. However, in the towns and open spaces of hinterlands, stretching from upstate New York to southern California, popular culture was making steady inroads into small communities, and small communities were shaping what was being depicted in the big cities.

There is perhaps no better illustration of these tendencies than the evolution of theater in this period. The segmentation of audiences and the fracturing of entertainment forms after the Civil War moved drama from its central place in the popular cultural world of the Jacksonian era. The period between 1865 and 1900 is widely considered a low point in the history of the theater, because so few interesting plays were produced. But if we shift our attention from the bright lights of Broadway to the hinterlands, and from critically acclaimed texts to large and attentive audiences, we find that in this period, millions of Americans from all walks of life found their lives and interests dramatized on small stages across the country.[12]

This was possible in part because the industrial transformations of the first half of the century had created a new cultural infrastructure. An ever more elaborate rail network reached a milestone in 1869, when Chinese workers moving east and Irish workers moving west met in Utah to connect the first transcontinental railroad. Controlled by cartels that received government money and land, railroad companies could be enormous oppressors of ordinary people, as the Great Railroad Strike of 1877 attested. In milder moments, though, they allowed large groups of people—such as theater companies—to visit previously inaccessible areas.

The staples of the stage in these years were plays that had been written in the antebellum era but enjoyed a long lease on life after the Civil War. Stage versions of *Uncle Tom's Cabin* continued to proliferate; indeed, the story was so popular that many companies, called "Tommers," presented it exclusively. As was the case before the war, liberties were often taken with Stowe's tale: its antislavery dimensions were toned down, and dramatic incidents, like Eliza's flight to freedom, were embellished (or even invented). Another popular favorite was *Ten Nights in a Barroom,* a highly sensationalistic temperance polemic based on T.S. Arthur's novel of the same name. *Ten Nights* was first presented in New York in 1858 and went on to become a popular standard in the rest of the country for the remainder of the century.[13]

Yet new issues were also pushing themselves to the fore, however ambivalently. A good example was *East Lynne,* an 1861 British melodrama that became very popular with U.S. audiences. It tells the story of a woman who, unjustly accused of infidelity by a controlling, philandering husband, falls in love with another man. She leaves her husband and their infant son, but is punished when her lover betrays her and the son falls fatally ill. Visiting the boy in disguise, she reveals her identity, and the two are reconciled before he dies. She then falls ill and is reconciled with her husband before *she* dies.

In terms of sexual politics, we can see how *East Lynne* stacks its cards against women: it is acceptable for men to indulge in adultery but the consequences for women are deadly. But however patriarchal its ending, the play suggests the increasing interest in, and anxiety generated by, the small but growing number of activists for suffrage, legal reform, and personal freedom for women. Edwin Forrest's attempt to alter the ending of the play is also revealing. In early performances as the cuckolded husband, he censured his dying wife for her adulterous offenses—and received hisses from an angry audience. So he adopted a milder approach. If the heroine is ultimately punished, she is also forgiven. A slight tilt in the sexual balance of power was underway.[14]

Another sign of social tension in late-nineteenth-century drama is suggested in the ways the past was romanticized. This is especially true of regional archetypes. In *The Old Homestead,* first mounted in 1876, the popular actor Denman Thompson played Uncle Joshua, a kindly New Hampshire farmer (a role he would perform for twenty-four years). If

Solomon Swap, Industrious Doolittle, or the other Brother Jonathan characters that dominated the early Jacksonian stage were comically shrewd but
also had a realistic edge, by the late nineteenth century they had become
kindly, sweet patriarchs like "Uncle Josh," who wisely eschews the city for
a long and happy country life. When actor Frank Mayo portrayed Davy
Crockett between 1872 and 1896, he turned the salty-tongued Indian
fighter into a noble Leatherstocking character. Similarly, Joseph Jefferson
III attained wide acclaim between 1865 and 1904 for his role as Rip Van
Winkle in a play based on the Washington Irving tale. Jefferson used the
character of Old Rip, who cannot quite come to terms with modern life, to
evoke the sense of a lost world. The hackneyed quality of these and other
plays suggests a widespread sense of uneasiness in a nation undergoing a
dramatic industrial transformation.[15]

But modern life brought a sense of excitement as well. If improved
communications and transportation made it possible to bring the pleasures
of the big city to the small town, they also made it possible to bring novelties
even farther afield, in a cultural form whose appeal reached its zenith in the
late nineteenth century: the circus.

Actually, the circus, defined here as a traveling show of people and
animals who perform within a ring, is a cultural institution that dates back
to the Middle Ages (the art of clowning, so central to the circus, dates back
even further). After a long period out of historical view, the circus reemerged
in London in the 1760s, when an equestrian named Philip Astley opened
a one-ring circus that featured horsemanship, clowns, acrobats, jugglers,
and other performers. The circus arrived in the United States in the 1790s,
when Scotsman John Bill Ricketts, a student of one of Astley's rivals, opened
a permanent exhibition in Philadelphia. Rickett's circus performed in New
York, Boston, and other cities, but it was not until after the Erie Canal opened
in 1825 that circuses began to regularly travel into the interior.

The first circus stars and attractions emerged in the Jacksonian era. The
first elephant was exhibited in 1796, but it was the second, "Old Bet," who
was an international star until she died in 1816. Lion tamers became
prominent in the 1820s, when the "Lion King," Isaac Van Amburgh, thrilled
audiences with his flamboyant style. And a Kentucky cardsharp and jockey
named Dan Rice became a star clown in the 1840s with his mangled
renditions of Shakespeare. The first circus parade, organized to attract
patrons, took place in 1837; rail was first used to transport a troupe in 1838.

But the golden age of the circus was the late nineteenth century, when railroads (and covered wagons) permitted ever larger and more spectacular exhibitions in regions previously untouched by modern popular culture. The decision as to exactly *where* to pitch the tents became a matter of intense calculation: planners tried to account for such factors as the weather, the previous year's receipts, rivals' intentions, and the prevailing labor situation. Playing the big cities was less important than maximizing the number of people and minimizing the distance they (and the circus itself) had to travel. The small town of Maryville, Missouri, for example, was considered a more attractive locale than St. Louis. So massive and complex were the logistics of organizing and moving circuses that army officials observed them in order to improve military efficiency.

One of the early masters of these new, more complex circuses was William Cameron Coup. Coup's major structural innovation was the additional of a second ring, which doubled the amount of activity the spectators could watch. He also excelled at promotion, using advance men to paper future circus sites with carefully timed advertising. In this regard, Coup was something of a latter-day P.T. Barnum. Perhaps recognizing this—and certainly aware of his promotional value and capital—Coup succeeded in coaxing an aging Barnum to form P.T. Barnum's Museum, Menagerie, and Circus in 1870.

Barnum's willingness to lend his name to shows other than Coup's led to a split between the two men in 1875. The old man demonstrated his entrepreneurial pluck when he dubbed his outfit "The Greatest Show on Earth," a slogan that has lasted to the present. In 1880, he merged with his competitor James Bailey to create the Barnum & Bailey circus. This three-ring circus was then gradually overtaken in popularity by that of the Ringling Brothers of Wisconsin. The sons of German immigrants, the Ringlings developed acrobatic skills that won them great acclaim in the 1880s, and this success allowed them to acquire such other circus elements as elephants (Barnum's Jumbo, acquired from a British circus, was until then considered the supreme specimen). Rivalry between the two companies lasted until 1904, when they agreed to focus on different markets. In 1919, they merged to form Ringling Brothers and Barnum & Bailey Circus, which remains in operation to this day. In part, these maneuvers represent the machinations of large corporate enterprises, but they also indicate a general decline in the popularity of circuses: after peaking at approximately ninety-eight in 1902, they have declined ever since.

Circuses were more than business arrangements, however. They were highly developed subcultures that had complex relationships with the communities they reached. All forms of nineteenth-century live entertainment tended to foster a sense of camaraderie among performers, but this was especially so for circus people, who lived for long stretches in self-contained communities that remained at any given location only temporarily. The outside world was fascinated by the mechanics and subtleties of circus life, as countless newspaper and magazine articles attest. But there was something of an adversarial relationship between the artists and their audiences. Until James Bailey expressly forbade it, circus owners routinely sold grift concessions—literally, licenses to defraud unsuspecting customers. And while Barnum labored mightily to improve the image of circuses, there remained an unsavory air about them. Those whose size, weight, or physical deformities were exploited as "freaks" were especially disdainful of the "marks" or "rubes" who attended the shows. Fights between "towners" and "sawdust eaters" (a general term for any kind of circus worker) were common. This combination of economic dependence and social hostility, communal celebration and ideological conflict, made the circus an unusually resonant arena for the expression, contestation, and mediation of cultural issues.

Although theaters and circuses occupied a prominent place in the cultural landscape of the West—a term that, in the late nineteenth century, described the territory beyond the Mississippi River—they usually originated elsewhere (and performed all over the country), even if they were particularly significant to the people of the plains or desert. The Wild West Show, however, was a Western original.

Unlike other forms of popular culture, the origins of the Wild West show are well known. Although elements were discernible as early as the 1820s, and while it has affinities with the rodeo (which, unlike the Wild West show, is a competitive sport in which contestants pay a fee in the hope of winning prize money), most historians agree that the form began with the work of William Frederick "Buffalo Bill" Cody. The real Cody was a pony express rider, Union army scout, spy, and Indian fighter, and a fictionalized version of Cody appeared in a number of 1860s dime novels written by Ned Buntline (who, it may be recalled, played a role in the Astor Place Riot of 1849; see Chapter 2). In 1872, Buntline persuaded Cody to leave Nebraska, where he was fighting Indians and serving in the state legislature, to star in *The Scouts of the Prairie,* a play loosely based on his life. Despite its slapdash quality, the show was a major hit.

But show business in the East made Cody restless, so he periodically returned to the West, where, among other activities, he fought the Cheyenne Indians who had crushed George Custer (Cody was fighting elsewhere during the Last Stand). After that war, he allegedly avenged Custer's death by scalping a war chief who challenged him to a duel, an act that would be ritually re-enacted in years to come.

In the early 1880s, he teamed up with a theatrical producer to develop outdoor exhibitions of his skill as a hunter, fighter, and all-around frontiersman. Over the course of the decade, the show grew to include bears, elk, and buffalo, and featured appearances from Sioux chieftain Sitting Bull and the celebrated markswoman Annie Oakley. It was extremely popular but also extremely expensive to produce, and it was only when it went East, where travel costs and distances were smaller, that it began to make money. Cody went on to become an international star, entertaining Queen Victoria, receiving the blessing of the Pope, and shooting the ash off the Kaiser's cigar in Berlin (Annie Oakley nicked off the end of his cigarette). In Paris, Cody created a fashion craze for buffalo robes, bear skins, Mexican saddles, and Indian crafts. (Despite this success, Cody, a spendthrift and drunk, remained chronically in debt until his death in 1917.)

There was an element of irony in this. For both Americans and Europeans, Cody was the quintessential Yankee, taming the wilderness for white society even as he retained a distinctive patina of that wilderness. In this regard, he inherited Davy Crockett's mantle. Yet many of the elements of his performance actually originated in other civilizations, especially the cowboy culture of Latin America and a number of Native American arts that spanned the continent. The quintessential American was at heart a multicultural creation.

Indians and Mexicans were not the only supposedly non-civilized peoples against whom whites measured themselves. Though they were seldom represented, or even discussed, African Americans were a significant presence in the West, especially after the Civil War (when up to a third of the U.S. army was black).[16] It has only been in the late twentieth century that songs like Bob Marley's "Buffalo Soldiers" and movies like *Silverado* (1983), *Unforgiven* (1992), and *Posse* (1993) have situated blacks in popular culture forms about the West.

Asian Americans were also a significant presence in the late- nineteenth-century West. By 1870, for example, Chinese made up 8.6 percent of California's population and 25 percent of its wage-earning labor force. They became part of the popular culture in the 1870s, when Bret Harte's famous poem "The Heathen Chinee" was published in a Western magazine and widely reprinted in newspapers across the nation. (Harte collaborated with Mark Twain on a play, based on this poem, that premiered in 1877.) Although he considered himself something of a friend to Asians—the poem depicts a Chinese man's triumph in cards over an unscrupulous white man—Harte's depiction drew on an emerging stereotype of Asians as childlike but wily, people with odd habits alien to a republican society. This stereotype is not unlike that of blacks, which is not surprising since all racial and ethnic minorities in nineteenth-century America were lumped together in the popular white mind. However, Asian differences, particularly their languages, were also satirized, especially in minstrel shows. Minstrels often imitated the Japanese, more of whom lived in the Northeast than did Chinese in the late 1860s.[17]

Some racial and ethnic groups were able to ignore stereotypical representation in white popular culture and produce culture on terms that reflected their American milieu. Mexican Americans, for example, developed *conjunto*, a distinctive working-class, Tex-Mex musical style, while the Chinese became a presence in twentieth-century vaudeville.[18] Yet this took time, and not every group was able to make the transition. The most important exceptions were Native Americans, who remained outside mainstream society well into the twentieth century. Largely unindustrialized, they had a vibrant and varied folk culture that never became popular culture on its own terms.

But in the 1870s and 1880s Indian fictional characters were a fixture of a genre of popular culture that would show great resilience, first as a literary form and then as a cinematic one: the Western. The storylines and structure of Westerns varied widely, but as literary critic and historian John Cawelti has observed, it is the symbolic landscape and its influence on the hero that most clearly defines the Western.[19] (Such a designation sets the genre apart, for example, from detective novels, in which the main character's occupation is central, or the gothic romance, where the determining factor is mood.) Metaphorically, Cawelti notes, the Western landscape is the meeting place between civilization and nature, East and West, legal society and lawless isolation. The links between these spaces are in constant danger of being cut off—by Indians, outlaws, or other antagonists—and the central drama is the epic confrontation that ultimately affirms those links.

Many of the Western's core components can be traced back to James

Fenimore Cooper's Leatherstocking novels, which put the same emphasis on the role of environment in shaping character and the same often tenuous links between civil society and frontier life. Yet Cooper showed more ambivalence about the frontier than many writers of Westerns, and his depictions of Indians, even if they included the "noble savage" stereotype so common in early-nineteenth-century popular culture, were more nuanced than those of his immediate successors. Robert Montgomery Bird's *Nick of the Woods* (1837), for example, exhibited a more realistic and dramatic quality than the Leatherstocking tales, but was more racist in its Indian portrayals. Bird's frontiersman was a former Quaker named Nathan Slaughter who ultimately saw the need to kill Indians. Cooper's Natty Bumpo, by contrast, adopted a Pawnee as his son and died among the Plains Indians.

A major milestone in the development of the Western was the advent of the dime novel. As discussed in Chapter 2, these cheap paperbacks first appeared in the 1840s, but generally focused on urban themes. After the Civil War, however, the Western became the dominant genre of dime novel. In 1858, a Buffalo-based publisher and former journeyman printer named Erastus Beadle moved to New York and formed Beadle and Adams, the most famous and successful of the dime novel companies. In 1860, after profitably selling a number of songbooks and handbooks, Beadle decided to launch a fiction series and hired an Ohio newspaperman named Orville J. Victor to edit it. Beadle formed an association with the American News Company, which held a virtual monopoly on dime novel distribution from its formation in 1864 until the end of the century. The usual print run for Beadle and Adams novels was 60,000, but many were repeatedly reprinted.[20]

Given the Western's reputation as a decidedly male genre, it is somewhat ironic that Beadle's first Western, *Malaeska: Indian Wife of the White Hunter* (1860), was written by a woman, Ann S. Stephens. It sold 300,000 copies. Stephens was unlike later Western writers because of her willingness to allow interracial sex between whites and Native Americans. In general, Cooper's rigid sexual segregation continued to be the rule, although there were always squaws who turned out to be white women raised by Indians. Stephens was also the author of *Esther: A Story of the Oregon Trail* (1869), which featured the archetypal Kirk Waltermyer, a perfect specimen of "that pioneer race who, scorning the ease and fashionable fetters of city life," blazes a trail through the vast and mysterious West.[21]

But the most popular Western hero of the late nineteenth century was

Seth Jones, the protagonist of Edward S. Ellis's *Seth Jones; or, The Captives of the Frontier,* which sold over 400,000 copies and was the eighth novel in Beadle's series. Jones symbolized a convergence between the natural nobleman of Cooper's fiction and the Down East and Southwestern humor of Jacksonian journalism—a seriocomic, gunslinging, natural democrat. Yet this persona is undercut at the end of the story, when the reader learns that Jones is actually Eugene Morton, a Revolutionary War hero and the scion of an elite New England family. Such character shifts were a common convention in Westerns: nature's nobleman often turned out to be society's nobleman as well. Those whose exploits were far from noble, like the semi-fictional Kit Carson or George Custer, were gradually sanitized or gentrified. And those whose origins were avowedly humble, like the main character in Owen Wister's *The Virginian* (1902), one of the most popular novels at the turn of the century, often married into money and became men of stature. Leatherstocking may have been doomed to dwell in a liminal space between nature and civilization, but the Virginian—who foils the evil designs of the suspicious Mexican Trampas—can have it all.[22]

   This is not to say that all Westerns lacked a class-conscious edge. The best example was Deadwood Dick, the enormously popular protagonist of a series of novels by Edward L. Wheeler. Deadwood Dick first appeared in 1877 as part of Beadle's Half Dime Library, and went on to figure in a total of thirty-three stories (other writers wrote ninety-seven more for Deadwood Dick, Jr.). Deadwood Dick represented a distinct break in the Western tradition because he was an outlaw. His world was one in which the social order is corrupt and the dream of conventional upward mobility a sham. His sidekick was the proficient markswoman Calamity Jane, who joined him (starting in 1878) in a series of highly episodic novels that included highway robberies, narrow escapes, dramatic confrontations, and numerous cases of characters disguising themselves as members of the opposite sex. With immigration reaching new heights, capital being concentrated in ever fewer hands, and a nascent labor movement organizing with fitful urgency, the popularity of the Deadwood Dick/Calamity Jane series and other outlaw tales suggests the appeal of subversive fiction at a time of some of the most severe class conflict and tension in U.S. history.[23]

   Meanwhile, the conflicts with Indians in the great open spaces in Westerns were changing to conflicts and intrigues in Western towns. The gap between nature and civilization was closing. But there was plenty of action in the city, too. Deadwood Dick, Jr. went on to become a detective—a role that was equally captivating to the Easterners and urbanites who read the fictions inspired by the vast West of the imagination.

Entertaining Propositions:
The Culture of the Urban Working Class

Cities are, by definition, places of teeming activity. But U.S. cities in the late nineteenth century were sites of unprecedented development and struggle. The Haymarket riots of 1886 and the Pullman strike of 1894 were only two of the most dramatic signs of a labor movement whose numbers and militancy were growing rapidly. Conflicts went beyond organized strikes, and crossed racial, ethnic, and gender lines. For many, class struggle was also cultural struggle and there were controversies over the proper use of parks, the right to consume alcohol, and the meanings assigned to historical events like the Civil War.

Some of the most important arenas of cultural conflict were the dime novels and story papers with urban themes published by Beadle, Robert Bonner, and other cheap fiction publishers. From Ned Buntline's "Mysteries of the City" in the 1840s to the tales of factory women written by Laura Jean Libbey in the 1880s and 1890s, these works exhibited the same class-conscious edge that had characterized the work of George Lippard (see Chapter 2). Certainly, a number of these tales, like those of the middle-class writer Horatio Alger, focused on the opportunities supposedly available to all (although the heroes of *Strive and Succeed, Forging Ahead,* and other Alger stories never seem to actually *work* for their fortunes. Instead, they come by them through sudden discoveries, fortunate marriages, or the revelation of elite lineage).[24] But others, like Frederick Whittaker's 1883-1884 serialized novel *Larry Locke, the Man of Iron*—whose subtitle was *A Story of Labor and Capital*—rejected the Alger dream in favor of the solidarity afforded by the Knights of Labor. "I'd rather be a Master Workman than own a mill, anytime," says Locke, a craneman in a steel mill. "When the time comes that every honest workman in America belongs to the Order, and all stick together, as we should do, every workingman will see more happiness, than he ever saw before. Heaven send the time, and God speed the just aims of the KNIGHTS OF LABOR!" Libbey's tale of Locke's sister, *Leonie Locke; or, the Romance of a Beautiful New York Working-Girl,* appeared in 1884.[25]

Some dime novels retained the lurid quality of Lippard's *Quaker City* and provoked hostility from the elite. After the Civil War, a young New York reformer named Anthony Comstock won financial backing from the city's business community to form the Society for the Suppression of Vice, which led a campaign to censor what it considered obscene material. His efforts led in 1873 to the "Comstock Law," which banned the mailing of "indecent" material, and Comstock himself became a post office special agent assigned to enforce the law. At times, such anti-smut campaigns took on more direct political overtones, as when the Postmaster General forced publisher Frank Tousey to withdraw his outlaw tales of the James brothers in August 1883. Comstock later called dime novel publishers "Satan's efficient agents to advance his kingdom."[26]

The title of Michael Denning's 1987 study of dime novels, *Mechanic Accents,* is apt for two reasons. First, in their "fusion of the emblems and political language of the Republic with the labor relations and social traditions of the crafts," a significant amount of dime novel fiction reflected the persistence of an artisanal radicalism that had first been articulated early in the Jacksonian period. The other meaning for "mechanic" refers to the books' means of production: they were rapidly written and manufactured, and the industry gradually "shifted from selling an 'author,' who was a free laborer, to selling a 'character,' a trademark whose stories could be written by a host of anonymous hack writers and protected in court." By the end of the century, much dime novel fiction had a factory-made feel to it, appropriate for an art produced for the masses in a machine age.[27]

In terms of its production and audience, then, cheap fiction was consonant with the broader intellectual temper of the late nineteenth century. This was a time of preoccupation with the impact of industrialization on the human condition. Some of the misgivings and yearnings of the age were vividly captured by newspaper editor Edward Bellamy's hugely bestselling *Looking Backward* (1888), which speculated on the Boston of the future and found it a world of plenty governed with order, efficiency, and benevolence. So attractive was Bellamy's vision that dozens of clubs dedicated to exploring his ideas further sprang up around the country, and a utopian community, modeled on his principles, formed in California in 1897 and lasted for over forty years. For some readers today, the regimentation of Bellamy's "industrial army" evokes totalitarianism, although many a leftist then and since has been inspired by an industrial order predicated on what

Bellamy considered a kind of Christian socialism. The novel remained among the most popular books for the next fifty years, but it was only the best known of a number of works that explored the new industrial order, from William Dean Howells's uncertain *A Hazard of New Fortunes* (1894) to assembly-line theorist Frederick W. Taylor's optimistic *The Principles of Scientific Management* (1911).[28]

This preoccupation also had a profound effect on the style of literary fiction. The romantic sensibility, with its highly ornamental language and transcendental symbolism, persisted for decades after the Civil War—epitomized by Elizabeth Stuart Phelps's *The Gates of Ajar* (1872), an enormously popular novel that served as balm for the grief wrought by the war by offering its (largely female) readers a soothing vision of the afterlife. But it was accompanied by a growing impatience with moral pieties and cosmic certainties, and a desire to represent life on more empirical terms. This led to the literary movement known as realism.[29]

Realism took a variety of forms. In some cases, it was an effort to break free of the didactic quality of Victorian fiction, humorously captured by Mark Twain's warning that anyone seeking a moral in *The Adventures of Huckleberry Finn* (1885) would be punished.[30] In other cases, it took the form of a genre called "local color," writings firmly rooted in a particular location, ranging from the grim Midwestern stories of Hamlin Garland to descriptions of New England life in Sarah Orne Jewett's *The Country of the Pointed Firs* (1896). In still other cases, it reflected a fascination with technology and with the implacable hand of science. At the end of the century, realism culminated in a more deterministic approach, called naturalism, that drew on the social Darwinism of the elite. The writings of Stephen Crane, especially *The Red Badge of Courage* (1894-95), demonstrated a fascination with the levers of industrialism and its impact on character, while *Maggie: A Girl of the Streets* (1896) evoked a starker mood. Crane's attempt to represent working-class life as accurately as possible—he roamed the Bowery in order to write *Maggie*—reflected a growing determination on the part of reformers to understand, in the words of journalist Jacob Riis, "how the other half lives."

This realistic thrust reflected and reinforced a much more powerful, and literal, realism in the visual media. The arrival of photography as a fact of everyday life in working-class homes in the late nineteenth century was one of the most dramatic developments of the era. The technological roots of photographic reproduction dated back to a half-century earlier, but it was not until the decades following the Civil War that the visual image diffused down from the top of society to the masses.

Photography began with the discovery that certain chemicals interacted with light in a particular way to create a lasting image. The first person known to try this was Frenchman Joseph Nicephore Niepce in 1824. In 1837, Niepce formed a partnership with L.J.M. Daguerre, who had in the meantime improved the process: these early photographs went by the name of daguerreotypes. At about the same time, Englishman William Henry Fox Talbot found a way of making pictures that had the added advantage of being reproducible. Before long, a host of scientist/entrepreneurs (among them Samuel Morse of telegraphy fame) went into the reproduction business.

Family portraits of members of the aspiring middle class were the first common use for such pictures. By 1850, some 3 million daguerreotypes had been sold.[31] During the Civil War, *cartes de visites* (card photographs) became common, as inexpensive reproduction techniques and the anxieties of wartime made small pictures a kind of personal treasure for soldiers, their families, and friends to give each other. *Cartes de visites* of objects, picturesque places, and celebrities also became common.

By the end of the century, various means of visual reproduction had proliferated to the point of being woven into the fabric of everyday life, and the means for people to take their own pictures had become commonplace enough—George Eastman's famous personal camera was introduced in 1888—that the *New York Times* felt compelled to chastise the "Kodak camera fiends" who stalked the Metropolitan Museum of Art and other public places. A postcard craze also took root late in the century, encouraging a more clipped writing style as well as interest in faraway places. Nowhere, however, was the new visual orientation more evident than in the nation's newspapers and magazines.

Lithography, a reproduction process that uses greasy ink applied to stone, was invented by Alois Senefelder in Germany in 1796. A series of modifications created the process of chromo-, or color, lithography, which was introduced in the United States in 1840 by English immigrant William Sharp. Chromolithography was used to decorate calendars, advertisements, sheet music, and fine art prints, like those sold by the now-fabled firm of Currier and Ives. By the 1870s, this form of reproduction had become so common that Edwin Lawrence Godkin, editor of the *Nation,* called the United States as "a chromo civilization."

Godkin was unhappy about this state of affairs, and his reasoning reveals a familiar fear of mass access to what had once been an elite preserve. "Chromos," as they were called, "diffused in the community a kind of smattering of all sorts of knowledge, as taste for 'art'—that is, a desire to see and own pictures—which, taken together, pass with a large body of slenderly equipped persons as 'culture,' and give them unprecedented self-confidence in dealing with the problems of life, and raise them in their own minds to a plane on which they see nothing higher, greater, or better than themselves." In 1884, Godkin's remarks were echoed in the highbrow *North American Review* by a writer who was concerned about "the intellectual indolence that a habit of indulgence in picture-gazing" would bring. Such remarks were echoed in the next century with the advent of movies, television, video games, and other visual media.[32]

In the 1850s, the first attempts at illustration in publications like Frank Leslie's *Illustrated Newspaper* and *Harper's Weekly* used photoengravings of woodcuts—images based on daguerreotypes that were etched onto wooden blocks. Over the course of the next two decades, a series of techniques improved this process, but the real breakthrough came in the 1880s when a "half-tone" technique was developed by Cornell University professor Frederick E. Ives. Halftones turned pictures into collections of tiny black and white dots, which made it possible to reproduce photographs by the same mechanical means used on editorial copy.

However potent, illustration was only one factor in the ongoing expansion of the world of journalism. As discussed in Chapter 2, the birth of the penny press before the Civil War had led to an explosion in the volume, impact, and audience for newspapers. In the last third of the century, this growth continued at a breakneck pace that would have boggled the minds of the early journeymen-entrepreneurs. The number of newspapers almost doubled, to 7,000, in the 1870s alone. Since the population had increased by 30 percent in these years, this growth was both absolute and relative. The ratio of newspapers to readers slackened in the 1880s, but the absolute number almost doubled again, to around 12,000.[33]

In addition to changing its look, the late-nineteenth-century penny press became more independent politically. Papers that were partisan during the Jacksonian era were mostly independent by the time of the Civil War, although their party orientation (usually Democratic) remained evident. During the 1870s, 1880s, and 1890s, however, the press became less predictable as control over editorial content moved from politicians to reporters. In fact, reporting came into its own as a profession in these years, and many writers were influenced by the increasingly scientific and managerial temper of the middle class. This emphasis on objectivity was epitomized by the *New York Times,* which by the end of the century had begun to cement its reputation as the nation's "newspaper of record."

One aspect of the press became distinctly less independent, however, and that was the telegraph. As noted in Chapter 2, the antebellum period ended with the Associated Press and Western Union in respective control of wire reporting and transmission. In 1865, the Western Associated Press was founded to provide an alternative to the northeastern bias of AP reporting. In 1867, the two companies agreed to divide the territory. Meanwhile, Western Union swallowed up the last of its major rivals and assumed control over the telegraph lines. It then struck a deal with the eastern and western wings of AP, which gave it a monopoly over wire news service operations. Despite efforts by the National Grange, the Populist Party, the Knights of Labor, and the American Federation of Labor, as well as the introduction of over seventy telegraph reform bills in Congress, the monopoly was not broken. Its power was apparent in 1879, when AP refused to sell news to land reformer Henry George when he tried to publish a Democratic newspaper in San Francisco. George then founded an alternative news service, which WU was able to crush. The AP-WU axis never did altogether choke off journalistic discourse—a series of successful rivals emerged toward the end of the century—but its power in the nineteenth century serves as a pointed reminder that the "free" press has long been something of a misnomer.[34]

The late-nineteenth-century newspapers were also marked by the ascendance of non-news elements that were designed to attract readers. In addition to a continued reliance on local human interest stories, more effort was put into attracting women readers with articles on fashion, domestic advice, and consumer goods—clearly, the papers' interest in the nascent women's movement was primarily commercial. Newspapers were smaller, articles more tightly written, and illustrations more plentiful, so that they could be more easily read by the burgeoning population of commuters riding horse-drawn buses, subways, and trains to work. Sunday papers, which included sports writing, cartoons, and political opinion, became a fixture of working-class life: in 1889, one out of every two New Yorkers bought one. Recognizing the appeal of feature stories, editors increasingly included them in the daily papers as well.[35]

The late nineteenth and early twentieth centuries were also the golden age of the foreign-language press. Until the Civil War, immigrants into the United States were primarily English-speaking people from the British Isles, although Germans were an important journalistic presence. Around 1880, however, a significant demographic reorientation took place, as a flood of immigrants arrived from southern and eastern Europe. A series of foreign-language papers sprang up to service these communities, the most successful of which imitated the style and substance of the mass-circulation English-language dailies. These papers also served as a vital source of information about the homeland—ethnic nationalism was a potent force in immigrant communities—and also provided clues for those seeking to adapt to life in a new land. Especially notable in this regard was the *Jewish Daily Forward,* first edited by the noted Yiddish-American writer Abraham Cahan, which avoided difficult-to-understand expressions and instead used English words immigrants would or should have known.[36]

As for the major New York metropolitan dailies, many of the first published papers in the 1830s, 1840s, and 1850s—the *Sun,* the *Herald,* the *Times,* and others—were still major players at the end of the century. There was some waxing and waning of their individual fortunes; the *Times,* for example, struggled financially until it was purchased by the powerful Ochs family in 1896.[37] The major factor in the city's bitterly contested news market during this period was the emergence of two maverick papers: Joseph Pulitzer's *World* and William Randolph Hearst's *Journal,* both of which spurred the creation of the epithet "yellow journalism."

Joseph Pulitzer was a man of great talent (and arrogance). The son of a wealthy Magyar-Jewish father and an Austro-German mother, Pulitzer came to the United States during the last year of the Civil War and served an undistinguished stint in the Union cavalry. Drifting west with little more than the clothes on his back, he settled in St. Louis, where he was hired by Carl Schurz as a reporter for the *Westliche Post.* (Schurz, who had participated in the revolutions of 1848, had helped Abraham Lincoln build a bridge to the German-American community in 1860.) After dabbling in politics for a few years, as a journalist as well as a representative in the Missouri legislature, Pulitzer bought the virtually worthless St. Louis *Dispatch* at a sheriff's sale. Three days later, he merged it with the *Post,* another city paper, to form the St. Louis *Post-Dispatch,* which was to become one of the nation's great newspapers. Pulitzer's success allowed him to buy the sagging New York *World* in 1883 and increase its circulation from about

15,000 to 60,000 a year later, and to 250,000 by the fall of 1886. Pulitzer then launched an evening edition; by 1892 the two papers had a combined circulation of 374,000.[38]

The *World*'s success was predicated on a number of factors. Its penny price was so attractive that many of its competitors were forced to lower their prices. Pulitzer also rationalized the relationship between the paper and its advertisers, pricing space on the basis of circulation and allowing for different-sized ads. In editorial terms, the *World* commanded attention because of its news coverage, its convenient size, its plentiful illustrations, Pulitzer's tireless promotion and, last but not least, its pro-labor, anti-monopoly editorial stance.

Perhaps the most important element, however, was the paper's sensationalism. The *World* was well-known for its habit of having writers—especially its stunt reporter "Nellie Bly" (Elizabeth Cochran)—visit hospitals, slums, or asylums in disguise in order to write exposés. The paper also led crusades against Standard Oil, Bell Telephone, and other big companies, for which it was censured by "responsible" critics. In addition, Pulitzer orchestrated a number of highly publicized events, sending Bly around the world in an effort to beat Jules Verne's record of eighty days (she did it in seventy-two, and the contest to predict how long it would take drew almost 1 million entries) and leading the charge to fund the Statue of Liberty (he raised $100,000 in small contributions within five months). By the end of the century, the *World* was the paper to beat.

The man who tried to beat it was William Randolph Hearst. The son of a mining magnate who had struck it rich at Nevada's Comstock Lode, Hearst embarked on a newspaper career when he bought the New York *Journal* from Pulitzer's brother Albert in 1895. Hearst modeled the *Journal* on the *World*—so much so that he hired the entire Sunday *World* staff for his own Sunday edition. One of the artists he snared was Richard F. Outcault, who became well known for his weekly drawings of "The Yellow Kid"—a funny-looking boy who wore a garish yellow dress. The word "yellow" became a synonym for bad taste, and eventually came to refer to sensationalistic papers like the *World* and the *Journal*.[39]

Hearst's role in the provocation of the Spanish-American War was the incident most commonly associated with the advent of yellow journalism. In December 1896, he sent reporter Richard Harding Davis (son of novelist Rebecca Harding Davis) and illustrator Frederic Remington to Havana to cover the Cuban revolt against Spanish rule. When Davis wired Hearst that nothing was happening that was worth reporting, the publisher replied, "PLEASE REMAIN. YOU FURNISH THE PICTURES AND I'LL FURNISH THE WAR." About six weeks later, Davis sent a story about Spanish police boarding an American ship to search for three Cuban passengers. Hearst splashed the story on page one under the headline, "Does Our Flag Protect Women?" Subsequent stories goaded President William McKinley to prepare for war, and the intense publicity led the normally anti-imperialist World to join the swelling chorus calling for the United States to take a hard line. When the battleship Maine was blown up under mysterious circumstances in Havana harbor in February 1898, the Journal made an unsubstantiated charge of Spanish guilt. Before long, Hearst had his war, and while he could not singlehandedly claim credit for it, he and a number of other city newspapers certainly played a part in the crude appropriation of Cuba and subsequent brutal suppression of unrest in the Philippines.[40]

The role of the press in precipitating the Spanish-American War serves as a pointed reminder of the ability of the media to distort and manipulate its readers, and remains one of the more troubling chapters in U.S. history. But while the press—and the public at large—overwhelmingly supported the war, a persistent and vocal minority opposed it. Part of this minority was driven by a racist fear of contamination by nonwhite peoples, but another part had honorable motives. This was the case with the African-American and labor press. "Are the tender-hearted expansionists in the United States Congress really actuated by the desire to save the Filipinos from self-destruction or is it the worldly greed for gain?" asked the Indianapolis Recorder in 1899. The Railroad Telegrapher expressed dismay that "working people are willing to lose blood and treasure fighting another man's battle."[41]

For all its power to inform and manipulate, however, printed matter was only one facet of a varied urban cultural scene in the late nineteenth century. As often as not, dominance and resistance created a complex dynamic that worked in a number of ways. Nowhere was this complexity more evident than in the stage entertainment of the period.

The post-Civil War era opened with older stage entertainments in relative decline. As noted earlier, this was a period of growth for dramatic plays in the hinterlands and of intensifying class stratification in the cities. While "legitimate" theater remained a presence in the cities straight through this period, it became increasingly expensive. On the other hand, many plays and productions, especially melodramas, filtered down to the less well-heeled crowd through so-called "10-20-30" theaters, named for their prices (in cents). But serious stage drama was losing ground to new forms of comedy. In 1879, when the writing team of Edward Harrigan and Tony Hart opened their play *The Mulligan Guards* on the Bowery, they introduced ethnic characters as featured players on the stage. Relations between blacks and the Irish were a major element in this and subsequent plays, but Harrigan and Hart productions also explored the lives of Germans, Chinese, and other ethnic groups on New York's diverse Lower East Side. While to some extent these plays drew on stereotypes, there was affection and humanity in their comedy, which was laced with songs, dances, slapstick, and ethnic humor. Harrigan and Hart's focus on ordinary people stood in marked contrast to that of Gilbert and Sullivan, the British team with whom they were often compared. While their work had become dated by the end of the century, it created precedents that would be echoed in vaudeville, radio, and early television.[42]

Where Harrigan and Hart relied on a faithfulness to the fabric of everyday life, another kind of stage entertainment, the musical comedy, relied on extravagance and scale. Combining dance, humor, and drama, these shows rose steadily in popularity. Some, like *Evangeline* (1874), a parody of a Henry Wadsworth Longfellow poem of the same name, were based on American sources. Others, like *Excelsior* (1883), drew on European traditions—indeed, these extravaganzas owed much to the operettas that had evolved on the continent. A vast new 5,000-seat theater, the Hippodrome, opened in 1905 to house such spectacles. It later became the site for indoor circuses, Wild West shows, and other large cultural events.[43]

Some elements of musical comedy—skits, songs, and dances—were adapted from minstrel shows, which, like traditional theater, were increasingly being forced into a losing competition with their own progeny. But the reason for minstrelsy's decline also lay in its own history and ideology. Its roots were in the plantation, an institution that was fundamentally altered by the Civil War and that became progressively more remote as the century wore on. And while the racial supremacy that had been a cornerstone of minstrelsy certainly did not disappear, its dynamics shifted, turning entertainment based on older versions into a form of perverse nostalgia.

Nevertheless, a number of efforts were made to update the minstrel show, the most striking of which was to include African Americans. One way of doing this was to incorporate spirituals into the quieter, more sentimental component of the shows. This was an ironic development, because while minstrel shows usually celebrated racial subordination, black jubilee singers were often able to perform African-American music more faithfully in minstrel houses than in the more refined, Europeanized concert halls.

The second and perhaps more dramatic change in late-nineteenth-century minstrelsy was the advent of African-American men in blackface. The first black minstrel troupes appeared in the 1850s, but it was at least a decade before they became common. To a great extent, this was the logical outcome of an entertainment form that prided itself on authenticity: who, after all, could better portray slave life than former slaves?

It is easy to see how minstrelsy represented a two-edged sword for African Americans, the symbol of a dilemma that would haunt them for the next century. On the positive side, minstrelsy provided them with the first significant opportunity to enter the entertainment business, and to reap economic and artistic rewards denied them in virtually all other areas of U.S. life. It also empowered them to perform, whether in minstrelsy or other genres, for other African Americans, with whom they had a special rapport and with whom they could experiment with, or subvert, white conventions. At the same time, however, the price of this success was often complicity in demeaning stereotypes.

Some black performers, like songwriter James Bland (composer of such minstrel song favorites as "Carry Me Back to Old Virginny"), and performing artist Sam Lucas, struggled hard to escape this straightjacket. The simplest way to do this was to leave minstrelsy altogether. Lucas, for instance, teamed up with singers Anna and Emma Hyer to produce three critically acclaimed dramatic/operatic productions. There were also a number of relatively progressive "negro musicals," most notably *Clorindy* (1898), a show written by the classically trained African-American musician Will Marion Cook. After some delay, *Clorindy* opened on Broadway and met with great success. More often than not, however, support for such projects was lacking, and many of the compromises that made minstrelsy so frustrating reappeared in other stage forms.

A closer look:

THE DARK HUMOR OF BERT WILLIAMS

A black man is brought before a white judge for stealing chickens. The judge, surprised that the prisoner could steal chickens when there were dogs in the yard, asks him how he did it. "Hit wouldn't be no use judge, to try to explain things to you all," the black man says. "If you was to try you would like as not get your hide full of shot an' get no chickens either. If you want to engage in any rascality, judge, you bettah stick to de bench whar you am familiar."

This joke, with its underlying message about the resourcefulness of black people, the inequities of power in a white-dominated society, and the (often intended) misunderstandings that animate the best humor, came from the comedy routine of Bert Williams, one of the most successful African-American entertainers of the late nineteenth and early twentieth centuries. Yet that very success served as a painful reminder of the severe limits imposed on even the most gifted black people, and the corrupting compromises forced on those who tried to escape them. From the sly slave stories of Brer Rabbit to the tart observations of Richard Pryor, humor has long been a vital instrument for African Americans seeking to navigate these waters, and Bert Williams fits squarely in this tradition.

Williams was born on the Caribbean island of Antigua in 1874.

His family relocated to Riverside, California, in 1885, where his father worked as a railroad conductor. Williams received a better education than most black people of the time, finishing high school and enrolling at Stanford University. But early successes as a performer at saloons and with a Hawaiian song-and-dance group led him to pursue a show business career. He joined a minstrel troupe in northern California and toured the lumber camps. He then tried to succeed as a serious singer, but got nowhere.

By then it was 1893. Resigning himself to working as a minstrel, Williams mastered the exaggerated speech of the minstrel show—"as much a foreign dialect as that of Italian," he later said—and joined a troupe in San Francisco. There he met another black minstrel, George Walker, who became his partner for the next sixteen years. In general, Walker played the smooth, graceful member of the team, while Williams was his comic, inept foil. Moving from small-time minstrel shows to big-time vaudeville, Williams and Walker sang, cross-dressed, clowned, and cakewalked their way to stardom—in blackface.

There were all kinds of irony in this. Originally, white minstrels had applied burnt cork to their faces so they would look more like the African Americans they portrayed. By the 1870s, when blacks entered minstrelsy, this convention was so entrenched that they continued it. Although blackface was most often used as a tool for the denigration of African Americans, it could also, like whiteface for clowns, be liberating. At first, Williams had avoided it. "Then I began to find myself," he explained. "It was not until I was able to see myself as another person that my sense of humor developed." Yet this means of expression (and of coping—seeing oneself as another person is a common strategy for dealing with personal trauma) was also a straightjacket. "The public knows me for certain things," he once said. "If I attempt anything outside of those things I am not Bert Williams."

In the 1890s, however, Williams and Walker felt they still had possibilities. In 1899 they attained new heights when they opened their own show, *The Lucky Coon,* and toured the nation's second-tier theaters. They followed it with two other hit variety shows, *The Policy Players* and *The Sons of Ham.* Then, in 1903, the duo opened the biggest black musical of its time, *Dahomey.* The play was about the financial shenanigans surrounding efforts to fund a black colony in Africa. It tried to evoke certain elements of African culture, but its real function was to serve as a vehicle for big production numbers and for the team's humor. *Dahomey* opened on Broadway—*Theatre Magazine* called Williams "a vastly funnier man than any white comedian now on stage"—and then went on an English tour that included a command performance at Buckingham Palace.

England was something of a revelation for Williams because the racism there was relatively muted. He joined an interracial Masonic fraternal order, something that would have been impossible in the United States. The indignities the team had to endure seemed less difficult for Walker, who was something of a dandy offstage as well as on, and who took great pride in his success as a performer and as manager of the troupe (which included his wife, Ada Overton Walker).

Williams and Walker followed the success of *Dahomey* with a series of musicals that featured exotic locations, flashy musical numbers, choice parts for Ada Walker, strutting leads for her husband, and a simpleton's role for Williams. But in 1909 Walker fell seriously ill, and he died two years later without returning to show business. Williams fulfilled the team's advance bookings, but he lacked his partner's managerial skills, so he turned to a new career as a stand-up comedian, joining Florenz Ziegfeld's Follies, the celebrated revue that represented the apogee of the show business world in the 1910s and 1920s.

This phase of Williams's life was dogged by painful ambivalence. The advent of Jim Crow segregation in the South at turn of the century was accompanied by increasing hostility toward blacks in the North, whose numbers were growing as a result of the mass migrations to major urban areas like New York, Chicago, and Cleveland. Williams might have been a VIP on stage, but he was a second-class citizen everywhere else.

He also occupied an ambiguous place in the black community. An African-American college teacher once wrote to Williams to criticize him for legitimizing white stereotypes of blacks, and for serving as a poor model for black youth. Williams acknowledged that the teacher had a point, but maintained that his black characters were drawn "from the mass and not the few." If such an answer suggested condescension, Williams' finely observed portrayals of African Americans won him an appreciative black audience in Harlem, the new mecca of New York culture. Another Williams joke suggests the solidarity he felt with this community: An unemployed black man finds a job posing as a lion in a circus. In his first appearance, he is put in a cage with a ferocious tiger. Unable to escape, he drops to his knees and prays. The tiger bounds over to him and whispers, "Don't be skeered, pal. I'm colored same as you."

Despite chronic depression, heavy drinking, and exhaustion, Williams continued to perform. He appeared frequently with the Ziegfeld troupe, and financed his own review, *Broadway Brevities*. He had just landed a starring role in a new play when he contracted pneumonia in early 1922. He insisted on going on with the show, but collapsed during an evening performance after having struggled through a matinee. He died a week later and was buried with his Masonic medallion.

"Bert Williams is the funniest man I ever saw, and the saddest man I ever knew," W.C. Fields once said. "The burnt cork weighed him down," journalist Heywood Broun concluded in his obituary. Eddie Cantor, who rose from the Jewish ghetto to become a major star on stage and screen, later wrote of his Ziegfeld Follies partner, "Whatever sense of timing I have, I learned from him." Cantor had heard Williams express his anguish first-hand. One New Year's Eve, the two friends returned to the luxury hotel where Williams lived and paused outside the back door he was forced to use. "It wouldn't be so bad, Eddie," Williams told him, "if I didn't still hear the applause ringing in my ears."

———————

Meanwhile, down on the Bowery, a struggle that had important gender dimensions was being fought in a new arena: the concert saloon. These eating, drinking, and entertainment establishments began to appear in the 1850s and flourished with the infusion of Union troops in the early 1860s. As legitimate theaters banished alcohol, installed new standards of decorum, and sanitized productions for its heterosexual middle-class clientele, such lost elements of the Jacksonian theater reappeared in these male enclaves, which had a cross-class presence of "slumming" white-collar workers and laborers. Concert saloons emphasized female sexuality, not only in the "waiter girls" who served drinks, but in the brief comedic sketches that were part of the variety shows that were the staple of concert saloons.

For those trying to police what they considered the city's moral and social excesses, the concert saloons presented a veritable catalog of sins: alcoholic consumption, male rowdiness, and above all, the dreaded specter of prostitution. It is impossible to know how much actual sexual barter took place, although the reformers' fears that it did (and even that it posed a danger to some women) were plausible. Yet in nineteenth-century terms prostitution—or, as it was commonly called, "white slavery"—hinted at full female participation in sexual and economic activity, which both separately and together threatened notions of Victorian womanhood.[44] Such concerns led the New York State Legislature to pass a law in 1862 that effectively banned concert saloons; this drove the saloons underground in New York, although they emerged in other cities, often with a measure of official tolerance. In the late 1860s, for example, Minneapolis concert saloons began advertising in the local newspapers.

There were a number of cultural forms that centered around female sexuality in this period. One was ballet. Dance had long been a part of theatrical entertainment, usually as a brief *entr'acte* performance or occasionally within a play, and ballet had been imported from France in the 1820s. Although its sensuality aroused the ire of some members of the elite—"Let an institution that has dared to insult you be forever proscribed," abolitionist Arthur Tappan urged women—ballet's aesthetic appeal outweighed concerns about lasciviousness (and dancers wore much more than they do today). By the middle of the century, the elements of sexual spectacle became harder to contain as "living pictures," or live female models striking classical poses, became increasingly common in theaters, concert saloons, dime museums, and even advertising. Once again, however, strategically placed clothing and claims of aesthetic uplift kept the censors at bay.[45]

Women were taking center stage in male bastions as well. The first female minstrel troupe, which appeared in 1870, performed the basic three-part format. Women were also taking male roles in plays. In 1861, the famed actress Adah Menken performed the lead in *Mazeppa,* a popular melodrama. Not only was Mazeppa a male role, but the part called for the actor to be bound, naked and face-up, while riding offstage on a stallion (actually a tamed mare or pony, and often ridden by a double). Despite advertising that suggested she was unclothed and acted as a male, Menken wore a body stocking and light tunic, but she performed the stunt herself, which created a sensation.

Nowhere were women performers more evident than in musical comedies. The most famous of these was *The Black Crook,* a musical with a largely female cast that opened in 1866 and was revived in 1877. *The Black Crook* was a mythic story about an evil count, a malevolent magician (the black crook), and the lovers who had to overcome their machinations; it was less a tightly scripted play than a loosely bound collection of vignettes and skits, and had more in common with a concert saloon variety show than a traditional play. The same was true of *Ixion* (1869), a similar musical extravaganza put on by a British troupe led by Lydia Thompson, one of the most celebrated stage performers of her time. *Ixion*'s cast was all female except for one actor—who played a woman. In both shows, women cross-dressed to play the male roles, performed the can-can and other dances in revealing costumes, parodied well-known works and performers, and conducted a social commentary on current affairs and fashions. By the 1870s, these performances were known as burlesques.

Burlesque was initially greeted enthusiastically by the middle class. Men and women attended, and performances were held in "respectable" venues. As the form spread and grew in popularity, however, negative reaction grew. There were the usual complaints about "nudity" and the aura of sexual exchange, but sexual license was not the only issue. One of the fiercest attacks was led by Olive Logan, an actress and woman's rights activist who lectured and wrote widely on the topic. While there was an element of prudery in Logan's outrage, the issue for her was also tactical: "leg work" demeaned women, *all* women, and set back the struggle for equality in other areas by allowing, even encouraging, men to look upon women as sexual objects.[46]

Logan was right to some extent. But as with blacks in minstrel shows, burlesque cut two ways for women, at least in its earliest formulations. Not only did it (along with related cultural forms) give otherwise disenfranchised women social and economic power—Adah Menken lived a highly publicized bohemian life that included three divorces, great wealth, and renown as a writer of proto-Zionist poetry and essays—but it gave women who were not performers but admired and emulated the actresses' clothing, expressions, and style a hint of its subversive cultural power.

We can sense this power in William Dean Howells's anxious fascination with burlesque. The novelist and *Atlantic Monthly* editor, who by 1900 had become the epitome of the high-culture literary writer, was troubled by "women who, though not like men, were in most things as unlike women, and seemed creatures of an alien sex, parodying both. It was certainly a shocking thing to look upon them with their horrible prettiness, their archness in which was no charm, their grace which put to shame." Howells seemed unnerved by the frank exertion of sexual power, as well as by the ways it could comment on other kinds of male power.[47]

Interestingly enough, there was a class dimension to this subversion, for men as well as women. Many advertisements for burlesque shows featured gigantic women towering over enthralled tuxedo-clad gentlemen. Burlesque was one way bourgeois men went "slumming" in the nineteenth century, and such ads suggest working-class male solidarity with the women with whom they had much in common, at least in economic terms. Intra-class sexual subordination never disappeared, however, and by the early twentieth century, women performers were literally and figuratively silenced as performances focused on the strip-tease to the exclusion of everything else.[48]

A closer look:
CONEY ISLAND

In our day, a brief vacation is not unusual even for people of limited means, and a huge tourism industry makes long-distance travel a commonplace event. But a hundred years ago, most working people didn't get any days off (other than Sunday), let alone vacation, and the popular slogan "Eight hours for work, eight hours for rest, and eight hours for what we will" was an uphill battle that labor unions had only begun to fight. This is what made the opening of amusement parks at Coney Island such a remarkable event: a day at the beach was no longer an impossible dream.

Before subways, buses, and other forms of modern transportation, Coney Island, which sits directly off the southern coast of Brooklyn and is a mere nine miles from Manhattan, was a remote place. The only way to get there was by boat, which was difficult and expensive. The first Coney Island hotel to cater to an elite clientele was built in 1829. The opposite end of the island, known as Norton's Point, attracted gamblers, prostitutes, and other social outcasts. Over the course of the nineteenth century, travel to Coney Island became easier as horsecars, trolleys, trains, and ferries grew more common and less expensive. By 1895, nickel trolleys and cheap ferries put Coney Island within the reach of New York's multitudes.

A new entertainment industry saw profit in such advances and

LUNA PARK, CONEY ISLAND, IN 1905

developed new means to tap their vast commercial potential. The tremendous success of rides and attractions at Vienna's "Prater" in 1873 and Chicago's "Midway" in 1893 showed that a self-contained, permanent amusement park could be economically viable. Moreover, since the 1880s, state fairs had increasingly included professional companies. On Coney Island, all these elements came together with the opening of Sea Lion Park in 1895. Sea Lion was followed by three major enclosed facilities: Steeplechase Park (1897), Luna Park (1903), and Dreamland (1904).

Each of these amusement parks had its own distinguishing feature. Sea Lion was the most basic, but the appeal of its famous ride, called shoot-the-chutes, proved durable. Steeplechase's major draw was its namesake ride, a kind of rollercoaster. Luna Park, which had more of a luxury feel, was lit by 250,000 incandescent lights. Dreamland was the most lavish of all, lit by a million bulbs and built for the phenomenal cost of $3.5 million. Steeplechase was a working-class bastion, while Luna and Dreamland had more of a middle-class reputation. But all were relatively affordable, and their dance pavilions, boardwalks, and proximity to the beach promoted the mingling of classes and ethnic groups.

Indeed, period photographs of Coney Island suggest an informal, easygoing air that was in marked contrast to the fast pace of the city. The resort loosened some of the strictures of Victorian life: for example, the Pavilion of Fun at Steeplechase featured rides like the Dew Drop, which jostled people into each other, and the Blow Hole theater, where jets of air lifted skirts and sent hats flying.

No group found more opportunities at Coney Island than young single women. Often forced to work long hours for poor wages, and then to turn over most, if not all, of their earnings to their families, these women found a degree of freedom at Coney Island that was difficult to come by at home. Many grew adept at "treating," a complex ritual during which they allowed men to buy them tickets, food, or transportation in return for their attentions (which ranged from simple company to sexual intercourse). This conversation, overheard by a magazine journalist in 1904, is revealing:

"What sort of time did you have?"
"Great. He blew in $5.00 on the blow out."
"You beat me again. My chump only spent $2.55."

Treating offered young women partial power at best, and they often risked failure or compromise. Nevertheless, many used it to maximize the minimal opportunities available to them.

Coney Island achieved its cultural preeminence in the twenty years following 1895, when its attractions were new and competitors (from movie theaters to other resorts) were still undeveloped. Dreamland was destroyed by fire in 1911, and Luna went into a slow decline after 1920, until it was consumed by a series of blazes in the 1940s. Steeplechase was also hit by fire in 1907, but was rebuilt and survived, in gradually shrinking form, through the twentieth century. These parks were replaced by newer, bigger—and more genteel— facilities, the epitome of which is Disneyworld in Orlando, Florida. In a relative sense, though, not even Disneyworld has surpassed its ancestor; adjusted for population, 20 percent more people visited Coney Island in 1909 than the combined 1989 attendance at Disneyworld in Orlando and Disneyland in Anaheim, California.

More broadly, Coney Island looked backward as well as forward. In one sense, it was the latest manifestation of the carnival, a cultural institution that dates back at least to the Middle Ages. Seasonal celebrations that marked any number of events or traditions, carnivals encouraged deceptive appearances, sanctioned illicit behavior, and overturned established hierarchies. But in its industrialized, commercial setting, Coney Island also marked a transition from the folk culture of the carnival to the popular culture of the amusement park. If both permitted only temporary departures from the worka- day world, at least the latter allowed the adaptation of the engines of modernity to provide age-old pleasures in new settings.

Drama, comedy, variety shows, minstrelsy, musicals, and burlesque were the major forms of stage culture in the late nineteenth century. Other kinds of performance, including pantomime and female impersonation,[49] did not stand on their own but, like ballet in Jacksonian theater, were integrated into other kinds of shows. At the end of the century, all these forms came together into vaudeville.

The most immediate roots of vaudeville (the term came from nineteenth-century French pastoral plays, although U.S. vaudeville was very much a native form) were in the concert saloon, from which it drew its audience, structure, and performers. In virtually all accounts, the key figure in its development was "the father of vaudeville," Tony Pastor. Born in the early 1830s, Pastor began his theatrical career as a child, singing songs about the evils of alcohol at temperance meetings. He also performed at Barnum's dime museum, with a minstrel troupe, and in a circus. During the Civil War, he staged and performed in variety shows at concert saloons on the Bowery and on Broadway, and he became known for his topical songs about war, labor issues, and women's fashions. The lyrics were published in book form, so that patrons could sing along in the saloon or at home. All the pieces were set to tunes presumed to be familiar to Pastor's audience.

Pastor's songs, which were not only highly class-conscious and racy but often racist, were tailored for the white, working-class male audience that attended the concert saloon. But by the mid-1870s, crackdowns on the saloons, a restlessness with their narrow clientele, and perhaps a residual middle-class streak from his temperance days led Pastor to consider alternate forms of entertainment. "During my stay at 444 [a Broadway concert saloon], I studied the situation closely and determined that if women could be induced to attend, the patronage could be materially extended," he later explained. In 1865, he opened Pastor's 201 Bowery Opera House, and he spent the next ten years successfully riding a fine line between retaining his concert saloon base and trying to expand his audience. He moved to Broadway in 1875, where he went head-to-head with Harrigan and Hart shows and musical extravaganzas. In 1881, he moved again, this time to a theater at Tammany Hall, in the heart of what was then the city's theater district. By this time, he had removed liquor from his venue, although the theater was connected to a bar in the Tammany building. This strategy, combined with a series of promotions designed to attract women—advertising, door prizes, and drawings for major items like silk dresses or sewing machines—not only made him a rich man but demonstrated the economic and cultural viability of vaudeville.[50]

For all his success, however, Tony Pastor was something of a throwback, more like the journeymen-printers so crucial to the development of the penny press than such newspaper magnates as Pulitzer and Hearst. The true moguls of vaudeville were B.F. Keith and Edward Albee, men who had begun their careers in the circus and then moved on to dime museums. In the 1880s, they turned to vaudeville and began acquiring a chain of theaters in the northeast. Far more than Pastor, Keith and Albee sought to restrict audience behavior through ticket prices and printed instructions. They also made a greater effort to create an aura of opulence, with lavish lobbies, plush seating, and a well-mannered staff. The goal was to make vaudeville a thoroughly respectable form of entertainment for the whole family—and, by offering continuous shows from morning to night, a legitimate pastime for women during shopping expeditions.

Keith and Albee also changed the content of the vaudeville show. By the time they finished building their empire, vaudeville had a highly orchestrated structure of animal acts, singers, dancers, comedy skits, magicians, and other performers that had one climax before an intermission, and another toward the end of the show, when the headliners—who ranged from escape artists like Harry Houdini to comedians like W.C. Fields—took the stage. Keith and Albee exerted tight control over their performers, especially by rooting out what they considered inappropriate material. The term "Sunday School Circuit" came to refer to the family-oriented shows for which their theaters were known. But although they usually featured "gold-brick" or "dignity" acts, they could stretch the bounds of propriety when they considered it in their interest to do so, with performers like burlesque artist Eva Tanguay or muscleman Eugene Sandow, whose sexuality translated into box office appeal.

Keith and Albee also took some behind-the-scenes measures to ensure their economic hegemony over vaudeville. Taking their cue from The Syndicate, a group of theater entrepreneurs who in 1896 had formed a cartel in order to control theater ownership, booking, and production, they teamed up in 1900 with other vaudeville managers to form the similar Association of Vaudeville Managers of the United States. In addition to paving the way for integrating the eastern and western circuits, further reducing competition and simplifying touring routes, the Association created a booking mechanism that paid it a 5 percent commission whenever a performer received a contract (this was in addition to the 5 percent the performer usually paid his or her agent). Vaudeville performers responded by forming the White Rats, a labor organization modeled on the craft union. Unfortunately, the White Rats lacked both the means and the organizational savvy of the Association and were never able to mount effective resistance. The formation of a company union, the use of blacklisting, and rampant fraud and evasion weakened its efforts. Vaudeville became a vertically integrated industry controlled by a corporate elite.

Still, if vaudeville's economic structure was controlled from the top and a growing proportion of its audience came from the middle, there remained much about it that was rooted in the working class. The only statistical survey ever made of vaudeville audiences, conducted in 1911, reported that 60 percent were "working" class, with another 36 percent "clerical."[51] This is only a snapshot, and a relatively crude one at that. Nonetheless, it seems fair to say that working people represented a very significant constituency, especially in the "small time" theaters in residential neighborhoods. There is no doubt, at any rate, as to the origins of vaudeville's *performers,* virtually all of whom were of working-class origin, and many of whom retained ties to their communities. Singer Sophie Tucker was the daughter of immigrant parents in Hartford, Connecticut, and worked in their Jewish delicatessen before breaking into show business. Throughout her career, she performed in largely working-class Yiddish theater. Similarly, comedian Eddie Cantor found that material which flopped in English drew an enthusiastic response when performed in Yiddish.[52]

Of course, these examples reveal the power of ethnicity at least as much as class, but in this period, ethnic identity virtually guaranteed working-class status. Between 1890 and 1920, over three-fourths of New York's population was comprised of immigrants and their children.[53] As a number of observers have noted, vaudeville served as a means for different communities within the working class to meet, observe, and laugh at each other. Early performers and humor focused on the Irish and Germans; later in the century, the focus switched to Southern and Eastern Europeans, especially Jews.

Race also played a role in vaudeville. African-American acts, especially black bands, had become an important presence by the turn of the century, and some performers, such as Bert Williams, became major stars. But the widespread custom of including only one black per show narrowed opportunities. Blackface, a convention borrowed from minstrelsy, was widely used by both black and white artists, including Cantor, Williams, and even Sophie Tucker (who first blacked up for a burlesque show in 1908). African-American influences also worked their way into ethnic cultures. Singers like Tucker and Al Jolson fused black and Yiddish elements—Tucker's smash hit "The Yiddishe Mama" (1925) is a classic example.[54]

As noted earlier, vaudeville emerged after the Civil War as part of an effort to bring working-class culture to a wider audience. In that regard, it helped reunify a popular culture that had been steadily splintering since the Astor Place riot. It should be noted, however, that by the end of the century it was the *middle* class that was doing much of the adapting. As early as 1890, the moral, social, and sexual underpinnings of Victorianism were weakening, and a fresh interest in the vitality of working-class and African-American culture was taking hold, especially among the young. Vaudeville offered an intriguing glimpse of a culture where the joys of ragtime, the burlesque of Eva Tanguay, or the spicy lyrics of Sophie Tucker could be experienced.[55]

Vaudeville made one further contribution to modernity as well. Always on the lookout for newer—and cheaper—attractions, turn-of-the-century managers were especially pleased with a form of entertainment that seemed particularly popular as a "chaser," or an act that signalled the close of the show. This attraction consisted of crude images of parades, horse races, and other sights projected onto a screen. Though merely a novelty for the moment, these acts—called "movies"—would become one of the most important forms of popular culture in the new century.

4

Mediating Communities:
Popular Culture
and Modern Technology,
1900-1945

"I AM VERY DOUBTFUL there is any commercial feature in it, and fear that they will not earn their cost," Thomas Alva Edison wrote of his latest invention in 1893. "These zoetropic devices are of too sentimental a value to get the public to invest in."[1] Strictly speaking, Edison was right: his "zoetropic device" had only limited appeal. As he knew, though, it was an important step toward what would become motion pictures, in which the public ultimately invested a great deal indeed. But it took a decade and the contributions of Edison's competitors before the movie camera's financial potential became clear, and even longer for that potential to take a specific form. When it finally did, Edison tried desperately, but unsuccessfully, to form a profitable monopoly in the nascent film industry. Ultimately, however, he lacked the vision to apply this new machine in ways that the public would invest in, and so others reaped the benefits.

Edison's difficulty in predicting and controlling the uses of technological innovation was hardly unique. In fact, when it comes to the major innovations that would shape popular culture in the twentieth century, such unpredictability was the rule rather than the exception. It was decades before another of Edison's inventions, the phonograph, was widely adopted to play music. In 1900, most people familiar with wireless telegraphy—or radio— could foresee its use in shipping and warfare, but would not have predicted its expansion into mass broadcasting twenty-five years later. Moreover, the relationship *between* these new forms was by no means clear. For the first three or four decades of this century, for instance, radio and records were seen as competing, even antagonistic, forms of popular culture. It was only after World War II that it was widely assumed that radio promoted records and vice-versa.

If there was one constant in all of this uncertainty, it was that in the United States all these new technological forms would sooner or later be used for private profit. It sometimes took quite a while for entrepreneurs to figure out ways to do this. In the case of radio, for example, commercial broadcasting was the end result of a long process marked by competing possibilities and failed experiments. Things could have turned out differently, as

---

Reverse page: Clark Gable on the set of Dancing Lady *(1933). A typical MGM moneymaker, the film showcased the studio's package of creative and technical talent. This early semi-musical about backstage life on Broadway also starred Joan Crawford and featured Franchot Tone, May Robson, Nelson Eddy, Robert Benchley, the Three Stooges, a young Eve Arden, and Fred Astaire in his film debut.*

anyone familiar with public broadcasting in England today will attest. And things may still change, depending on what forms of technology emerge and how older ones are adapted or reconfigured.

One of the ironies of popular culture in the twentieth century—especially the first half of the twentieth century, the focus of this chapter—is that inventors and investors pinned their hopes for profit on technological *hardware* while the real future of the new media lay in *software*. To use the example of radio again, its full economic and cultural potential became apparent only after manufacturers switched from trying to figure out ways to sell machinery to focusing on the entertainment that could be broadcast over it. Similarly, movie cameras were a necessary prerequisite for a film industry, but that industry did not come into its own until individual films became desirable commodities. And the phonograph would not become a staple of the American household until records could play music passably and promote dancing.

Historically, new cultural hardware has been developed by elites with access to capital, equipment, and training. But the lasting power of any cultural form has rested with the working and middle classes in three important ways. First, to be successful, any hardware must be relatively accessible. This access can be direct (e.g., affordably priced radios) or indirect (film projectors cheap enough for small theaters to earn back the outlay by showing movies to their patrons). Second, the steady source of profit for any hardware depends on the software, whose appeal must be sufficiently compelling to elicit small earnings (from movie tickets, records, or the patronage of advertisers) that become very large in the aggregate. Finally, many of the most successful creators of software have sprung from the ranks of working people. The artistic vitality and economic viability of every popular cultural form has depended on steady infusions of talent from economically, socially, and/or politically marginalized people. This was the case for domestic novels, minstrel shows, and popular theater in nineteenth century, and remains so for Hollywood films, television comedy, and popular music in the twentieth.

Of course, we should not underestimate the powerful anti-democratic forces that have marked the mass media. For most of the twentieth century the most important forms of communication have been dominated by large private interests that have often restricted cultural interchange and stifled dissent. The danger of totalitarian control of the media is a real, and ongoing, threat. At the same time, however, the history of the modern media is also one of utopian expression, popular protest, and social commentary. Its future vitality will rest on this established tradition.

Many histories of popular culture discuss the intense commercialization of U.S. life in the early twentieth century, the beginning of what has come to be called "consumer culture." The inter-war decades in particular have been singled out as crucial to this process, although there are clear indications that it both pre- and post-dated the 1920s and 1930s. During these years, modern advertising, whose roots lay in the late nineteenth century, reached its peak of influence, and the nation's immense productive capacity was increasingly oriented toward leisure goods. As a number of scholars have noted, the very idea of consumption was intrinsic to the production and marketing of popular culture.

There is no denying the validity of such observations, or the often implicit (and sometimes explicit) concern that consumerism has deferred or deflected Americans from reforming the persistent inequities in their society. Taken too far, however, a stringent attitude toward consumerism portrays the great mass of ordinary Americans as doltish fools unable to make rational choices—only a person who never does laundry would look disdainfully on someone who coveted a washing machine—and suggests a moralistic elitism that cuts across the political spectrum: ideologues of left and right tend to use the same language of corruption when the masses do not do what they want them to.[2] Moreover, unlike other consumer products, popular culture is art. No matter how intensely packaged it is, it will always have a value that cannot be commodified.

Such tensions go to the very heart of what modern media do: they *mediate,* linking ideas and communities, often instantly. In 1900, for example, African-American music was still largely localized in the southeastern corner of the United States. But by the end of World War II, radio and records had allowed a number of black musical strains to coalesce into the new art of jazz, which was then transformed from a regional subculture into a national—and even international—phenomenon that came to be seen as quintessentially American.

The new twentieth-century technologies did not simply move ideas: they also filtered and changed them. To be transmitted, information has to be packaged into a portable form that not only captures the essence of an experience but also formats it for the sake of intelligibility. In the process of doing this, however, the arrangers of information unconsciously *interpret* and subtly alter it. (This is no less true of newspapers than of feature films, because even the most factual stories are shaped by *which* facts are chosen and the order in which they are presented.) In many cases, the added messages reflect the interests of the elites who control the transmission of the information. In others, these messages are coded (a brash haircut, a raised eyebrow, or even a joke) to compensate for, if not actually overcome, a lack of control over transmission.

Such tussling over the larger meaning of information can be discerned long before the opening decades of the twentieth century. But the breadth and depth of it increased exponentially in these years, when some of the factors noted above—the rise of mass advertising, the acceleration of technological innovation, and the incursion of industrialization into virtually every corner of life—made many people feel that they were living in an entirely new world. This was an exciting and disturbing experience, one that the makers of popular culture repeatedly sought to explore. In doing so, they added to the very culture they were trying to understand.

Offering an integrated narrative of popular culture in the nineteenth century is a difficult task, but it pales in comparison to doing so for the twentieth century. In one sense, however, the job is easier because in the twentieth century popular culture became truly national. As late as the 1890s, a number of forms—African-American music, popular theater, and much popular fiction—had a decidedly regional orientation that reflected the specific conditions of their formation and the still-limited networks for their dissemination. Much of this changed dramatically in the twentieth century, not only for technological reasons, but also because of large-scale migrations from South to North, from East to West, and from country to city. A sense of place did not altogether vanish, as the profile of Los Lobos in the next chapter should make clear. But more than ever before, inhabitants of disparate points on the continent shared experiences. And popular culture was often at the center of these experiences.

But while popular culture did become national in the twentieth century, the profusion of new forms, and the persistence of old ones, makes telling a comprehensive story in a small amount of space impossible. The focus here will be on the major forms and on a few of the practitioners, with the goal of suggesting a framework that can be applied more widely. I will begin with a discussion of film, the most influential cultural form of the early twentieth century.

Moving Images:
The Rise of Film Culture

Of all the popular arts, film is the most structurally complex. Besides drawing on a number of cultural forms—including literature, theater, music, and dance—modern filmmaking requires large numbers of people performing highly specialized technical tasks. It is an intensely collective enterprise.

This was not always the case, however. The first films were relatively crude affairs, drawing on a simple illusion that remains the basic building block of cinema: the appearance of motion when a progression of still photographs are shown in rapid succession. Such simulations had been the basis of toys for centuries—called zoetropes in the nineteenth century—but these were relatively simple and not subject to visual manipulation.

The first people to experiment with motion pictures, French scientist Etienne Jules Marey and British-born U.S. photographer Eadweard Muybridge, had little interest in popular entertainment. In the 1870s, Marey sought to use photography in order to simulate Darwinian evolution; Muybridge was hired by California railroad tycoon Leland Stanford to shoot a series of pictures to see if running horses lift all four legs off the ground when galloping, something that could not be ascertained with the naked eye (they do). Marey hailed Muybridge's work, which was otherwise widely ignored. Muybridge went on to develop a device called the zoopraxiscope for displaying his images, while Marey adopted and refined Muybridge's methods and developed an early version of a motion picture camera in the 1890s.

Meanwhile, in New Jersey, Thomas Edison—ever keen to exploit his inventions for profit—was developing another machine to show photographic images, drawing on Marey and Muybridge's work. With the help of his assistant, Scotsman W. Laurie Dickson, Edison's laboratory produced the kinetoscope, a simple device that showed one-minute silent films to individual viewers in peep-show fashion. The kinetoscope was most notable for its use of celluloid film with sprockets on either side, so as to move smoothly past the lens, a method that remains in use to the present day. Despite some early reservations about the commercial viability of his new product, Edison aggressively promoted it at the Columbian Exposition of 1893, hoping that it could be sold on a retail basis. This was a fruitless effort, however, although he was able to sell a few kinetoscopes to arcades, which charged a quarter to view a series of five machines, and over the next few years kinetoscopes sprang up around the country and even in Mexico. Dickson, who had left Edison's employment, weighed in with the "mutoscope," a hand-cranked movie device that relied on flip cards. Another Edison variant, called the kinetophone, played nonsynchronized music along with the picture. (Edison's great hope was an invention that would coordinate audio from his phonograph with the visual images in a film projector, something that did not become possible until the 1920s.)

These machines' inability to reach more than one viewer at a time was a limitation that both Edison and his competitors wanted to overcome. The race to develop a practical movie projector became a fierce international contest involving inventors in the United States, Great Britain, France, and Germany. Edison's most serious rival turned out to be Dickson, who had developed what he called the biograph projector. Two other projectors were developed in 1895-1896, one in the United States by Thomas Armat and C. Francis Jenkins, and the other in France by two brothers, Louis and Auguste Lumière. Edison persuaded these two sets of inventors to pool their resources to create a product they called the Vitascope, which Edison marketed in the United States.

Edison then set about creating a trust to control the nascent motion-picture industry. He did this by acquiring control of the key patents for film, cameras, and projectors. He forced any buyers or renters of his films (which were of far less interest to him than the hardware) to use only his cameras (under license), and used strong-arm legal tactics to conquer his competitors and/or bring them into the fold. The last holdout was Dickson, who won repeated lawsuits brought by Edison but was eventually worn down by the legal costs. By 1909, Edison had set up the Motion Picture Patents Company, more simply known as "The Trust." The Trust then made a deal with the Eastman Kodak company, the only manufacturer of film stock, whereby Kodak agreed to sell its product to any prospective filmmakers who paid a fee to The Trust. The Trust consolidated still further in 1912 by acquiring a film exchange, thereby effectively controlling the exhibitor rental market. All of this was flagrantly illegal under the terms of the Sherman Antitrust Act of 1890, but it was not until Democratic presidential candidate Woodrow Wilson pointed this out during the presidential campaign of 1912 that the Republican Taft administration finally acted. Three years later, a federal court ruled that the Motion Picture Patents Company was engaged in an illegal conspiracy in restraint of trade.

By that point, however, it hardly mattered, because Trust members had failed to see that the greatest profits would be not in the hardware, but in the software. Edison was never involved in film production, and the Trust was a top-down commercial structure with relatively little interest in adapting to the rapidly evolving movie culture. The future belonged to those who understood the average moviegoer, the true foundation of the movie industry.

There is little empirical data on early film audiences, and most efforts involve a good deal of speculation. There does appear to have been a strong middle-class component in film's early years, especially in the arcades. "Illustrated" lectures for the bourgeoisie were also popular. But very early on, a large constituency of working-class people flocked to the new medium, and they quickly dominated it. As noted at the end of Chapter 3, the advent of movie projectors allowed films to be used as "chasers" in vaudeville theaters to signal the end of a show, but their appeal was so quickly apparent that they became an important attraction in their own right. To meet this new demand, a large number of small-time entrepreneurs set up improvised storefront or tenement loft theaters that charged five cents admission—hence the nickname "nickelodeons." A 1909 comparison between the price of movies and other forms of popular culture in Boston suggests films' value as a cheap amusement: the average major vaudeville ticket sold for fifty cents, the theater cost a dollar, and the Boston Opera charged two dollars (which was the average workingman's daily pay).[3] Moreover, since early movies were silent, they transcended language barriers in cities with enormous immigrant populations, virtually all of which were working class.

The growth of nickelodeons in the early twentieth century was nothing short of astounding. The first opened in 1905, and five years later there were 10,000. New York City had 600 alone, with an estimated daily attendance between 300,000 and 400,000. By 1910, tens of millions of Americans were going to the movies every week, many more than once. A 1905 article in Harper's Weekly described the phenomenon as "nickel madness."[4]

Nowadays, we think of going to the movies as a matter of viewing 90-minute-plus fictional (or fictionalized) narratives, but for technical and cultural reasons, it took a full generation for popular filmmaking to take this form. The first movies produced for Edison's kinetoscope featured vaudeville performers, boxing matches, circus acts, and other scenes in a self-contained, black-and-white loop that lasted about ninety seconds. Since these "movies" were viewed in peep-show fashion, they did not have the literally larger-than-life quality that projection would bring. With the advent of film projection, however, new possibilities began to emerge. During the Spanish-American War, for example, producers began filming spectacular patriotic renditions of events there (all of which were completely fictional, since no footage of the conflict was shot, although newsreels soon became common). A few years later, a film exhibitor named George C. Hale made millions by decorating his theater like a railroad car and showing outdoor scenery shot from the front of a moving train. Hale recognized the power of film to do what no form of live entertainment could ever do: transcend time and space. In the most literal sense, it offered escapism.

It seems apropos that it was a magician who first tapped the more expressive, metaphorical, and imaginative dimensions of this escapist—yet almost palpably real—power. French filmmaker and illusionist George Méliès was best known for *Voyage to the Moon* (1902), which marked the beginnings of the science fiction film. Méliès's arresting and often surreal imagery was widely copied in the United States, which did not have a motion-picture copyright law until 1912; the purchaser of a print simply put his name on it. If such exploitation was unfair, these years nevertheless marked the greatest impact of European cinema on the U.S. market, with the French and Italians widely recognized as producing the best films.

Meanwhile, U.S. producers were beginning to tap film's imaginative storytelling power. Perhaps the greatest filmmaker in the first decade of the twentieth century was Edwin S. Porter. Porter began his career as a projectionist and joined Edison's company in 1899 to produce motion pictures. Most early films had used a single, still camera to shoot a scene, as if from a seat in a theater, but Porter employed a variety of techniques—abrupt cuts between shots, dissolves, and multiple points of view—to bring new levels of excitement into filmmaking. These elements came together forcefully in his most famous work, *The Great Train Robbery* (1903), the first cinematic Western.

Porter's work also demonstrated a class-conscious edge. The lawmen of *The Great Train Robbery,* for example, were just as ruthless as the criminals. In *Kleptomaniac* (1906), two women are arrested for shoplifting, but the rich woman's lawyers secure her release, while the poor woman is jailed. Porter was by no means unique in this regard. A few years later, comedic filmmaker Mack Sennett, best known for his "Keystone Cops" films, used humor to suggest the capriciousness, foolishness, or corruption of authority figures. Such assumptions, whether explicit or (often disarmingly) implied, were common in early movie history.

Perhaps the most striking aspect of U.S. filmmaking in these years was the extent to which overtly sexual issues dominated content. The titles of many of these films suggest their flavor: *Trapeze Disrobing Act* (1901), *How They Do Things on the Bowery* (1902), and *The Corset Model* (1903) were typical. One movie with the innocuous title *The Typewriter* (1902) was about marital infidelity; *What Demoralized the Barbershop* (1901) depicted men swooning over a woman adjusting her stockings. And male titillation was not the only gender-related issue: in *Down with Women* (1907), a well-dressed man condemns suffrage, only to encounter a series of women performing "male" tasks—including one who saves his life. Such themes and images represented an emphatic rejection of a residual Victorianism in middle-class America.

For the first few years of the nickelodeon explosion, middle-class Progressive reformers largely ignored the fledgling movie culture. As the extent of film's impact grew, however, it attracted increased attention. Some reformers, notably Jane Addams, recognized the appeal of movies for poor youth, even as they lamented the unhealthy (to the point of being dangerous) conditions in many movie theaters and the misleading messages that some films promoted. Others, however, were less interested in weighing these issues than in simply seizing control over the movies' content, even shutting them down altogether. Vice crusaders like Charles Parkhurst and Anthony Comstock (still on the scene over three decades after his first attacks on dime novels) fulminated over the proximity of movie houses to saloons, and called for public action against films like *The Great Thaw Trial* (1908), the Dickson company's film about a sensational turn-of-the-century murder case. On Christmas Day of that year, New York Mayor George B. McClellan, Jr., finally complied with these demands, ordering the city's police to shut down approximately 550 movie houses and nickelodeons. Local exhibitors, who were often of humble backgrounds like their audiences, were an easier target than producers, who were better able to elude official control. The exhibitors succeeded in reopening their theaters, but were now subject to higher municipal licensing fees and police jurisdiction.[5]

The closing of the New York theaters in 1908 was something of a watershed in movie history, less because government action had a direct impact than because of a subsequent change of stance on the part of some reformers and producers. Progressives moved from attacking the kinds of movies they did not like to praising those they did, and the Trust set up a "National Board of Review of Motion Pictures" to censor films likely to raise objections. (Such groups were periodically reorganized, most recently in the case of the Motion Pictures Producers Association, which rates sex and violence with codes of G, PG, PG-13, R, and NC-17.)

This reorientation was part of an effort to broaden the demographic base and the appeal of movie-going, observable on both the production and consumption ends of the industry. On the production side, there was a new willingness to take film seriously, a tendency embodied by D.W. Griffith. A modestly successful actor and writer, Griffith began directing films for Edison's and Dickson's companies between 1908 and 1913. Here he began drawing on the techniques of Porter, Sennett, and other filmmakers, forging them into a unique cinematic style. Griffith also lengthened his films to run over a series of reels, and incorporated literary themes. In 1913 he formed his own company and began writing, producing, and directing a huge epic on the Civil War and Reconstruction based on two novels by fellow Southerner Thomas Dixon. That movie, *Birth of a Nation* (1915), is a landmark in film history for a number of reasons: it was the first film to be widely hailed as a major work of art; it legitimated movie-going for middle-class audiences; and it was one of the most racist movies ever produced (the film is essentially a celebration of the early Ku Klux Klan). Ironically, Griffith saw himself as something of a reformer and movies as the medium of universal truth. Ultimately, his messianic streak led to heavy-handed flops like *Intolerance* (1916), which, however technically accomplished, was the work of a man whose sensibility was in many ways rooted in the past.

Among those whose sensibility was more forward-looking were a remarkable group of Jewish immigrants from Eastern Europe who broke Edison's monopoly and essentially achieved his goal of controlling the industry. They did this by exploiting segments of the market that the Trust considered relatively unimportant: film production and exhibition. A number of these immigrants, including Adolph Zukor and Marcus Loew, got their start managing movie theaters. Others, like Carl Laemmle, were involved in production and distribution, and were willing to make the multi-reel films that the Trust considered too difficult and expensive to produce. By side-stepping (or secretly trespassing on) the Trust's territory, these producer/distributors, known as "independents," gradually eroded the strength of the Trust until they became the dominant force in the industry. Through a series of complex legal maneuvers, corporate intrigues, and a knack for anticipating the public's taste, these men consolidated their hold over segments of the market, expanded into new ones, and "verticalized" their organizations by handling production, distribution, and exhibition. Zukor went on to run Paramount Pictures; Laemmle became the head of Universal. Loew helped found what ultimately became Metro-Goldwyn-Mayer (MGM). And they were only a few of the many Jewish immigrants (including the four siblings who founded Warner Brothers, Harry Cohn at Columbia, and William Fox of what became 20th-Century Fox) who broke into a WASP-dominated industry—and a WASP-dominated society.[6]

To paraphrase Tammany Hall politician William Riordon, these were men who saw their opportunities and took 'em. The outbreak of World War I crippled the European film industry, and the United States was able to become the overwhelmingly dominant film-producing nation by capturing key foreign and domestic markets. By the end of the war, the United States was producing 85 percent of the films shown throughout the world and 98 percent of those shown domestically.[7] For the rest of the century, film remained a major—perhaps *the* major—product and symbol of U.S. culture.

At home, the "movie moguls," as they were called, consolidated their hold over domestic production through a technique known as block booking. Under this system, a studio rented films to theaters it owned (and those it didn't) on a package basis—if you rented one, you rented them all. The technique was first used by Adolph Zukor at Paramount in the late 1910s and quickly spread to the other major studios. Legally, it was a highly questionable practice, and one the government would half-heartedly investigate for the next twenty-five years. While it lasted, however, block booking gave the studios enough income to support their expensive movie houses, the high salaries of their stars, and a steady flow of product. In a limited way, it also fostered new talent, because it allowed the studios to make inexpensive films with relative unknowns ("B-movies") which were then grouped with the high-priced features sought by exhibitors. Many major actors, writers, and directors, from Humphrey Bogart to Clint Eastwood, started as B-movie actors and worked their way up.

Taking a page from the vaudevillians' book, the movie moguls also went to great lengths to make their theaters more attractive places to see movies. Movie "palaces" became ever more ornate, and large orchestras were hired to accompany feature films. At the same time, ticket prices remained relatively low, allowing working people a sanctuary from the wear-and-tear of a laboring life.[8]

The moguls made one other move that would have tremendous ramifications. Taking their cue from Griffith and other early filmmakers, they kept their financial operations in New York while shifting film production to a small California town that boasted scenic settings, cheap real estate, and a pliable labor force. Its name, of course, was Hollywood.

By the 1920s, Hollywood had become more than an eminently practical locale for film production; it had begun to take on the symbolic dimensions that have grown in the decades since. The standard-bearers for the Hollywood myth were the movie stars. Featured performers who could draw audiences—and large salaries—had been common in other areas of show business since the early nineteenth century, but the members of Edison's Trust had consciously avoided cultivating a star system so as to hold down costs. From a very early date, however, moviegoers identified figures to whom they gave their ticket-buying loyalty, and more flexible producers responded by paying for the services of those who received the most attention. Good-girl types like Lillian Gish (who starred in a number of Griffith's films) and bad-girl types like the vampish Theda Bara were among those who enjoyed early fame and fortune.

Movies also offered opportunities for ethnic "hyphenated Americans." Theda Bara, for instance, was Jewish; Pola Negri a Pole. Rudolph Valentino's enormous popularity among women was the result of his appeal as an "exotic," but he nevertheless helped integrate southern Europeans into the U.S. mainstream. The anarchic humor of the Marx Brothers grew out of the (Jewish) brothers' experience in vaudeville, where they had specialized in Dutch (Groucho), Irish (Harpo), and Italian (Chico) jokes. At the same time, "Anglo" stars like Gish and Norma Talmadge offered immigrants important visual and stylistic cues to help navigate the often choppy waters of everyday life in the United States.

These actors represented stylized archetypes rather than specific personas, which had a great deal to do with the fact that many were women, and were thus even more likely to be objectified than the men of the time. But with the rise of Mary Pickford and Douglas Fairbanks, we can see the emergence of a slightly different phenomenon: not merely archetypal figures (though the supposedly virginal Pickford and the masculine Fairbanks were surely that), but people who epitomized the new consumer culture. The two were married from 1920 until 1930, living highly public lives in a palatial Hollywood mansion they named Pickfair, making playful films, fraternizing with famous friends, and having lots of good clean fun. In this regard, they represented a retreat from the more libertine Hollywood that had prevailed in its first years, an era that came to an abrupt end in 1921 after a raucous party hosted by the famed actor/writer/director Roscoe "Fatty" Arbuckle resulted in the accidental death of an actress, creating a national scandal. Film stars like Pickford and Fairbanks, as well as filmmakers like Cecil B. DeMille (whose slightly racy romantic sagas always ended up affirming the sanctity—and pleasures—of marriage), helped create a new moral center in American culture, one that tried to build a bridge between older notions of character and newer ones of personality.[9]

This was classic liberal ideology in action, diffusing potentially radical ideas about sexual expression, women in the workplace, and industrial discipline through partial incorporation. But there were strong pressures on both sides of this middle ground. In the aftermath of the Arbuckle affair, industry leaders appointed Will Hays, Postmaster General in the Harding administration, to police films from within and promote the industry to outsiders in order to forestall government regulation. Nevertheless, Hollywood film never lost the ability to critique the social order, and its power of suggestion—whether in the provocative garb of a working-class flapper like Clara Bow, the subversive pratfall of a Keystone Cop comedy, or the pathos of Charlie Chaplin's Tramp—became even stronger.

A closer look:
CHAPLIN'S BUSINESS

Back in the 1980s, the International Business Machines Company, or IBM, introduced its new personal computers with a series of print and television advertisements that sought to emphasize the product's elegance, versatility, and user-friendliness. The ads featured a mustachioed man in black with a bowler cap and a cane immediately recognizable to many viewers as the tramp, a character created by filmmaker Charlie Chaplin in the 1910s. In their sparse clarity, the ads were effective in linking these new machines with one of the great geniuses of U.S. culture. They were also effective in obscuring one aspect of Chaplin's life: his lifelong antipathy toward gigantic corporations like IBM and skepticism about the technology they sold—literally and figuratively—as an unalloyed good for all people.

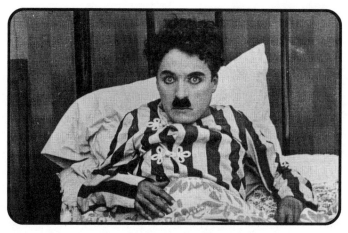

CHAPLIN IN *THE ADVENTURER,* 1917

Born in 1889 to a show-business English family but placed in an orphanage as a small child, the young Chaplin wandered the streets of London before he and his brother joined a dance troupe on the strength of his mentally ill mother's personal connections. The company toured the United States in 1910 and 1912, and during the latter tour Chaplin attracted the attention of Mack Sennett, who hired him to act in movies with established stars like Fatty Arbuckle and Mabel Normand. Within months, however, Chaplin began making his own movies, where he introduced the persona of "The Tramp," a character who would make him internationally famous. By 1915 he had joined a new company and made *The Tramp,* a success now regarded as his first masterpiece. Chaplin's greatest films, among them *The Kid* (1921), *The Gold Rush* (1925), and *The Circus* (1928), were marked by visually stunning imagery, droll (and often stunningly graceful) physical comedy, and above all a powerful gift for inviting sympathy for the downtrodden.

Chaplin is also a pivotal figure in film history because his commitment to his craft led him to make far-sighted and often principled economic, artistic, and political decisions. In 1920, he teamed up with Pickford and Fairbanks to form United Artists, a film distribution company that gave them independence from the major studios. For the next sixty years, UA was an alternative way for filmmakers to reach audiences.

Like many performers who had flourished in the early days of the film industry, the introduction of sound in the late 1920s posed a challenge to Chaplin, whose humor depended heavily on mime and other silent sources of humor. He dealt with it by reaffirming his commitment to his own style, a decision that was a great artistic and financial risk. And despite his track record, none of the major studios, all of which had hopped on the sound-technology bandwagon, was willing to finance his next work, *City Lights* (1931), forcing him to do so himself. It turned out to be one of the highest grossing films of the year and continues to be regarded as a masterpiece.

Chaplin's rejection of the corporate mentality found its way into the content of his films as well. Although many of his earlier works had threaded social critiques through the Tramp's quest for romance, by the 1930s his arguments had become more explicit. They are most obvious in *Modern Times* (1936), an often hilarious commentary on the ravages of industrial labor. Scenes of the protagonist suffering a nervous breakdown under the pressure of trying perform like a machine—and wandering the streets when he is thrown out of work—resonated with Depression-era viewers. So did the Tramp's unwitting but inevitable transformation into a radical in one of the film's most amusing sequences. A few years later, Chaplin addressed the issue of fascism in *The Great Dictator* (1940), playing a buffoonish Hitler. Although he strongly supported the Allied effort in both world wars, Chaplin was attacked by conservatives for his series of marriages to young women, for not acquiring U.S. citizenship, and especially for his refusal to name names during the anti-Communist hysteria of the 1940s and 1950s (he spent most of the postwar era, until his death in 1977, in Europe, and wired a description of himself as a "peacemonger" to the House Un-American Activities Committee). By the 1960s, he was dismissed as either a Communist "pinko" or seen as a legend whose recent works— *Monsieur Verdoux* (1947), *Limelight* (1953), *A King in New York* (1957), and *The Countess from Hong Kong* (1966)—were considered either dated or uninspired. Nevertheless, Chaplin had set a standard for comedic contemporaries like Harold Lloyd and Buster Keaton, and was a role model for subsequent cinematic giants, ranging from David O. Selznick to Woody Allen (who also released many of his films through United Artists). Today he is considered one of the greatest artists of the twentieth century.

This is why, ironies notwithstanding, IBM sought to exploit Chaplin's aura in its advertising campaign for personal computers.

> In the twentieth century, *no* popular culture has proved immune to exploitation by those who wish to channel it for private profit. But popular art also transcends the narrow purposes for which it is often used, and a closer look at it can keep alive a memory—and thus a future—of alternatives.

———————

Even as the star system was maturing, however, a new technological development revolutionized filmmaking yet again in the late 1920s: sound movies. Actually, motion picture sound was not new. As noted earlier, Edison himself had long sought to link the phonograph with the movie camera, although not until the early 1920s were the technical problems resolved. Nevertheless, there was no rush to produce sound pictures at this point; the industry had invested too much in silent films to make the expensive changes that sound recording necessitated. But in 1926, Warner Brothers, which was struggling compared to its more established competitors, decided to experiment with sound as a way to catch up. It released a few sound shorts and one feature film, *Don Juan*, that included a sound track recorded by the New York Philharmonic. None had much impact. The following year it released *The Jazz Singer,* starring Al Jolson, a movie based on a Broadway musical. The script had no dialogue, but at one point during filming the irrepressible vaudeville star had blurted out "You ain't heard nuthin' yet, folks! Listen to this!" Sam Warner, struck by the remark, added another 250 words of dialogue to the film, which became a huge hit. The rush to sound was on, with Warner Brothers leading the way.[10]

Besides the enormous sums needed to refit equipment and theaters, sound had other effects on film culture. Because recording sound required confined sets, indoor shooting, and less movement than silent pictures, filmmaking temporarily retreated into the photographing of staged plays. Sound also had an effect on who did, and who did not, become a star. Celluloid magic had always been somewhat fickle: Griffith collaborator Harry E. Aitken went broke when his company paid Broadway stars large salaries to act in movies that never caught on. Now those who could not easily speak Hollywood's language (literally, in the case of Pola Negri, or figuratively, in the case of British actors with clipped accents) were at a distinct disadvantage, and others with relevant experience, like the Marx Brothers or Jean

Harlow, could flourish. Some screen actors changed personas: Greta Garbo played the vamp in silent movies but became more the tragic heroine in the age of sound. Most fundamentally, however, the advent of sound consolidated the movies' position in the center of popular culture. Previously, vaudeville, Broadway, and new cultural forms like radio had provided elements—voices and music—that movies could not. Now, however, film could compete with, and in some cases overwhelm, such forms (as will be discussed below).

For the film industry, the sound boom in the late 1920s initially muffled the impact of the stock market crash that inaugurated the Great Depression. Theater attendance actually rose in 1930, and while it declined in 1931, the major studios and exhibitors remained in the black. By 1932, however, Paramount, RKO, Universal, and Fox were either in bankruptcy or undergoing major reorganization.[11] Even so, such setbacks ultimately proved only temporary. President Franklin Roosevelt's first attempt to deal with the crisis, the National Recovery Administration (NRA), granted companies like the studios concessions that allowed them to regain—and in some cases, strengthen—their positions. But the NRA was later declared unconstitutional, and the passage of the Wagner Act in 1937 gave new legitimacy to unions, a salutary development in Hollywood. Somewhat reversing its earlier course, in 1938 the Justice Department filed an antitrust suit against the largest studios, a process that was slowed by the outbreak of World War II and a desire to use Hollywood for propaganda purposes. The day of reckoning for the moguls was postponed.

The period between the onset of the Great Depression and the end of World War II has been widely viewed as Hollywood's "Golden Age." During these years the industry created a densely interlocking infrastructure of talent, production facilities, managers, and capital in a way that one historian has described as "the genius of the system."[12] Actors signed with a studio, which paid them a flat salary and had the right to use them in any film they wished. A studio could also "loan" an actor's services to another studio, pocketing the difference between the fee and the actor's salary. In addition, companies rented studio space to each other, and bought, financed, or distributed pictures by their main competitors or smaller concerns. Such techniques allowed the major studios to produce a large number of movies with factory-like efficiency.

Hollywood operated with a similar mass-production mentality on the aesthetic plane, producing a line of genres that would satisfy different segments of the population. Of course, not all movies could be slotted into a particular category, but a series of discrete storytelling traditions—the Western, the horror film, the screwball comedy, the musical, and so on—emerged. By high-cultural standards of uniqueness and elite appeal, such films were not considered "serious" art. But by drawing upon, adapting, and subverting widely known aesthetic conventions and organizing them into individual works, the resulting films had tremendous appeal. So while from the standpoint of technical experimentation a film like *Casablanca* (1942) might leave a lot to be desired, its combination of brisk direction by Michael Curtiz, nuanced acting by Humphrey Bogart and Ingrid Bergman, and above all its imaginative manipulations of cultural conventions (a romantic love story where the guy *doesn't* get the girl; a fable of political commitment set in an atmosphere of cynicism and corruption) have made it justly famed as one of the great films of all time.

Given the teamwork responsible for so many films, and the profit motive that impelled such combinations, it should not be surprising that studios became known for particular genres. Universal, for example, specialized in low-cost horror movies, aided by the successive talents of Bela Lugosi, best known for his *Dracula* (1931), and of Boris Karloff, star of *Frankenstein* (also 1931). MGM, the "Tiffany" of the industry, made a string of highly successful musicals, beginning with *Broadway Melody* (1929) and culminating in *Singin' in the Rain* (1952). RKO gave MGM a run for its money in the 1930s, particularly with its Fred Astaire-Ginger Rogers films, which included *Top Hat* (1935) and *Shall We Dance?* (1937).

Warner Brothers was responsible for some of the most contentious films of this era. It made a series of films starring the sexually frank "come-up-and-see-me-some-time" Mae West. It was also responsible for one of the most durable of Hollywood genres, the gangster movie. *Little Caesar, Public Enemy,* and *Smart Money* (all 1931), as well as the independent production *Scarface* (1932) portrayed powerful people who took matters into their own hands, defying conventional behavior in favor of their own codes of honor.[13]

The relative frankness with which these movies depicted sex and violence generated a backlash from the Catholic church and other moralists, leading to the implementation of a new form of censorship, the Production Code Administration, in 1934. Thereafter, producers were more likely to portray law enforcement officers more sympathetically and to undermine the credibility of criminals. As one indication of this shift, James Cagney, the celebrated gangster character in *Public Enemy,* starred in *G-Men* the following year.

Skepticism about conventional wisdom and civic authority re-emerged a decade later in the genre of *film noir.* Such movies featured individualistic loners who tried to maintain their integrity amid the casual corruptions of public life and the private perversities they encountered in their work. The quintessential *film noir* movies were *The Maltese Falcon* (1941) and *The Big Sleep* (1946), both of which, not coincidentally, were Warner Brothers pictures. (It should be noted, however, that two other *noir* classics, *Double Indemnity* (1944) and *Sunset Boulevard* (1950), were released by Paramount, perhaps the most eclectic of the major studios.) Cagney reverted to form in *White Heat* (1949), the story of a psychopathic gangster.

Another of Hollywood's most famous genres was the Western. As noted in Chapter 3, the roots of the Western are literary, and as discussed earlier in this chapter, *The Great Train Robbery* brought the Western to the screen very early in film history. In the 1910s, actor William S. Hart became a major figure in the genre, playing relatively realistic roles overlaid with sentimentality (he was usually reformed by a good woman). Actor/director Gilbert M. Anderson played Bronco Billy in colorful Westerns that owed a debt to Buffalo Bill Cody. A similar debt can be seen in the work of Tom Mix, the star of a series of 1920s cowboy films.

But the Westerns that occupy the collective national imagination—the Westerns of expansive vistas, stirring music, and the larger-than-life acting of figures like John Wayne—did not really emerge until the Western went to Hollywood. No man did more to bring the genre to life than director John Ford, whose forty-five-year directing career ranged from silents like *The Iron Horse* (1924) to such classics as *Stagecoach* (1939), *The Searchers* (1956), and *The Man Who Shot Liberty Valance* (1962). Though stereotypically associated with conservative values and unalloyed racism, some Westerns went beyond stock assumptions and raised discerning questions about society. The 1952 Western *High Noon,* for example, was a parable of McCarthyism written by Carl Foreman, a screenwriter blacklisted for his leftist politics (see Chapter 5).

Both gangster films and Westerns were largely male-oriented in appeal, but there were also genres produced at least partially (and in some cases, primarily) with women in mind. One of these was the screwball comedy, typically a light romance that appealed to all classes. The prototype was *It Happened One Night* (1934), starring Clark Gable and Claudette Colbert, but the genre was perfected by Katharine Hepburn, beginning with *Bringing Up Baby* (1938) and *The Philadelphia Story* (1940) and culminating in the movies she made with the stolid Spencer Tracy (1942's *Woman of the Year,* 1949's *Adam's Rib,* among others). Hepburn was a pioneering figure in cinematic history because of her ability, in art and life, to have at least some control over her career (she acquired the rights to *The Philadelphia Story* when her stock in Hollywood was low). While her elite New England background and the circumscribed limits of her freedom are obvious— *Woman of the Year,* after all, ends with Hepburn in the kitchen—she nevertheless became a useful role model to millions of women. So did Rosalind Russell, Jean Arthur, and the stars of other screwball comedies.

Dramas were also made for women. In fact, in the 1930s and 1940s there was an entire genre known as "the woman's film." As film historian Molly Haskell has asked rhetorically, "What more damning comment on the relations between men and women than the very notion of something called 'the woman's film'?" Yet if its existence was a telling indication of the marginality of women on screen and off, the woman's film did provide a cultural site where women's concerns—their friendships, their relationships with their mothers and children, and their positions vis-à-vis the men in their life—were central. And the actresses who specialized in these movies, including Joan Crawford *(Mildred Pierce,* 1945) and the incomparable Bette Davis *(All About Eve,* 1950), were among the most impressive artists Hollywood has ever produced.

Even more than women, African Americans were subject to stereotyped roles: the coon, the Uncle Tom, and the savage black buck; or, if one happened to be an African-American woman, the mammy or the tragic mulatto. Sometimes several of these figures were present in the same movie, as was the case in *Birth of a Nation.* Sometimes these characters were inserted into what were widely considered sensitive (but painfully conde-scending) treatments of interracial relations, such as the women's film *Imitation of Life* (1934). Almost never, however, were such archetypes blurred or recombined to allow the kind of complexity routinely accorded white men or even women. Yet despite such straitjackets, some black actors became well-known, including the comedians Stepin Fetchit and Bill "Mr. Bojangles" Robinson, along with the mammy-portraying Hattie McDaniel, who won an Academy Award for her performance in *Gone with the Wind* (1939).

Like women's films, the most nuanced treatments of blacks were generally in those movies specifically targeted at blacks—"race films," as they were known in the industry. Among the most important were *Scar of Shame* (1927), which dramatized the obstacles in the way of upward mobility for middle-class blacks; *Stormy Weather* (1943), a musical about the life of black entertainer Bill Robinson that starred Lena Horne and jazz musicians Fats Waller and Cab Calloway; and *Intruder in the Dust* (1949), an often overlooked drama about a man, played by the black Puerto Rican actor Juano Hernandez, who refuses to knuckle under to white pressure. Despite their audience *orientation,* however, the *production* of these movies did not move squarely into African-American hands until the 1970s and 1980s, when directors like Spike Lee and John Singleton began to exert control over their own films.[14]

Despite the genre films that characterized Hollywood during its Golden Age, there were a number of filmmakers who developed their own imme- diately recognizable styles. Some, like John Ford, were best known for their work within particular genres (though not all of his films were Westerns, as 1939's *Young Mr. Lincoln* and 1940's *The Grapes of Wrath* attest). Others, such as Orson Welles, defied categorization. Like D.W. Griffith, Welles developed his own particular visual grammar, expressed most bril- liantly in the unnerving angles and striking lighting of *Citizen Kane* (1941), a fictionalized biography of William Randolph Hearst that is widely cited as the greatest Hollywood film of all time. Still other directors singlehandedly developed formulas that could be considered genres in their own right. In films like *Mr. Smith Goes to Washington* (1939) and *It's a Wonderful Life* (1946), Frank Capra expounded a sentimental (but often surprisingly shaded) movie formula that critics have dubbed "Capracorn." Arriving in Hollywood in the early 1940s, British director Alfred Hitchcock used clever camera techniques, psychological drama, black humor, and accomplished actors to become the unrivalled master of suspense, with movies like *Rebecca* (1940), *Spellbound* (1944), *Notorious* (1946), and *Psycho* (1960).

By the late 1930s, it was becoming apparent that alternatives to the studios' mass-production style were emerging. David O. Selznick, the executive who first brought Hitchcock to the United States, had set up his own company, which he used to produce a small number of very expensive films that were distributed by the major studios. His greatest success was *Gone with the Wind,* probably the most popular movie of all time. Selznick was eventually superseded by more nimble competitors, including talent agencies, which "packaged" prospective movies by lining up script, talent, finance, and production facilities and then selling them to a studio and/or distributor. One such agency, the Music Corporation of America, which was founded in the 1920s, eventually swallowed Universal to create MCA/Universal.[15]

Meanwhile, a series of external forces was also reshaping the film industry. In 1946, the Justice Department finally ruled against the studios' monopolistic form of organization and declared the practice of block booking illegal. Anti-communist hysteria whipped up by the onset of the Cold War damaged morale and ruined careers. And the growth of television steadily reduced the size of the film audience. All these developments will be explored in further depth in Chapter 5. Here I will trace other popular cultural forms, and examine how older forms fared amid the growth of film and the other media of the modern age.

Receding Lines: Old Forms in a New Century

The rise of motion pictures and other new media brought about a profound reordering of the cultural landscape. For most of the nineteenth century, the printed word and the live performance had been the two pillars of the popular arts. In the twentieth century, they retained their attraction—people did not stop reading novels or going to plays—but they became less central. And some old forms became building blocks for new ones.

The penny press was the first manifestation of popular culture in modern industrial society, and on a day-to-day basis it had a broader reach and more intimate contact with the multitudes than any other form. Newspapers have remained a powerful cultural force in the twentieth century, and have even gained a new sense of authority despite the fact that radio, television, and computer networks have taken over some of their functions, but they no longer have the impact they once did.

The major innovation in the world of newspapers was the tabloid. The term at first referred to the publication's smaller size, which made it easier to read on the subway or streetcar. The first major newspaper to adapt the new form was Joseph's Pulitzer's New York *World,* which published a special tabloid edition on January 1, 1901. The format was launched on a daily basis by a new paper, the New York *Illustrated Daily News,* in 1919.

After a slow start, the *Daily News* (it dropped the word "illustrated" during its first year) picked up momentum, and by 1940 it had a circulation of 2 million, the largest in the United States.

In the 1920s, as the *Daily News* and a host of competitors entered the scene, the word "tabloid" began to take on connotations that went beyond the paper's size. Photography had been making steady inroads into journalism since the late nineteenth century, when the process of using halftones first became common. Pulitzer's *World* was known for its lavish use of halftones, but the tabloids gained a reputation for displaying them in dramatic ways, especially on their covers. This sense of drama was mirrored by the papers' reportage, which tended toward sensationalistic stories written in a brisk style. For all their novelty, however, the tabloids were the direct inheritors of the penny press tradition, and they continued to attract a largely working-class readership. They also exhibited many of the ideological strengths and weaknesses of the New York *Sun* or *Journal*. Such tendencies are apparent in the tabloids of today.[16]

From the Lindbergh kidnapping of the 1920s to the Watergate scandal of the 1970s, newspapers have played a vital role in informing the public, and their features—from comic strips to recipes—have been a part of the warp and woof of daily life. But by the 1920s, there were new outlets for such material, outlets that drew on newspaper talent and reportage even as they competed with the printed press. One was the newsreel, a staple of moviegoing in the 1920s, 1930s, and 1940s. Another was the emerging medium of radio, which will be discussed below.

The literary landscape was sprawling and fragmented in the years following 1900. Among intellectuals, the realistic sensibility that animated writers like Stephen Crane was giving way to the nascent ideology of Modernism, a more skeptical, self-consciously experimental perspective that focused on psychological perceptions rather than concrete realities. Such values ran directly counter to the tenets of popular fiction, which generally drew on familiar themes and language, narrative clarity, and a rejection of the irony that is so central to the modernist aesthetic.[17] Modernist writers like T.S. Eliot or those of the "lost generation" that wandered through Parisian cafés had little interest in the shopworn pieties of the Western bourgeoisie. But the angst of Eliot's "The Wasteland" (1922) contained overtones of condescension, if not contempt, for ordinary people that were all too common in modernist literature.

Meanwhile, another literary sensibility, called "middlebrow culture," was taking root among the growing ranks of white-collar workers. Middlebrow was important in the first half of the century because it mediated between older notions of culture as a form of uplift and the new emphasis on personal expression. (Broadway musicals, with their classical musical embellishments and vernacular language, can be seen as theatrical examples of middlebrow culture.) Generally rejecting the tenets of modernism, novelists like John Erskine offered readers the promise of both edification and entertainment. In a similar vein, historians like H.G. Wells and Will Durant enjoyed successful careers synthesizing and summarizing large bodies of knowledge. At its best, middlebrow was genuinely democratic, for it made culture more widely accessible. At its worst, it packaged information into a cocktail party format.[18]

At the bottom of the literary pyramid in terms of esteem, cost, and the status of its readership were the "pulps," the most truly popular fiction of the early twentieth century. The pulps, named for the cheap paper on which they were printed, were the latest inheritors of a tradition that had begun with chapbooks and been followed by dime novels. But Beadle and Adams went out of business in the 1890s, and the cheap libraries that survived increasingly turned their focus toward children. Perhaps the best evidence of the dime novel's decline were the lamentations in the press. *The Atlantic*—hardly a champion of popular culture—sentimentalized the form in a 1907 eulogy. "What boy of the sixties can ever forget Beadle's novels!" exclaimed the author of "The Dime Novel in American Life." The aim of such fiction, this writer claimed somewhat misleadingly, "was to give, in wholesome form, a picture of American wild life." Deadwood Dick? wholesome?[19]

It can be argued that the demise of dime-novel fiction stemmed from this sentimentalization and middle-class appropriation, or more generally that the form was supplanted by the movies. In one sense, however, the dime novel did not disappear, but took on a new shape. Around the same time that story papers and dime novels went into eclipse, a series of new magazines devoted solely to fiction—*The Argosy, The All-Story Weekly,* and *The Cavalier,* among others—emerged. *The Argosy* enjoyed particular success, and had a circulation of half a million by 1907.

As the pulps grew in number and size, they too began to specialize in particular genres. The Western remained popular—Zane Grey's 1912 novel *Riders of the Purple Sage* was a landmark in the evolution of the genre. Mystery fiction, whose origins can be traced back to Edgar Allen Poe,

George Lippard, and "mysteries of the city" dime novels of the 1840s, also flourished, particularly in *Black Mask,* a monthly action pulp of the 1920s that plumbed mystery, horror, and even the supernatural. *Love Story Magazine* appeared in 1921 to meet the demand for romance, and a number of publications—*Weird Tales, Amazing Stories, Astounding Stories of Super-Science*—emerged to meet a growing, and lasting, demand for science fiction and fantasy. Prohibition and the Great Depression stimulated interest in gangster sagas, and pulps like *Prison Stories* and *Public Enemy* offered sensationalistic accounts of crime.

The most original development in twentieth century popular fiction, however, was the emergence of the detective and his related archetype, the spy. In a sense, such figures were urban cowboys: free agents in a highly bureaucratized society, operating on their own terms outside socially structured limits. By the 1930s, much of this fiction had a terse, skeptical edge, reflecting a widespread cynicism about official authority. Raymond Chandler's Philip Marlowe and Dashiell Hammett's Sam Spade were the premiere examples of such "hard-boiled" fictional heroes, and these men's works—Chandler's *The Big Sleep* (1939) and Hammett's *The Maltese Falcon* (1930)—influenced both the *film noir* aesthetic and radio programming.[20]

But none of these rough categories of literature was airtight. Readers of all stripes read and valued F. Scott Fitzgerald's *The Great Gatsby* (1925) and appreciated Chandler's innovations in detective fiction. And there were moments when particular novels broke through the usual conventions and audiences to become cultural events. The best example is Margaret Mitchell's *Gone with the Wind.* An instant bestseller when it was published in June 1936, the novel sold 50,000 copies in one day, 1 million—at a hefty $3 a copy during the middle of the Depression—within six months, and averaged 3,700 copies a day for the rest of the year. The novel has continued to sell roughly 40,000 copies a year, except in years like 1986 (the book's fiftieth anniversary) and 1991 (the year Alexandra Ripley's sequel *Scarlett* was published), when it returned to the *New York Times* bestseller list. The film version has been an even bigger phenomenon: it has been estimated that 90 percent of the U.S. population has seen it at least once, and countless numbers have seen it worldwide.[21]

Gone with the Wind represented the culmination of a century-long effort to dislodge *Uncle Tom's Cabin* as the dominant work of U.S. popular culture. In telling the story of Scarlett O'Hara and the fall and rise of the American South, Mitchell substituted a vision of victimized whites burdened by negroes and vicious white radicals for Stowe's indictment of slavery. Her vision of the Civil War and its aftermath continues to have enormous influence, largely negative, because of its unremitting racism (far more marked in the book than the later movie). At the same time, however, while the novel's protagonist Scarlett O'Hara was far from an attractive character, her grit and determination have led millions of women to identify with her ever since.[22]

Gone with the Wind's success on page and screen typified the mutual dependence between the literary and cinematic media: while the written word became a prerequisite for the visual image, the movies brought fiction to vast new audiences. The relationship between movies and the popular stage, by contrast, was more complex.

In some cases, films absorbed older stage forms. This is what happened to vaudeville, which had, in *its* beginnings, appropriated elements of the dissolving minstrel show. By 1900, vaudeville had arguably become the premiere form of popular culture. Its success was based on the diversity of its entertainment (and its audience), its vast (though primarily urban) reach, and its adaptability (typified by its incorporation of film exhibition). Vaudeville continued to flourish in the opening decade of the twentieth century, when the nascent film industry was undergoing rapid, but fitful, growth. Small-time vaudeville felt the impact of film when it began to siphon off working-class audiences into nickelodeons, but the glamor, color, sound, and high quality of the live entertainment in big-time vaudeville allowed it to hold its own into the 1920s.

Thereafter, however, a variety of forces began to undermine its survival. As long as films were silent, vaudeville's verbal comedy and musical renditions offered something that movies could not. This ceased to be the case once *The Jazz Singer* had demonstrated the cultural and economic viability of sound projection. The fact that the film starred Al Jolson illustrates a second problem for vaudeville: its stars had a new outlet. In addition, performers like Eddie Cantor made a smooth transition to radio (and later television), while Bert Williams moved into the Ziegfeld Follies, a sophisticated Broadway variety revue that ran between 1907 and 1927 (see previous chapter). And it was not only entertainers who made such moves: financiers did, too. In 1928, the Keith-Albee colossus joined the emerging Radio Corporation of America (RCA) to form Radio-Keith-Orpheum (RKO), which remains a large entertainment conglomerate today. All these developments were intensified by the Great Depression, which decimated vaudeville's financial structure. By 1928, there were only four theaters in the United States that offered vaudeville without films; in 1932, the majestic Palace Theater, formerly a vaudeville bastion, capitulated to the movies. An era had ended.

The decline of burlesque was less dramatic. Unlike vaudeville, which added new performance elements throughout its lifespan, burlesque grew narrower, becoming ever more preoccupied with striptease acts. There was a brief flowering in the early years of the Great Depression, when many major vaudeville talents turned to stints in burlesque in order to make a living, including comedians Bud Abbott and Lou Costello, Jackie Gleason, and Red Skelton, as well as chorus girls Ruby Keeler and Joan Crawford. These entertainers went on to success in film, radio, and television, but their sojourns in burlesque temporarily reinvigorated the form, and in the case of the comedians provided forums for honing their craft.[23] But the striptease aspect generated a steady stream of police harassment, culminating in the shutdown of burlesque theaters in New York in 1937. From then on, burlesque was regarded as little more than a furtive red-light-district attraction.

Traditional stage entertainment did not experience as severe a decline. It had a more established history and repertory to draw upon, and, like vaudeville and burlesque, could offer elements that movies could not. New York theater in particular offered a unique sense of spectacle, typified by Ziegfeld's Follies: lavish production numbers, verbal wordplay, or simple dramatic immediacy. In drawing people to the city—or in symbolizing the city's glamor as shows toured the country—New York theater continues to have a significant presence in popular culture to this day.

But it was no longer popular culture in quite the same way. At the turn of the century Broadway became *Broadway*—not simply a group of theaters gathered on or near 42nd Street, but a theatrical institution of renown and even reverence. Playgoing was no longer the cheap entertainment it had been in the Jacksonian era, and its audience and artistic orientation reflected this change. To be sure, working people never altogether gave up on the theater. Indeed, it retained an excitement that a night in front of the radio or even a trip to the movies have never had. For precisely this reason, though, it was less often a fixture of everyday life.

The principal legacy of Broadway in the twentieth century is the musical, a series of songs and dances framed by a dramatic plot. The origins of this form lie in European light opera, and grew directly out of the stage traditions developed in burlesque, the variety show, and the work of performers like Harrigan and Hart and Williams and Walker. The first major figure in modern musical history was George M. Cohan, best known for his highly patriotic songs. Cohan's *Little Johnny Jones* (1904) spawned the hits "Give My Regards to Broadway" and "Yankee Doodle Boy," and his "Over There" became an American anthem during World War I. His fusion of street smarts and cheery patriotism did not fit the postwar mood, however, and his fierce opposition to labor organizing in the theater—he closed his production company after the Actor's Equity Association won recognition—tarnished him in the eyes of working people.[24]

Cohan had a number of distinguished heirs, including Jerome Kern, Oscar Hammerstein II, George Gershwin, Richard Rodgers, and Leonard Bernstein. The works these men produced for Broadway—Kern and Hammerstein's *Showboat* (1927), Gershwin's popular opera *Porgy and Bess* (1935), and Bernstein's *On the Town* (1944)—all became among the best-known and best-loved works of the stage. Significantly, all of these writer/composers drew at least some inspiration from black musical traditions.

There are the usual caveats, however. While Gershwin and Bernstein were clearly influenced by black music, especially jazz—Gershwin's symphonic composition "Rhapsody in Blue" (1924) is a landmark in the history of classical music for that very reason—they tended to use African-American elements in ornamental or highly attenuated ways. *Showboat* was relatively daring in its exploration of interracial relationships, as was Rodgers and Hammerstein's 1944 musical *South Pacific,* but both seem condescending, if not outright racist, today. Nonetheless, they demonstrate the influence of African-American culture and they also offered important opportunities for black performers: the multi-talented Paul Robeson, for example, won wide acclaim for his performance in the 1936 movie version of *Showboat.*

In fact, there were three cinematic versions of *Showboat* between 1929 and 1951, suggesting a key aspect of Broadway's influence: its value as a source for movies after the silent era. Unlike vaudeville and burlesque, which could provide talent but not material for feature films, many Broadway plays made a smooth transition from stage to screen, keeping interest alive for the inevitable revivals, community productions, and musical recordings that followed in subsequent decades. In recent years, moreover, transmission has worked the other way, as popular films have been made into successful plays *(La Cage aux Folles, Kiss of the Spider Woman,* The Who's *Tommy).* The

Broadway-Hollywood connection illustrates the synergetic relationship that can exist between popular cultural forms.

By the end of the World War I, film was the dominant partner in all these interactions. By the 1920s, however, it had a serious rival in the new medium of radio. Though radio's place in the sun was relatively brief—about twenty-five years, after which it was elbowed aside by television—it played a pivotal role in shaping popular culture for the rest of the century.

Making Waves:
The Dawn of Broadcasting in the United States

Few American institutions developed as unpredictably as radio. Originally valued for its nautical and military applications, virtually no one in 1900 imagined its primary use a quarter-century later would be for the transmission of information and entertainment. When it became clear that this *was* to be radio's most common application, it remained unclear how the industry would be organized and who would control it. And even once it was clear that commercial interests would emerge ascendant, it was not clear *which* interests and companies would dominate.

Samuel Morse's invention of the telegraph created the possibility of instantaneous communication between two points connected by a wire; the next step was to imagine a process whereby the wire itself would become unnecessary. Wireless telegraphy became a subject of scientific investigation in the late nineteenth century when British physicist James Clerk Maxwell, German physicist Heinrich Hertz, the ever present Edison, and a number of others confirmed that electric waves could travel through the air from one point to another. Building on their work, the Italian scientist and entrepreneur Gugliemo Marconi developed a practical device for transmitting Morse or other coded messages using these wireless, or radio, waves, and in 1897 formed a company to market his invention, backed by British capital. Marconi's company sold and operated radio equipment on lighthouses and ships along the English coast.

Rapid innovations by Marconi and others refined the new radio machinery, and opened up new uses for it. In 1902, Marconi succeeded in transmitting a message across the Atlantic. There were obvious military applications here, and by World War I, radio was being used in air, land, and sea operations. But the new technology had peacetime uses as well.

Thousands of hobbyists began to acquire equipment themselves, and these "hams," as they were known, communicated with one another, boasting about the amount of distance they could cover. Hundreds of thousands of others bought receiving kits, which they used to listen to transmissions without sending any themselves.

Meanwhile, innovations—and complications— proceeded apace. By 1910, inventors Reginald Fesseden and Lee De Forest had separately transmitted the human voice over radio waves. De Forest then refined the power of radio to project voices and music over long distances. By this point, however, the airwaves were crowded with hams who faced increasing interference, and the industry was being crowded with companies trying to get a piece of the action. De Forest sold the rights to a crucial invention, the audion, to the American Telephone and Telegraph company (AT&T), which wanted to use it for long distance telephony. AT&T feared competition from radio and gained control of the vacuum tube technology that was crucial to the future of the industry. Another company, General Electric, became a leader in the manufacture of transmitters and vacuum tubes.

The other major participant in the development of radio was the U.S. government, which began regulating the industry in 1904. The Navy worked with AT&T to develop transcontinental and transoceanic transmission capability, and in 1912, the Radio Act attempted to deal with the crowded airwaves by requiring that radio operators be licensed, that stations transmit over assigned wavelengths, and that distress signals take priority (the law was prompted by the role—or *lack* of role—of radio in rescuing survivors from the sinking *Titanic*). When World War I broke out, the government took control of all radio stations. But the Wilson administration failed in its attempt to keep them for government use after the war, a decisive moment in making new electronic media, like the telegraph before it, an instrument of private gain. The administration did step in when British Marconi tried to buy General Electric, however, thereby preserving GE's autonomy and aiding in the creation of the Radio Corporation of America, or RCA. (So much for *laissez faire.*)

By the early 1920s, GE, RCA, and AT&T had pooled their various patents to form a cartel. As with the early film industry, it was assumed that the major source of profits would be the hardware, with the other legs of the business providing the support that would justify purchasing equipment to send and receive private messages. Once again, however, it was the "software"—in this case, radio programs—that proved decisive to radio's development.

Westinghouse, a company that been something of an also-ran in the radio sweepstakes, stumbled onto the potential of broadcasting. An executive noticed that an employee who was broadcasting records in East Pittsburgh had attracted attention in the local press, and that a department store was advertising radio receivers for their ability to pick up the concerts. In 1920, the company moved this operation to its nearby station, known by the call letters KDKA, and, beginning with the presidential election returns that year, began nightly broadcasts in order to sell cheap receivers.

The radio boom was on. Between 1912 and May 1922, the Commerce Department had granted only 300 licenses for broadcasting; seven months later, the number had almost doubled. Some of these early stations, like KDKA, existed solely as a means of promoting the medium itself. But schools, churches, newspapers, and department stores all owned stations. By 1930, radio was reaching 40 percent of homes—12 million in all.[25]

What did these people listen to? We can never know for sure, because there was no way to record this programming. It is clear, however, that early radio was a varied, even freewheeling, affair. Schools broadcast educational programming; newspapers reported current events; churches transmitted religious services. Individual stations had large blocks of time to fill, even though they only broadcast part of the day. Amateur performers were common, if not dominant. Talk shows, sporting events, and lectures were staples.

The one common denominator in all this programming was its low cost: people were not generally paid to speak, nor did they pay for the publicity radio provided. For churches, schools, and newspapers, broadcasting represented a form of community service. For department stores and other commercial interests, it was a goodwill gesture that they hoped would indirectly aid sales. For Westinghouse, GE, and other manufacturers that owned stations, broadcasting was a form of product support, much in the same way computer companies today hire staff to advise users of their products or set up hotlines to answer questions about them. None of these broadcasters expected to make money from radio programming per se.

But AT&T did. Much more than equipment manufacturing, it was telephony, whether wired or wireless, that remained the company's primary domain, and one that it hoped would be a source of profit. In the early twenties, AT&T set up a radio station, WEAF, and sought to charge users for its transmitter much in the same way it charged telephone customers for the use of its wires to make phone calls. In August 1922 a Long Island real estate corporation paid $50 for the right to broadcast a ten-minute talk on the advantages of living in its apartment complex. A short while later, a department store paid for some entertainment to be broadcast by WEAF—in other words, it sponsored a program.

It took about a decade for sponsored programming to catch on; when it finally did, advertising—and, more pointedly, advertisers—came to dominate radio, a corporate force to be reckoned with. At first, agencies put together programs and bought time on behalf of advertisers. By the 1930s, the stations themselves were producing programming for advertisers directly. So in addition to the dubious claims that mark the industry—for instance, that cigarette smoking is actually *good* for your health—advertisers subtly (and not so subtly) dictate the kinds of ideas and entertainment that best serve their interests.

With the advent of paid advertising there came the desire to project radio over greater distances. Given the limits of technology, the crowding of airwaves, and the persistence of old patterns, early radio broadcasts tended to be localized. But the "urge for distance"[26] that characterized the earliest ham radio communications was fully shared by early listeners seeking contact with the outside world and by commercial interests seeking to create a national market. (Some cities had "silent nights" one evening a week when local stations suspended broadcasting so that distant signals could be heard by residents.) In January 1923, WEAF broadcast a concert that was simultaneously transmitted to Boston station WNAC, demonstrating the feasibility of networks of affiliated stations. While the industry as a whole considered two other methods for creating national radio—powerful superstations that would cover large areas, and short-wave transmission between stations, which would then broadcast to individual listeners—wired networks were the most technologically feasible option at the time and the only one that AT&T, which still controlled the key patents, would sanction.

The stage was now set for a new broadcasting order. In 1926, RCA joined with GE and Westinghouse to create the National Broadcasting Company. NBC in turn struck a deal with AT&T that allowed NBC to lease AT&T lines, and AT&T then sold or closed its broadcast operations. NBC was actually made up of two networks; a "red" one anchored by WEAF (acquired from AT&T), and a "blue" one anchored by Newark, NJ, station WJZ. Less than a year later, the Columbia Broadcasting System was created. The government gave its blessing to these arrangements, and the Radio Act of 1927, which created the Federal Radio Commission (FRC) to regulate the industry, basically gave large broadcasters a free hand.

A large segment of the public was not happy about the seemingly unstoppable growth of private control of the airwaves. Some actively fought it. Throughout the late 1920s and early 1930s, a variety of constituencies—labor unions, educational institutions, churches—used public appeals, funding drives, and appeals to legislators to resist the power of the private stations. A proposal to allocate a quarter of the radio spectrum for non-commercial use was narrowly defeated only after a furious corporate lobbying campaign. The only notable exception to the government's acquiescence to such interests was a 1941 ruling that NBC must divest itself of one of its two networks. It sold the "blue" one, which became the American Broadcasting Company, or ABC.

Thus modern U.S. radio—privatized, commercial, oligopolistic—was born. It did not have to be so. The government lost an important opportunity when it returned control of radio back to the private sector after World War I; many nations, including England, Canada, and Australia, did not. All these countries developed public broadcasting traditions that have flourished. Even in the 1920s, the government might have exerted an influence by creating a federal network and/or raising funds for programming through a tax on receivers. Instead, the FRC stood by as commercial stations elbowed aside non-profit ones, and relegated those that remained to either end of the broadcast dial, where transmission quality was poorest. Nonetheless, those that survived have provided a crucial alternative to commercial radio, and have demonstrated that the medium can indeed be organized in another way.

No matter how powerful the corporate radio system became, radio listeners refused to tolerate a continuous stream of advertisements. Stations, sponsors, and the advertising agencies that acted as brokers between them had to avoid offending listeners by offering them something in return for their attention. The first attempt to do this was the Happiness Boys, a singing/comedy duo whose half-hour weekly performances on WEAF in the 1920s were underwritten by the Happiness Candy Company. The Happiness Boys (Billy Jones and Ernie Hare) were experienced vaudeville entertainers and recording artists, and were thus more polished than most performers in early radio. Similar acts—the A&P Gypsies, the Goodrich Silver Masked Tenor, and the Clicquot Club Eskimos (Clicquot Club was a soda company)—offered quality entertainment accompanied by relatively soft-sell advertising. Companies also sponsored more varied forms of entertainment: *The Eveready Hour* became one of the most popular programs after its debut in 1923. The advent of networks made it possible to broadcast these programs in many cities around the country, saving individual stations the time and expense of producing their own shows and giving the networks advertising markets they could sell to companies.

The 1920s thus witnessed the formation of a broadcast radio culture; the 1930s saw its consolidation. One of the most prominent aspects of this culture was the rise of the first radio stars. With the exception of the Happiness Boys, company-sponsored acts had been largely anonymous in order to keep the focus on the products being promoted. Yet as part of the complex negotiation between media and their audiences, listeners channelled their loyalties to performers, who in turn had to negotiate between the sponsors who paid their salaries and their own artistic identities. Many of these people were already established in other cultural venues; the folksy cowboy Will Rogers, for example, was a featured player in the Ziegfeld Follies, while comedians Jack Benny, Fanny Brice, and George Burns began their careers in vaudeville. Benny, Brice, and Burns were all children of Jewish immigrants, and their success gave working-class and ethnic voices a place on the airwaves.[27]

Another important outlet for such voices was the radio serial. A (usually weekly) program with recurring characters and an ongoing narrative, the serial owed obvious debts to both drama and cheap fiction. But like the television situation comedy it inspired, radio serials developed distinctive styles and techniques to suit their aural medium. For instance, actors used their voices in nuanced ways to compensate for the lack of literary scaffolding or visual imagery, and producers came up with innovative methods to make sounds.

Radio serials were developed in a variety of genres—Westerns, detective shows, traditional dramas, and others.[28] Perhaps the most important was the soap opera, named for its early sponsors. The soaps were aimed at female listeners, who had replaced ham-operating men as the target audience for radio by the early 1930s. They usually focused on a strong central character who provided advice and succor to less mature friends, and emphasized character development and situations that were relevant to the lives of ordinary listeners. By 1940, soaps made up almost 60 percent of daytime radio programming.[29]

Then as now, the soaps were widely dismissed as overwrought tripe and their listeners as sentimental fools. It seems likely, however, that these early soap consumers were similar to the romance novel readers studied by one recent historian: a group of people with a well-defined sense of what they liked, and decided opinions about which romances worked well and why.[30] The same is true of other popular culture genres: their artistry becomes clearer if we set aside modernistic criteria of uniqueness, self-conscious complexity, and irony, and instead look at the material on its own terms.

This does not mean, however, that all popular culture should be accepted uncritically, or that its possible meanings are transparent. This is especially true for the most popular radio serial of all: *Amos 'n' Andy.* The program, which ran from the late 1920s into the 1950s (when it became one of the first television shows), once again demonstrates the pattern of old cultural wine being placed in new technological bottles. In this case, the wine was the minstrel show. Charles Correll and Freeman Gosden, white men with varied entertainment backgrounds that included minstrelsy, originally teamed up as a singing team on a Chicago radio station in 1925. A year later, they developed a comedy program, *Sam 'n' Henry,* which was based on the misadventures of two Southern black men who had migrated to the big city. In 1928, they switched to a network affiliate in Chicago and retitled their show *Amos 'n' Andy;* it went on to run nationally five or six nights a week in fifteen-minute segments (extended to a half-hour in 1943). Gosden played Amos, a stereotypical Sambo. Correll portrayed Andy, a sly, dandified Zip Coon. The two augmented these core characters by playing a number of others, including a few middle-class blacks.[31]

Amos 'n' Andy was a huge hit. By the 1930s, an estimated 40 million people—about one in three Americans—listened to it. Movie theaters played it in their lobbies; Atlantic City merchants broadcast it on the boardwalk. Utility companies reported drops in water pressure as people flushed toilets after the show ended, and one sponsor, Pepsodent toothpaste, saw a massive rise in sales. Rarely has popular culture been more popular.[32]

In part, the success of *Amos 'n' Andy* stemmed from the intimacy with which the audience came to know the characters and the topicality of their humor. This topicality encompassed race relations—millions of African Americans were migrating to work in Northern urban factories from the 1920s through the 1940s—as well as other issues that may not have had an obvious racial orientation to some but did to others. Take, for example, this conversation between Andy and Lightnin', an unemployed black man seeking work with Andy's taxi company. It was broadcast on October 30, 1929, the day after the stockmarket crash:

> *Andy:* Well, Lightnin', 'course I would like to give you a job but de bizness repression is on right now.
> *Lightnin':* Whut is dat you say, Mr. Andy?
> *Andy:* Is you been keepin' yo' eye on de stock market?
> *Lightnin':* Nosah, I aint never seed it.
> *Andy:* Well, de stock market crashed.
> *Lightnin':* Anybody get hurt?
> *Andy:* Well, 'course Lightnin', when de stock market crashes, it hurts us bizness men. Dat's what puts de repression on things . . .[33]

The humor in this exchange stemmed from Lightnin's uncannily appropriate concern over people being hurt and Andy's evocative malapropism for the Depression *("Amos 'n' Andy's* term 'repression' is a better one than is generally used," an Illinois newspaper later editorialized).[34] Yet it seems possible that "repression" was a more accurate way of describing the impact of the crash on black people than Correll himself imagined, an irony that some African Americans may have perceived.

Amos 'n' Andy was racist in its indulgence of black stereotypes, and its careful avoidance of racial confrontation made it more a white fantasy about blacks than the "authentic" representation the show and its followers claimed it was. In this regard, it was very much like the nineteenth-century minstrel shows. In 1931, a weekly black newspaper in Pittsburgh circulated a highly publicized petition asking the station to take the show off the air. Yet it had a large black following, perhaps because many middle-class African Americans were willing to laugh at their poor counterparts, because working-class blacks were willing to laugh with other listeners, or because both were able to subvert the show's racism through their own interpretations of it. In any case, *Amos 'n' Andy* remains a touchstone of twentieth-century popular culture, a revealing, if ambiguous, prism of white and black attitudes about race, and a demonstration of an ongoing fascination with African-American culture.

Just as radio adapted and reshaped such print narratives as westerns, mysteries, and other genres, so too did it reconfigure popular music. Most musical performances were limited by radio's technological capabilities, but the situation improved in the mid-1920s with the development of the electric microphone, which could transmit a greater range of voices. The rise of "sweet music," or "crooning," followed. The big, brassy voice of Al Jolson (who had never been much of a radio star in any case) was downplayed in favor of the mellow singing of Bing Crosby, one of the most durable singing stars of this era. Whatever the artistic merit of crooners—one critic acidly commented that when one group sang, you could hear a mashed potato drop—they vividly demonstrated how technology could shape aesthetics.[35]

Perhaps the most obvious example of radio's impact on popular culture was in broadcast journalism. To some extent, the rise of radio ordained the fall of newspapers, but their relationship was too complex to be characterized as narrowly adversarial. Radio interests used newspapers to advertise the new medium, and newspapers invested in radio (sixty-nine papers owned stations by the end of 1922). The United Press wire service cooperated with WEAF to report the election returns in 1924, and at different points in the 1920s the Associated Press allowed its reports to be broadcast.[36]

From very early on, however, rivalry marked the relationship. The Associated Press remained uneasy about radio straight through the 1920s, and in the early 1930s joined with the other wire services in an effort to drive radio out of newsgathering. They stopped when it became clear that the stations could produce news themselves, and by the mid-1930s the networks (notably CBS) had developed sophisticated newsgathering operations. News shows tripled in frequency over the decade, and by 1940 comprised 14 percent of network evening programs. A *Fortune* magazine survey undertaken in 1939 found that 70 percent of Americans considered radio their primary source of news, and that 58 percent considered radio more reliable than the press.[37]

While print and broadcasting media reported many of the same events, radio stories had a distinctive style. Radio offered listeners a sense of immediacy, drama, and even credibility that newspapers lacked (a credibility epitomized by the hysteria precipitated by Orson Welles's fictional "War of the Worlds," broadcast of 1938, in which Welles reported that creatures from another planet had invaded earth). Radio journalism made the most of these characteristics. Compare, for example, the way the UP wire service led off the same 1939 story for its print and radio clients. First, the newspaper version:

London, April 26 — (UP) — Prime Minister Neville Chamberlain announced today that Great Britain had decided to conscript all men between the ages of 20 and 21 for six months of military training.

Conscription, he said, would be provided in a bill to be introduced in the House of Commons. In addition, he said, the bill would empower the government to call up any and all reserves.

Now, the radio version:

> Great Britain cast off centuries of tradition today in a desperate move to preserve the delicately balanced peace of Europe.
> Prime Minister Neville Chamberlain announced England will expand her army by compulsory military service. A bill would be introduced at once to conscript all men between 20 and 21 years for six months of military training.[38]

The radio version is clearly both more dramatic and more interpretive. It can be argued that such a style was just what was needed for the dark days preceding the war—or that, as many critics of television news say today, such a style is misleading. Of course, any media can use either style: tabloid newspapers are more sensationalistic than public radio news, for instance. The primacy of one over the other is a stylistic choice (in the case of radio, a bid for differentiation), not an inherently structural or ideological one.

One of the best illustrations of the fluidity of media interactions is the relationship between radio and recorded music. For a contemporary radio listener, it may be surprising to learn that the one kind of programming *not* frequently heard over the airwaves in these decades was records, which had begun to emerge as a major form of popular culture at the turn of the century. There were a number of reasons for this. One was the poor sound quality of records when sent over the airwaves. Another was a feeling, fostered by networks seeking primacy over rivals who could not afford live acts, that records represented cheap corner-cutting compared to live music. But a third and perhaps more important reason was the demands by the American Society of Composers, Arrangers and Publishers (ASCAP) that it receive licensing fees for ASCAP-member records played over the air. Rather than pay such fees, some programmers avoided records altogether.

One reason for the record industry's intransigence was a well-justified fear that radio hurt record sales. Why this was true is not clear. Perhaps people reasoned that radio equipment was a better investment than phonographic equipment (you pay for a radio once and receive free music thereafter, while each record must be paid for separately), or that they could hear the music they liked live and/or on the radio rather than on generally inferior records. After peaking in 1921, record sales declined in the 1920s—the years of radio's ascendance.[39] The Great Depression almost destroyed the record industry (as will be discussed below), but beginning in the 1940s, a number of factors began to change the situation, and the more symbiotic relationship that exists today began to develop. For the moment, however, the story of popular music was independent of radio, and thus merits separate examination.

Giant Steps:
The Emergence of Modern Popular Music and Dance

As long as there has been popular culture, there has been popular music. On concert stages, on sheets of paper, or as part of shows, music has been an integral element of many forms of culture, and has had an independent identity as well. But the advent of recording marked a decisive moment in popular musical history. Before exploring the genres that formed, however, it is useful to look at popular music on the eve of the recording era.

Before the nineteenth century, the most important means for disseminating music was performance. Religious ceremonies, communal celebrations, family gatherings, and other performance events offered singers, instrumentalists, and listeners the opportunity to learn songs through repeated personal contact. Repertoires were also expanded by varying the lyrics that accompanied the same tune (in some cases, sexually suggestive lyrics co-existed with more conventional ones). Such patterns cut across race, class, and gender lines, although they were intensely localized. Later varieties of popular music drew their vitality by tapping these particularistic traditions.

The spread of the press in the early nineteenth century allowed many song lyrics to be published in broadsheet form. Farmers, merchants, and travelers helped distribute such music, which was usually set to familiar tunes. To aid the process—and to help spread new melodies—"song hawkers" performed on city streets. The lyrics included political commentary ("American Taxation" narrated events surrounding the American Revolution); catastrophic events ("The Dreadful Hurricane at New Orleans"); or everyday events ("The Lawyer Outwitted," "The Old Maid's Last Prayer"). In more affluent circles, the spread of the pianoforte, a modified piano popular among bourgeois women, helped circulate "parlor songs," which tended to be more sentimental than the highly realistic, even graphic, songs in the peasant Anglo-Celtic tradition or the religious and work songs of slave communities.[40]

Meanwhile, the stage provided another important venue for the diffusion of popular music. Minstrel shows, Broadway plays, and vaudeville all spawned songs that were subsequently published and performed off-stage (some even ended up as parodies in burlesque shows). Charles Hoyt, a writer of musicals at the turn of the century, was especially successful in this regard; his *A Trip to Chinatown* (1890) included a series of hits, including "Reuben, Reuben, I've Been Thinking" and "After the Ball." The latter, one of the most popular pieces of the era, was written by Charles K. Harris, who paid $500 and gave up a share of the royalties for it to be included in *A Trip to Chinatown*. Long before the payola scandals of the 1950s (see Chapter 5), such schemes were a common way for writers to promote their music.[41]

Popular music also spread via dance halls. Dancing has, of course, been an accompaniment for music since the dawn of civilization. As discussed in Chapter 2, by the early nineteenth century it had become a performance art that was viewed (somewhat uneasily) by patrons of the fine arts and (often more enthusiastically) by the audiences of popular theater. In the closing decades of the century, however, public dancing become a form of popular culture—a commodified experience in an industrial society. The number of public halls available for rental in New York rose by 50 percent between 1895 and 1910, and while not all of these venues were available for dancing, the number does not include the large number of more informal sites—saloons, rooms, or upstairs halls—that ran dancing operations without licenses.

This "dance madness," as it was known, cut across gender and class lines. The writer of a 1913 book on New York nightlife reported that the dance craze created "a social mixture such as was never before dreamed of in this country—a hodge-podge of people in which respectable young married and unmarried women, and even debutantes, dance, not only under the same roof, but in the same room with women of the town." Racial segregation almost always prevailed on the dance floor, however, although black music and musicians were central to the movement and black dancers enthusiastically frequented their own halls and clubs. There were a few "black and tan" venues that allowed interracial mixing, albeit on a very limited basis (high prices kept most blacks away). Almost all dance halls were adjacent to saloons, and the sale of liquor was a major reason that unions, social clubs, and private companies sponsored these affairs. Such an environment favored a less rigid sexual atmosphere, as indicated by this 1912 joke in the *Harvard Lampoon* about the bunny hug, one of the more popular dances of the period:

> *He:* Shall we bunny?
> *She:* No: let us just sit down and hug.[42]

By the 1910s, the mania had become so pronounced that a number of halls designed specifically for dancing—the Grand Central, the Roseland Ballroom, and others—sprang up. These dance palaces had a largely working-class constituency, mostly young people. They were particularly important to female factory and office workers, who balanced the possibilities of personal and sexual expression and the dangers of exploitation by the men they accompanied or met there.

Such opportunities and dangers led many Progressives to pay close attention to dance culture and try to reform it, often by using paid inspectors who filed reports for organizations like the Chicago Juvenile Protective Association. Progressives also promoted more modern "dating" rituals to structure the dance experience and prevent unchaperoned women from meeting men at dance halls. Yet women continued to flock to the clubs because they offered a combination of excitement and relative safety they could find nowhere else.

Social dancing was only one facet of early-twentieth-century dance culture. In addition to becoming a mass-participation activity, dance was also a spectator sport. Famous couples like Vernon and Irene Castle of Britain adapted popular dance styles for elite U.S. audiences in cabarets and nightclubs in the 1910s, while Fred Astaire and Ginger Rogers enchanted millions of moviegoers in their films of the 1930s. While these people greatly (though not completely) muted the sexual, class, and racial accents of popular dancing, their activities provided strong evidence of weakening Victorian mores and the power of popular culture to move from the bottom to the top of U.S. society.

A far less refined sensibility marked the dance marathon craze of the 1920s and 1930s. These grueling contests, which could draw hundreds, if not thousands, of spectators, offered cash prizes to those who could remain on their feet the longest. In their early years, dance marathons had the air of a lark undertaken by young collegians; by the dark days of the Great Depression, they had become an often grim, almost Darwinian spectacle (a mood captured in Sydney Pollack's 1970 film *They Shoot Horses, Don't*

They?). In their better moments, however, dance marathons offered cheap entertainment and excitement in big cities and small towns across the country.

All music has powerful associative potential, and exposure to popular songs in live settings increased the demand for them outside the theater or dance hall. Around 1885, music publishers began producing sheet music for home use, allowing the growing number of people who could afford mass-manufactured pianos to sing and play music at home. By the end of World War I, around 200 million pieces of sheet music, costing as little as ten cents each, were being sold every year from department stores like Woolworth's. One song, the wartime ballad "Till We Meet Again," sold 3.5 million copies. Clearly, popular music had become big business.[43]

To meet the growing demand for songs, a number of music publishing houses clustered together in what was then mid-town Manhattan, hiring staff writers—many of them classically trained Jewish musicians—to produce material. For reasons that remain unclear, this area was known as Tin Pan Alley. Tin Pan Alley composers wrote catchy urban songs that drew on ragtime without really embodying it. Irving Berlin's "Alexander's Ragtime Band," for example, was more a march than a rag. Berlin's subsequent hits—among them "White Christmas" and "God Blessed America"—typified the white, largely middle-class orientation of this music. Similarly, the dances that accompanied Tin Pan Alley rags—the Turkey Trot, the Bunny Hug, the Grizzly Bear—were often diluted forms of the African-American cakewalk. A few years later, a tango craze led to an interest in Latin music.

Even in diluted form, urban dwellers found these songs and dances novel, and the music industry rapidly developed techniques to make the most of the demand. One of the most tirelessly used techniques was the "song plugger," a publicist who tried to gain exposure for his product. (Before Irving Berlin was Irving Berlin, he was Israel Baline, a New York song plugger.) Sometimes this meant slipping money to the piano player at a nightclub; other times it meant breaking into song in the middle of a busy street. While it is impossible to know how effective song-plugging was, the large number of pluggers seems to suggest it worked.

The point of plugging was to get the song widely adopted, not only in sheet music form but by generating fees for other uses. In 1914, the American Society of Composers, Authors, and Publishers (ASCAP) was formed to further this process. Five years earlier, Congress had passed a copyright law that included protection for published music, and ASCAP planned to use it to extract licensing fees from orchestras, musicians, sheet-music salesmen, and (later) from broadcasters. It was some time before ASCAP became a powerful legal force in the music industry, but its ultimate success demonstrates capitalism's ability to commodify ideas and expressions, a tendency that intensified over the course of the century. While this was unquestionably a boon to those who never received proper remuneration for their work—Stephen Foster might not have died a penniless drunk had there been an ASCAP in the mid-nineteenth century—intellectual property ownership practices constrict cultural discourse. A 1994 U.S. Supreme Court decision upholding the right of the rap group 2 Live Crew to satirize Roy Orbison's 1964 hit "Pretty Woman" was an important victory for free cultural dialogue, but the fact that the case went to the courts at all is a troubling precedent.

Another pivotal cultural event of the early·twentieth century was the introduction of the phonograph, which not only had a dramatic impact on the ways music was heard and used, but also on the way music was produced, particularly in those genres that had been shaped for hundreds of years by local traditions. The phonograph was another invention that Edison had a role in, and another that had an unpredictable trajectory. The immediate technological impetus was the telephone. Building on Alexander Graham Bell's work, Edison received a patent for the phonograph in 1878 (his first recording, in December 1877, was "Mary Had a Little Lamb"). But Edison quickly lost interest in the phonograph, both failing to see how he could make money from it and preoccupied with his efforts to perfect the electric light. Bell continued to refine his own version, called the graphophone (he switched the two syllables in the name of Edison's invention), until Edison resumed work on his phonograph. The two men worked together briefly, but their rivalry drove them apart, each believing that the ultimate application for the new technology would be to aid businessmen who wanted to record messages. By the early 1890s, however, the most popular use for the phonograph was in arcades like the ones where kinetoscopes would soon be placed. Visitors who dropped a coin in a slot and heard recorded music were awed by the novelty of it.

Meanwhile, other inventors refined recording technology. One such innovator, Emile Berliner, replaced the awkward cylinders Edison was using with flat plates, or records. After a series of patent struggles and financial manipulations that lasted for thirty years, the modern record player resembled Berliner's "gramophone" more than Edison's phonograph.

These struggles carried over into the manufacturing end of the business, which became increasingly focused on machines for home use. By 1901, two companies had emerged as major players. Columbia Phonograph, which had origins in Bell's company, became part of the RCA empire, was acquired by RCA's rival CBS in the Great Depression, and remains a force in the record industry today (under Japanese ownership as part of Sony Music). At the start of the century, Columbia's major rival was The Victor Talking Machine Company, which designed relatively user-friendly machines—so-called "Victrolas"—that turned the unwieldy contraption into a piece of furniture for the middle-class home. Together, these companies and others had sold more than 500,000 phonographs by 1914. By 1921, annual production exceeded 100 million.[44]

The growing popularity of records helped feed the dance crazes of the 1910s, providing a relatively convenient means of supplying music for those who had neither the money nor the space to hire a full-fledged band. Victor hired Vernon and Irene Castle to supervise the making of all the company's dance records, suggesting the degree of symbiosis between the two forms. Meanwhile, the rise of recording reshaped the parameters of the music industry. Sheet music sales dropped once music could be produced mechanically. Pop songs became shorter, to fit the three-minute capacity of most records, but they also became more complex, since they no longer had to be simple enough to be performed at home or to rely solely on the piano.[45]

As noted earlier, however, the birth of radio hurt the record industry. Sales peaked in 1921, but had fallen to half that four years later. And the Great Depression was devastating: a mere 6 million records were sold in 1932, less than a tenth as many as in 1921. As a result of such crippling declines, the major record companies were acquired by other entertainment media: RCA bought Victor in 1929, Warner Brothers acquired Brunswick in 1930, and Columbia Records, which had been instrumental in launching CBS a decade before, was swallowed by the same network in 1938. The end of the Depression would mark the start of a reversal in the industry's fortunes, but for the moment the medium was in eclipse.[46]

Throughout these years, records had been primarily an urban and middle-class pastime, with Tin Pan Alley the dominant musical genre. Yet a major revolution in music unfolded when the phonograph and radio receiver extended their reach into the nation's hinterlands, especially the South. Working-class people, black and white, responded with an enthusiasm that led to a dramatic transformation of vernacular music in previously isolated communities. Just as importantly, its dissemination allowed local artistic achievements to reach the rest of the country—and the world.

The first major musical genre to emerge was jazz. As noted in Chapter 3, a variety of musical strains in African-American culture coalesced in New Orleans (and elsewhere) at the turn of the century. The first important manifestation of this convergence was in ragtime, which appeared in the South in the 1890s and played a large role in the evolution of Tin Pan Alley and the dance crazes of the 1910s. By adding instrumentation (ragtime was primarily music for the piano) and blending in elements from other African-American musical styles like blues and spirituals, black musicians were able to develop a new musical idiom.

Jazz is a varied and subtle art, with numerous submovements and interrelationships with other musical genres, ranging from classical to country & western. But for a century, it has been sustained by a sturdy dialectic: On the one hand, it is generally a collaboration between instruments (or voices and instruments, or hands on a piano) performing within a basic chordal structure rooted in the blues. On the other, it depends on improvised solos performed by individual musicians, connoting freedom in two separate ways: freedom within the instrumental arrangement, and freedom to elaborate, embellish, or otherwise enhance the basic chordal structure. This combination of individual effort and collective enterprise is central to such African musical traditions as the griot, suggesting the amazing resilience and adaptability of that culture. Such resilience and adaptability lie at the heart of the African-American artistic tradition and its enduring power to revitalize U.S. culture as a whole.

The first jazz emerged in New Orleans around 1900. As noted in the last chapter, the city had a unique matrix of disenfranchised creoles with musical training, blacks who had arrived from other parts of the South, and access to instruments owing to the relative wealth of creoles and the city's position as a military center. The first jazz combinations were modified marching bands and generally included cornets, trombones, and other brass instruments; a clarinet or piccolo; a snare drum; and bass and tuba. There might also have been a banjo, piano, or string bass. (The saxophone, invented by Belgian instrument maker Adolph Sax in the mid-nineteenth century, did not come into wide use until jazz musicians adopted it after the music fanned out from New Orleans in the 1910s.)

While the particulars surrounding jazz's development will probably always be a mystery, it was clearly a familiar musical style by the time it was first recorded in 1917—it had to have been, because in one of those annoying twists of history, the first jazz record was made by white musicians. The Dixieland Jass Band, as it was known, went from New Orleans to the Victor company's studios in New York to record "Livery Stable Blues" and "Dixieland Jass Band One-Step." The group's members were instant celebrities in New York until the mid-1920s, re-forming again in the 1930s. By the standards of what came later—or of working black musicians of the time—the music was fairly tepid. But even in its diluted form, it created a good deal of excitement, marking the beginning of jazz's transformation from a regional curiosity to an international sensation.

Meanwhile, more lastingly influential jazz musicians were also coming to the fore. Sidney Bechet, a New Orleans creole, wandered from Chicago to Paris over the course of his long life, becoming the first major jazz saxophonist. Joseph "King" Oliver, a cornetist, led the fabled King Oliver's Creole Jazz Band, which included a young cornet player named Louis Armstrong. Still another creole, Ferdinand La Menthe—a.k.a. Jelly Roll Morton—began his career as a gambler and pimp in Storyville, the red-light district of New Orleans. He mastered a number of instruments but settled on the piano. As the leader of Jelly Roll Morton and His Red Hot Peppers, he made a number of recordings and was also the first true jazz composer, shaping compositions more self-consciously thanprevious jazz musicians.

Yet however artistically accomplished jazz became in its first two decades, it was frequently met with hostility and scorn. A well-known 1918 diatribe in the New Orleans *Times-Picayune* is revealing in this regard:

> Why is the jass music and, therefore the jass band? As well as ask why is the dime novel or the grease-dripping doughnut. All are manifestations of a low stream in man's tastes that has not yet come out in civilization's wash. Indeed, one might go further and say that jass music is the indecent story syncopated and counterpointed. Like the improper anecdote, also, in its youth, it was listened to blushing behind closed doors and drawn curtains, but, like all vice, it grew bolder until it dared decent surroundings and there was tolerated because of its oddity.[47]

However crude such opinions were, in connecting the rise of jazz with the dime novel the writer recognized the essential kinship between this new music and other cultural forms. In transgressing old boundaries of respectability and giving voice to "lower" elements—both practitioners and audiences—jazz belongs to a long and varied tradition within African-American culture and U.S. society as a whole.

Such screeds aside, jazz made remarkably fast inroads into the nation's cultural life, rapidly becoming not only the dominant form of popular music but a symbol of its time—as the very phrase the "Jazz Age" suggests. Of course, not everyone partook of this culture; prohibitionists, Protestant fundamentalists, and rear-guard Victorians were opposed to jazz and all it stood for—its subversion of regularized musical patterns (and all *that* stood for), the sexual expressiveness so apparent in the dances it inspired, and, above all, the black and interracial elements that challenged a segregated, white-supremacist society. As a 1921 article in the *Ladies' Home Journal* explained to its middle-class readers, "Jazz originally was the accompaniment of the voodoo dancer, stimulating the half-crazed barbarian to the vilest deeds."[48] Nevertheless, the allure of jazz was so powerful that even the relatively staid Castles used a proto-jazz band for their dances, and performers ranging from Sophie Tucker to George Gershwin tried, with varying success, to integrate jazz into their work.

Meanwhile, the most compelling jazz was performed in New York venues like Harlem's Cotton Club, which featured black jazz musicians playing for white audiences. Such policies demonstrate the racism that persisted even amid white appreciation for African-American art, which in itself was all too often cast in terms of sentimental or exotic appeal. Fortunately, black Americans had their own clubs, such as the Savoy, and the Cotton Club opened to them in the 1930s. In the meantime, white-only clubs provided livelihoods for black musicians and places where they could refine their work. Some of the greatest names in jazz history—Duke Ellington, Cab Calloway, Lena Horne—came of age in the Cotton Club.

Perhaps the first person to bridge the varied jazz audiences was Louis Armstrong. Unlike Bechet, Morton, or Oliver, Armstrong was not a creole but a poor New Orleans black who learned a number of instruments at a reformatory. He settled on the cornet, and played with a number of bands, including King Oliver's. In 1925, he made a series of acclaimed recordings for Okeh, a black recording label, which helped spread his reputation. Throughout the 1930s he was a featured performer, and in the ensuing decades he made a reputation for himself as a singer and even as a movie star. Given the extent of his success with white audiences, and his willingness to play "mere" pop music, Armstrong has been looked down upon as an

Uncle Tom by some jazz musicians in subsequent generations. His talent, however, has never been in question.

Perhaps the most revered jazz musician was Edward Kennedy Ellington. The son of a butler who occasionally worked at the White House, Ellington acquired the nickname "Duke" for his sartorial dress when he was a young man. He exhibited strong leadership abilities early on and began directing his own bands in the early 1920s. Over the course of the next fifty years, he produced an extraordinary body of work, as a pianist, composer, and arranger, that ran the gamut from pop standards like "Take the A Train" (written by a band member) to symphonic set pieces. More than any other performer, Ellington demonstrated the transcendent power of jazz as an art.

A closer look:
BILLIE HOLIDAY, THE JAZZ SINGER

Billie Holiday was desperate. Certainly, this was nothing new: in her short life, she had already been raped, sent to reform school, and had eked out the most precarious of existences scrubbing whorehouse floors. As she said of her family and her neighbors in the Harlem of the early 1930s, "A depression was nothing new to us, we'd always had it." But now, with her mother ill and refusing to accept the money she'd occasionally wheedle from the father who had abandoned them to play in jazz bands, Billie knew she'd have to try something different. So she went to a nightclub seeking a job as a dancer. Sent over to the piano player, she gave an audition that was, in her own words, "pitiful." Feeling sorry for her, the piano player asked her if she could sing. In the awed (even tearful) silence that fell over the club audience during her performance, it was clear that Billie Holiday could indeed sing. She went home that night with two chickens, $57 in tips, and the beginnings of a musical career that would transform her life.

But not quite save it. Given the brutality that surrounded her, perhaps nothing could. She was born Eleanora Fagan in Baltimore around 1915 (her 1956 autobiography *Lady Sings the Blues,* the source of the above story, is fuzzy or inaccurate about many details). Her then-unmarried parents, virtually children themselves, parted when she was very young, forcing her mother to leave her behind

BILLIE HOLIDAY IN 1937

with relatives while she sought work as a maid in New York. Her father, Clarence Holiday, was gassed in World War I, which destroyed his trumpet-playing ambitions; he later turned to the guitar and played with the famed bandleader Fletcher Henderson. Mother and daughter (who adopted "Billie" as a diminutive of her tomboy nickname of "Bill") were permanently reunited in Harlem in 1929, by which time Billie had already had a harsh life. Performing in jazz clubs was not much easier. Singers were required to pick up their tips with their labia; it was Billie's refusal to do this that earned her the nickname "Lady," later modified to "Lady Day" by saxophonist Lester Young.

The one source of wealth in her life was music. While most careful listeners have been struck by Holiday's originality as an interpreter of even the most banal material, it is also clear that she drew inspiration from blues great Bessie Smith and jazz legend Louis Armstrong. (While Armstrong had an uncanny way of making a horn evoke a human voice, Holiday could endow a voice with the richness and fluidity of a horn.) Most of Holiday's records in the 1930s were made quickly and cheaply to fill the expanding jukebox market, recorded with easily available session players. But she was fortunate in who these players were: many, including Benny Goodman, Lester

Young, and Teddy Wilson, went on to become some of the most important figures in the history of jazz. She also proved herself a gifted lyricist whose classics include "God Save the Child" and "Don't Explain," songs she wrote directly out of her own experiences. Perhaps her most famous work is "Strange Fruit," a Lewis Allen poem about lynched black men hanging from trees that she and accompanist Sonny White set to music in 1939.

Because she was only paid a flat fee of between $25 and $50 for most of her hundreds of recordings—black artists were routinely denied royalties—Holiday's livelihood rested on her nightclub performances. She did, however, tour with the Count Basie and Artie Shaw bands in the late 1930s, an experience marred by the racism in cities like Detroit and especially the vicissitudes of the segregated South (the lone African American in Shaw's white band, she would often sit in the tour bus outside restaurants while members brought her food). A child of the city, Holiday could not abide such limitations. She was most at home in New York, the site of her greatest artistic triumphs.

Tragedy, however, followed her everywhere. Both her parents died young (her father unable to get adequate medical care while on tour in the South), and Holiday was involved in a series of unhappy relationships. By 1942, she had become addicted to heroin. Convicted on narcotics charges in 1947, she was sentenced to a year in jail in West Virginia. Upon her release, she found that as a convicted felon she was barred by New York law from working in clubs where liquor was sold, which effectively deprived her of her primary source of income. An unscrupulous manager was able to circumvent the problem, but he exploited her ruthlessly and her second arrest for possession in 1949 may have been a frame-up. She was acquitted, but charged again in 1956, along with her second husband, whom she later divorced. While the trial was repeatedly delayed, alcohol displaced heroin as her drug of choice, gradually ravaging her glorious voice (just when she entered irreversible decline is a matter of some debate). Her liver destroyed, she went into cardiac arrest in May 1959 and died that July.

Billie Holiday's life resembled that of far too many of her contemporaries in an era when even the most gifted African Americans were barely considered second-class citizens. But her work stands as a testament to the way exquisite beauty can be wrought from the ugliest circumstances. There is probably no art that can singlehandedly save a person's life, but work like hers made it one eminently worth living, at least for those who can hear her voice.

――――――――

While generally a black musical form, a few whites did rise to prominence as jazz musicians. There were those, like the unironically named bandleader Paul Whiteman, who tried to give jazz classical music pretensions. Others, notably trumpeter Bix Beiderbecke (who played with Whiteman), performed with an artistry that earned them the respect of many blacks. And a number of whites—most notably Benny Goodman—were prominent in the phase jazz entered in the 1930s: swing.

The swing boom was the next wave in black music, after ragtime and dixieland (and followed by rock & roll), that seized the imagination of a generation. A music by and for young people, swing was loud, flashy, and highly rhythmic, characterized by call and response patterns between wind and brass instruments pioneered by black band leader Fletcher Henderson. But swing was more than music; it was also a cultural style of zoot suits, "hep" talk, and a series of dances (the Suzie-Q, the lindy, the jitterbug, among others) whose buoyancy belied the dark political mood of the late 1930s and early 1940s. Years after his conversion to Islam, a weary Malcolm X vividly recalled his baptism into the world of Boston and New York dance halls:

> "*Showtime!*" people would start hollering about the last hour of the dance. Then a couple of dozen really wild couples would stay on the floor, the girls changing to low white sneakers. The band would now really be blasting, and all the other dancers would form a clapping, shouting circle to watch that wild competition as it began, covering only a quarter or so of the ballroom floor. The band, the spectators, and the dancers, would be making the Roseland Ballroom [in Boston] feel like a big rocking ship. The spotlight would be turning, pink, yellow, green, and blue, picking up the couples lindy-hopping as if they had gone mad. "*Wail, man, wail!*" people would be shouting at the band; and it *would* be wailing, until first one and then another couple just ran out of strength and stumbled off toward the crowd, exhausted and soaked with sweat. Sometimes I would be down there inside the door jumping up and down in my gray jacket with the whiskbroom in the pocket [he was a shoe-shine boy at the time], and

the manager would have to come and shout at me that I had customers upstairs.[49]

For all his skepticism about so many aspects of American life, Malcolm X saw his early immersion in popular culture with a clarity and affection he carried to his death. (This clarity and affection is vividly captured in director Spike Lee's 1992 film *Malcolm X*.)

The popularity of swing in the 1930s and 1940s, which affected the more mainstream pop played by largely white "Big Band" orchestras led by Tommy Dorsey, Glenn Miller, and others, generated two responses from jazz aficionados. One was a return to "trad," or dixieland, which took place in the 1940s. In the most fundamental sense, this was a conservative movement. Another, much more radical, movement was "bebop" or simply "bop," as practiced by a generation of musicians that included Charlie Parker, Dizzy Gillespie, and John Coltrane. Bop musicians rejected the Armstrong sensibility and self-consciously cultivated a complex musical style designed to resist popular appropriation. Cool, cerebral, and modernist in outlook, bop was an important artistic subculture in the 1940s and 1950s. For precisely these reasons, it removed jazz from the center of popular culture.

Despite the breadth of its impact, jazz was not the only African-American musical genre to come into its own in the first half of the twentieth century. Another was gospel. As noted in Chapter 3, the sacred tradition in African-American music gave rise to the spiritual in the late nineteenth century, as black singers came into contact with the more formalized structures of European art music. An important constituency in the black evangelical churches resisted this tendency, however, retaining the more expressive, improvisatory quality that marked older religious songs. A pivotal figure in the development of what was to become gospel music was Charles Albert Tindley, a preacher, publisher, and writer of a number of classic songs at the turn of the century, including "We'll Understand It Better By and By," "Stand By Me," and "The Storm Is Passing Over." Tindley's mantle was later inherited by Lucie E. Campbell, Thomas Dorsey, and others in the 1920s and 1930s. In the 1950s and 1960s, a number of important figures, among them Sam Cooke and Aretha Franklin, drew on their gospel training in making their classic secular records.

Another major musical genre, one closely allied with jazz, was the blues, which continued along the evolutionary path that it had embarked upon in the late nineteenth century. Among the most noted practitioners working along the blues/jazz seam were two women who dominated the field, Ma Rainey and Bessie Smith. Ma Rainey, who was born in the late nineteenth century and recorded prolifically in the 1920s, collaborated with Thomas Dorsey, among others, and sang in a tremendously powerful, dusky style. Bessie Smith, widely considered the greatest singer of her time, enjoyed much success before her premature death in an automobile accident in 1937. These women laid the musical foundations for the great jazz singers of the 1930s and 1940s: Ethel Waters, Sarah Vaughan, Lena Horne, Ella Fitzgerald, and, of course, Billie Holiday. Many of these women led lives punctuated by alcohol and drug abuse, faithless lovers, and unremitting racist treatment. Their achievements lay in bringing their gifts to bear in expressing their sorrows, and in doing so in a way that transcended their limitations.

Another important blues variant was country blues, which was produced by poor, itinerant rural black men with only the simplest accompaniment on acoustic guitar. Many of these players—including Skip James, Charley Patton, and Blind Lemon Jefferson—lacked the polish of more refined musicians like Ellington, but their work had a raw power that proved enormously influential later in the century. The most famous country blues musician was Robert Johnson, who, the story goes, sold his soul to the devil to gain his prodigious talent. Johnson's life is shrouded in mystery, and he died in 1938 when he was only 27, allegedly at the hands of a jealous lover. But in five days of recording between 1936 and 1937, he produced a body of work—including the now-classic "Dust My Broom" and "Stones in My Passway," as well as the widely re-recorded "Crossroads"—that has stood the test of time.

Many of these country blues musicians, who were concentrated in the Mississippi River Delta, left the South in the 1940s and settled in Chicago. There the blues were filtered through new urban experiences and the use of the electric guitar to create a grittier sound expounded by performers like Muddy Waters and B.B. King, men who laid the foundation for rock & roll—again illustrating how local (and changing) conditions can cause cultural effects that subsequently ripple outward.

African-American music was not alone in experiencing rapid development in the first half of the twentieth century. The period is also notable for the emergence of country & western, another of the nation's great musical traditions. Perhaps more than any other musical form, country has retained a strong working-class flavor, which is why it has repeatedly been dismissed—and why it continues to have international appeal. In its early days, country went by the name of "hillbilly music," a term that could be a slur or a badge of honor, depending on who was using it.

Like blues, gospel, and jazz, country & western is fundamentally a music of the American South. And like those black forms, its roots lie before the twentieth century and in the nation's interior, where it was fostered by isolated groups of people (especially in Appalachia and the Ozark mountain ranges) performing highly localized styles. The taproot was the Anglo-Celtic tradition, itself very old, marked by a plaintive, often highly realistic sensibility. Death and sorrow are common themes, usually rendered in a spare, muted voice—in marked contrast to the loud sentimentality of Tin Pan Alley, for instance.

For all its influence, the Anglo-Celtic strain was not the only force shaping country music. African-American music played a role as well. If African Americans learned to play the guitar (a Spanish import that drifted down from the plantation elite to poor whites and blacks), white Americans appropriated the banjo so thoroughly that this originally African instrument is often considered quintessentially white American. And instrumentation was not the only site of such exchanges: themes, melodies, and various embellishments were passed back and forth so frequently that it is often hard to pinpoint origins. In the 1960s, Mick Jagger of the Rolling Stones self-consciously emulated the gruff singing style of black Chicago bluesman Howlin' Wolf, who himself reputedly got his name trying to imitate white country singer Jimmie Rodgers. Rodgers, for his part, drew on nineteenth-century black traditions—and on the English culture that later produced a twentieth-century middle-class white youth like Jagger who wanted to sing like a poor black American.

Ethnic influences also played a role in making country & western. German and Eastern European settlers brought their polkas, waltzes, and other songs (and dances) to eastern Texas, where they were a major influence on a country derivative known as western swing. Mexican *canciones* and guitar playing lent a further western dimension to country; the popular waltz "Over the Waves" was originally written by a Mexican (as "Sobre las Obras").[50]

The sounds of the city were never far from country, either. Minstrel shows, circuses, and medicine shows, all of which originated in cities, penetrated deep into the nation's interior and introduced urban sounds to country folk. When Dr. Humphrey Bate, one of the most popular country music fiddlers, died in 1936, he left behind a repertoire of 125 songs. Of those whose origins could be traced, thirteen were vaudeville and minstrel songs, twenty were popular songs from the late nineteenth century, twelve were pop songs from the 1920s, and three were rags.[51] In other words, almost 40 percent of his material had either originated or circulated in urban contexts.

Nevertheless, such familiar methods of musical transmission paled in comparison to the impact of radio and records. The effect of these was even more dramatic in rural America than in the cities, where contact between different races and cultures was far more common. Moreover, the relative lack of radio interference in the South and West meant that stations could cover much greater distances, creating a broader regional musical community. Some stations were able to evade U.S. regulations by setting up just over the Mexican border, where they could be two or three times more powerful than if they were licensed in the United States, sometimes reaching clear into Canada. Mexico ignored any complaints, because the United States and Canada had unilaterally assigned the long-wave frequencies to themselves.

By the mid-1920s, the most important institution for the dissemination and elaboration of country music was the "Grand Ole Opry," a national weekly program from radio station WSM in Nashville, Tennessee. The "Grand Ole Opry," like "National Barn Dance" out of Chicago, had live country music performers, vaudevillian entertainers, and a generally intimate feeling that resonated with rural people and those who had left the South to find jobs in California or the Midwest. Instrumental music predominated, though over time singers developed a greater presence.

Like other art forms rooted in a specific milieu, country music reflected the social tensions of its time and place. One of the most important was a dialectic between the sacred and the profane. Country drew on a Methodist pentecostal musical tradition that emphasized the spiritual dimensions of everyday life in standards like "This World Is Not My Home" and "Farther Along," songs performed by whites and blacks alike. Yet country was also "the devil's music," a vehicle for hell-raising and the rejection of authority in a very conservative society. Along similar lines, country could express a profound appreciation for the joys of home or the same restless spirit that moved black country bluesmen. Of course, such strains were not mutually exclusive: a number of great country artists (e.g., Hank Williams) were able to fuse such contradictions into a single compelling musical vision.

Perhaps the first great purveyors of country's domestic tradition was the Carter Family. The group was founded by Alvin Pleasant (A.P.) Carter, who was born into a deeply religious western Virginia family, and his wife Sara, an accomplished singer and instrumentalist. They married in 1915, and the couple's singing and playing became a neighborhood attraction. When Sara's sister Maybelle married A.P.'s brother Ezra in 1926, she began contributing by playing autoharp, banjo, and guitar. Discovered by legendary talent scout Ralph Peer, the Carter Family made over three hundred records in the 1920s, 1930s, and 1940s. Though they never toured outside the schoolhouses, churches, and movie houses of the upper South, their music was broadcast all over the country, especially on the Mexican border stations.

The Carters performed their own material as well as traditional tunes (some of which, like "Will the Circle Be Unbroken?" and "The Wabash Cannonball," were copyrighted by A.P. Carter at the insistence of Peer). Both eulogized a vanishing culture that the Carters themselves symbolized to millions of Americans. There is some irony in this, since A.P. and Sara divorced in 1933, though they continued to perform together for another decade. Like the seemingly intimate "barn dance" radio shows that relied on sophisticated technology for their transmission, country looked backward even as it was propelled forward—a tendency that was not, of course, limited to country music specifically or popular culture generally.[52]

Country's first major star was Jimmie Rodgers, a prime exemplar of the itinerant strain. He was born in Mississippi in 1897, the son of a gang foreman on the Mobile and Ohio Railroad. Rodgers himself worked the roads intermittently in his youth—hence his later nickname of the "singing brakeman"—but tried to develop a musical career. In 1925 he was able to give up railroading altogether when he became a minstrel in a medicine show in the upper South and Midwest, and later turned to making records. Drawing on black musical traditions as well as his distinctive yodeling, Rodgers rose to fame in much of the country with hits like "Waiting for a Train," "High Powered Mama," and "Blue Yodel No. 1." Collaborating with his sister-in-law in writing and arranging much of his varied repertoire, Rodgers became a household name in the South in the late 1920s and early 1930s, touring widely with vaudeville shows, though never north of Washington. A bona fide product of the working class, he was probably the most beloved entertainer of his generation in the white South, famed for his generosity, his freewheeling lifestyle, and his humor, which he maintained even after being diagnosed with tuberculosis (as his songs "TB Blues" and "Whipping that Old TB" suggest). He retained his artistic determination: though gravely ill, he traveled to New York to make his last records in 1933, using a special cot provided by the record company to rest between takes. He died two days later.

Rodgers's legacy is vast. His fusion of blues and yodeling, though only a component of his performing style, decisively shaped the future of country music, and his songs were later recorded by performers ranging from Crystal Gayle ("Miss the Mississippi in You") to the Southern rock band Lynyrd Skynyrd ("T for Texas"). His use of instruments like the steel guitar paved the way for their incorporation into the musical grammar of country. And his persona—a rakish-yet-sentimental man in cowboy garb performing alone with a guitar—has become a virtual archetype. Many of the subsequent giants of country music—Gene Autry, Roy Acuff, Ernest Tubb, and others— began their careers in conscious emulation of Rodgers.[53]

Like all cultural genres, country music did not operate within strict definitions, and a number of important artists departed from its sensibility even as they owed a great deal to it. One such figure was Woody Guthrie, who today is primarily known as a folk singer—a term that, ironically, usually connotes the urban balladeers who first came to prominence in the 1950s and 1960s. Born in the flatlands of Oklahoma in 1912, Guthrie absorbed a good deal of hillbilly music in his youth, including that of Rodgers, the Carter Family, and others. In the late 1930s, he became part of the Okie migration to California made famous by John Steinbeck's 1939 novel *The Grapes of Wrath* and began performing on a Los Angeles radio station. In 1940, he came to New York, where he befriended Huddie Ledbetter, or "Leadbelly," a country bluesman discovered by ethnomusicologist Alan Lomax in the 1930s. Leadbelly, best known for "Goodnight Irene," his haunting tale of an abandoned lover on the cusp of suicide, had a large following in New York intellectual circles and the two often performed together. Over the course of the next three decades, Guthrie gradually grew in fame until his tragic death from Huntington's chorea, a progressive neurological disease, in 1967.[54]

Guthrie's greatness as a songwriter lay in his ability to infuse his music with a deeply felt radical edge rooted in personal experience. His most famous songs, like "Oklahoma Hills" and "Philadelphia Lawyer," are based on traditional melodies, but feature distinctive lyrics with a sharp, class-conscious edge. His most famous composition, "This Land Is Your Land," was written as an angry response to Irving Berlin's "God Blessed America."[55] In his flat claim that "this land was made for you and me," Guthrie was pointedly commenting that it did *not* belong to the faceless corporate and bureaucratic interests that were impoverishing the spirit of Okies and other poor people. A Communist sympathizer at a time when such sentiments were widely held to be anti-American, Guthrie almost singlehandedly cleared a space for the patriotic radical.

As noted earlier, the primary roots of country music were in the South, especially Appalachia. By the late 1930s, however, themes and styles deriving from Louisiana, Texas, Oklahoma, and California became more prominent—thus the "western" in "country & western." These western elements were the result of the more varied racial and ethnic accents present in the music produced in this region, from cajun-styled accordions to waltz tempos. But the most distinctive aspect of Western music was the cowboy mentality that pervaded it, from the themes of the songs to the garb of the performers. Ernest Tubb, Bob Wills and the Texas Playboys, and Gene Autry (later a movie star) were among the major figures in Western music.

The focal point of the production—and mythology—of Western music was the honky-tonk, or bar, where such songs were played. Stimulated by the oil boom of the 1930s, honky-tonks sprang up to serve illegal liquor on the edge of towns, where tax rates were lower, police supervision was lax, and access was greatest for both rural and city dwellers. In these liminal spaces, which usually had an air of danger as well as pleasure about them, Western music was particularly effective; its insistent beat (for dancing), fuller instrumentation (including pianos, drums, and even electric guitar) and melodramatic themes ("Born to Lose," "Driving Nails in My Coffin") went over well.

Because not all honky-tonks could afford live musicians, they turned to the jukebox, a machine for playing records that entered the market in the 1920s. The repeal of Prohibition in 1933 allowed for a greater proliferation of honky-tonks and other music-playing venues, stimulating a demand for jukeboxes and thus for records. By 1939, some 225,000 jukeboxes were using 13 million records, giving that flagging industry a boost.[56]

It needed one. The outbreak of World War II led to a government ban on non-military uses for shellac, then a necessary material for the manufacture of records. And a dispute between the music publishing and broadcasting industries further paralyzed the industry. At the end of 1940, a five-year contract between ASCAP and the National Association of Broadcasters expired. Expecting demands for higher licensing fees, the Broadcasters created a new company, Broadcast Music Inc. (BMI), which it hoped would compete with ASCAP for the loyalty of songwriters and publishers. When

ASCAP and the NAB failed to reach an agreement, the broadcasters slapped a ban on all ASCAP music. The ban was fortuitous for country musicians, however, since they had been generally looked down upon by ASCAP and eagerly joined BMI. By the time ASCAP and the NAB resolved their dispute at the end of 1941, ASCAP's dominance—and its Tin Pan Alley orientation—had been broken. The following year, country songwriter Roy Acuff took his Nashville publishing company, Acuff-Rose, from ASCAP to BMI, and then merged it with another important company, Hill and Range. This move effectively made Nashville the center of country music and broke New York's lock on the music publishing industry.

Then, in 1942, a strike erupted between the record companies and the American Federation of Musicians. The industry increased production so that it could hold out against the musicians, but by 1943 its reserves were getting thin. Eventually the companies gave in, but not before the relatively marginalized hillbilly and race records had gained access to the record and radio industries. In the 1950s, the growing presence and vitality of this music sparked rock & roll.

Although World War II, the ASCAP/NAB dispute, and the musicians' strike all disrupted popular music, their long-run impact was salutary, decentralizing the industry and bringing new performers to the fore. In a sense, however, these developments were only a prelude to a much more fundamental reorganization of popular culture as a whole. By the beginning of the second half of the twentieth century, television had completely restructured the relationship between radio and records, reoriented the film industry, revolutionized journalism, and effected a series of other changes. A new era—one that is perhaps still underway—was unfolding.

5

Channeled Energy:
Popular Culture in the
Age of Television,
1945-1990

FROM OUR VANTAGE POINT at the end of the twentieth century, with the United States' dominance of the world on the wane and the costs of its inability to achieve lasting social justice increasingly evident, the period immediately following World War II may appear as a charmed moment in U.S. history. Compared to its European and Asian allies and enemies, the United States risked the least and gained the most from the war, emerging as the preeminent power, with seemingly inexhaustible economic, political, and military resources. Rarely, if ever, has any nation wielded such clout or offered more promise. Today's college student may well imagine that those were simpler times, when the enemies (Hitler, then Stalin) were obvious and the problems (such as racial discrimination) lent themselves to straightforward solutions.

Yet for many Americans in the early postwar era, life was anything but charmed or simple. A suggestion of the national mood can be glimpsed from the Oscar-sweeping film *The Best Years of Our Lives* (1946), which depicted weary and cynical war veterans facing an uncertain future.[1] Millions of lives were shattered by war casualties, and the Great Depression was no distant memory—indeed, many feared that it would return with military demobilization. Moreover, while victory over the Axis powers had supposedly made the world "safe for democracy" (something World War I was supposed to do), the treatment of some groups within U.S. society, notably African and Japanese Americans, raised troubling questions about the degree of difference between the victors and the vanquished. Such questions were again raised during the anti-Communist hysteria of the late 1940s and early 1950s, when dissent was crushed in the name of freedom.

Besides reflecting the tensions of the times, films like *The Best Years of Our Lives* symbolized the intensely contradictory character of the film industry during the immediate postwar years. In some important ways, it was indeed the best of times: in the fifty years since the advent of the motion picture, film had become the premiere form of popular culture in America. In 1946, its popularity stood at an all-time high: nearly 75 percent of the potential audience (in other words, excluding young children, the elderly, and the infirm) went to the movies at least once a week.[2] And with Europe once again shattered by war, the United States could further tighten its grip

---

Reverse page: Lucille Ball and Desi Arnaz around the time of the debut of I Love Lucy *(1951). The show raised the hackles of programmers, who feared that an interracial couple would not be accepted by the American public. It is now remembered as one of the most beloved situation comedies in television history.*

over the world market. For the rest of the century, films have remained among the most reliable of U.S. exports, with the country's large domestic market, extensive distribution infrastructure, and strong-arm tactics effectively blocking serious international competition, as will be discussed later.

The industry was also being subjected to pressures that would ultimately challenge its legitimacy and displace its centrality. The first of these was the "Red Scare." By the late 1940s, anti-Communism had become a powerful force in U.S. life; the end of World War I had been followed by a virulent crackdown on left-wing activity, and hostility continued even during the most hopeful days of the Popular Front of the 1930s. In 1940, Texas Congressman Martin Dies, chairman of the recently formed House Committee on Un-American Activities (HUAC), launched an investigation of Communist activities in Hollywood. Dies's probe did not amount to much, but when a labor dispute broke out five years later over whether set decorators would be represented by a company union or a craft guild, disgruntled company union sympathizers claimed that members of the guild were Communist subversives. This charge, which was made in a general climate of paranoia—a 1945 Chamber of Commerce Report had claimed that Communists were trying to take over the media and the film industry in Hollywood had organized the Motion Picture Alliance for the Preservation of American Values (MPA) in 1944—led to a 1947 HUAC investigation. In those hearings, ten witnesses refused to say whether they had been members of the Communist Party (saying no would have been a lie; saying yes would have created even more pressure to name others). All of the "Hollywood Ten" went to jail for contempt of Congress.

Film historian Robert Sklar has eloquently described the impact of the Red Scare on Hollywood:

> For the first half-century of American movies, the industry had had a fascinating and curious relationship with the American public. It had always stood slightly aslant the mainstream of American cultural values and expressions, seeking to hold its working-class audience while making movies attractive to middle-class tastes, and therefore never quite in step with other forms of cultural communication. Movies were always less courageous than some organs of information and entertainment, but they were more iconoclastic than most, offering a version of American behavior and values more risqué, violent, comic, and fantastic than the standard interpretation of traditional cultural elites.

It was this trait that gave the movies their popularity and their mythmaking power.

And it was this trait that the anti-Communist crusade destroyed.[3]

One of the great ironies of the anti-Communist hysteria was that Hollywood was a highly patriotic institution, churning out war movies during both world wars and making stars out of people like Ronald Reagan, who epitomized what were widely held to be old-fashioned American values. Even more ironic was the intensely capitalistic tenor of the industry. By the 1940s, the immigrant ethnics of the turn of the century—Warner, Zukor, Cohn, and others—had become corporate autocrats, dependent on Wall Street for capital but running their empires like late-nineteenth-century robber barons. Once independent mavericks who had to overcome Edison's powerful Trust, they now controlled a monopoly through the instrument of block booking (see Chapter 4).

Indeed, the major studios' control over the industry had become so extensive by the late 1930s that the federal government initiated an antitrust suit against them. Because of the lengthy legal process and the war, it was not until 1949 that the Supreme Court ruled (in *United States* v. *Paramount Pictures, Inc., et al.*) that block booking was illegal. No longer allowed the vertical structure of production, distribution, and exhibition that had ensured its profits, the industry had to change its ways.

Meanwhile, movie attendance began to decline. After peaking in 1946, both attendance and box-office receipts fell for the next seven years; by 1953 they had gone down 50 percent.[4] Many factors were involved, but the most obvious was the new cultural medium that was rapidly emerging in these years: television.

Of all the forms of popular culture discussed in this book, television is indisputably the most pervasive. Newspapers had an unprecedented reach in the Jacksonian era, trips to the movies became weekly facts of life for the majority of Americans in the early twentieth century, and radio had attained a unique access to private lives by the 1930s. But none of these had the breadth of television, which reached 85 percent of U.S. homes by 1957 (by the early 1980s, 98 percent had television sets, which were in use for 6.5 hours a day).[5] For better and worse, the second half of the twentieth century has been the Age of Television, affecting even those who professed to be hostile or indifferent to popular culture.

That hostility and indifference continued to be common, particularly on the part of those schooled in Modernist aesthetics (see Chapter 4). But by the end of the century resistance to popular culture has become less focused than it was at the start. For sure, there have continued to be plenty of complaints—FCC Chairman Newton Minow's 1961 description of television as a "vast wasteland"[6] is still widely accepted over three decades later—and new cultural forms like rap have been subject to familiar criticisms about tastelessness and degeneracy. At the same time, other forms (like movies, to be discussed shortly) have moved up the cultural ladder. But more importantly, so have people. While there has continued to be a powerful class hierarchy in the United States, a combination of New Deal reforms, economic prosperity, and the ubiquity of television partially blurred class lines, at least until the Reagan administration in the 1980s. By that time, however, many forms of popular culture had attained enough legitimacy to have become the subject of scholarly study; indeed, this book is a product of that process. Nonetheless, popular culture has never completely lost touch with its class or racial origins, as the history of rock & roll that follows should make clear. It remains, and probably always will remain, contested—or, more accurately, contesting—terrain.

Moreover, for all their novelty, television and the other forms of culture discussed in this chapter are also a distillation of their antecedents. They assumed the shape they did because decisions made long before they were conceived channeled them in particular directions. Those decisions were made on minstrel stages, in private laboratories, and in corporate boardrooms. Television may have made history, but history also made television.

Shows of Force:
The Birth of Television

Television's immediate roots lie in radio. Unlike with radio, however, there was relatively little confusion about how TV would be used, and the victory of commercial interests in radio broadcasting gave those interests an almost insuperable advantage in shaping this newer form of broadcasting. Television's course was not inevitable, however; indeed, its development took longer and was marked by more detours than even the most far-sighted observers could have foreseen.

One of the most far-sighted—and ruthless—of those observers was David Sarnoff. A Russian immigrant who began his career with the American Marconi company (he earned early fame as the telegraph operator who picked up the signal from the sinking *Titanic* in 1912), Sarnoff rose rapidly through the ranks of RCA after World War I, becoming president of the company in 1930. Throughout the 1920s, Sarnoff had been deeply interested in experimental attempts to transmit visual images, an effort underwritten by RCA and its allies (AT&T, Westinghouse, General Electric, and the United Fruit Company, which got involved in radio as a means of coordinating its shipping empire). Radio profits from the companies' network, NBC, were poured into television research, a demonstration of the extent to which technological innovation was increasingly under corporate control. In 1928, an ebullient Sarnoff predicted that television would overtake radio within five years.

He was off by about twenty. One reason for the delay was the persistence of the pesky little independent inventor. Some, like Charles Francis Jenkins and John L. Baird in England, and the entrepreneurial Allen B. Dumont, who founded his own network, were competitors for a while. Philo T. Farnsworth, an inventive young Mormon, was more of a problem, because in 1930 he acquired a key patent that RCA needed. The company contested the patent in court, and when that failed, tried to intimidate Farnsworth into selling his rights. He stood his ground and the corporate colossus reluctantly agreed to pay royalties for the right to draw on his work.[7]

A bigger challenge to Sarnoff's plan for RCA's ascendancy came from Edwin H. Armstrong, a personal friend of Sarnoff's since college who became a millionaire when he sold RCA a patent in 1922. At Sarnoff's suggestion, Armstrong then plunged into the research that laid the groundwork for higher quality transmission by means of frequency modulation— i.e., FM radio. But by the time Armstrong presented his work in the early 1930s, Sarnoff had moved on to television, and brushed him off. Armstrong's bitter enmity with Sarnoff continued into the 1950s, because, unlike other manufacturers, RCA never paid Armstrong royalties for building an FM capability into its radios and televisions. A bitter legal struggle drove Armstrong to suicide, but his estate won every suit after his death.[8]

The government made only fitful efforts to slow private control of the media. In 1930, the Justice Department sued RCA, GE, Westinghouse, and AT&T over their interlocking patents and ownership. AT&T, which had already separated itself somewhat as a result of the Radio Act of 1927, withdrew from its licensing agreements (the patents were expiring anyway). Sarnoff, meanwhile, engineered a scheme whereby RCA would buy out GE and Westinghouse, leaving him in sole control of their formerly shared network, NBC. By 1933, this deal was complete. After industry pressure helped defeat a move to limit advertising (part of the Communications Act of 1934, which also created the Federal Communications Commission, or FCC, to replace the FRC), the road appeared clear for RCA/NBC to leap into television, with CBS moving quickly to catch up.[9]

Once again, however, events conspired to slow things down. An RCA demonstration of television at the 1939 World's Fair in New York generated excitement, but the outbreak of the war put the new medium on hold, as manufacturing capacity was directed toward war needs and technology was directed toward military uses (television research was used in radar communications). In 1945, however, the FCC began to make a series of crucial decisions, ultimately giving RCA the best wave lengths (over Armstrong's objections) and rejecting a CBS attempt to persuade the commission to adopt its as-yet-unperfected color television technology as the industry standard. Then the gathering momentum of set manufacturing, station licensing, and program development was slowed again when the FCC froze further licensing first because of interference problems and then because of the outbreak of the Korean War. It was not until the mid-1950s that the floodgates finally opened.[10]

By this point, television was overwhelmingly in the hands of big business. Although some channels were allocated for the use of public television stations, these were usually on poor-quality ultra-high-frequency (UHF) channels rather than the very-high-frequency (VHF) wavelengths given to the major private networks. Public stations were chronically starved for funds and under constant pressure from private interests. Not until the late 1960s, with the help of foundation grants, the establishment of the Public Broadcasting System, and the success of television shows like *Sesame Street* did a few public stations begin to flourish.

Coming on the heels of radio, and controlled by many of the same people, television soon developed a system of stations affiliated with major networks; local and national programming were both paid for by advertising. This strategy, while it had the advantage of offering programs at no cost, exacted a more subtle but no less real price. Strictly speaking, TV shows were (and are) not produced for the pleasure of the viewing audience. Rather, they are produced in order to create an audience that can be sold to an advertiser. The *audience,* not the show, is the real product being sold by a station or network. Obviously, broadcasters tried to put on shows that they believed people would like. But in the event of a conflict of interest, they were beholden to the advertiser. So, for example, Camel Cigarettes, which sponsored the 1950s show *Man Against Crime,* distributed the following instructions to its writers: "Do not have the heavy or any disreputable person smoking a cigarette. Do not associate the smoking of cigarettes with undesirable scenes or situations plot-wise."[11] (In 1970, with the health dangers of smoking apparent, Congress banned all cigarette advertising from television.) The networks later acquired some autonomy by moving from the radio-era strategy of having one advertiser pay for an entire program (e.g., *The Eveready Hour*) toward a "magazine" format, selling particular slots on a particular episode of a show, the method that obtains today. Yet this has only marginally enhanced the power of viewers.

Coming of age at the height of the Cold War, television was also tainted by anti-Communist hysteria, with results comparable to those of the film industry. In 1950, *Counterattack: The Newsletter of Facts on Communism* published *Red Channels*, a 215-page report that cited 151 people in the entertainment industry for their possible Communist sympathies. Ed Sullivan, host of a popular variety show, used *Counterattack* as a guide for which guests were appropriate for his program. In the wake of *Red Channels,* a television series based on the radio series *The Aldrich Family* (1949-53) was cancelled because its star, Jean Muir, was cited in the report. (Muir frankly admitted, for example, to signing a cable of congratulations to the Moscow Art Theater on its fiftieth anniversary.) Many writers could not find jobs for years, or, like their cinematic counterparts, were forced to write screenplays under assumed names. To avoid being charged with harboring subversives, CBS used "blacklisting" as a standard administrative practice.[12]

For such reasons, television might well be considered the least democratic of the popular arts. Of course, newspapers had been financed through paid advertising for centuries (although those that relied on subscription revenue were at least partially sensitive to the popular will), while radio was just as dependent on sponsors as television. Moreover, while movies were self-contained works sold directly to the public, the highly technical, bureaucratic, and expensive nature of the industry made it less than the populist arena its boosters claimed it was. And all three media have been mouthpieces for intolerance and bigotry. But television has magnified these faults, in part because of its enormous reach. Critics on the left and right feared that it would debase cultural discourse and have narcotic tendencies; the doctor who predicted children would develop stunted feet from watching too much

TV is only an exaggerated example of concerns that have persisted to this day.[13]

Nevertheless, television has repeatedly, if fitfully, demonstrated its demo-cratic power. The most celebrated example is its role in bringing an end to the "Red Scare" that dogged it so persistently. In the early 1950s, *See It Now,* a news program written, produced, and hosted by Edward R. Murrow, examined the evidence of Communist subversion being presented by Wisconsin Senator Joseph McCarthy. This show raised doubts about McCarthy's honesty and character, but they were nothing compared to the effects of the televised hearings he conducted in 1954. McCarthy's blustery, arrogant appearance, during which he claimed that the U.S. army (of all institutions!) was riddled with Communists, made for riveting television, an opportunity exploited most fully by ABC, which lacked the fully sponsored daytime schedule of CBS and NBC. Shortly afterward, McCarthy was censured by the Senate and ceased to be a major political figure. Though rabid anti-Communism was not dead, it was no longer so influential. McCarthy's downfall was only the first of a number of cases of political malfeasance that would be vividly revealed on television, including Water-gate, Vietnam, and the Iran-Contra scandal.

Indeed, however real the concerns over television's hypnotic effects and its encouragement of violence, it can also show a number of activities—po-litical decisions, military operations, exercises of privilege, or simply author-ity figures in casual settings—previously unseen and having something of a mystique. One communications scholar has argued that a merging of male and female behavior (even feminism itself), a blurring of childhood and adulthood, and a new skepticism about politics have all been engendered by the simultaneous intimacy and scope of television, which has removed spatial barriers that previously shaped and segmented human behavior.[14]

Finally, while it is clear that ruling elites have the greatest power to shape television's content, this control has never been monolithic. Despite re-peated attempts to gauge audience response, viewer taste has always been unpredictable. Networks receive regular statistics on the number of people who have watched a given program, but even if these numbers are considered accurate (a dubious proposition, given the varied attention spans and record keeping of the viewers who are solicited to record their choices), no one knows for sure why certain shows succeed while others fail, and why those that do succeed last for widely different lengths of time. Nor, of course, is it clear *how* shows are being watched. Networks and advertisers cannot tell if viewers are "surfing" the channels, "zapping" commercials, ignoring everything they see because they are talking, or have even left the room. The power not to watch is limited, but it is a real power nonetheless. Indeed, it is precisely this power that motivates programmers to produce shows that people—or particular groups of people, like those with large disposable incomes—will seek out, within the limits restraining them.

However positive or negative its effects, virtually all observers have agreed on television's dramatic penetration into everyday life by the early 1950s. During the years of the FCC's licensing freeze (1948-1952), access was confined to a series of what media people called "television cities." These areas (e.g., metropolitan Boston, Chicago, New York) signalled the changes to come. In 1951, for example, most television cities reported a 20 to 40 percent drop in attendance at movie theaters, while those without television reported steady or even growing attendance. In television cities, radio listening dropped, restaurant receipts fell, library circulation declined, and jukebox earnings went down. Lipstick manufacturer Hazel Bishop had a $50,000 business in 1950. In 1952, after the company began advertising on television, sales were $4.5 million and rising.[15]

When licensing resumed, the rest of the country experienced similar effects. In 1950, there were 3 million television sets in use in the United States. Three years later, there were 21 million, a 700 percent increase.[16] Of course, most of these sets were watched by more than one person, so the actual number of viewers could be at least two or three times that figure. At the same time, however, this unprecedented growth in audience was accompanied by a growing sense of privatization: television arrived at the very moment of the mass exodus to the new suburbs, with its attendant loss of shared community spaces. In this regard, the rise of television echoed the middle- and elite-class exodus from Jacksonian theaters a century earlier. Although television viewership crossed race, class, and gender lines, it had the odd effect of fostering isolation, not only between groups of people but even within families, because individuals had different programming inter-ests—or would rather watch television than interact with each other. Again, such tendencies were already evident in movie watching (which was, however, both an intensely private *and* a public experience), as well as in the growth of radio in the 1930s and 1940s. But the intensity was far greater with television, and it generated some anxiety. Marketers, programmers, and consumers all sought to allay this, either by invoking the new mantra of "family entertainment" or by packaging television sets as pieces of furniture (with traditional names like "Pioneer") that would fit right into a middle-class home.[17]

But what kinds of programming did viewers actually watch? This was perhaps the most crucial aspect of the rise of the television. Obviously, programming varied greatly; nonetheless, there were clearly some major types of shows, and what is especially striking is the degree to which they derived from earlier forms of popular culture even as they were remade into something new. What follows are a few examples of this dynamic at work.

We might suppose that the primary influence on early television was film, because these two media had so much in common. But for a variety of reasons this was not the case. One reason was the film industry's initial hostility to television, a hostility that was the result of the mortal threat TV seemed to pose to the movies. Another reason was that the television industry was based in New York, not Los Angeles. Not until Hollywood began to realize the potential in cooperating with television by producing and selling shows to the networks—a process that only began in the mid-1950s—did the axis of the newer industry tip to the West.

The primary influence on early television was stage drama. One explanation was that New York was the capital of the theater industry. Early television was broadcast live rather than filmed (or later videotaped), and technical and financial limits favored the small, interior settings common to the stage over the panoramic vistas common to cinema. One of the fixtures of TV in the 1950s was the "anthology"—a different one-hour play each week sponsored by a single advertiser. These were among the most intelligent shows ever produced, and one reason why the mid-1950s was widely considered the "golden age" of television. Rod Serling (creator of the famed TV show *The Twilight Zone)*, Arthur Penn (director of the classic 1967 film *Bonnie and Clyde),* and Paul Newman (the distinguished film actor) were among the talents who made their mark in these years. Screenwriter Paddy Cheyefsky's *Marty* (1953), a low-key story of a homely working-class butcher's search for romance, exploited TV's intimacy by eschewing the glitzy production values of Hollywood and the ultra-commercial instincts common to broadcasting. Eventually, however, network and sponsor strictures on content led many of these people to leave TV for the relative freedom of film.

Other theatrical forms—minstrel shows, burlesque, vaudeville, and revues—were instrumental in the creation of another important television genre, the variety show. Television variety shows were modified versions of performances not unlike those of the nineteenth century—a combination of comedy skits, novelty acts, stand-up routines, and music. Milton Berle's *Texaco Star Theater* (1948-1956) and Sid Caesar and Imogene Coca's *Your Show of Shows* (1950-1961) were two of the most popular of this period. Broadcast live and including new material each week, variety shows exuded a sense of vitality that made them another reason people called this TV's golden age.

Another program type, with roots in fiction, film, and radio, was the Western. Cinematically speaking, the genre had been largely eclipsed in the 1930s by gangster movies, to which Westerns are thematically related, but they made a comeback in the late 1940s and into the 1950s. Westerns first appeared on the small screen in 1954, when Warner Brothers agreed to produce a weekly series for ABC. Though TV Westerns could not match movies in their visual scope, they nevertheless became a mainstay of the medium. In 1956, four new Westerns entered the network schedule; by 1957 there were nine more. By 1958 there were at least twenty-five prime-time Westerns, and they accounted for seven of the top ten shows. Two of the most popular were *Bonanza* (1959-1973) and *Gunsmoke* (1955-1975).[18]

Yet for all their appeal, anthologies, variety shows, and Westerns had ceased to dominate television by the 1960s. The reasons are unclear. The sponsors' desire for more predictable programming was a factor in the demise of anthologies, and the relative weakness of film Westerns during the 1930s and of TV Westerns in the 1960s suggests that political upheaval and reform (the New Deal, the Civil Rights and antiwar movements) were factors. But a number of other programming formats, also derived from older cultural forms, had considerably greater staying power, despite changes in the political or commercial climate.

The most durable of these was the daytime soap opera, whose thematic origins can be traced to early women's fiction, although the immediate source for TV soaps was radio. *The Guiding Light,* a soap developed by Ohio schoolteacher Irma Phillips, first appeared on radio in 1937 and made the transition to television in 1952, where it has remained ever since.[19] Soaps that reflected the interests of their (mostly female) audiences, like *Search for Tomorrow* and *As the World Turns,* had long lifespans. Over the course of the last fifty years, soaps have developed a visual grammar and dramatic style (the use of music to underline a character's emotions, for example) that gives them a sense of intimacy and also allows intermittent viewers to pick up the narrative threads.[20] In the 1980s, programmers introduced nighttime soaps like *Dallas* (1978-1991) and *Dynasty* (1981-1989), which were also very popular. But in the 1990s, competition from talk shows, which are far cheaper to produce and at least as profitable, cut into soap programming, although 40 percent of U.S. women still watch at least one soap a week.[21]

Another lasting type of television program is the dramatic series, a variation on the radio serial. These shows, which have ranged from *Lassie* (1954-1974) to *Star Trek* (1966-1969), are too varied for useful generalizations to be possible, except to say that they feature recurring characters and situations that are resolved within the course of an hour that is marked by periodic commercials. Even this rule has many exceptions, however, including *Hill Street Blues* (1982-1988) and its heirs, *L.A. Law* (1986-1994) and *NYPD Blue* (1993-).

Somewhat more uniform was a genre that has come to be considered television's unique province: the situation comedy, or "sitcom." This too derived from radio serials, the best-known of which, *Amos 'n' Andy,* became a television show between 1951 and 1953 and lasted in syndication (reruns shown on individual stations) until 1966, when protests over its racist humor finally forced it off the air. Like dramas, sitcoms feature recurring characters, usually based in a particular setting. The bonds between the characters are often familial metaphorically, if not in actual fact: in *The Mary Tyler Moore Show* (1970-1977), the "family" was made up of colleagues at the workplace, while in *Cheers* (1981-1993) it was the patrons of a Boston bar. In many cases, sitcoms feature unlikely pairings, as in *The Odd Couple* (1968-1975), and most rely on stock characters who often, over the life of the show, become caricatures of themselves. Yet despite their tightly circumscribed format and dramatic limitations, the best sitcoms have exploited TV's opportunity to develop characters, as well as its own past. Perhaps the most striking example of this was the final episode of *Newhart* (1982-1990) in which Bob Newhart's character, an innkeeper, awakes to find that the previous few seasons were a dream and that his "reality" was his life as a psychiatrist on *The Bob Newhart Show* (1972-1978). The joke alluded not only to Newhart's previous television career, but to a similar plot device used by the prime-time soap *Dallas* in 1981.

Situation comedies have also been television's most accessible arena for exploring issues of class, gender, ethnicity, and (later) race. Perhaps the most striking early example is *I Love Lucy* (1951-1961). In the early 1950s,

Lucille Ball was a successful radio comedienne, starring in a radio serial called *My Favorite Husband*. When CBS asked her to join a number of other successful CBS radio actors (George Burns, Jack Benny, et al.) and switch to television, Ball refused unless she could co-star with her husband, the Cuban-born bandleader Desi Arnaz. The network said no, arguing that the public would not accept an Anglo woman married to a Latino man. But after the couple took a successful stage show on tour, CBS agreed to give them a chance. Bucking established conventions, Ball and Arnaz declined to do the show live in New York and borrowed money to create Desilu, a production company based in Hollywood. This meant that they retained the rights for the shows, including later syndication rights. *I Love Lucy* was thus notable not only because it was one of the most successful television shows of all time, but because it established new methods and strategies for television production.

On the other hand, *I Love Lucy* was typical in its upholding of suburban norms—indeed, Ball and Arnaz moved to Connecticut during the show's run. Arnaz's Ricky Ricardo was a patriarchal husband (and later father) who expected his wife to be submissive and feminine. Yet as television historian David Marc argues, something always seemed to get in the way of Lucy's behaving as she was supposed to:

> Lucy is in no way the imperturbable wife and mother embodied in her contemporary, Margaret Anderson [of *Father Knows Best*]. She overspends her budget, acts on impulse, and does not hesitate to drop Little Ricky with [neighbor] Mrs. Trumble at the slightest hint that her dream of something more than a hausfrau existence might be satisfied by an audition for a show at the Tropicana. Lucy refuses to allow bourgeois role destiny to stifle her organic desires, no matter how often she is repressed. Her attempts to escape from what Ricky and society define as "her place in the home" turn her into a buffoon, and this is the center of the show. By the end of each episode she has been whipped back into middle-class-housewife shape. Her weekly lapse into "childish" behavior, however, makes her into a freak whose comic talents are far more compelling than the authoritarian morality that surrounds her.[22]

It would be foolish to argue that *I Love Lucy* was a feminist show, but it would be equally foolish to argue that it lacked implicit, if not incipient, protests against a repressive social order. (Marc notes that the Saudi Arabian government refused to broadcast the show in 1961 because the censors felt

Lucy dominated Ricky.[23]) Watching *I Love Lucy* could be an experience not unlike reading *Charlotte Temple:* on the surface, the message is clear, but just underneath, conflict and contradiction lurk.

Similar dialectical currents could be discerned in other sitcoms from the 1950s. *The Goldbergs* (1949-1957) depicted urban Jewish working-class life at a time when anti-semitism was still a potent force; *Mama* (1949-1956) represented Norwegian-Americans. These shows portrayed family life with a rosy glow, but not without problems, such as difficulties acquiring status-conferring consumer goods. Conversely, *The Honeymooners* (1952-1957) presented working-class busdriver Ralph Kramden with comedy and sympathy, but his frequent outbursts toward his wife—"One of these days, Alice, pow! Right in the kisser!"—raised the troubling specter of gender conflict and even abuse.[24]

A closer look:
A BUNKER MENTALITY

Historically, the television situation comedy has offered viewers a world both familiar and unreal. The very premise of the genre rests on depicting details from everyday life that everyone can relate to. Doing so, however, has meant avoiding issues that segments of a national audience may find objectionable. For example, many 1950s sitcoms with working-class and/or ethnic characters and settings—

WITH SAMMY DAVIS, JR., IN "SAMMY'S VISIT," JUNE 1972

The Honeymooners, The Goldbergs, and *The Life of Riley*—muted aspects of their characters' cultural lives. Similarly, a character like Samantha Stevens (Elizabeth Montgomery) in *Bewitched* sought to eschew her magical powers in favor of becoming a middle-class housewife and mother. Of course, she found this difficult, and by the end of the 1960s, the very notion of remaining a stay-at-home middle-class housewife and mother was itself becoming exotic amid the tremendous social and political upheaval of the decade. It was these changes that opened up space for *All in the Family,* which for all its artifice was one of the most bracing, incisive, and humorous shows ever to appear on U.S. television.

All in the Family was developed by producers Norman Lear and Bud Yorkin, two television veterans who modeled the show on *Till Death Do Us Part,* a British sitcom about a reactionary Cockney and his tumultuous relationship with his son-in-law. Their version, as it evolved over the course of two pilots (trial shows) for ABC and subsequent rewrites, featured Carroll O'Connor as the bigoted dockworker Archie Bunker and Jean Stapleton as his dimwitted but saintly wife Edith. The couple's daughter, Gloria (Sally Struthers), was married to hippie Polish-American graduate student Mike Stivic (played by future film writer/director Rob Reiner, son of the TV and film writer/director Carl Reiner). Lacking a regular income, Mike and Gloria lived with the Bunkers, a situation that provided endless opportunities for verbal jousting and comic mishaps.

In the social context of television production in the late 1960s, a TV show that offered relatively frank talk about racism, sexism, homophobia, and other prejudices made a number of television executives nervous. Lear and Yorkin offered the show to ABC because it was the network in last place, which they figured would make its programmers more receptive. It was too skittish, however, and CBS, which was in first place but had an aging, downscale audience, decided to take the risk. As CBS founder William Paley said later, "We felt the time had come to catch up with some of the developments that had taken place in the United States." CBS nevertheless delayed inserting *All in the Family* into the network schedule until halfway through the 1970-1971 season.

When it finally aired, on January 12, 1971, the show became an instant hit; it was first in the ratings by the end of its first full season in 1972, and it remained there for the next five years. At its peak, one-fifth of all Americans, or 50 million people, watched each weekly episode. In 1978, Edith and Archie's familiar living room chairs were placed in the Smithsonian Institution "to be preserved as part of the cultural legacy of our country," in the words of Congressman John Brademas, who led the effort.

Why did *All in the Family* command such attention and affection? Part of the answer lies in the brilliant writing and acting that marked the show. But even more important, its language, subject matter, and humor shattered generations of radio and television taboos. Week after week, Archie railed against "your coloreds," "your gay homosexuals," and "your women of the female persuasion," only to find his opinions and actions lead him into sticky situations. Among the most hilarious were those where he exhibited his racial prejudices, as he did in his frequent encounters with his black neighbors, the Jeffersons. One classic episode starred Sammy Davis, Jr., who left his briefcase in Archie's taxicab and then had to go to Archie's house to reclaim it.

For some, Archie's behavior illustrated the stupidity of prejudice; for others, it ventilated opinions too crude for them to express themselves. Either way, the show created a space for public conversation that had been sorely lacking in situation comedy. When Lucille Ball's character in *I Love Lucy* gave birth to a son, the word "pregnancy" was deemed too shocking to transmit over the airwaves. But the middle-aged Edith Bunker experienced menopause, confronted a rapist, and (furtively) expressed her sexuality to her highly repressed husband. Instead of the often stifling image of the "happy family," *All in the Family* showed a household where husbands called wives "dingbats" and parents, in-laws, and children had vicious fights that those living outside of TV land could relate to.

There were, of course, strict limits to such transgressions. However serious the tensions, they were usually settled by the end of the twenty-two or so minutes of any given episode. Archie referred to African-Americans as "coloreds," not "niggers," and Jews as "Hebes," not "kikes." Such highly charged words would have been censored, even if the writers had wanted to use them. On the other hand, by remaining inside the most basic social conventions, the show was able to retain its large audience. Because popular culture by its very nature is the result of social and political compromise, it will almost always strike a middle-of-the-road path. At its best, however, it reveals, and promotes, the movement of the middle to a new location—which is what *All in the Family* did in the 1970s.

The series spawned a number of spinoffs. *Maude* (1972-1978) became a vehicle for exploring feminist issues. (In 1972, the lead character, played by Bea Arthur, decided to have an abortion. After thousands of protests, some stations refused to repeat this highly controversial two-part episode.) Meanwhile, *The Jeffersons* (1975-1986) explored class and racial tensions in an upwardly mobile African-American family. It became one of a number of Lear-Yorkin shows, including *Good Times* (1974-1979) and *Sanford and Son* (1972-1977—starring burlesque and vaudeville comedian Redd Foxx, whom Malcolm X called "the funniest man I ever met"), that marked the entry of a significant number of black characters into prime-time television.

By the late 1970s, *All in the Family* began losing momentum. When Mike and Gloria left for California in 1979, the show continued in modified form as *Archie Bunker's Place.* Jean Stapleton left the show in 1980—Edith died off-screen between seasons—and it finally went off the air in 1983.

Although the conservatism of the 1980s did not lend itself to the same type of pointed, socially conscious situation comedy, *All in the Family* had a lasting impact. More recent sitcoms about working-class life, notably *Roseanne,* are direct inheritors of the traditions it established. And the archetypal protagonist it depicted, a staunch Nixon supporter, remains—and helps to explain attitudes that are the bulwark of the modern Republican coalition. Like most other TV shows, *All in the Family* was an ephemeral product whose major purpose was to sell advertising. But it also attested to the reflections on life that can emerge despite such strictures.

The final major type of television show is the news program. In its accessibility to wide audiences and its general appeal, daily local and network broadcasts, documentary specials, and "magazine" shows like *60 Minutes* (1968-) and *20/20* (1978-) are the inheritors of the Jacksonian newspaper tradition. Television news also has roots in radio, not only in terms of personnel, like Edward R. Murrow, but also in its reportorial style (see the comparison of print and radio reporting in Chapter 3).

But the very first network broadcasts were modeled on the cinematic newsreel. Network news programs in the 1940s lasted fifteen minutes and included several film clips. By later technical and journalistic standards, these were crude affairs: anchormen read copy on those stories (the majority) that were not recorded on film. This situation changed rapidly, however, and by the late 1950s, NBC, CBS, and a trailing ABC were on their way to establishing sophisticated professional newsgathering teams.

Television news has always been a visual medium, deriving its power more from pictures than words—indeed, after subtracting commercials and station breaks, the script for the average NBC newscast fills less than two-thirds of the *New York Times'* front page.[25] Generally speaking, TV lacks the analytical power of the best newspaper reporting, although it offers a sense of immediacy other media cannot match. Ideologically speaking, this cuts two ways: analysis can break through appearances to reveal underlying dynamics, or it can become a means of obfuscation. Similarly, pictures can provide clarity or create misconceptions by stinting on context.

Despite its obvious radical potential, television has not been at the forefront in breaking stories about major political and social issues. It is striking that some of the most important events of the postwar era—the Civil Rights movement, government deception over Vietnam, Watergate, and the Iran-Contra scandal—were first reported in print. On the other hand, television's power to move the nation and shape social policy has occasionally reached awesome proportions. The intensity of grief over the assassination of President John F. Kennedy in 1963 was partially influenced by the sense of simultaneity experienced by the hundreds of millions who watched its aftermath (including the murder of alleged assassin Lee Harvey Oswald) live on television. The sight of racist whites jeering or attacking peaceful civil rights protesters in Southern cities played a major role in persuading President Lyndon B. Johnson to push for the Voting Rights Act of 1965. And the unending stream of images from Vietnam in the late 1960s helped turn national sentiment against that war.

In addition, television played a crucial role in the rising tide of skepticism about official authority of the 1960s. In fact, one of the first incidents to puncture public confidence in large institutions was the scandal surrounding a television show, *The $64,000 Question*. Game shows were another example of radio programs that made the successful transition to television, and *The $64,000 Question* was one of the most spectacular of those (although in its radio days, prizes of $64 were more common). In 1959, it was revealed the one of the show's most popular contestants, a young Columbia lecturer named Charles Van Doren, had been given the correct answers by the show's producers in order to manipulate the game's results. In the inquiry that followed, Congressional investigators learned that the sponsor, Revlon Cosmetics, had routinely told the show's personnel which contestants could stay in further rounds and which could go. The entire affair (fictionalized in the 1994 film *Quiz Show*) revealed the extent to which corporate interests were dictating programming content, as well as the moral laxity of government supervision over the airwaves.

That laxity came into even sharper focus in 1960, when an American U-2 spy plane was shot down over the Soviet Union. The Eisenhower administration denied that the plane had violated Soviet airspace, only to be severely embarrassed when the Soviets broadcast footage of the wreckage and a confession by the pilot, Francis Gary Powers. Whether or not Powers' confession was coerced, this degree of government deception was new to Americans. It was repeated the following year during President Kennedy's botched Bay of Pigs invasion of Cuba, and again when Lyndon Johnson used a trumped-up attack on a U.S. warship as a pretext for launching the Vietnam War in 1964.

Even powerful people cannot control the unintended consequences of intended acts, and for Johnson and his successor Richard Nixon, television played a large role in the price they paid for their deceptions. Johnson, whose wife owned an Austin television station, was keenly attuned to the power of the medium and cajoled, wheedled, and even bullied newsmen into seeing things from his point of view. But not even he could reverse the tide once television finally began to show the resistance his war was generating abroad and the dissent it was generating at home. Richard Nixon's case is even more ironic. In 1972, he vetoed a bill to provide $155 million for public broadcasting because he did not want public stations to compete with commercial ones. The ensuing austerity led many PBS stations to show the Watergate hearings the following summer as a low-cost alternative to producing new programs. The hearings quickly outdrew the networks' daytime shows, which they had not wanted to preempt for fear of losing advertising dollars. By July 1973, when White House counsel John Dean detailed the corruption at the Nixon White House, the Watergate hearings had become one of the most dramatic "shows" in the history of television.[26]

By the early 1970s, Civil Rights protests, the Vietnam war, and the Watergate hearings had punctured TV's shiny veneer. While television never attained the political edge that, for example, characterized popular music in this period, important changes of tone were nonetheless evident. These changes were most obvious in situation comedy, which experienced a quantum leap in sophistication. *All in the Family* turned the placid family archetype on its head and dealt with social issues like race and gender in ways they had never before been discussed on television. *M*A*S*H* (1972-1983) took an unlikely setting for a comedy—a hospital army unit during the Korean War—and turned it into an affecting and often incisive parable of Vietnam. Somewhat less daring but still important was *The Mary Tyler Moore Show,* which portrayed a single professional woman who did not need a man on whom to stake her identity.[27] Television comedy also broke new ground in other genres. *Saturday Night Live* (1975-) was a hip variation on the variety show that (initially, at least) was bracing in its razor-sharp irony, while *Mary Hartman, Mary Hartman* (1976-1978) and *Fernwood 2-Nite* (1977-1978) satirized soap operas and talk shows respectively.

The late 1960s and early 1970s were also a relative high point for African Americans, although as always, dramatic and comedic treatments of black life in white America generally left a good deal to be desired. Indeed, one reason we can see an improvement by the late 1960s is that television's early standards were pathetically low—witness *Amos 'n' Andy* and *Beulah* (1950), a shameless exploitation of the Aunt Jemima stereotype. Shows where blacks were *not* reduced to caricatures at first were met with indifference and even hostility. In 1952, vaudeville and radio star Eddie Cantor invited newcomer Sammy Davis, Jr., onto *The Colgate Comedy Hour.* At the end of Davis's performance, Cantor used his own handkerchief to wipe the black entertainer's brow, precipitating baskets of hate mail for both men. Nat King Cole, another urbane black popular singer, could not find a sponsor for his variety show in 1956 and was forced off the air after one season.[28]

Coverage of the Civil Rights movement by television news organizations pried open some space for black interests, characters, and programming. Perhaps the most striking example of a fresh perspective was the public television series *PBL,* whose first installment in 1967, "Day of Absence," depicted a southern town whose blacks had disappeared (the residents were unable to function). "Day of Absence" also reversed the conventions of the minstrel show by having its white characters portrayed by blacks in white-face.[29] More conventional was *Julia* (1968-1971), an NBC dramatic series about a black nurse (played by Diahann Carroll) whose beauty, professionalism, and peaceful coexistence with whites in an integrated neighborhood made it something of a white liberal fantasy about race.

Nevertheless, times had clearly changed from the days when Nat King Cole could not find a sponsor, and the clearest demonstration of this was *Roots,* the 1977 miniseries based on the slave family saga by Alex Haley. The eighth and final installment was one of the most widely watched shows of all time. The series started a genealogy craze around the country, and spawned a number of imitators, including *Holocaust* (one of the highest rated programs of 1978) and a number of *Roots* sequels.

In terms of regular programming, the most promising arena for a black television sensibility has been comedy. *The Flip Wilson Show* (1970-1974), a variety hour, was widely hailed as the first truly black-led program, although some critics considered it merely an updated minstrel show. A number of situation comedies, especially those produced by *All in the Family* creator Norman Lear, attained great popularity, among them *The Jeffersons* (1975-1986), a show about a petit-bourgeois owner of a laundromat and his wife, and *Sanford and Son* (1972-1977), starring longtime vaudeville and burlesque comedian Redd Foxx as the owner of a junk dealership in the black Los Angeles neighborhood of Watts. Then there is the case of Bill Cosby, who appeared on a variety of shows, the best known of which, *The Cosby Show* (1984-1992), was a squeaky clean view of black life on the order of *Julia.* A more earthy perspective did not become common until the late 1980s, when the maverick Fox network began programming a spate of shows with black characters and themes, most notably *In Living Color* (1990-1994), a variety show developed by comedian Keenan Ivory Wayans.

In fact, for all the signs of life in television in the 1970s, the overall tendency was far from progressive, and became less progressive as the decade wore on. The self-consciously liberal vision of producers like Norman Lear gave way to the more nostalgic approach of Garry Marshall in shows like *Happy Days* (1974-1984) and *Laverne and Shirley* (1976-1983), both set in a highly white-bread 1950s America, although the latter was more rooted in a working-class milieu. And the ethical, professional, and personal concerns facing Mary Richards on the *Mary Tyler Moore Show* were replaced by "tits-and-ass" sitcoms like *Three's Company* (1977-1984). In the age of Reagan, commercial broadcasting values became more crass then ever, and shows that needed time to develop an audience were rarely given a chance. As always, however, some notable shows broke through. Distinguished dramas like *Hill Street Blues,* for example, expanded the parameters of television drama. And *Roseanne* (1988-), an unusual sitcom in which unemployment, crushing debt, and physical abuse were facts of life, sug · gested the mounting injuries of class as the Reagan era drew to a close under the stewardship of George Bush.

By this point, however, the networks, which had dominated television at the start, were beginning to suffer mounting injuries. In the late 1970s and early 1980s, cable television, the videocassette recorder, new networks, public television, and such new forms of popular culture as videogames all posed a serious challenge to the networks' supremacy. These technologies and forms will be discussed in further detail in Chapter 6. But first, I will look at how other forms of popular culture were faring in the decades that followed World War II.

Smaller Roles:
Movies in the Age of TV

For all its considerable problems, the film industry was still a force to be reckoned with in the late 1940s, and one that did not respond passively to the challenge posed by television. As viewership declined, Hollywood responded in a number of ways, some more successful than others.

Hollywood had never shown much interest in broadcasting. The exception was Adolph Zukor of Paramount, who acquired 49 percent of CBS when the network was founded in 1927, perhaps as a hedge against Warner's production of sound movies that same year. But the Great Depression hit Paramount hard, harder than it hit CBS, and when the. studio went into bankruptcy, the network bought back the stock. Hollywood blocked contract players from appearing on radio until the late 1930s, when its publicity value became unmistakably apparent, but otherwise had little to do with it. As television developed, some studios bought stock in individual stations, but they never became involved in their operation—not least because the Justice Department would not look positively on their entering a new medium at the very moment it was pursuing an antitrust action against them.[30]

Television had the greatest impact on the B-movie segment of the film market. These were the assembly-line pictures that the studios produced in abundance in order to feed their small neighborhood theaters, which were now deserted as filmgoers found cheaper and more convenient entertainment at home (and which the government, in the aftermath of the *Para-*

mount case, no longer allowed the studios to own). In response, the industry began to focus on its A-line features, whose high production values and sense of spectacle television could not hope to match. This period marked the final flowering of the musical in films like *An American in Paris* (1951) and *Singin' in the Rain* (1952); legendary Westerns like *Red River* (1948) and *High Noon* (1951); and huge epics like *The Ten Commandments* (1956) and *Ben Hur* (1959).

In its quest to maintain visual supremacy, Hollywood also turned to gimmicks. The most notable was the introduction, in 1952, of three-dimensional (or 3-D) movies, which required viewers to wear cheap disposable glasses. The effect was especially dramatic in horror films, but the novelty wore off after a few months. A more lasting innovation was the wide-angle lens, which allowed for spectacular vistas in big-budget epics and emphasized the visual differences between movies and television.

These tactics had the desired effect, and in 1953 film attendance rose for the first time since 1946. But although rising ticket prices and a growing population kept the industry afloat, it was no longer the fixture of everyday life it had been in the first half of the century.[31]

In this new popular cultural order, some film executives began to see the wisdom in the maxim, "If you can't beat 'em, join 'em." In 1954, ABC, then the also-ran network, struck a deal with Disney whereby the studio (a minor player in Hollywood in those days) would produce weekly films for a series called *Disneyland.* This impressed Jack Warner of Warner Bros. He had seen television as the enemy: he even refused to allow shots of TV sets in any of his studio's films. But people were advising him to change his stance—his son-in-law described the thousands of antennas he had seen when flying over a Chicago slum—and he sensed an opportunity to make a lot of money. So he too struck a deal with ABC: he agreed to produce forty one-hour TV films for $75,000 apiece, receiving in turn ten free minutes to plug movies that were about to be released in theaters. The show, to be called *Warner Brothers Presents,* was actually three film series—one based on *Casablanca,* one on *King's Row,* and one on the B-class Western, *Cheyenne*—which were shown in rotation. As it turned out, the audience stopped watching during the long commercial breaks, and the *Casablanca* and *King's Row* series did not draw as many viewers as the *Cheyenne* series, which came to occupy the time slot. The Western mania, along with the TV drama series, was born.[32]

Television's voracious demand for programming was a boon to the film industry in another way: it created a new market for the studios' enormous catalog of old films. Once the film-TV relationship ceased to be adversarial, Hollywood began to sell broadcast rights for its chestnuts to the networks, with immensely profitable results. The economic motive was clear: an old Hollywood movie—or even a previously broadcast episode of a show ("rerun" or "repeat")—had already been made and paid for, so the studios could sell broadcast rights at a reduced price, since all the money made would be pure profit. Television could in turn sell advertising time for less, since *its* costs were lower, which allowed it to gain a market share on print and radio. This drastically changed the nature of some types of programming. For instance, in 1954, New York station WOR-TV showed a live drama every night. Two years later, 88 percent of its programming was film, mostly Hollywood features.[33]

The impact on the international market was especially dramatic. Because both film and television companies had already earned back costs and even made profits at home, they could undercut any foreign competition: whatever it cost to produce a show in, say, South Korea, a U.S. advertising agency would simply offer a U.S. show to a sponsor (either the state or a private company) for less, and hawk its wares on commercials as well. Foreign television might need subtitles to be linguistically intelligible, but from lighting to car chases, native film industries could seldom match U.S. production values. Television rode the crest of an imperial cultural wave that has lasted for the rest of the century. Moreover, even as U.S. power and influence ebbs, film and television continue to maintain a hold on the international imagination.

But while television in some ways revitalized the film industry, it also dramatically changed its structure. "They're going to tell us how to make pictures?" an incredulous Jack Warner asked when he learned that the advertising agency involved in *Cheyenne* wanted to consult over the script. Warner still wielded enough power to veto such a proposal, but his successors did not.

The reasons were varied, but one of the most important was the rise of the independent producer, who increasingly sidestepped the collapsing studio system. This development can be traced back to the mid-1930s, when David O. Selznick left MGM to create his own production company. Selznick's protégé, writer/director Alfred Hitchcock, took this idea to its logical conclusion for his films (and later television shows). Instead of relying on a corporate executive like Selznick to line things up, he did it himself—and held on to artistic control and a percentage of the profits.[34] This was the model followed by Lucille Ball and Desi Arnaz for *I Love Lucy,* and to the extent that it allowed the actual creators of popular culture to exert more control over their own work, it represented a real democratization of these media.

The growth in power of key actors, writers, directors, and producers led to a sharp rise in the influence of talent agencies, which acted as brokers between talent and capital—and between media like film, television, and music. This role eventually became so encompassing that the agencies in effect became producers. The most spectacular example was the Music Corporation of America, or MCA, which was founded in the 1920s to handle booking for musicians in Chicago. By the early 1940s, MCA had established a presence in Hollywood, and by the 1950s it had become the dominant agency. In 1959, MCA bought Universal Studios, a company that had specialized in the kinds of films now routinely produced for television. Too financially battered to launch its own TV shows, Universal rented its facilities to outside producers until MCA's capital allowed it to enter the fray. To this day, MCA/Universal remains a prominent studio in Hollywood, while the role of talent agents is greater than ever.

Universal was able to survive only by being taken over by a larger company. The *Paramount* case, the rise of independent producers, and the damage done by television—a damage to the old order that was greater than the opportunities it had afforded—left all the major studios in a badly weakened condition. Hollywood, of course, had long been dependent on Wall Street capital, but now it began to be swallowed by companies with no previous stake in the entertainment industry in general or movies in particular. In the late 1960s and early 1970s, Gulf & Western bought Paramount; Kinney bought Warner Bros.; and Coca-Cola bought Columbia. Some studios have since changed hands and become spoils in multi-media empires, a development that will be discussed in the next chapter. The days of the working-class immigrant Jews who became media moguls are long gone.

For all the studio system's drawbacks—its monopolistic, even autocratic behavior; its reluctance to confront social issues on screen; its even greater timidity in responding to the anti-Communist threat off screen—it did bequeath a valuable legacy to popular culture. The best films of the era projected a confidence that reached millions of Americans, even as they (often subtly) revealed their fears about race, gender, economic unrest, and global conflict. These movies cannot really be considered mirrors of their times, for they are too partial and distorted for that role. But, like abstract portrait paintings that bear little obvious resemblance to their subject, they nonetheless reveal something essential.

The Hollywood film world has never been prone to dwell on the past and it continued to churn out features and telefilms, even if they did not match past glories in the eyes of critics or older generations of moviegoers. In the 1950s and 1960s, a number of factors gave the film industry a boost. One was a new interest in foreign cinema. The shrinking of the moviegoing audience created an incentive to cultivate small but loyal audiences that could be counted on to support features tailored to their tastes. One such audience was the "art house" crowd, for whom the term "film" was more appropriate than "movie" and who took the form seriously as art. These were many of the same people who became interested in jazz, once again demonstrating the upward mobility of popular culture over time. Less likely to be troubled by language barriers and more willing to tolerate deviations from U.S. filmmaking traditions, these viewers helped bring the work of many distinguished foreign filmmakers to the United States, among them Italian writer/director Roberto Rossellini, best known for his intensely realistic *Rome, Open City* (1945) and *Paisan* (1948), both co-written by future director Federico Fellini. The psychological dramas of Swedish director Ingmar Bergman and the arch anti-narrative approach of Frenchman Jean Luc Godard also claimed devotees. For the most part, the context in which such films were viewed made them an elite pastime, and Godard's obvious contempt for the "discreet charm of the bourgeoisie" (the title of one of his films) shaded into a form of snobbery that brooked no compromise with mass taste. But these films not only introduced fresh perspectives into U.S. cinema; they also became part of a vital cultural repository, as film became an increasingly common subject of study in the nation's colleges and universities.

Another source of vitality grew out of the *Paramount* decision. In supporting the dismantling of the studio monopoly, the Supreme Court explicitly granted movies free-speech protection under the First Amendment, a right that had been denied since 1915. The impetus was provided by *The Miracle,* a 1950 Rossellini/Fellini film that had been banned in New York after pressure from outraged Catholics. The Court's decision helped weaken the cultural force of the old production code that had been shaping and censoring motion picture content since the 1930s. (The code was replaced in 1966 with the G, PG, R, and X ratings that obtain today—still coercive to filmmakers who wish to work outside established boundaries, but less restrictive nonetheless.) Moreover, European films, which were less sexually prudish, conferred an intellectual respectability on more expressiveness and provided workable models for U.S. filmmakers.

These tendencies, combined with the general loosening of restrictions that marked the late 1950s and all of the 1960s, coalesced in the rise of two other specialty interests: pornographic and action-adventure films, each with much greater proportions of explicit sex and violence than was then possible on television (or had been possible in movies). In 1973, the pornographic *Deep Throat* and *The Devil in Miss Jones* ranked sixth and eleventh respectively in box office grosses,[35] while Charles Bronson's *Death Wish* (1974) mined a paranoid, murderous mentality that would later be exploited by Clint Eastwood's *Dirty Harry* and Sylvester Stallone's *Rambo* movies. Sex and violence also became more common in already well-defined genres, such as the horror film. Another major popular success was *The Exorcist* (1973), widely considered one of the most shocking and disturbing movies of all time.

Such developments provoked indignation on the left and right. Yet the legal and cultural freedoms of the late 1960s also offered filmmakers an opportunity to make movies of great artistic power. One of the first was *Bonnie and Clyde* (1967), a critically acclaimed film directed by Arthur Penn that ended in a vividly depicted hail of bullets. Similarly, *Easy Rider* and *Midnight Cowboy* (both 1969) used casual violence, sex, and drug use to raise deeply troubling questions about longstanding assumptions of the existence of freedom, upward mobility, and moral clarity.

Indeed, in terms of the degree to which Hollywood's machinery was used to fashion a thoroughgoing critique of society, the years between the late 1960s and the late 1970s were the *real* golden age of cinema. *The Deer Hunter* (1978) and *Apocalypse Now* (1979) explored U.S. involvement in Vietnam; *The Candidate* (1972) satirized the vacuity of U.S. politics; *Up the Sandbox* (1972) was the first serious attempt to wrestle with feminism on screen; *Network* (1975, written by *Marty* creator Paddy Cheyevsky) savaged television, albeit with too much misogyny; *Shaft* (1971) and *Superfly* (1973) went further than any previous mainstream films in presenting an urban African-American perspective, although they too treated women shabbily. Some of these films had more artistry and staying power than others, but they are collectively notable for the degree to which they inverted, revised, or simply rejected some of the most basic premises governing the status quo.

The 1970s were also notable for the individual talents whose work came to fullest expression in this decade. Francis Ford Coppola's *Godfather* trilogy (1972-1992) remains a critical and popular landmark, while Robert Altman—director of *M*A*S*H* (1970), the unconventional Western *McCabe and Mrs. Miller* (1971), and the documentary-like *Nashville* (1975)—established a reputation that would be further enhanced by his caustic Hollywood satire *The Player* (1992). Martin Scorsese earned enormous acclaim for a series of vivid depictions of underground life in *Mean Streets* (1972), *Taxi Driver* (1976), and *GoodFellas* (1990). Each of these directors operated at least partially outside mainstream Hollywood values, and in so doing broadened the thematic and ideological scope of American movies.

By the late 1970s, however, a reaction to this cinematic soul-searching was apparent. As in the case of television, it was typified by a rejection of ambiguity and an indulgence in nostalgia. In fact, the quintessential television manifestation of this change, *Happy Days,* was modeled on the 1973 hit movie *American Graffiti,* directed by the young George Lucas. Lucas and his University of Southern California film-school friend Steven Spielberg were unquestioned masters of filmic technique, but unlike Coppola or Scorsese, they used their talents to craft ingenious visual extravaganzas with mythic overtones. The prototype for what followed was Lucas's *Star Wars* (1977). With its romantic evocation of good guys in white fighting an evil empire in black, and its reluctant hero (Harrison Ford) a direct transplant from classic Westerns, *Star Wars* hailed back to old Hollywood models, its futuristic setting masking its essential conservatism. At the same time, its high-tech glitz was sold relentlessly through commercial tie-ins (dolls, posters, and a huge new company created to produce special effects for other movies). For these reasons, *Star Wars* can be considered the first film of the 1980s. Lucas followed it with *The Empire Strikes Back* (1980) and *Return of the Jedi* (1983), which also drew large audiences.

Spielberg took strategies like those of Lucas to even greater heights. After enjoying his first major success with *Jaws* (1975), a kind of pop-culture *Moby Dick,* he proceeded to direct a string of movies that made his name a household word. *Close Encounters of the Third Kind* (1977) tapped a widespread fascination with purported alien encounters; *Raiders of the Lost Ark* (produced by Lucas in 1981, with sequels in 1984 and 1989) offered unabashed swashbuckling; and *E.T.: The Extraterrestrial* (1982) resurrected the fairy tale in the form of a special-effects laden story about a benign visitor from outer space. In a sense, Spielberg was like Ronald Reagan: he allowed Americans to feel good about themselves in an unironic way. He had difficulty handling serious material—his 1985 film version of Alice Walker's novel *The Color Purple* was too sunny to be credible—and his baroque sensibility could be distasteful, as in the case of *Hook,* his overly lush 1991 update of *Peter Pan*.

Whatever political or aesthetic qualms there may have been about Spielberg and Lucas, their economic power was undeniable. After the commercial lassitude of the 1960s and early 1970s, Hollywood began developing a "blockbuster mentality" whereby a studio's financial resources were marshalled into making a few major movies that were then sold in a variety of ways: commercial exhibition in the United States and abroad; sales to network television; and tie-ins to other media, particularly music soundtracks. This approach yielded gigantic profits in the case of *Saturday Night Fever* (1977), a movie about disco culture, and *Grease* (1978), another willfully naive celebration of the 1950s. There was always the chance that studio miscalculations could fail, as was the case with Lucas's hapless *Howard the Duck* (1986), but the potential returns were great, and budgets ballooned straight through the 1980s.

The potential returns became even greater when such newer media as videocassettes, cable television, and even amusement park rides created additional avenues for profit. Though this process was disorienting to the television industry, especially the networks, it was a great boon to moviemakers, and Hollywood enjoyed an economic vitality unknown since the 1940s. At the same time, movie production companies were being sucked into new communications conglomerates, ranging from cellular phone companies to textbook publishers, a phenomenon that will be further discussed in the next chapter.

Amid—and despite—all this intense packaging (and repackaging) of blockbusters, sequels, and other formula products, some powerful Hollywood movies were made in the 1980s and 1990s. *Wall Street* (1987), for example, is already a classic portrait of a decade of greed. And despite the intense politicking that goes into the Academy Awards, some "Best Picture" winners in recent years have all been worthy efforts. *The Silence of the Lambs* (1991) turned the horror movie into a powerful (feminist) statement about the cunning complexity of evil; Clint Eastwood single-handedly reinvigorated the Western from within in *Unforgiven* (1992); and Steven Spielberg overcame his worst impulses to direct *Schindler's List* (1993), a towering document about the Holocaust. Hollywood's future cultural legitimacy will depend on the extent to which such works continue to be possible.

New Chapters:
The "Paperback Revolution"

Not all cultural forms declined in television's wake. Although audiovisual media like radio and film could overcome the barrier of literacy, the written word remained the basic unit for the construction of most popular cultural forms. So while, for example, television news displaced newspapers and radio as the primary source of information, both retained the allegiance of millions of Americans, and demonstrated a greater degree of independence than other media. To this day, magazine publishing remains a vital industry catering to all races, classes, and genders. With the exception of computer typesetting and layout, however, print journalism has not undergone any fundamental structural revolution in the last half-century, and changes in its production and editorial methods have been evolutionary rather than revolutionary. But in the roughly twenty-five years after World War II, book publishing experienced a major transformation with the introduction of a new format: the paperback. Although their impact on reading and mass literacy have declined in recent decades, paperbacks continue to have a major democratizing effect.

As is clear from previous chapters, the idea of producing and distributing inexpensive books on a mass basis is certainly not new. Chapbooks (see Chapter 1), dime novels (see Chapters 2 and 3), and pulp fiction (see Chapter 4) are the ancestors of the modern paperback. To a certain extent, however, the paperback was intended as an *antidote* to its predecessors. The pulps were considered by many as seedy, with poor quality paper, ink, and bindings. The first paperback publishers tried to provide what they considered the highest quality fiction in an accessible format at the tightest possible profit margin. If it was inevitable that the margin would widen, perhaps it was also inevitable that the breadth of what was offered would also widen to meet mass tastes. And by selling a product—the book—rather than selling advertising, as the television and radio industries did, publishing came closer to capitalism's often invoked, but never fulfilled, goal of providing a market-place of ideas.

Ironically, given the plethora of American antecedents, the immediate model for the paperback was European. Beginning in the 1840s, a German publisher, Tauchnitz, began issuing inexpensive English-language editions of British and U.S. fiction. Tauchnitz had the field to itself until the 1930s, when he ran into competition from Albatross, a European firm that later absorbed it. (One of the founders of Albatross, Kurt Enoch, was a German Jew who later fled Nazi Germany for the United States and still later helped to launch New American Library, a major paperback publishing house from the 1950s through the 1970s.) A third major entrant, Penguin Books, was also founded in the 1930s and also went on to become a major international publisher (it acquired New American Library).

All these efforts focused on classics, or "high" literature, that presumably transcended mass appeal. The books usually had plain covers, not only to keep costs down but also to suggest their seriousness and to distance them from dime novels or pulps. Similar projects were attempted in the United States. In the 1830s, for example, newspapermen Park Benjamin and Rufus Griswold tried publishing writers like Balzac and Hugo in a tabloid format, while book publisher Charles Boni experimented with illustration in his "Boni Paper Books" from 1929 to 1931. Both ventures were sold on a subscription basis. Another attempt at early paperback publishing, Modern Age Books, sold literary classics through newsstands from 1937 to 1942.

One notable exception to this string of failed attempts to bring "culture" to the masses was the index-card-sized "Little Blue Books" published by socialist Emanuel Haldeman-Julius out of Kansas between 1919 and 1964. Little Blue Books ranged from Shakespeare to psycho-analysis and sold hundreds of millions of copies at a nickel each. Tax-evasion charges (allegedly political in motivation), Haldeman-Julius's death in 1951, and increasing competition eventually drove the company out of business, but not before it demonstrated the demand for inexpen-sively priced classics.

That demand was finally tapped on a mass scale in the United States by Robert DeGraff, who founded Pocket Books with capital from hardcover publisher Simon & Schuster in 1939. DeGraff pared his costs and maxi-mized his profits by paying reduced royalties to publishers and authors for the right to reprint their books; limiting the discount to the newsstands or bookstores; using cheaper binding methods and reusing the plates from the hardcover version (which was published first); and above all, publishing large quantities, which allowed an economy of scale that became even more dramatic when press runs began to exceed 100,000 copies. Such tactics allowed DeGraff to sell Pocket Books for a quarter, an amount within the reach of many Americans.

Besides the price, the other key factor in these books' success was their penetration into the nooks and crannies of everyday life. At a time when bookstores and libraries were few and far between, paperbacks were displayed on racks at newsstands, train stations, drugstores, lunch counters, and other commercial establishments. Indeed, hardcover publishers allowed their books to be reprinted in paperback because they knew they could not achieve such results themselves, and because paperbacks were generally *not* sold in bookstores (that came later). Authors were similarly delighted. "I am always glad when any of my books can be put into an inexpensive edition, because I like to think that any people who might wish to read them can do so," wrote Nobel Prize laureate Pearl Buck on the dedication page of the paperback edition of *The Good Earth* (1931). "Surely books ought to be within the reach of everybody." By the end of World War II, *The Good Earth* had sold over half a million copies, many of which must have had more than one reader.

The war itself was a major stimulant of the paperback revolution. Despite paper shortages and transportation obstacles, Pocket Books in the United States and Penguin in Britain churned out millions of paperbacks, many of which were sent overseas. Military manuals, how-to books, history, and fiction were avidly read on planes, trains, and even in the trenches. In 1941, Pocket Books sold 12 million books; by the end of the war, it had sold 40 million. Nor did the pace lessen: 214 million paperbacks were sold in 1950, more than one book per person in the United States.[36]

One of the more striking aspects of this phenomenal growth was the eclecticism of the books that were reprinted. Pocket Book's initial list of ten titles included bestsellers like James Hilton's *Lost Horizon* and Thorne Smith's *Topper* (both of which were made into popular movies), as well as *Five Great Tragedies* by William Shakespeare, which had sold 141,000 copies by 1941. By that point Emily Bronte's *Wuthering Heights* had sold over 300,000—and was later listed as the eleventh most popular title in Pocket Book's survey of army camps.[37] In the years after the war, Pocket Books and a host of competitors published the works of James Joyce, William Faulkner, and other major canonized writers, putting this literature within easy reach of curious readers, including former soldiers who were receiving a free college education through the GI Bill of 1946.

A more systematic outreach strategy was successfully implemented by highbrow companies like Pelican, Anchor, and Vintage (the softcover branches of Penguin, Doubleday, and Random House respectively). These "imprints," as such subsidiaries are known, published scholarly books—called "trade paperbacks"—at slightly higher prices. Ruth Benedict's *Patterns of Culture,* a major work of anthropology, sold a few hundred copies when it was first published in hardcover by Houghton Mifflin in 1934, but it sold *1 million* in the fifteen years following its first appearance in paperback in 1945.[38] Books like David Riesman's sociological study *The Lonely Crowd* (1950), Eldridge Cleaver's Black Power manifesto *Soul on Ice* (1968), and Kate Millet's feminist polemic *Sexual Politics* (1971) were not simply important works that entered the stream of popular culture; they were important works at least to some degree *because* they entered the stream of popular culture.

We should not exaggerate the extent of this taste for serious fare—more people probably watched one episode of *I Love Lucy* on a single night in the early 1950s than ever read Joyce's 1922 masterwork *Ulysses* (the subject of a landmark 1933 court decision that struck down a ban on the book for obscenity). Moreover, *how* people read these books—and what, if any, consequences there were—is unknown. But in creating a diverse arena for the exchange of ideas, styles, and readers, the paperback revolution of the 1940s and 1950s represented an important democratizing moment in popular culture.

Of course, classics and scholarly books were only one facet of paperback publishing. The huge success stories of the postwar era—Dr. Benjamin Spock's *Baby and Child Care* (1946; over 45 million and counting); *The Merriam-Webster Pocket Dictionary* (1947; 15.5 million by the mid-1960s alone) and Dale Carnegie's *How to Win Friends and Influence People* (5 million at that same point)—pointed to a hunger for self-help that was satisfied by sources of varying credibility. Blockbuster novels like Grace Metalious's *Peyton Place* (1957) explored the seamy side of small-town life at a time when the myth of the happy nuclear family was at its height. And William Lederer and Eugene Burdick's *The Ugly American* (1960) brought readers the apparently shocking news that the United States was not viewed with universal admiration in the rest of the world.

But perhaps the most distinctive element of paperback publishing, and one that tied it to other forms of popular culture, was the flourishing of genre fiction, Westerns, science fiction, mysteries, crime, and romance. Moved from their previous incarnations into the new format, these genres won large audiences and evolved an aesthetic that went unrecognized among professional literary critics. Just as movie studios came to specialize in particular genres, so too did publishers. Bantam Books, for example, became known for its Westerns, while Ballantine developed a reputation for science fiction. Perhaps the greatest genre success story was Harlequin Books, which was founded as a general trade publisher in Canada in 1949, but has issued only romances since 1964. By the end of the 1970s, Harlequin claimed a regular readership of 16 million women in North America and had sold 168 million copies of its books worldwide.[39] Since that time, the company has launched a series of imprints appealing to specific segments of the romance audience, such as those who like more (or less) overt sexuality.

Unlike other paperback houses, Harlequin's success was not predicated on reprinting books that had already appeared in hardcover but on publishing "paperback originals." This approach was pioneered in the 1950s by Fawcett Books, an imprint of New American Library, and remains a common (though not dominant) practice today. The rise of the paperback original, coupled with the expansion of the trade paperback, led to a gradual acceptance of softcover books in bookstores. The common practice today is a two-tiered approach, whereby a hardcover edition of a book is followed about a year later by a mass market or trade paper edition (trade paperbacks tend to be larger and more expensive than rack-sized mass-market paperbacks).

The paperback revolution was not without its opponents, who saw the diffusion of material they did not like as a major problem. And as in other areas of popular culture, the Red Scare was an issue for the publishing industry. One-time Communist author Howard Fast was jailed and then blacklisted for refusing to name his associates. Vanguard Books, a hardcover left-wing press that specialized in economics and politics in the 1920s, was investigated by HUAC, an act for which the committee later apologized. (Ray Bradbury's science-fiction story "Fahrenheit 451," published in paperback in 1953, was a parable of McCarthyism.) On the whole, however, explicitly political censorship was less pronounced than in other media, in large measure because writers were not subject to the defensive reactions of sponsors or networks. In a less tangible way, book censorship may have

seemed too flagrant a violation of the First Amendment for officials accustomed to professing respect for the written word, if not other cultural forms
(as noted above, First Amendment protection for films was denied from
1915 until the late 1940s).

More sustained threats to cultural expression have come from those
seeking to ban books on grounds of obscenity. In 1952, the House of
Representatives convened a committee under the chairmanship of E.C.
Gathings, a Democrat from Kansas, to investigate "the kind of filthy sex
books which are affecting the youth of our country."[40] Nothing much came
of the hearings, but harassment of publishers, libraries, and readers has been
continual ever since. J.D. Salinger's novel of youthful alienation, *Catcher
in the Rye* (1951), is still widely banned because of its frank language, and
Grove Press, a daring publisher of important books (it took on *The
Autobiography of Malcolm X* in 1965 when Doubleday, which had
contracted the book, dropped it), was forced to go to court to defend its
right to publish an edition of D.H. Lawrence's *Lady Chatterly's Lover.* The
difficulty in establishing a precise definition of obscenity—or perhaps more
accurately, a questionable insistence that the term can and should be legally
fixed—is likely to result in future conflicts.

This is not to say, of course, that debates over morality or politics were
always high-minded affairs. Plenty of offensive books have been published
in the last fifty years, ranging from the misogyny of Mickey Spillane's
swaggering private detective Mike Hammer to the racism of countless
Westerns. Moreover, the industry's tendency to package even fairly straight-
laced novels in pseudo-pornographic covers with titillating come-ons—"A
subject only whispered about!" proclaims a blurb for the 1952 novel *Cage
of Lust*—shows a desire to mislead and to pander to the most prurient tastes.

It is precisely such objections that have led elite critics to dismiss the effects
of the paperback revolution. While acknowledging that there have been
some good paperbacks, such people note that they were more the exception
than the rule and that even classics were marred by tasteless marketing (the
first Bantam cover of Sinclair Lewis's 1922 novel *Babbitt* featured a
smug-looking man in an apparent love triangle beneath the words "What
did this man want?"). This view was cogently expressed by historian Bernard
DeVoto in a 1954 article for *Harper's* magazine. "Tripe has always been
the basis of the publishing business, and in the two-bit book it is performing
the functions of all popular literature in all ages," he observed. "At worst it
is preventing boredom, assisting digestion and peristalsis, feeding people's

appetites for daydreams, giving the imagination something to work on and taking the reader out of a momentarily unsatisfactory life into a more enjoyable one. At best, or so the theory of revolution holds, it is plowing, harrowing, and seeding the soil."[41] At worst, DeVoto's description is contemptuous of non-professional readers; at best, it underestimates the promise, necessity, and satisfaction of "seeding the soil."

Whatever its effects, the impact of the paperback revolution began to ebb in the 1970s. Sales peaked in 1968, when over 350 million books were sold; after that publishers compensated for falling sales with rising prices.[42] A blockbuster mentality then took hold. As with the movie studios in these years, the publishing industry became less interested in a small-margin, high-diversity business than in making killings with a few big hits. And as with the studios, individual houses were swallowed by larger companies that had no previous experience in the business. When publishing houses failed to meet quick-profit expectations, as Fawcett Books did after CBS acquired it in the early 1980s, the imprint was summarily dismantled.

Nevertheless, reading remains a popular passion at the end of the twentieth century. Concerns about the intensifying commercialization of publishing and declining literacy are real, even if they were also lamented a century *before* the paperback revolution. But two full centuries after it became the first modern form of popular culture, the written word continues to play an important role in U.S. life.

Rewired:
Radio's Transformation

A paperback "revolution" may accurately describe what happened to publishing in the 1940s and 1950s, but no branch of the media underwent as dramatic a change as radio broadcasting in these years. As noted above, movie culture made significant adaptations in response to television, but such accommodations paled compared to the wholesale overhaul of radio: from being the centerpiece of the U.S. home, it moved to fill niches in everyday life (e.g., as an accompaniment to driving).

In one sense, the writing had been on the wall almost from the beginning. Leading industry figures like Sarnoff had been laying the foundations for television since the 1920s, financing its development with radio profits. Yet the Depression, World War II, and the TV-station licensing freeze of

1948-1952 held back television's arrival as a major force, and radio broadcasts continued to proliferate. Five hundred new stations took to the airwaves in 1946, followed by 400 more the next year. From the end of the war to 1952, the number of stations more than doubled, to almost 2,400. Perhaps, some speculated, predictions of radio's demise were greatly exaggerated.

When TV did begin to make inroads, radio tried to meet the challenge by persisting with programming that was now also on television. But it quickly became apparent that this approach was fruitless. Besides the inherent visual appeal of being able to see performers, many of radio's brightest stars—Berle, Benny, Burns, Ball—were defecting to television. Even more damaging, the networks had now largely shifted their attention to TV, cutting allocations for new radio shows and lowering advertising rates (and thus income for the increasingly disenchanted affiliates). By 1952, radio's prime-time audience was only a third of what it had been at its peak.[43]

Faced with this challenge, individual stations began to specialize. Shedding network affiliations that were doing them more harm than good, they began to focus on their own communities and to develop inexpensive programming, or "formats." Among the most popular were news and/or talk stations, religious stations, and above all, music stations that played records, that once maligned but now cost-effective means of broadcasting. In its intensely localized, relatively modest approach, this type of radio programming harkened back to the days before network dominance. But its ongoing dependence on advertising and ever more systematic segmenting of its audience showed the extent to which private interests continued to control the medium.

There were important exceptions to this rule, however. One of the most important was the Pacifica network, which began in the late 1940s, when pacifist radio journalist Lewis Kimball Hill received an FCC license for a radio station in Berkeley, California, after failing to secure one in San Francisco. The station became a network after it acquired another station in Los Angeles in 1959, and went national in 1960, when philanthropist Louis Schweitzer donated a New York station. It has since picked up affiliates in other cities, surviving on listener contributions and offering eclectic, generally progressive, and decidedly noncommercial programming.

A more centralized form of alternative broadcasting, National Public Radio, came on the scene in the late 1960s. When Congress passed the legislation establishing the Public Broadcasting System, funding was included for a similar radio network. NPR member stations have local autonomy and local programming, but pay dues so that they can draw on a series of Washington-based programs and news reports that have a national orientation. Although NPR has been criticized for being insufficiently diverse, it has become an important presence in the largely commercial world of broadcasting, a major reason for conservative hostility.

One final example of alternative radio is college and university stations. Besides serving as a training ground for future broadcasters and providing information services to communities that might not otherwise have them, college radio has been an important arena for experimentation in music, news, and other programming in the last thirty years. This has been possible because such stations are often (but not always) free of the formatting strictures and staid conventions of both commercial and public radio.

Occasionally, economic and/or technological changes can open up space *within* commercial radio. One case is the development in the late 1960s of stations using Lee Armstrong's frequency modulation, or FM, method of broadcasting. Because this was a frontier compared to the dense AM dial, and also because it offered higher quality musical transmission, early FM radio was an expansive affair that was characterized by the counterculture's hopeful ebullience (more on this below). Like so much before it, however, FM was subsequently harnessed to generate profits more effectively.[44]

Postwar radio's greatest contribution to popular culture has been in fostering the development of new styles and forms of music and disseminating them. By the early 1950s, record companies no longer believed that radio was a threat and began to cultivate it assiduously. This conferred new power on the person who chose and played the records—the "disc jockey"— who in those days was more likely to determine a station's playlist. This disc jockey was often a connoisseur of what was regarded as obscure music, especially rural white and African-American varieties, which were met with increasing enthusiasm, especially among young people. It was because of this that radio became the midwife of rock & roll. But in order to understand this development, and radio's role in it, we must return to the story of black and white musical forms in the twentieth century.

Postwar Popular Music:
The Rise and Fall of Rock & Roll

In the world of popular music, the period from the late 1950s to the present is considered the age of rock & roll. Rock & roll was not the only genre of popular music in this period, of course, but it dominated both because it was a powerful musical force in its own right and because of its seemingly inexhaustible ability to absorb and adapt older genres and styles.

The foundation for rock was African-American music, especially the blues. The blues were rock's cornerstone, whether the criterion is musical scales, AAB lyrical forms, or the themes of the lyrics. Gospel music contributed a call-and-response vocal pattern that was vitally important, and jazz provided a model of improvisation that was widely appropriated, especially by electric guitarists. These musical traits have become so pervasive, so taken for granted, that it is all too easy to overlook just how distinctive they are, and how wonderfully elastic.

While the musical prerequisites for rock & roll were firmly in place by the end of the nineteenth century, the social, economic, and technological ingredients did not fully coalesce until the mid-twentieth. Many of the forms have already been discussed. The mass migration of African Americans from the South to other parts of the country, for example, began after the Civil War and intensified with World War I. But neither came close to matching the migration during World War II; between 1939 and 1945 over a million blacks left the South to take jobs in cities like Los Angeles and Detroit.[45] The culture the people brought with them underwent subtle changes in the process. The soothing blues of the Mississippi Delta retained their emotional power in Chicago, but were electrified in urban nightclubs instead of being sung in the moonlight, reflecting a grittier, faster paced milieu.

One of the characteristics that distinguished World War II-era black migration was that it took place at a time when newer media, like radio and records, were proliferating and the access African-Americans had to them was growing. Radio stations that played black music and black record labels like Okeh existed well before the 1940s, but the scale of such activities was much larger this time around. A big part of the reason was the wartime and postwar prosperity, which generated more disposable income for the American worker. Although African-Americans earned less than their white counterparts, African-American communities were more able than before to support a popular cultural infrastructure of artists, nightclubs, radio stations, and record labels. The establishment of Atlantic Records in 1947 and Chess Records in 1948 are important in this regard. Although still marginal in an industry dominated by New York companies that focused on Tin Pan Alley material, these "race" labels recorded and distributed a form that was becoming known as "rhythm and blues" (or r&b), tapping into a groundswell that would soon shake the music world.

Meanwhile, the musical map was also being redrawn by white performers extending the frontiers of country music. As discussed in Chapter 4, the Western boom in states like Texas and Oklahoma had broadened country's musical base, while its popularity in honky-tonks, jukeboxes, and on radio consolidated its appeal across the nation. Yet country never lost contact with its Southern roots, and even reaffirmed its Appalachian origins in a subgenre known as bluegrass, which was based on folk models and used acoustic instruments. The best-known bluegrass musician is Bill Monroe, who dominated the form throughout the 1940s and 1950s, and bluegrass retains a relatively small but loyal following of players and listeners to this day.[46]

The person most responsible for synthesizing country's varied strands and giving them a compelling new configuration was Hank Williams. Williams was born in 1923 and grew up in a rural Alabama family, absorbing white gospel music, black blues, and country & western. After a few difficult years as a laborer and welder in Mobile shipyards, he began to experience some success as a singer; by the late 1940s he had begun to build a national reputation with songs like "Your Cheatin' Heart," "Lovesick Blues," and "Jambalaya." Embedded in Williams' more lighthearted songs, like "Settin' the Woods on Fire," was the archetypal image of the redneck rake (a persona that would be embodied in his country-singing son, Hank Williams, Jr., in the 1970s and 1980s), but his more blues-derived songs, like "Cold, Cold Heart," had a haunting power. By the time of his death at age 29 in 1953, Williams had secured a place as one of the major figures in U.S. vernacular music.

In self-consciously drawing on black musical expressions, or capturing a less concrete but still-real blues sensibility, Williams was part of a growing move toward racial integration in country & western. One of the most important signs of this change was the popularity of white "boogie-woogie," which drew on the lively black rhythms that were also propelling big band and r&b material in the 1940s. Country acts like the Delmore Brothers (who between 1945 and 1952 recorded at least eleven songs with the term "boogie"), Tennessee Ernie Ford, and Moon Mullican were examples of this trend.[47] They also paved the way for the boogie-woogie variant called "rockabilly," which was taken up by Johnny Cash, Carl Perkins, and others in the 1950s.

Much of this music was being produced by small, regionally based record companies that were more in touch with these trends than the big New York companies. One of the most important was King Records of Cincinnati, which recorded performers ranging from the Delmore Brothers to James Brown, one of the seminal figures in African-American music. By releasing the music of blacks and whites alike—and in throwing them together in the recording studio—companies like King became hothouses of musical experimentation and cross-fertilization.

Back in the nation's cities and suburbs, a number of other forces were contributing to the emerging postwar musical culture. Although their power was on the wane, Broadway and Tin Pan Alley continued to dominate. But mainstream pop was also being reinvigorated from below by the first modern pop idol: Frank Sinatra. A product of the working-class shipyard culture of Hoboken, New Jersey, Sinatra began working as a jazz performer with big band leaders Harry James and Tommy Dorsey in the early years of World War II. By 1944, when there was a riot after 30,000 fans showed up at a 3,600-seat New York theater, Sinatra had become the preeminent figure in urban popular music. As such, he was the generational successor to Bing Crosby and the direct antecedent of such future hysteria-inducing figures as Elvis Presley and the Beatles. Sinatra's role as a cultural icon (especially to working-class Italian-Americans), his connections with questionable characters (ranging from gangsters to Nancy Reagan), and his hostility to 1960s counterculture should not obscure his musical achievements. His highly idiosyncratic vocal style—marked, for example, by improvised lines in the middle of a song—has made him one of the most influential singers of the twentieth century.

Even as these diverse musical subcultures matured, another set of technological and economic developments was having a decisive impact on popular music. The end of wartime rationing of shellac, combined with the demand from jukeboxes and the increasingly symbiotic relationship between records and radio, revitalized the lagging music industry. So did a series of innovations that were changing the way music was made. In the closing days of the war, U.S. intelligence discovered that Adolf Hitler had been using a tape-recording device that made it appear as if he was making live "broadcasts" at the battlefront when in fact he was hundreds of miles away. A few years later, Columbia Records introduced the "long-playing" or "lp" record. Made of vinyl, the lp rotated 33 times per minute, compared to 78 times for shellac records. It was more durable, had better quality sound, and made it possible to record a symphony on two sides of one disc or an entire opera on three or four discs (which indicates Columbia's musical priorities—Sinatra was its sole pop act on lp).[48] Around the same time, RCA introduced the 45 rpm record, which generally had one song on each side, and introduced a newfangled record player that made it possible to listen to a stack of records in succession. At first, the competition between the two formats was fierce, but eventually the 45 rpm "single" and the 33 rpm "album" developed a cozier relationship, with the former serving as an inexpensive way of introducing songs from the latter. Both lost out to 8-track and cassette tape formats in the 1960s and 1970s, and were supplanted by compact discs in the 1980s.

At stake in all this corporate jockeying were the vast profits to be earned from the burgeoning youth market of "baby boomers" born after World War II. Since the turn of the century, it had been clear that young people were an economically powerful constituency, one that had been crucial, for example, in making jazz a major form of popular music in the 1920s and 1930s. But the extension of adolescence into the college years, the explosion of the birth rate after the war, and the almost staggering rise in disposable incomes all created a postwar consumer culture unlike any the world had ever seen. The teenage market in 1959 was estimated at $10 billion—$1 billion more than General Motors grossed that same year. In 1960, the editor of *Seventeen* magazine estimated that young women under age 20 spent $20 million on lipstick, $25 million on deodorants, and comprised a large proportion of the $75 million market for 45 rpm records.[49]

And what did these young people listen to? By the early 1950s, this was being decided by the disc jockeys at the nation's major record stations. In search of novelty, some of these people, like Alan Freed at the Cleveland radio station WJW, began to play the heretofore largely marginalized music of the hinterlands. Freed's prominence in disseminating this music in Ohio is a major reason why the founders of the Rock & Roll Hall of Fame decided to build their museum in Cleveland.

And so, in one of the great ironies of U.S. history, millions upon millions of well-fed, well-educated, and thoroughly respectable youth embraced a series of musical forms that had been shaped by the sorrows of their ill-fed, barely literate, and impoverished elders. In the decades to come, this music would be merchandised by those with little feeling for it. But it would also receive the honor and respect it deserved, while enlightening—and even transforming—the lives of some with great feeling for it. "I know that rock and roll changed my life," rock artist Bruce Springsteen, the son of a bus driver and legal secretary, once said. "It was something for me to hold onto. I had nothing. Before then the whole thing was a washout for me. It really gave me a sense of myself, and it allowed me to become useful, which is what I think most people want to be."[50] Not all rock fans became rock stars, of course, but listeners could have a similar experience with it.

In the heat of this moment, however, the founding fathers of rock & roll—the mothers came along a little later—were less interested in meditating on the music than in seizing opportunities. Among them was Sam Phillips, a native Alabaman and former disc jockey who established his own record label, Sun, in 1951. Sun was based in Memphis, an important musical crossroads, and Phillips made the most of it by recording both white and black acts (performers whose work he nurtured included bluesmen Howlin' Wolf and B.B. King, black country singer Charlie Pride, and piano wizard Jerry Lee Lewis).

Phillips ran a relatively small operation and leased many of his recordings—like Jackie Breston's 1951 single "Rocket 88," featuring Tina Turner's husband Ike and widely cited as the first rock & roll record—to larger companies like Chess. He did, however, keep some of them for Sun, especially rockabilly acts like Johnny Cash, Carl Perkins, and Roy Orbison. Aware of the potentially huge market for the music he recorded, but also of the racism that constricted it, he reputedly told his secretary Marion Keisker, "If I could find a white boy with the Negro sound and the Negro feel, I could make a million dollars."[51]

That boy—whose name of course was Elvis Presley—was born in Tupelo, Mississippi, in 1935 (a twin brother died in childbirth).[52] His father, a sharecropper and truck driver among other professions, spent time in jail for check forgery when his son was three years old. Most biographers consider his mother a pivotal figure in his life, someone who, among other things, instilled in him a lasting love of gospel music. The family moved to Memphis when Presley was an adolescent, and after graduation from high school, he took a job as a truck driver.

Around the time Phillips was lamenting the absence of a compelling white singer of black music, Presley wandered into the Sun Records studio, presumably to make a vanity record for his mother's birthday. Phillips wasn't there, but Marion Keisker took note of him and encouraged the producer to give him a call. Phillips finally did, but it took months of practice and false starts before his protégé began to exhibit the ease and spontaneity of a first-rate rock singer. The performer who emerged from what are now known as the "Sun Sessions" of 1954 is not quite the cocky, charismatic vocalist of "Hound Dog" and "Jailhouse Rock"—his voice is higher, sweeter, and more lighthearted—but the vitality of the music is unmistakable. Indeed, some critics regard the Sun Sessions as Presley's finest moment. Unable to meet the almost instant demand for Presley's records, Phillips sold his contract to RCA, which was seeking a franchise for the new youth market. There were then dozens of hit records and a string of mediocre movies, followed by a slow decline punctuated by occasional successes (like the celebrated comeback of 1968-1969). To many, Presley's death in 1977 only underscored an artistic collapse that had taken place years before.

But in those first years following his explosion into popular consciousness in the 1950s, it seemed as if Presley had entered the world stage fully formed, offering a dazzling vision of possibility in an era of unprecedented prosperity as well as stifling conformity. Yet Presley succeeded not only because he presented something new, but because he distilled some very old—and very powerful—tensions.

Those tensions included technology vs. tradition, the sacred vs. the profane, and poverty vs. crass materialism, but the most central was racial. Growing up as a poor white in the South during the Great Depression, Presley was in close contact with African-American culture and evangelical religion, both of which had a powerful influence on his musical development. By the time of his first recordings, he had acquired an almost effortless ability to evoke and adapt a wide variety of styles—blues, gospel, bluegrass, country & western, even urban pop (Sinatra crony Dean Martin was one of his models). Presley's first record for Sun was Mississippi Delta bluesman Arthur Crudup's "That's All Right," backed with Bill Monroe's bluegrass standard, "Blue Moon of Kentucky." The selection was revealing: Presley took black and white music and made them two sides of the same record, etching each with a sense of style (in this case, a jaunty one) wholly his own.

Contrary to popular myth, however, Presley did not invent rock & roll, and he was only one of a number of its significant practitioners. Western swing bandleader Bill Haley's "Rock Around the Clock" (1954) had wide currency before Presley's records did, and Jerry Lee Lewis may have had more raw performing talent. And there were many exceptionally gifted African Americans who were as deserving of fame and stature as Presley but who were denied it because of their race. Songwriter and guitar hero Chuck Berry, for example, showed a similar gift for musical synthesis and a knack for articulating youthful concerns on records like "Maybelline" (1955), "Roll Over Beethoven" (1956), and "School Day" (1957). Little Richard (Penniman) displayed amazing vocal intensity on the sexually subversive "Tutti Frutti" and "Long Tall Sally" (1956). And Ray Charles probably outdid all comers in musical versatility, being as comfortable with country as he was with the emerging subgenre of soul. Given the racism that pervaded so many aspects of U.S. society in the 1950s, however, it was inevitable that wealth and fame would be conferred on a white rock star rather than a black one.

At the same time, it is important to remember the immense challenge rock music posed to the established cultural and political order. The music implicitly expressed in cultural form what Civil Rights leaders like Martin Luther King expressed in political form: a desire for, and belief in, racial integration. To a great extent, the severe backlash that rock generated was rooted in fear of such a prospect. In church pulpits, in high school auditoriums, and in the editorial columns of newspapers, rock was attacked as a source of juvenile delinquency, often in highly charged racial language. "Rock and roll inflames and excites youth like the jungle tom-toms readying warriors for battle," Boston priest John P. Carroll told the Teachers' Institute of the Archdiocese of Boston. A poster urged parents to "Help Save the Youth of America" by boycotting radio stations that played "negro records." Disc jockey Alan Freed (who left Cleveland in 1954 for a high-profile job in New York) was labeled a "nigger lover" who played "jungle music" on the radio, and his own television show was canceled after he hosted a show in which black singer Frankie Lymon danced with a white woman. Freed was later blackballed by the industry after confessing that he had accepted bribes to play records (part of a "payola" witchhunt in the late 1950s and early 1960s). While his manipulation of the airwaves for personal gain was hardly laudable, many observers felt the intensity with which he was pursued, and the calumny that was heaped on him, was the result of his identification with African-American music.[53]

The most powerful challenges to rock & roll came not from moralists, however, but from the record industry itself. In their never-ending quest to make an easily digestible product, executives, managers, and promoters were constantly pushing performers with highly attenuated connections to rock's sources—often at the expense of those who *were* connected to those sources. A classic case in point was the Penguins, a Los Angeles r&b act who were masters of the proto-rock vocal form called "doo-wop" (a style resurrected recently by the black pop group Boyz II Men). Their 1954 hits "Sh-Boom" and "Earth Angel" were recorded—"covered," to use the industry term—by a white group, the Crew Cuts, who remain identified with the songs. Today, white versions of early rock hits, like the Little Richard and Pat Boone versions of "Tutti Frutti," are laughable for their utter evisceration of the black versions.

The consequences of these maneuvers were not so laughable, however. Indeed, many popular music historians and critics consider the late 1950s and early 1960s a relative low point in rock's fortunes. The growing number of mediocre white acts (many promoted by disc jockey and TV dance-show host Dick Clark, a starched version of Freed) was part of the problem. So was the series of misfortunes that afflicted rock's brightest stars. Presley was drafted into the army between 1958 and 1960, and while he went on to make a number of distinguished records in the years that followed, he never again recaptured the intensity of his earlier work. Chuck Berry spent two years in prison in the early 1960s for having sex with a fourteen-year-old Apache Indian prostitute. Jerry Lee Lewis was considered a public disgrace after 1958 for marrying his thirteen-year-old cousin. And the exceptionally promising Texas rockabilly singer Buddy Holly was killed in a plane crash in 1959, cutting short a career that had already been marked by a string of hits (including "Peggy Sue," "That'll Be the Day," and "Rave On") and a number of innovative musical practices (producing his own records, using a widely emulated four-piece lineup of two guitars, bass, and drums, and so on). Los Angeles Latino singer Richie Valens was killed in the same plane crash; he had generated great excitement with his 1957 recording of "La Bamba," a traditional Mexican standard. A number of distinguished artists continued to make fine music, among them Ray Charles, the r&b vocal group The Drifters, and a series of "girl groups" produced by the brilliant Phil Spector. Nevertheless, some momentum had clearly been lost.

But in one of what would become a series of revitalizations, rock & roll then received a shot in the arm, this time in the form of a group of English performers who called themselves the Beatles. Hailing from the old industrial city of Liverpool, these four young men of working-class backgrounds began their careers in what was then viewed as a pop music backwater. Influenced by Presley, Holly, Little Richard, and others, their attempts to emulate U.S. music led to an Anglo-American synthesis that was arresting both in its novelty and its familiarity. Although their first U.S. releases (in 1963) received little notice, a widely publicized tour in 1964 ignited "Beatlemania"—mass adolescent hysteria on the order of Sinatra or Presley. The Beatles were at the vanguard of what came to be known as the "British invasion," which included the Rolling Stones, Eric Clapton, and the Who, all of whom became important later in the 1960s and established a pattern of English adaptation of black music for white American audiences.

However fresh and exciting songs like "I Wanna Hold Your Hand" or "She Loves You" (both 1964) may have been, the Beatles would have quickly faded in popular memory had they not demonstrated an astonishing ability to expand their artistic parameters. Sometimes this versatility took the form of growing thematic sophistication, as in the case of John Lennon's uncommonly honest depiction of vulnerability in "Help!" (1965) or Paul McCartney's vivid representations of personal isolation in "Yesterday" (1965) and "Eleanor Rigby" (1966). Beginning in 1965, the group also showed an increasing willingness to experiment musically, drawing on Eastern influences, studio technology, and even improvised instruments, innovations that may have been fostered by the use of hallucinogenic drugs. In writing and performing their own material, and in placing more emphasis on carefully wrought recordings than live performances, the Beatles made the 33 rpm record the primary rock format. *Rubber Soul* (1965), *Revolver* (1966), and especially *Sgt. Pepper's Lonely Hearts Club Band* (1967), a key document in the rock subculture of "psychedelia," demonstrated rock's potential as a form of artistic expression.

The Beatles were not alone in this pursuit. Indeed, a key influence (and a major admirer) was folk singer Bob Dylan. A Minnesotan migrant to New York City, Dylan was a self-conscious inheritor of the radical protest tradition embodied by Woody Guthrie. Ironically, by the early 1960s, this music—which covered a political spectrum that ran from the Kingston Trio to Joan Baez to Pete Seeger—had become a largely urban, middle-class phenomenon, and to some degree an implicit rebuke of rock. Between 1961 and 1965, this was Dylan's constituency, much of it white college students who welded their brand of intellectual politics with emotionally charged music.

In the mid-1960s, however, Dylan underwent an abrupt change of direction, one vividly documented on his albums *Highway 61 Revisited* (1965) and *Blonde on Blonde* (1966). If Elvis Presley integrated blues and country in the 1950s, Dylan integrated rock and folk in the 1960s (at least after his controversial appearance at the Newport Folk Festival of 1965). In drawing new attention to political polemic and verbal wordplay, Dylan paved the way for a generation of performers, including the Beatles (who in a sense combined Presley and Dylan into one potent package), Simon and Garfunkel, Jefferson Airplane, and many, many others. For these people, rock was a vehicle—or at the very least the soundtrack—for the "counterculture," a cultural revolution that wanted to end racial strife, imperialist wars, and the conservative lifestyle choices of the previous generation.

Meanwhile, African-American music was attaining new heights of excitement and power. Before and during the years the Beatles, the Rolling Stones, and Dylan were in their heyday, a series of black performers extended their own rich heritage. Many of these people came out of church singing and infused their blues-based songs with gospel-inspired urgency. Perhaps the most lastingly influential was James Brown, the so-called "Godfather of Soul." Emerging from rural Georgia with his group the Famous Flames, Brown developed a style that featured his rough, powerful voice, brass sections that played terse, staccato phrases, and an incantatory use of repetition that thrilled live audiences. From his first 1956 single "Please, Please, Please" to his 1986 hit "Living in America" and beyond, Brown has been cited again and again by critics, fellow artists, and fans as an essential force in the articulation of r&b, soul, disco, and rap.

Another giant of modern black music was Sam Cooke. The son of a Baptist minister, Cooke sang sacred and secular music—hits like "You Send Me" (1957), "Twistin' the Night Away" (1962), and his gorgeous "A Change Is Gonna Come" (1964)—in a smooth voice and urbane style that moved millions of listeners. His premature death at the hands of an angry lover in 1964 cut short his career at its height. Cooke was also an important figure in black musical history because he owned his own record label (Sar/Derby), as well as a publishing company and a management firm. As such, he was a pioneer among African-Americans seeking to successfully play the white capitalist game.

The most pivotal figure in this regard was Berry Gordy, founder of Motown Records. A Detroit songwriter and entrepreneur, Gordy founded the label in 1959 and proceeded to forge an immensely successful musical organization. In some ways it resembled an automobile production line; Gordy assembled a crack studio band, an efficient stable of songwriters (most notably the team of Lamont Dozier, Eddie Holland, and Dozier's brother

Brian), and a roster of stars who churned out dozens of hits. Many of these artists—The Temptations, Diana Ross and the Supremes, Smokey Robinson and the Miracles, Martha and the Vandellas, Marvin Gaye, Stevie Wonder, and others—remain popular today.

Although Motown was very clearly rooted in black traditions, Gordy consciously sought a white audience and cultivated it by sending his acts to charm school, booking them in "class" venues, and avoiding racial controversy. In time, this approach came to seem dated, and Berry's authoritarian style provoked resentment from his artists, but at first Motown was ideally suited to the optimism of the mid-1960s, when Martin Luther King was winning his greatest victories, the walls of segregation seemed to be collapsing, and the passage of the Voting Rights Act (1965) was beginning to transform Southern politics. Motown's lasting glow may reflect its identification with that moment.

Yet even as Gordy's performers were beginning to succeed on what might be called white terms, others were beginning to do so on more avowedly black ones, with soul music. Motown was an urban, Northern music for the upwardly mobile; soul was rural, Southern, and more closely aligned with black folk. Its foundations had already been laid by Ray Charles, Sam Cooke, and James Brown in the 1950s and early 1960s, but the term "soul" generally refers to a group of singers and songs that were in the popular musical spotlight from the mid- to late 1960s. Many of these artists recorded for the Atlantic Records subsidiary Stax, and many were backed by Booker T and the MGs, an interracial Stax house band that became legendary among soul aficionados. As with Motown, some soul records from this era have become classics, among them Percy Sledge's "When a Man Loves a Woman" (1966), Wilson Pickett's "The Midnight Hour" (1967), and Otis Redding's "(Sittin' on) The Dock of the Bay" (1967). Besides his numerous other hits, Redding, who died in a plane crash in 1967, is notable for having written "Respect" (1965), a song that would become a defining hit for Aretha Franklin, the "Queen of Soul." Franklin, for her part, has proved to be the most durable of the major soul artists of the 1960s, commanding a large following into the 1990s.

By the late 1960s, the British invasion, Dylanesque folk-rock, Motown, soul, and other styles had converged into a heady countercultural mix. The meeting place for this sprawling musical world was radio, especially FM radio, which for a brief moment in the late 1960s could contain the multitudes that comprised rock & roll, a term that was already losing its precision. More concretely, this diverse culture was represented at major rock festivals, notably Monterey (1967), Woodstock (1969), and Altamont (also 1969). In their own way, rock festivals can be seen as microcosms of the 1960s counterculture, one loosely united in its support of civil rights and opposition to the Vietnam war.

But we must emphasize the word "loosely." Actually, by the end of the 1960s the centrifugal tendencies within this coalition were increasingly apparent. While the "Movement," as it was called, was overwhelmingly young, by no means were all young people a part of it. To some extent, the counterculture was marked by class fissures: working-class youth who could not get draft deferments went off to war while middle-class kids with money and time to burn on drugs listened to psychedelic music and attended protests. Furthermore, while some members of the counterculture were clearly committed to political activity, others saw it as primarily a revolution in lifestyle. Finally, the counterculture had its own race problem. The original energy had come from the Civil Rights movement, but by the 1970s Vietnam, the women's movement, and the struggles of gays and lesbians, Chicanos and Chicanas, were increasingly competing for attention. Many whites became less interested in racial issues. Woodstock was telling in this regard: relatively few of the acts that performed there were black (Jimi Hendrix being a notable exception), and only Sly and the Family Stone was interracial. Such fragmentation was augmented by a series of shocks in 1968: the assassinations of Martin Luther King, Jr., and Robert Kennedy, rioting at the Democratic National Convention in Chicago, and the election of Republican Richard Nixon later that year. By December 1969, when the Altamont festival ended in the death of four people after the Stones and the Grateful Dead hired the Hells Angels as security guards, it seemed that the 1960s were truly over.

A closer look:
THE INTEGRATED SOUND OF LOS LOBOS

For much of the last two hundred years, the issue of race has largely been a black-and-white affair. Certainly, Native and Asian Americans have been common *subjects* of such popular cultural forms as Westerns and minstrel shows, but only with the recent

THE BAND TODAY

widespread recognition that the United States is a multicultural society have these minorities received attention on their own terms (e.g., in the work of popular writers like Louise Erdrich and Amy Tan). At the end of the twentieth century, one of the finest examples of a truly multicultural sensibility, one that integrates a variety of racial and ethnic traditions, is the Chicano rock band Los Lobos.

There is a decades-old Mexican-American rock & roll tradition. Big band leader and record producer Johnny Otis, a Greek-American who identified intensely with black culture, performed for large Chicano audiences in the 1950s and recorded some songs by Li'l Julio Herrera, a r&b singer, for his own record label. (Herrera was actually Ron Gregory, a Hungarian Jew who decided to become Chicano much in the way Otis decided he was black.) More directly, the music of Richie Valens (the teenage rocker whose 1959 recording of the classic Latino folk dance "La Bamba" became an enduring classic) and Carlos Santana (the immensely gifted Mexican-born guitarist whose fusion of black and Latino musical styles created a sensation at Woodstock) laid musical foundations for others to follow. In recent years, pop-rock singer Linda Ronstadt, the daughter of a Mexican immigrant, has affirmed her heritage on albums like *Canciones de Mi Padre* (1988).

The founding members of Los Lobos—David Hildago, Louie Perez, César Rosas, and Conrad Lozano—were all born in the

Chicano barrio of East Los Angeles in the early 1950s. The band they formed in the early 1970s featured cover versions of songs by the Beatles and others. In mid-1970s, the group, now named Los Lobos, began exploring Mexican folk songs, especially regional Mexican styles. They built a local following in Los Angeles, and made their first album, *Just Another Band from East L.A.* (1978), on a small record label. Until this point, most of Los Lobos's material was performed on acoustic instruments, but when they began to add electric guitars and blues arrangements, they attracted more attention (including that of saxophonist/keyboardist Steve Berlin, who joined the group), and they were signed onto the Warner Brothers subsidiary Slash Records in 1983. Their first record, ... *And a Time to Dance,* won the record industry's coveted Grammy Award for the best Mexican/American performance of 1983. Their next, *How Will the Wolf Survive?* (1984), won major critical and musical acclaim, and the group has been prominent on the rock scene ever since.

At the heart of Los Lobos's expansive musical vision is a series of interlocking dualities. The most obvious is the relationship between their Mexican and American heritage, which plays itself out in language (Spanish and English), instrumentation, and theme. Another is a dialogue between blues-based African-American music and Latino folk songs—the band plays both with seemingly effortless mastery, imbuing each with the best qualities of the other.

A third duality is a frank embrace of both realism and mysticism. At times, lead vocalist Hildago seems to sing with almost documentary clarity. On songs like "One Time, Night" (from the 1987 album *By the Light of the Moon),* he charts the destruction of ordinary lives with stark simplicity, lamenting our inability to grasp grief even as he embodies it. On songs like "Saint Behind the Glass" (from the band's 1992 album *Kiko),* singer Perez draws on surreal imagery associated with charismatic Catholicism.

Finally, Los Lobos suggest the rich connection between past and present. The most vivid example is their delightful 1987 rendition of "La Bamba," the No. 1 single from the movie and soundtrack of the same name about the life of Richie Valens. With its Norteña-flavored instrumentation and acoustic *guitarrón* coda, the band paid homage to both Valens and the well from which he drew in a nuanced recording of a song that sounds as fresh today as it must have in 1959 (or even 1859). All told, "La Bamba" sums up the Los Lobos aesthetic: recognizing and affirming one's heritage even while synthesizing varied strands to create something new.

In this regard, Los Lobos are not multicultural, they are *inter*cultural, and as such are truly representative Americans. The vitality of popular culture in the twenty-first century will depend on artists like them.

―――――――

The cultural diffusion and fragmentation of rock—a diffusion and fragmentation that reflected a wider culture engulfed by war, civil unrest, and adolescent self-absorption—created a profound sense of disorientation across U.S. society. One of the first people to sense this was Bob Dylan. He suffered a near-fatal motorcycle accident in 1966 and was off the scene for two years. When he returned, the unpredictable demigod did the unthinkable: he went country. *John Wesley Harding,* recorded in Nashville, was released in 1968 and was followed by *Nashville Skyline* in 1969. The acerbic, byzantine, raspy folk-rocker was now writing and singing unironic songs celebrating the joys of rural living. By the early 1970s, Dylan had spawned a generation of singer-songwriters from more privileged backgrounds—James Taylor, Jackson Browne, Joni Mitchell—who emphasized acoustic sounds and personal themes.

Meanwhile, the powerful cultural energy of figures like Presley, Hendrix, and the Beatles passed from the scene. Motown enjoyed a final flowering in the late 1960s and early 1970s, when acts like Marvin Gaye and Stevie Wonder responded to the tumult of the decade with more aggressively black sounds and/or themes. Gordy also scored a coup in signing the Jackson Five, featuring the talented eleven-year-old Michael. But Gordy's overbearing style led many of his acts to leave the label by the mid-1970s, and his migration to Los Angeles in 1971 marked the end of an era.

Times had changed. Richard Nixon was in the White House: he made it there with the help of a "Southern strategy" that would allow him to break the post-Reconstruction Democratic hold on the region completely by 1972. Nixon's compilation of an "enemies list," along with the kind of harassment that was typified by the immigration problems of John Lennon, shows how seriously he took the cultural dimension of the political left as he headed into the quagmire of Watergate.[54] But that power had clearly ebbed. Record companies like Motown and Stax, which had crossed musical lines and built multiracial audiences, lost their cachet. Radio resegregated as mainstream rock became increasingly white, while black music was confined to "urban" programming formats. In the eyes of many observers then and since, the mid-1970s were another dark age of popular music.

There were two major developments in the decade, however, that brought new vitality into the world of popular music. The first was disco. Building—as had so much black music since the 1950s—on the music of James Brown, late Motown, and especially the early 1970s material of Sly and the Family Stone, disco was a highly urban, technology-driven form that exploited repetition and elaborate nightclub settings to achieve its effects. Among its key practitioners were Donna Summer and the British pop trio the Bee Gees, who helped disco gain mass acceptance with their wildly popular soundtrack for the 1977 film *Saturday Night Fever.* Disco was an escapist form that repudiated social or political themes in favor of pure hedonism, spawning a subculture that included elaborate costumes, frenetic dancing, drug-taking, and sexual expressiveness. Gay men were especially prominent in popularizing the genre, which may be one reason—along with the prominence of blacks and women—that it generated a fierce backlash, most appallingly evident in a 1979 baseball-stadium record burning hosted by a Chicago rock station. Disco disappeared as a discrete musical genre in the early 1980s, but its influence has extended into the decades since, shaping the work of Michael Jackson, Madonna, and many others.[55]

The other major pop music explosion of the 1970s was punk rock. Like disco, punk was a response to the frustration and enervation that followed the 1960s. But instead of escapism, the punk response was anger. Punk originated in England, where the severity of that nation's economic situation contributed to widespread youth unemployment and the rise of fascist gangs called "skinheads." At the same time, the corporatization of rock, and its increasing pretentiousness (typified by "art rock" bands like Yes and Emerson, Lake, and Palmer, which fancied themselves as pseudo-classical virtuosos), made it irrelevant and even alienating to many British youth. This was the context for the formation of the first major punk band, the Sex Pistols, 1975. In such a climate, *not* being able to play an instrument competently became an artistic statement, a willful refusal to buy into the arid musical professionalism promoted by the record labels. And by seeking to erase what had become an enormous gap between performer and audience, the Sex Pistols and their heirs offered listeners the closest thing many had ever heard to a true musical democracy. So when Sex Pistols lead singer Johnny Rotten told the listeners of "God Save the Queen," the band's venomous response to Queen Elizabeth II's silver jubilee in 1977, that they had "no future," he was offering them a truth that was invigorating in a manner not unlike the way the blues had proved cathartic for generations of African Americans.[56]

Nevertheless, a musical philosophy built on willful ignorance and frustration, however potent, is inherently limited (if not dangerous), and by January 1978, the Sex Pistols had imploded. Their mantle was passed on to the Clash, who sought to focus youth anger in a coherent form of political protest that borrowed from third world ideology and musical styles such as reggae (their 1979 album *London Calling* is considered one of the great rock albums of all time). Meanwhile, a punk scene sprang up in downtown New York. It was a varied movement that ranged from the mindless mayhem of the Ramones (gleefully expressed in their 1978 hit "I Wanna Be Sedated") to the inventive work of the Talking Heads, whose increasingly complex rhythms anticipated a new fascination with Caribbean, African, and other "World Music" currents in the 1980s and 1990s. By the early 1980s, punk had diffused into a catch-all category called "New Wave," which included performers who had little direct link to the Sex Pistols or the Clash but who sought alternatives to mainstream fare.

During these years, the recording and radio industries were largely preoccupied with such white male subgenres as "Southern rock" (a country-rock hybrid) and heavy metal, both of which could be interesting but were also often insular and even ignorant about their (largely black) musical sources. Mainstream rock was also invigorated by reggae, whose greatest practitioner, Bob Marley, attained global influence before and after his untimely death in 1981.

Technological forces played a significant role in consolidating rock's position. The birth of the Music Television network (MTV) in 1981 brought together two previously separate media, boosting both. (This will be discussed in greater detail in Chapter 6.) Compact discs, or "CDs," which arrived in the early 1980s, had displaced vinyl as a musical format by the end of the decade (cassette tapes, which had replaced the 8-track developed in the 1960s, survived as a kind of junior, "paperback" format). Although they had their detractors, most music listeners agreed that CDs offered higher quality sound and greater flexibility—longer albums, the ability for the listener to program the order of the songs, and, best of all, the reintroduction of old favorites in a new format. Such reissues were a windfall for the record companies, which racked up unprecedented profits from the cheaper-to-produce CDs, which sold at higher prices.

By this point, rock & roll had been fully absorbed into U.S. life. This was both its strength and its weakness. On the plus side, seasoned performers like Bruce Springsteen, the Rolling Stones, and Tina Turner showed that it was possible to make compelling music in what had always been considered a youthful, even juvenile, genre. In 1965, the proto-punk band the Who had declared their wish to die before they got old (in "My Generation"), but now artists (including the Who themselves) showed that aging, parenthood, and even death could be explored within the form.

Tina Turner is relevant here because she demonstrated the new power of women in rock, which took a variety of forms, ranging from the frankly feminine-but-feminist style of Cyndi Lauper to the more aggressive, punk-influenced style of Chrissie Hynde, lead singer for the Anglo-American band the Pretenders. Women wrote, performed, and produced their own music, winning a degree of control over their art that illustrated feminism's impact on what had previously been an predominantly male form. Indeed, by the end of the decade, Janet Jackson (Michael's sister) and Madonna had made the very issue of control—sexual as well as economic—a centerpiece of their work. Though this troubled some observers, their music dramatized important social issues in revealing ways.

Moreover, a number of artists also crossed color lines. Michael Jackson led the way with his 1983 album *Thriller*, whose No. 1 hit single "Beat It" featured a solo by heavy-metal virtuoso Eddie Van Halen. Prince, an intensely erotic singer and songwriter, demonstrated his mastery of white as well as black idioms on albums like *Purple Rain* (1984) and *Sign O' the Times* (1987), while the black heavy-metal band Living Color became the first major black inhabitants of the genre since Jimi Hendrix had virtually invented it a generation earlier. George Michael, a white British pop singer, topped the *Billboard* (a music-industry trade paper) "black" chart with his 1987 album *Faith*. And Tracy Chapman infused the largely white, middle-class audience for acoustic folk-rock with her distinctively black and feminist point of view in songs like "Fast Car" (1988). Nor was all this musical dialogue simply black-and-white. The Miami Sound Machine and the East Los Angeles Chicano band Los Lobos put varieties of Latino music into circulation (see Chapter 6). As Latinos become increasingly prominent nationally in the next few decades, we can expect their influence on popular culture to grow dramatically.

By the late 1980s, however, rock & roll was becoming a victim of its own success. The world of rock was so sprawling that it was difficult to use the term with any precision, but insofar as it had any meaning at all, it had a white male connotation that failed to reflect the increasing diversity of the musical mainstream. Only by stretching the definition to virtual meaninglessness could performers like Madonna or Gloria Estefan be considered rock. More important, the 1980s witnessed the rise of a new musical genre—rap. Like many genres before it, rap was influenced and partially absorbed by rock, but it also retained a distinct identity that ultimately challenged rock's commercial and ideological dominance.

Rap was a hybrid, this time of Jamaican and black New York cultures. From the Caribbean, rap took a reggae-inflected vocal tradition of "toasting," or verbal wordplay accompanied by music. From the New York borough of the Bronx, rap took a street-smart attitude and a series of techniques practiced by inner-city disc jockeys: scratching records, reversing the direction of turntables, and sampling snatches of well-known songs in the middle of others. By reducing the music to its most bare essentials—spoken (as opposed to sung) rhyming vocals, loud, mechanical percussion, and easily produced sound effects—rap surpassed even punk in its accessibility and communal character, and at the same time vividly dramatized the inherent musicality of vernacular language.

Rap lies at the center of the musical subculture of hip hop, which includes colorful styles of dance and clothing as well as music. It is yet one more example of the black genius for reinventing new cultural forms in the wake of white co-optation, of which rock & roll was only the most recent example. But it is also part of a long tradition that draws on varied strands of black music, ranging from blues to disco.

The first major rap record was the Sugar Hill Gang's playful "Rapper's Delight" (1979). In its wake, a number of other rappers sprang up, among them Grandmaster Flash and the Furious Five, whose highly influential "The Message" (1982) offered a stark vision of urban life. Between them, the two records suggested two lasting tendencies in rap: celebration of hip hop culture and sober social commentary. The latter was typified by Public Enemy, a tough-minded, Afrocentric group whose work in the late 1980s and early 1990s won the group a dedicated following among many blacks, and enemies among many whites, especially Jews appalled by the anti-semitic remarks of group member Professor Griff. By the mid-1990s, the artistic locus of rap migrated to the West coast, where a series of rappers, including N.W.A. (Niggas with Attitude) and Snoop Doggy Dogg became associated with "gangsta rap," a hip hop derivative glamorizing ghetto life. Songs like N.W.A.'s "Fuck tha Police" (1989) and Ice-T's "Cop Killer" (1992) provoked severe criticism among whites and even some blacks, who in the process of expressing concerns about the sex and violence of this music tended to overlook the social conditions that provoked it—or tarred all rap as socially deviant or dangerous.

Yet by the 1990s, rap was itself a diverse musical world that contained within it growing riches and sophistication. Female rappers like Salt 'N' Pepa and Queen Latifah offered powerful alternatives to the hyper-masculinity of the worst gangsta rap. The "New Jack Swing" sound pioneered by producer Teddy Riley offered a dense, more rhythmic variation on the form for artists Bobby Brown and even Michael Jackson. And rap was being more explicitly connected to its African-American antecedents. One of the more notable examples of this was jazz artist and record producer Quincy Jones's 1989 album *Back on the Block,* which explicitly connected rap with traditions ranging from bop to African music. Perhaps even more significant was the work of Arrested Development, whose debut album *3 Years, 5 Months and 2 Days in the Life of ...* (1992) forged dazzling musical and thematic links between African-Americans—male and female, old and young, rural and urban, and, above all, past and present. The expansive vision and talent of this group suggested, as Jesse Jackson said on the title track of *Back on the Block,* "Rap is here to stay."

So is country music. It is tempting to say that country underwent a renaissance in the late 1980s and early 1990s, but this would create the misleading impression that it had declined in popularity. From the 1950s through the 1970s, country had often maintained—and in some cases exceeded—the popularity of rock, especially in the South and Midwest. Country singers and songwriters like George Jones, Willie Nelson, and Merle Haggard each captured important audiences while achieving broad national prominence. Even some figures from rock, such as Jerry Lee Lewis and Elvis Presley, had had one foot planted firmly in Nashville. In the popular imagination, country has been identified with cultural and political conservatism—Haggard's 1969 hit single "Okie from Muskogee" was an explicit attack on the counterculture—but the genre can also vividly voice the concerns of the white working class, as Haggard's own portrayal of the ravages of unemployment, "If We Make It Through December," attests.

One of the more striking developments in country music since the 1960s was the growing presence and power of women. Of course, female performers had been important since the Carter Family, but the success of Kitty Wells in the 1950s marked the advent of the female country star. Wells was best known for her 1952 smash "It Wasn't God Who Made Honky-Tonk Angels," a proto-feminist reply to Hank Thompson's "The Wild Side of Life," which had been a hit a few months before. Another major figure in country in the 1950s and 1960s was Patsy Cline, whose death in a 1963 plane crash ended a promising career (one of her biggest hits, "Crazy," was written by Willie Nelson). But the first true feminist in country music was Loretta Lynn, whose compelling rise from poverty was dramatized in the 1980 film *Coal Miner's Daughter.* In hits like "Don't Come Home Drinkin' (With Lovin' on Your Mind)" (1966), "One's on the Way" (1971), and especially "The Pill" (1972), Lynn created a gritty persona that was an inspiration to millions of women.

The broad musical appeal of these country figures led their records to "cross over" to the pop charts, where they jostled against rock and r&b records. Meanwhile, a series of performers with relatively little musical or cultural connection to country—Conway Twitty, Barbara Mandrell, Kenny Rogers, and even Australian Olivia Newton-John—crossed over from pop to country, and then back again. In the wake of the success of the 1980 film *Urban Cowboy,* country became a fad, and while the rage for cowboy boots faded, the rage for cowboy music did not, as evidenced by the establishment of The Nashville Network (TNN) in 1984, which sought to be for country music what MTV was for rock.

In response to such currents, a new generation of performers went back to basics. Beginning in the mid-1980s, singers and songwriters like Dwight Yoakum and Steve Earle acknowledged country's ties to rock, producing records that affirmed country's working-class musical and thematic traditions. At the same time, a number of people who felt a profound admiration for country music but did not fit into the classic Nashville mold—Mary-Chapin Carpenter, Johnny Cash's daughter Roseanne, k.d. lang, and Lyle Lovett—helped redefine its parameters and attracted audiences that had previously seen country as boring or even reactionary. Although some of these people, among them lang and Cash, ultimately found Nashville too confining, they nevertheless made a lasting contribution to country music.

By the 1990s, then, musical forms like rap and country had become worlds unto themselves. Fans of k.d. lang seldom like Tammy Wynette; fans of Queen Latifah are often downright hostile to Dr. Dre. And it is increasingly unlikely that listeners to rap acts know, much less care for, any country music at all (and vice-versa). In one sense, this may be taken as evidence of a vast cultural democracy that gives people a wide number of cultural choices. In another, it suggests that the particular cultural fragmentation and even segregation that began at the end of the 1960s is intensifying. Certainly, there are forums like MTV that preserve a musical center—but it does so as one of dozens, if not hundreds, of television programming choices. Meanwhile, at the very moment these centrifugal forces are becoming increasingly discernible, an equally discernible—and alarming—centralization of popular culture industries and capital is becoming ever more clear, as we shall see in the next chapter. However ultimately salutary or dangerous, these are the circumstances under which popular culture enters the twenty-first century.

6

Electronic Frontiers:
Popular Culture
in Transition

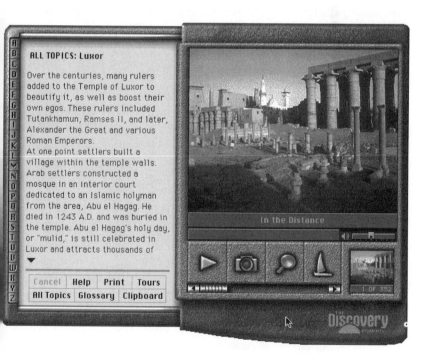

ALL TOPICS: Luxor

Over the centuries, many rulers
added to the Temple of Luxor to
beautify it, as well as boost their
own egos. These rulers included
Tutankhamun, Ramses II, and later,
Alexander the Great and various
Roman Emperors.
At one point settlers built a
village within the temple walls.
Arab settlers constructed a
mosque in an interior court
dedicated to an Islamic holyman
from the area, Abu el Hagag. He
died in 1243 A.D. and was buried in
the temple. Abu el Hagag's holy day,
or "mulid," is still celebrated in
Luxor and attracts thousands of
▼

| Cancel | Help | Print | Tours |
| All Topics | Glossary | Clipboard |

In the Distance

1 OF 352

Discovery

THE UNPREDICTABLE RESULTS of the rise of film, radio, and television in the twentieth century make for a healthy skepticism about predicting the contours of popular culture in the twenty-first. Moreover, given the sweep of human history, popular culture has not really been around that long, and could, given a dramatic change in Western economic organization comparable to that of industrialization in the eighteenth century, quickly become unrecognizable. History is at best an uncertain guide.

And yet it may be the best we have. If we assume that the world will not blow up tomorrow, it is possible to discern a series of technological and cultural developments in the last two decades that have already wrought enormous changes to everyday life and promise to play a decisive role in days to come. These include cable television, video, satellite technology, and fiber optics. While it remains unclear how such media will affect the ways popular culture is made and used in the next century, they will all probably play some role. This chapter will therefore chronicle the emergence of some of these technologies, and also suggest the ramifications of their use, ranging from an enlarged cultural democracy to unprecedented levels of social control.

Thus far, technology and big business play a major role in this story. Twenty-first-century popular culture is still very much in its "hardware" stage. Not until the much-vaunted "information superhighway" is fully built will the software traveling it become more central; until then, older cultural forms will continue to shape our perceptions. To put it another way, although the means of *delivery* of popular culture is in the middle of an epochal change, its *content,* with some notable exceptions, has been little affected. To a great extent, innovation is proceeding from the top down, not from the bottom up. Judging from the history of other forms, however, the bottom will eventually have a greater presence. There is one sense in which it already does: if manual labor in the early twentieth century meant performing repetitive tasks on industrial machinery, manual labor at the end of the twentieth century means performing repetitive tasks (like data entry) at a keyboard. As computers continue to spread throughout society and computer literacy increases, it is reasonable to expect that unforeseen new avenues of expression will open up. In many ways, the Internet (to be discussed below) is a model for these. Although, like most potential instru-

---

Reverse page: A screen from the CD-ROM Nile: Passage to Egypt. *Users travel down the Nile and "click" to visit and learn about such sights as the temple of Ramses II, the Aswan Dam, and the Sphinx. The tour includes sound, hypertext links, and a Print option.*

ments of democracy, corporate elites see new media as a "problem" to be solved—by which they mean technologically and financially controlled—we can hope that, as in the past, flourishing marginal cultures will continue to spring up, reinvigorating and challenging an increasingly micro-managed mainstream. Underground publications, called "zines", produced with desktop publishing programs, are one example of this process at work.

Whatever the future may hold, television is currently at the core of the new popular cultural forms. There are a number of reasons for this. One is that while some industries, like film and music, have long interfaced with it, their interactions having become sharply more intensive since the 1980s. Another is that, if all goes as planned, television itself will experience a major transformation with the introduction of High Definition Television (HDTV) in the next decade. At the same time, television as we have known it will become obsolete, superseded by computers or a TV/computer hybrid whose hallmark will be interactivity—i.e., the ability to conduct two-way communication (as on the telephone) instead of the one way programmer-to-viewer model of television.

As is so often the case, the radical changes television is undergoing have their roots in the origins of the form itself.

Fluid State:
The Transformation of Television

Early televisions were complicated and fragile devices that depended on liquid vacuum tubes wired by hand. These were superseded by mechanically installed computer circuits ("chips"), which had become universal by 1990. But if television sets are now "solid state," the medium is in a state of unprecedented flux.

In the beginning, there was broadcasting. Like radio, television programming was electronically encoded and transmitted via waves sent through the air (or "ether," as it was called), waves whose contents were picked up by millions of TV antennas and reconverted into images. The networks literally and figuratively dominated this finite airwave spectrum.

But during the charmed decades of the 1940s, 1950s, and 1960s, broadcasting's reach was not limitless. People living in remote rural areas often had a difficult time receiving their favorite shows. To serve such viewers (and to serve retailers trying to sell more television sets), a series of

Community Access Television (CATV) systems was established in 1948. Viewers paid a subscription fee of about $5 a month to have their homes connected, usually via cables strung on telephone poles, to large, centrally located antennas. What we had here, in other words, was the origin of cable TV.

Community Access Television spread rapidly. The 1948-1952 FCC freeze on the assignment of wavelengths for new television stations helped, as impatient viewers subscribed to CATV in order to receive the nearest broadcasts. By 1965 there were over 1,500 CATV systems, each serving about a thousand homes. Many of these belonged to the National Community Television Association, later named the National Cable Television Association.

The networks reacted to this development with alarm. They regarded cable operators as pirates who stole their programs and sold them to viewers without permission. But in 1964, the FCC ruled that it had no jurisdiction over cable television, since such systems did no actual broadcasting—they simply received and relayed the broadcasts of others. In 1966, the commission reversed itself, however, imposing a ban on new cable operations that lasted for six years.

By the time the ban was lifted, cable operators had more ambitious goals, especially once satellite technology permitted the rise of powerful superstations that could cover a much larger geographic area. Now some of them did become interested in broadcasting, although the idea that cable companies could generate their own programming dated back to the mid-1960s, when the New York Giants baseball team moved to California and one cable operator sold broadcasts of the games (since this service was wholly contained within the state of California, it was outside the FCC's federal jurisdiction). In 1977, New York's Madison Square Garden also started a cable network to broadcast its events, this one supported by advertising. The real source of cable's potential, however, lay in the ability to package new channels and offer subscribers an unprecedented choice.

By the early 1980s, a series of new networks had sprung up to exploit the vast television market: Home Box Office (HBO), which broadcasts recent Hollywood movies; the Entertainment and Sports Programming Network (ESPN), which specializes in professional sports; the Weather Channel, which provides round-the-clock local, national, and international forecasts; and so on. As is so often the case, these new channels relied on the tried and true—Nickelodeon, for example, is devoted to children's shows and reruns of old situation comedies—but they also demonstrated the potential for the evolution of new television formats. The most obvious example is MTV and its spinoffs (see below).

The one important area of programming innovation was news. In 1980, entrepreneur Ted Turner established the Cable News Network (CNN) in Atlanta, a continuous news operation that quickly became an international force in journalism. (Turner went on to found the more general Turner Broadcasting System [TBS], singlehandedly turning Atlanta into a major broadcasting center.) CNN provided the first serious alternative to network news, and its ability to go live instantly helped check the increasingly prepackaged and managed quality of television journalism. Even more innovative was Cable Satellite Public Affairs Network (C-SPAN), which offered live unedited coverage of the U.S. Congress, as well as of political events around the world.[1] These two networks vastly increased the amount of information available to viewers at any given time, although they were not without their deceptions. Congressman Newt Gingrich, for example, made C-SPAN his own personal soapbox in 1984 until House Speaker Tip O'Neill ordered the cameras to show him lecturing to an empty hall, while network acquiescence to government censorship of footage from Iraq during the Persian Gulf War compromised what much of the world considered "objective" coverage of the event. Such episodes showed that more news was not necessarily better news.

But whatever its weaknesses, cable's expansion shook conventional network television to its foundations. In 1976, 90 percent of television viewers watched evening shows broadcast by ABC, CBS, or NBC. By the mid-1980s, this figure had dropped to 75 percent; by the early 1990s, it was down to about 65 percent, and sometimes even less.[2] Although there were some signs that this slide had stopped by the mid-1990s, it nevertheless represented a major change in the networks' position.

A relative drop in the number of viewers was only one of the networks' problems, however. Even though a cable network's reach was almost always narrower than that of the "big three," it could count on income from subscriptions, as well as the paid advertising on which the networks also depended. Even companies that did not rely heavily on advertising, like Home Box Office, were financially secure enough to go into movie and television production, financing first-run theater releases that then became featured cable attractions, as well as productions (like the highly acclaimed 1993 film *Barbarians at the Gate)* specifically designated for cable broadcast. Moreover, cable's demographics (or "demos," as they are called in the industry) often made it possible to target the viewers advertisers wanted. Cable networks were also cheaper to run: in 1986 NBC was spending $276 million on its news division, which had not made a profit in seven years, while CNN, which broadcast news twenty-four hours a day, spent only $100 million.[3] Cable could not take on ABC, CBS, or NBC in one fell swoop, but by the 1990s all three feared losing a war of attrition.

A closer look:
THE MIXED MEDIA OF MTV

CYNDI LAUPER IN AN EARLY "ON-AIR" PROMO

In the 1950s, the most important site for rock & roll was Memphis, home of Elvis Presley and the legendary stars of Sun Records. In the 1960s, it was Liverpool, England, the point of departure for the Beatles and the other bands of the "British invasion." In the 1970s, it was London, which spawned punk rock and the New Wave. In the 1980s, however, the most important site for rock music was a television studio in Queens, New York. It was there that Music Television (MTV) was born, one more instance of the powerful conversion of technological and cultural forces at the end of the twentieth century.

The concept of pairing popular music with television imagery dates back to the 1930s and 1940s, when cartoons were synchronized to accompany the songs of jazz performers like Cab Calloway and Louis Armstrong. In the 1960s a device called the Scopitone offered viewers something resembling today's music videos, but it never attained widespread popularity, probably because it featured European singers rather than the far more popular American performers. More directly, such Beatles films as *A Hard Day's Night* (1964) and long-running British television like *Top of the Pops,* which featured long segments of musical performance and arresting imagery, were the inspiration for what became MTV.

But MTV's immediate precursor was *Popclips,* a music/video show developed by Michael Nesmith, a former member of the Monkees (themselves the subject of a hit TV show in the 1960s). *Popclips* featured video clips of music and image, and was hosted by stand-up comedian Howie Mandel; it first appeared on the Warner-Amex Satellite Entertainment company's Nickelodeon network in 1980. Recognizing its potential, Warner Bros. then financed a channel devoted to music videos, twenty-four hours a day. This was a relatively low-risk proposition because the programming was to be provided free by the record companies, which considered the videos a form of advertising. Expectations were modest: even the channel's strongest proponents believed profits would be years away. When it made its debut on August 1, 1981, MTV had a mere 125 videos, 13 advertisers, and access to a relatively meager 2.1 million households. It was not even carried in New York or Los Angeles.

But it soon became clear that the new format had a number of assets: engaging video disc jockeys (or "veejays," as they came to be known), hip sets, and astounding graphics that ran between the videos and commercials. The first video shown was the Buggles' "Video Killed the Radio Star," an audacious statement that would prove in some ways prophetic. In 1982, the network introduced its famous slogan "I Want My MTV" by having a variety of rock stars repeat it day and night. By 1984, Warner had spun MTV into a separate company that was showing a profit and claiming over 24 million viewers. Radio had not been killed, but it had become a poor relation to the video colossus.

Among the first to benefit from MTV were foreign acts, such as Australia's Men at Work and England's Culture Club, which were familiar with video production from British television and thus had material on hand to add to MTV's library. The result was a 1980s version of the "British invasion," as new acts like Duran Duran and more established ones like David Bowie and Elton John quickly seized the musical spotlight.

African Americans were conspicuously absent. Programmers apparently believed that their mostly white middle-class adolescent audience only wanted to see white performers. Media critics claimed the network was racist; more profit-minded record company executives were angry at the lack of access for some of their most creative acts. When Michael Jackson's *Thriller* topped the charts in early 1983 without the benefit of video exposure, CBS records reportedly threatened to stop providing videos for *any* of its artists until MTV started to play Jackson's work. The network complied, and the shortsightedness of its former policy quickly became apparent as Jackson and other black acts brought new excitement—and huge new audiences—to the medium.

One reason was that superb dancers like Jackson (and Madonna, another MTV giant) were able to bring an exciting visual element to their musical performances. This has always been important in rock, from Elvis's hip thrusts through the Beatles' stylish haircuts. But MTV created a showcase for charismatic performers, one that was exploited to the fullest extent by transvestites like Boy George of Culture Club and by special-effects-minded artists like Peter Gabriel. The more dubious aspects of this development became apparent in 1990, when it was revealed that the Grammy Award-winning Milli Vanilli were nothing more than lip-synching imposters.

A more subtle but equally significant aspect of MTV's impact was the push it temporarily gave to singles. By the late 1970s, the 33 rpm album largely supplanted the 453 rpm single, and some of the most successful artists had never had hit singles. With MTV, singles enjoyed a renaissance, and album-oriented performers were able to produce a string of hits from the same album. Billy Joel's 1983 album *An Innocent Man* spawned six Top 40 hits; Bruce Springsteen's *Born in the U.S.A.* contained seven. Performers who were already familiar to radio listeners, like Lionel Richie and Michael Jackson, got an even bigger boost. Jackson's *Thriller* shattered all-time sales records and became the first album in pop music history to hold six top ten singles.

Meanwhile, the fabulous success of MTV spawned a wave of imitators on cable television, local UHF stations, and the major networks, which began producing television shows like *Night Tracks* and *Friday Night Videos.* But the greatest potential challenge came from media mogul Ted Turner, who started a rival network, VH-1, that offered more family-oriented videos. Its ratings were low, however, and Turner sold it to MTV, where it survives in a more adult-oriented version. Meanwhile, The Nashville Network, or TNN, was founded in 1984 to reach fans of country music.

One important reason MTV has been able to thrive amid such challenges is the pace of innovation that has characterized it. For example, when rap began to dominate popular music in the late 1980s, MTV achieved a high profile in hip-hop culture with *Yo! MTV Raps,* a show devoted to that genre. In recent years, the network has added news services and has played an influential role in registering young voters and interesting them in the presidential election of 1992 (both Bill Clinton and George Bush appeared on the network during the campaign).

On the most obvious level, MTV has become a way for new performers to reach audiences; as a result, it has developed unprecedented power in its ability to make or break careers. By the 1990s, the network's decision to show a video clip was a major break for a fledgling artist, and a clip shown every few hours ("on heavy rotation") provided the kind of exposure no radio station or advertiser could hope to match. In a highly segmented music market, MTV and sister network VH-1 are the nearest approximation of a musical center, where diverse styles can influence a variety of performers and range of audiences alike.

But perhaps the most striking aspect of the MTV phenomenon is its impact on other cultural forms. What might be called the "MTV aesthetic"—bright images, rapid-fire editing, repeated motifs, and dream-like imagery, among other techniques—have been widely appropriated. Hit television shows like *Miami Vice* and *Pee Wee's Playhouse,* for instance, owed a great deal to MTV, as does much television and magazine advertising.

Not all observers see such developments as positive. Some critics believe that the MTV aesthetic is superficial, short-circuiting sustained analysis and accelerating the moved away from traditional forms of literacy, which are necessary for a truly educated citizenry. Others argue that MTV (and its related forms) represent a new visual order that will soon become the norm, much in the way the written word supplanted oral traditions.

In any case, MTV's audience has fallen off since the heady days of the early 1980s. The novelty wore off, and its audience is estimated at barely half of what it was at its peak. Yet it continues to be profitable because the (now global) youth market it targets is attractive to advertisers. If the day comes when viewers can program their own videos over telephone and/or cable systems, MTV may become obsolete—or dramatically changed in structure. But whether or not this happens, it will probably go down in history as the harbinger of the cultural order of the twenty-first century.

Cable represented only one front in the networks' struggle of the 1980s and 1990s, however. A second was the new non-cable networks. In 1986, conservative media baron Rupert Murdoch founded the Fox network, which had acquired about 150 affiliates by the mid-1990s and gained a secure toehold in the television market, especially after it acquired national football league broadcast rights in 1994—and convinced a bevy of individual stations to drop their CBS affiliation and join Fox. Its success led Paramount (now part of Viacom, a media conglomerate) and Warner (which merged with Time, Inc., in 1989) to either start their own networks or acquire existing ones. Both companies saw television as an outlet for other popular culture industries.

A third major issue was tumult from within. For their entire history, the major networks had been largely autonomous broadcast operations. This changed in 1985, when all three were sold: ABC to Capital Cities, a group of affiliates; NBC to the General Electric colossus; and CBS to the Tisch corporation, a real estate conglomerate. Back in the 1960s, a bid by the International Telephone and Telegraph Corporation (ITT) to acquire ABC had been blocked by antitrust regulators. But in the deregulatory mood of the Reagan era, such concerns were brushed aside. (Republicans in Congress now seek to relax limits on station ownership imposed on media barons like Rupert Murdoch). Of the three traditional networks, ABC has enjoyed the most stability, in part because it was bought by people with a bona fide interest in television. Its acquisition by Disney in 1995 promises to make it a formidable power in the entertainment industry. NBC has periodically been rumored to be for sale, while CBS, whose programming and profitability had suffered under the parsimonious Tisch, was tussled over by Westinghouse and CNN baron Ted Turner.

But the most serious challenge to the traditional networks came from movie studios and independent television producers. Back in the go-go years of the 1950s and 1960s, the networks made programs, paid their affiliate stations a fee to broadcast them locally, and then reaped the advertising profits. They also made money from reruns, selling ads without incurring additional programming costs, and making enormous profits by selling syndication rights to individual independent stations, which then used them as a cheap source of programming. Under a series of financial interest and syndication rule (or "fin-syn rule") regulatory decisions in the late 1970s, however, the networks lost the unlimited right to both own and broadcast programming. This opened the door to outsiders—small production companies, movie studios, and artist-entrepreneur types like Steven Bochco of *Hill Street Blues* and *NYPD Blue* fame—to become major forces in television. Only allowed to produce a few hours of programming a week, the networks became brokers, buying the right to broadcast shows (the producers held onto the syndication rights) and selling advertising time (individual stations continued to receive a fee from the networks, as well as a few slots to sell time for local ads). The Hollywood film industry had once feared television would swallow it whole; now the reverse seemed possible.

Such a fate does not seem imminent, however. For all their problems, the traditional networks have strengths their competitors do not have. The most important of these is an extensive system of affiliated stations that can deliver shows into homes. The government has again begun to favor the networks: not only has it allowed them to own more programming, but the expiration of syn-fin rules in 1995 may lead the networks to rely far more on their own production resources (one reason movie studios like Paramount, Time-Warner, and Disney are so interested in acquiring them). Moreover, after some early stumbling the big three have begun to dabble in cable; ESPN, for example, has long been a profitable asset in the ABC stable. Clearly, reports of the networks' death have been exaggerated.

Cable television, for its part, has its own problems. By the 1990s, most of the people who wanted cable had subscribed. Backlash against the industry's greed had also become a factor. During the 1980s, cable operators developed a two-tier system of services: "basic" service, which included access to programming (like CNN and the Weather Channel) and "premium" services (HBO and The Playboy Channel, for example) which cost extra. Operators packaged these channels in ways that minimized the viewers' control over what they could and could not have (e.g., you could not get

MTV unless you also got channels you did not want, while the premium services were further tiered to require multiple other charges). Moreover, the industry's pricing structure was deregulated during the free-market binge of the Reagan years, leading prices to double in many communities. When Congress overrode President George Bush's veto and re-regulated cable prices in 1992, the industry dragged its heels during the costly legal battle, thereby fulfilling the prophecy of higher costs. If cable had seemed to be a white knight during the days of network dominance, it quickly demonstrated its predatory character.

By the end of the century, however, this particular predator was facing a potentially mortal challenge from a different animal: the regional phone company, which could deliver programs over its own lines. As readers of Chapter 4 may remember, AT&T played a very large role in the birth of radio, and after a protracted legal and commercial struggle agreed to quit the radio and television programming business in return for gaining a monopoly over the wires that connect radio (and later television) stations. Local phone companies also played a crucial backstage role in the growth of cable television because cable companies had to contract with them for the right to string their wires along telephone poles.

Two major developments in the 1980s disrupted the cable/telephone equilibrium. The first was the successful conclusion of the U.S. government's antitrust suit against AT&T, which broke up the company into smaller regional units free to compete with each other and to enter previously forbidden segments of the telecommunications market. The other was the introduction of fiber optic wires to replace the copper wires long used in the telephone industry. Once fiber optics have replaced copper—a process that is well underway—its capacity to store and move electronically coded information could render the coaxial wires used in cable television obsolete.

Whether phone will actually conquer cable is unclear. Each has special strengths: cable in developing and delivering television programming, telephones in information distribution. As is common with large corporate interests, the two potential competitors are using mergers to avoid the market forces they ostensibly celebrate. Two such attempts, one by Bell Atlantic and Tele-Communications Inc. (TCI) and the other by Southwestern Bell and Cox Cable Communications, went sour. Even if they had not, the FCC might have stepped in to prevent such powerful combinations. Such technological, corporate, and regulatory jockeying is the hallmark of one of popular culture's most important frontiers.

A different frontier, this one with international implications, will have a more immediate impact on daily life. In 1995, U.S., Japanese, and European broadcasters were vying to determine global broadcast standards for HDTV, which will soon transform the experience of watching television. Such innovations as solid-state sets and satellite transmission notwithstanding, the technical standards of television broadcasting have not changed much since the 1940s, and the standards themselves were established in the 1930s. But HDTV is an entirely new broadcast system, and it promises not only flatter screens and dramatically sharper images, but a panoply of technical capabilities (such as allowing viewers to choose their own camera angles) that are indicative of the possibilities arising from the convergence between television and computers (a topic that will be discussed further below). This new communications order will require programmers and consumers to acquire an entirely new infrastructure, truly a marketer's dream: it is estimated that the HDTV business will be worth $100 billion by the year 2000. Promoters hope that the growth of HDTV will imitate, on a much larger scale, the surge in the recording industry that was prompted by compact discs, when consumers bought CD players and treasured recordings in CD format, along with new releases, generating enormous corporate profits.

For its part, the laser technology at the heart of compact discs is moving outside its base in popular music into other forms, such as filmmaking and computer software, where it will probably displace tape. Tape is a medium of information storage whose impact in the closing decades of the twentieth century has been dramatic. Indeed, we may in retrospect call this period the "age of tape."[4]

The Age of Tape:
Hollywood in the Video Era

Ever since the middle of the nineteenth century, various means of replaying lived experience—photography, records, and film—have been central to the creation of popular culture. None was flexible enough, however, or technically or financially practical enough, to allow individual consumers to play back their favorite television shows or movies on their own. But while television programmers soon found a solution to this problem, the long wait that consumers faced is a case study in the social forces that shape technology. When the issue was finally resolved, the result was a medium whose consequences were even more far-reaching than those of cable television.

The quest to record televised images, or video, dates back to the 1920s, when Scotsman John Logie Baird successfully recorded them on 78 rpm records. The results were crude, however, and most shows that were recorded were filmed on special cameras (known as kinescopes).

In the early 1950s, sound recording engineers discovered the usefulness of magnetized plastic tape in various widths. Television images required that much more information be packed onto tape than was necessary for music, and early efforts by the British Broadcasting Company (the BBC) and RCA were only partially successful. In 1956, however, the U.S. firm Ampex developed a workable machine, and began marketing it in 1957. But at $45,000 each, the Ampex video recorder was expensive, large, and unreliable. It was not until the German firm of Phillips developed a more advanced video recorder in 1959 that the networks began to tape news segments, situation comedies, and other shows, which they were then able to show at different times to audiences across the country.[5]

Magnetic tape was not the only common means for recording television, however. A record-like system called the videodisk was introduced in the 1960s and used for instant replay on football-game broadcasts. The debate over whether disk or tape would become the primary vehicle for video recording—and *which* particular variant of each format—continued for the next twenty years. Tape initially won out, but videodisks (now using laser technology) have recently made a comeback.

Beginning in the late 1960s, a number of companies attempted to perfect a small, reliable, and inexpensive video recorder for the consumer market. CBS was first with its Electronic Video Recorder (EVR), based on film technology. It was still expensive, however, and could record less than an hour of programming. Similar problems bedeviled the videotape machines developed by Ampex, Playtape, and Cartridge Television, Inc. RCA, which had not introduced any major new products since color television in the 1950s, also experimented with a tape recorder, but in the mid-1970s switched its focus to videodisk, which could play back but not record. In 1981, it unveiled its Selectavision VideoDisc, a system that relied on grooves and pits in a record-like device. Technologically speaking, it was far more cautious than the laser-driven optical videodisk developed by Phillips in 1972, which anticipated the future of CD technology. Neither disk system sold very well, however, and RCA ultimately wrote off its venture at a loss of over half a billion dollars.

Meanwhile, Phillips continued to work on videotape technology, while the Japanese firm Sony bought the rights to the work done by Ampex, which had foolishly (in retrospect, at least) left the field. Sony introduced a number of videocassette recorders, or VCRs, in the late 1960s and early 1970s, including its Beta system in 1975. The following year, Sony's rival JVC/Matsushita introduced a VCR based on its Video Home Service (VHS) tape format. As these products began to find their way into consumers' homes, the only remaining question was which format, Beta or VHS, would win out. Beta offered higher quality images, but VHS was cheaper and could hold more tape on its cassette, and the technologically inferior but more effectively practical VHS won out.

The manufacturers of VCRs and VHS tape made no attempt to sell software (i.e., TV shows, sports events, or movies), because they assumed the owners of their systems would simply tape from their televisions. Movie and television producers, arguing that this represented an infringement of their copyright, sought to prevent this, but in 1984 the U.S. Supreme Court (in *Sony* v. *Universal)* ruled that recording for personal use was legal. The technological, commercial, and legal pieces for a video revolution were finally in place.

It happened very quickly. There were 400,000 VCRs in U.S. homes in 1978, when the boom began to build. In 1983, 4.1 million machines were sold. The following year, the figure almost doubled. In 1985, 20 percent of all homes had VCRs; five years later, more than 75 percent did—more than had cable television.[6]

The VCR had a major impact on television viewing. One of the most important changes was the ability to time-shift, i.e., to tape shows at the time of broadcast but watch them later (although the difficulty of setting the VCR's controls was a running joke well into the 1990s). Time-shifting gave viewers more control, includes the ability to fast-forward past commercials or rewind to review a scene. The universal inclusion of remote controls for both VCRs and televisions by the 1980s enhanced the viewers' power to "zap" shows or commercials that bored or irritated them. Programmers and advertisers have sought to circumvent such developments through disguised commercials and other ruses, but video clearly presents a powerful challenge to the dominance of traditional network television.

This challenge is powerful in part because many viewers are forsaking network television altogether. Nowadays, we are accustomed to the ease of watching our favorite old movies on the videocassette, but those born before 1970 will still remember the aura that surrounded old films, even after the advent of television. They were only screened at repertory houses or by college film societies, or on an occasional television broadcast (punctuated by commercials and often heavy editing). At the same time, there was a widespread (though by no means universal) sense that, unlike songs or books, a movie was used up once it was seen. The former situation and the latter perception changed as film and television production companies began to distribute videocassettes of their products.

Most of this distribution has been done through video stores, which rent individual titles for from one to three nights for a few dollars. Relatively inexpensive to operate, video stores proliferated in the 1980s, becoming as common as gas stations or grocery stores (indeed, some gas stations and grocery stores added videos to their shelves). By 1985, revenues from video rentals had reached $1.2 billion; by 1988, they had more than doubled, to $2.5 billion. Although they were cheap to manufacture, the cassettes were expensive to buy, listing for about $100. By the late 1980s however, as owning movies became increasingly popular, prices came down swiftly, and many titles are now below $20. The number of videocassettes sold almost quadrupled between 1985 and 1988, from 22 million to 80 million.[7]

For the film studios, which had been declining in power and influence since the 1950s, the advent of video was a bonanza. As they had with television three decades before, the film studios fought hard against video, as the case of *Universal* v. *Sony* demonstrates. But like television, video provided the film industry with its greatest financial windfall since the earliest days of the medium. ("We know when to lose them, don't we?" Motion Picture Association of America President Jack Valenti asked in the aftermath of the decision.[8]) Now, in addition to domestic and foreign distribution, every movie could go onto video, much as hardcover books went into paperback. And any movie that was a flop in its first-run theatrical release could—and often did—go on to a profitable life in video. Some small-budget efforts went directly to video. Cable and network production companies also got into the act, putting successful series, mini-series, and specials on video, as well as financing their own feature films. Blockbuster Video, a national chain of rental stores, became so gorged with cash that it began to dabble in the production end of the industry.

In addition, the advent of portable, relatively inexpensive VHS-compatible video cameras made it possible for viewers to watch their own weddings and birthday parties, or to buy programming from outside sources—exercise tapes, self-help videos, educational documentaries, and so on.

The cultural effects of this flood of videotape were varied. In the case of music video, it fostered the creation of a bold new art form. It also accelerated the fragmentation of the television audience, a fragmentation abetted by cable television. More than ever, "broadcasting" was being replaced by "narrowcasting," as commercial interests sought to capture narrow but still relatively large and profitable segments of the viewing audience. Perhaps the most notable example of this was pornographic video. Because of the disreputable air surrounding pornography, many people shied away from viewing erotic films in theaters, which were usually squalid, if not dangerous, anyway. Once it became possible to watch pornography in the privacy and safety of one's own home, however, large numbers of men—and women— partook of it. More than half of all videocassette sales in the late 1970s were pornographic movies, a figure that had only declined to 40 percent after the huge surge in movie rentals of all kinds. In 1989, the combined rental and sale revenues of pornographic videos approached $1 billion.[9] Whether one views this as a hopeful sign of sexual freedom or an appalling illustration of national depravity, the advent of video satisfied hidden cultural tastes.

In a subtle but powerful way, videotape has been a key factor in what some scholars have described as the postmodern condition of late-twenti-eth-century life. For the purposes of this discussion, it is useful to note two widely agreed-upon attributes of postmodernity: (1) a skepticism about the hostility to popular culture that was characteristic of modernism; and (2) the ubiquity of popular culture and its recombinations and echoes (what literary scholars call "intertextuality"). Directly or indirectly, videotape figures promi-nently in both these attributes. As one small example, consider *The Brady Bunch* (1969-1974), a family-oriented sitcom that enjoyed a brief renais-sance during the early 1990s, when it was re-run on cable, was featured in a prime-time reunion special, inspired the paperback bestseller *Growing Up Brady,* and was the basis for a stage show that was produced around the country. This interest was both a nostalgic longing for a more innocent past and a knowingly cynical wink at the "family values" invoked by the Republican Party. Though it was not the primary product being sold to the consumer, the videocassette was the essential tissue—the collective memory of the series has been preserved on videotape—that connects the sequels, prequels, reruns, spoofs, and imitations of the last two decades.

For all its ubiquity, however, there are signs that our culture is becoming less video-driven. Despite its iconographic power as a symbol of modernity, the VCR is a relatively old-fashioned mechanical device with lots of moving parts and dated technology—in marked contrast to videodisks (now usually called laserdiscs), for instance. Moreover, "pay-per-view" cable service, which allows viewers to watch films without the bother of renting or returning VHS tapes, has become increasingly common. Indeed, the writing may be on the wall for the video store.

In fact, the very idea of owning cultural documents (like record albums or movies), even in a laser-driven format, may soon be obsolete, as the role of computers in the production, distribution, and use of popular culture reaches new levels of technological sophistication. This study would not complete without a discussion, however brief, of this trend.

The New Networks:
Computers and Popular Culture

For most of this book, I have used the terms "hardware" and "software" as a metaphorical shorthand to describe the structure and content of different kinds of popular culture. In contemporary life, however, these words are used more literally. Of course, computer technology has played an important role in popular culture for decades, as it has in U.S. life in general. But never have computers impinged on our lives as visibly as they do now—and their power will undoubtedly grow greater still.

As the very word implies, a computer is that which computes—i.e., performs mathematical calculations. A number of mechanical devices and tables were used during the nineteenth century to aid such tasks, but strictly speaking computers in the pre-electronic era were people, primarily women, who executed the work administered by managers and other authorities. Even after computers in the modern sense of the term have become common, women—many of them African-American or Latina—continue to be the ones who entered the data and run the programs. The information revolution, like the industrial revolution before it, rests squarely on the labor of working people.

Computer technology began to have a major impact on popular culture in the 1950s, when transistors (small devices made from germanium and silicon that move and amplify electronic information) began to be used in radios and televisions. Although they were a major improvement over vacuum tubes, they too became unwieldy as more and more of them were required for increasingly sophisticated machines. Manufacturers then developed ways to make boards filled with tiny linked transistors, or integrated circuits. These integrated circuits, which are called semiconductors (or the "chips" referred to earlier in this chapter), are the basic building blocks of contemporary computer technology—and to a great extent contemporary life.

Computers moved to the forefront of the national imagination with the advent of the personal computer, or "PC," in the 1980s. Early computers were gargantuan machines: individuals sat at one of any number of terminals that were hooked into the larger system, or mainframe. Mainframe computers continue be important in some industries (the newspaper industry, for instance), but by the late 1960s smaller, discrete machines were being built that were not as powerful as mainframes but cost a fraction of the price and were useful for many applications. In 1981, IBM introduced its PC, using widely available "open" architecture that invited copying by competitors who then "cloned" similar machines. Three years later, the small computer company Apple introduced its highly accessible, or "user-friendly," Macintosh. IBM, clone, and Macintosh PCs spread like wildfire. By 1981, there were more than 2 million personal computers in homes and offices; a year later there were more than 5.5 million.[10] The number has since tripled.

Even before the PC became common, however, computer technology was entering popular culture through mass-market video games. The first of these, which was played on a television set, introduced an element of interactivity whose ramifications are still emerging.

Video games were developed by computer experts at such major research centers as Long Island's Brookhaven National Laboratory and the Massachusetts Institute of Technology, who toyed with them in their spare time. They included "Pong," a ping-pong variant using relatively simple analog computing, and "Space War," a more complex digital game. These were essentially hi-tech versions of pinball that gave the players some control over the game's destiny. Indeed, pinball arcades (and bars) were among the first commercial sites for video games. The first consumer game was introduced in the early 1970s by the television manufacturer Magnavox. It was very profitable, since the computer chip cost $5 while the game sold for $99 (100,000 were sold). By 1976 there were more than seventy manufacturers vying for a piece of the video-game pie, the most successful of which was Atari. By 1982, over 16 percent of U.S. households owned game systems, and consumers spent $8 billion on video games in arcades and another $3 billion on home video systems, which were increasingly being run on personal computers, and the software cartridges used with them—more than was spent on movies and music combined. In fact, the decline in revenues in those industries was widely attributed to the video game boom.

Booms usually lead to busts, and the video game industry crashed with amazing rapidity: by the mid-1980s, merchandisers could barely give the games away. Atari lost over $500 million in 1983, and the total home video market for 1985 was a mere $100 million. A big part of the reason was boredom: most video games were easily mastered, and they were abandoned once the novelty wore off. In 1989, however, the Japanese firm of Nintendo introduced its hugely successful product line in the United States. Nintendo games were varied, graphically complex, and geared to different skill levels, and new games were regularly released to sustain interest. In the year of its debut, Nintendo had won 80 percent of the U.S. market. By the early 1990s, one in five homes had a Nintendo set and the company had sold more than all its rivals put together—one more example of Japanese dominance in an industry the United States had pioneered.[11]

The economic power of video games is clear, their cultural consequences less so. Demographic studies indicate that the majority of players are boys between the ages of eight and fifteen, and the prevalence of games with violent, militaristic themes has raised concerns comparable to, if not greater than, those surrounding network television. Conservative humorist P.J. O'Rourke glibly underlined this point during the Persian Gulf War, when he argued that U.S. soldiers who had grown up on video games were well prepared for the struggle at hand. "This is the mother of all Mario Brothers [a wildly popular Nintendo game]," he half-joked.[12] On a more positive note, some observers have argued that video games, and computer "hacking" in general, help cultivate skills vital to a twenty-first century epistemology that will be rooted in images and computer programs rather than words and books. Popular culture historian John Fiske even sees a hopeful political dynamic. He notes that the games are most popular among "subordinated males (subordinated by class, age, race, or any combination of the three), because they can be used to think through, to rehearse in practice, the experiential gap between masculine ideology of power and performance and the experience of powerlessness."[13] This is, to put it mildly, an optimistic reading from which women are conspicuously absent. It may nevertheless be a credible version of how adolescent males think of their video game avocation, translated into academic language.

Whatever their ideological impact, by the 1990s video games had completed their migration from the television set to the personal computer. The same compact disc technology that was revolutionizing music and video recordings was having an even more dramatic impact on computer games, where systems similar to those that can store encyclopedias give users far more control over images, text, and graphics than was possible with the older television-based games.

Meanwhile, personal computers are increasingly linked by modem into vast networks, including the Internet, the major thoroughfare on the "information highway." Here too TV and the PC are converging—to the extent that many observers believe that before long there will no longer be a line between the two. Even such services as pay-per-view will seem quaint because the new technology will allow viewers to choose any movie at any time, rewind, fast forward, and even edit at will. In fact, the very idea of collecting records, movies, and books may become obsolete, once the typical home is wired into gargantuan databases that can be instantly accessed—for a fee, of course. People will be able to do office work, send electronic mail, adjust their home heating systems, shop and pay for goods, and talk over video without ever leaving their living rooms.

Such prospects seem attractive to many people, but there are far less rosy scenarios, depending on the choices we as a people make in the years ahead.

Conclusion:
The Democratic Web

Back in 1980, before cable television was widespread, Warner Brothers teamed up with American Express to test-market an early interactive television service called Qube, in Columbus, Ohio. Although it was primitive by contemporary standards, Qube offered a variety of options: viewers could peruse merchandise, pay for it, vote in polls or surveys, and even take courses at local colleges, all using a device that resembled a small calculator. Qube even offered a home security service whereby sensors would both alert a security company and photograph intruders. "We're selling peace of mind," a publicist explained.[14]

Qube spread rapidly in Columbus and soon had 30,000 subscribers, 5,000 of whom bought the security service. Warner-Amex planned to expand into Houston, Cincinnati, Pittsburgh, and other cities. Even before the VCR conquered the living room, interactive television seemed to have arrived.

Then Qube began to lose subscribers. Questions were raised about the service: Would Warner-Amex start *tracking* customer preferences? If so, what would be done with this information? Assuming Warner-Amex would respect viewer privacy, would other interests—computer hackers, government agencies, political groups—be prevented from doing so? How, in short, would privacy be protected in a wholly electronic culture?

Warner-Amex pulled the plug on Qube in 1984, in part because of the spread of conventional cable service and VCRs in the aftermath of the *Sony v. Universal* decision, and the answers to such questions were largely deferred. But as the information superhighway expands and as ever more sophisticated, and potentially intrusive, interactive television systems make their debut, such issues will undoubtedly take on fresh urgency.

This urgency is made all the greater by the unprecedented levels of corporate consolidation of the media during the Reagan and Bush years. Sony's acquisition of the CBS music and movie empire in 1988 and the merger of Time, Inc., and Warner Brothers in 1989 typified these marriages of competitors (and hard/software combinations) and have a number of troubling implications. Once a set of government licensees with an explicit responsibility for public service (e.g., news, political debate, and other forms of nonprofit or low-profit broadcasting), the TV networks had come to be seen as cash cows ruled by the bottom line. Even electoral campaigns, when candidates should be given free air time as the price of a government license, have become one more opportunity for the media to make money.

The scope of such power goes beyond merchandising, however. When a group of companies whose interests include film, television, book publishing, computer software, and a host of other communication concerns controls the distribution of art and information, the temptation for private sector censorship is irresistible. So, for example, authors of less-than-flattering biographies of Walt Disney and Calvin Klein found themselves summarily dropped by their publishers when highly placed figures from within MCA and Paramount made it clear that such works were no longer welcome. Employees found themselves subject to brazen levels of corporate arrogance, as evidenced in this NBC memo "advising" its workers to contribute part of their pay to the networks:

> Employees who earn their living and support their families from the profits of our business must recognize a need to invest some portion of their earnings to ensure that the Company is well-represented in Washington, and that its important issues are clearly placed before congress. Employees who elect not to participate in a giving program of this type should question their own dedication to the Company and their expectations.[15]

The company management apparently never questioned the assumption that its interests and those of its workers were one and the same, much less that employees were hardly being paid for their labor out of profits!

Of course, corporate arrogance and domination have been facts of life for the last one hundred years. Never before, however, have big money and high technology been so closely and efficiently intertwined. Even the most optimistic among us must be aware that a terrifying dystopia awaits an unchecked accumulation of private media power.

At the same time, there are mitigating factors—emerging forms are no more inherently repressive than they are liberating. In the Soviet Union of the 1980s, for instance, the emergence of *magnitizdat*—loosely translated as magnetic (tape) self-publishing—opened new ways to overcome government censorship using the VCR. Copying machines were crucial tactical weapons for dissidents in Poland and China in these years, and technology may well serve similar purposes in other contexts. In the United States, perhaps the best example of technology being used for egalitarian purposes is the Internet—a kind of community without borders that allows people to send, receive, and collect information from all over the world at relatively low cost. The Internet is well-organized and governed by an informal etiquette that frowns on people who take advantage of it (by advertising, for example), although its growing commercialization may change this.

Another important factor that helps to retain a democratic element in popular culture is the people who produce the software. Within the fairly straitlaced world of computers, it is the programmers who have been the most colorful and creative players and the ones who make the machines work. Technology historian Steven Lubar's observation about software has wider reverberations in this regard:

> Software writing and testing is an art, not a science. In its half-century history, software has become easier to write, more powerful, and more

useful; it has also become increasingly important. Software is nearly ubiquitous, now, though it is still invisible. We rely on it every day, without thinking about it. But for all the effort that has gone into making programming easier, it remains the most difficult part of making the Information Age work.[16]

We can extrapolate Lubar's observation to popular culture as a whole. For all their pervasiveness and power, VCRs, TV stations, and computer systems are all designed to deliver information, not create it. And, to a great extent, that creation still depends on many "others"—the women, people of color, and workers of all kinds who provide the imaginative spark behind the records, TV shows, movies, and other documents with which their fellow citizens make sense of their lives. Ultimately, it will be people—not money or machines—that will endow popular culture with its vitality.

Nevertheless, if the dystopian vision of a corporate or governmental monopoly of culture is too dour, the assumption that cultural vitality will inevitably survive is excessively optimistic. A historical perspective implies a sense of contingency, a belief that we are continually faced with vital choices that have real consequences. As the various electronic media converge (i.e., toward transmission by fiber optic cable), there are two discrete models for the future: the "tree-and-branch" model and the "web" model. The tree-and-branch model is exemplified by television, with the trunk (the transmitting station) distributing data to the branches (individual homes). The web model, exemplified by telephone service, is a decentralized system whereby data is both generated from, and delivered to, a variety of sites. This is the case with the Internet, at least for now. In contrast to the more hierarchical tree-and-branch model, the web implies a smaller scale, producer-oriented order, which is why its premier advocate, the Electronic Frontier Foundation, describes it as "Jeffersonian."[17]

For the most part, media companies and important segments of the government prefer the tree-and-branch model, which has been the governing paradigm for the electronic media since the rise of radio. Limited as it may be, we live in a moment when a viable alternative is visible, a moment when popular attention and focused government action could restrain the status quo that puts profit first. If such an alternative were to be realized, the foundations of a truly democratic culture could be laid. In the meantime, we look to our art for a means of navigating our current lives and imagining better ones.

Notes and Further Reading

Notes

1. For a survey of objections raised against popular culture from ancient Rome to the post-World War II United States, see Patrick Bratlinger, *Bread and Circuses: Theories of Mass Culture as Social Decay* (Ithaca, NY: Cornell University Press, 1983). For a very brief but useful compendium of these objections (and responses to them), see Jackson Lears's essay on the subject in the third volume of *The Encyclopedia of American Social History*, edited by Mary Kupiec Cayton, Elliot J. Gorn, and Peter W. Williams (New York: Charles Scribner's Sons, 1993). While popular culture is enjoying perhaps more critical acceptance than ever before, it continues to have informed critics. For one notable example, albeit one more focused on retailing than the popular arts, see William Leach, *Land of Desire: Merchants, Power, and the Rise of a New American Culture* (New York: Pantheon, 1993).
2. The "hurts of history" is a term coined by the noted popular culture scholar George Lipsitz. See *Time Passages: Collective Memory and American Popular Culture* (Minneapolis: University of Minnesota Press, 1990).

1
NOVEL APPROACHES

For Further Reading

There are, of course, many ways of approaching the subject of popular culture. The strategy of this book is essentially narrative and historical, though much interesting and valuable work has been done from a more theoretical perspective. Those interested in exploring these dimensions of the subject are encouraged to seek out John Storey's *An Introductory Guide to Cultural Theory and Popular Culture* (Athens: University of Georgia Press, 1993), a brief, readable, and fairly comprehensive guide to the subject. For encyclopedic collections of subject-specific essays on particular forms of popular culture (many more than can be treated in this book), see *The Handbook of Popular Culture,* 2nd ed., edited by M. Thomas Inge (1978; Westport, CT: Greenwood Press, 1989), and *The Encyclopedia of American Social History,* edited by Mary Kupiec Cayton, Elliot J. Gorn, and Peter W. Williams (New York: Charles Scribner's Sons, 1993). For a smorgasbord of essays on topics ranging from comic books to sports novels, see *Popular Culture in America,* edited by Paul Buhle (Minneapolis: University of Minnesota Press, 1987). One of the best recent descriptions of popular culture is that offered by the renowned historian Lawrence Levine. See "The Folklore of Industrial Society: Popular Culture and Its Audiences," one of his collected essays in *The Unpredictable Past: Explorations in American Cultural History* (New York: Oxford University Press, 1993).

Students seeking information on the origins of popular culture are also likely to be interested in the social life of colonial and early national U.S. history. The HarperCollins Everyday Life in America series offers excellent introductions. See David Freeman Hawke's *Everyday Life in Early America* (1988) and Jack Larkin's *The Reshaping of Everyday Life, 1790-1840* (also 1988).

Most narrative histories of books and periodicals in the United States are quite old. Among those I consulted are the still-standard works of Frank Luther Mott, *A History of Newspapers in the United States Through 250 Years, 1690-1940* (New York: Macmillan, 1940) and *A History of American Magazines, Vol I: 1741-1850* (Cambridge, MA: Harvard University Press, 1938). For books, see Hellmut Lehmann-Haupt with Lawrence C. Wroth and Rollo G. Silver, *The Book in America: A History of the Making and Selling of Books in the United States,* 2nd ed. (New York: R.R. Bowker, 1952); and James D. Hart, *The Popular Book: A History of America's Literary Taste* (New York: Oxford University Press, 1950). The foremost recent scholar of book publishing is John Tebbel. See his four-volume *History of Book Publishing in the United States* (New York: R.R. Bowker, 1972-81). Tebbel has also written a one-volume synthesis of this work, called *Between Covers: The Rise and Transformation of Book Publishing in America* (New York: Oxford University Press, 1987).

My perspective on early U.S. fiction was especially shaped by a group of books on the subject that were published during the 1980s (some of these will be cited at the end of the next chapter, where their influence is most clear). The most important for this chapter was Cathy Davidson's groundbreaking *Revolution and the Word: The Rise of the Novel in America* (New York: Oxford University Press, 1986). See also

Jane Tompkins, *Sensational Designs: The Cultural Work of American Fiction, 1790-1860* (New York: Oxford University Press, 1985) and especially the diverse collection of essays in Cathy Davidson, ed., *Reading in America: Literature and Social History* (Baltimore, MD: The Johns Hopkins University Press, 1989). The most definitive recent work on the rise of the U.S. literary infrastructure is Ronald J. Zboray, *A Fictive People: Antebellum Economic Development and the American Reading Public* (New York: Oxford University Press, 1993). Carefully noting the ironies and paradoxes that surround this subject, Zboray uses the word "fictive" to connote not only the popularity of fiction in the nineteenth century, but also the unconfirmable—and even false—perceptions that have marked books and reading for both contemporaries and later scholars.

As is true of many of the works to be cited in the chapters that follow, these references are rich sources of further leads for those who wish to pursue specific issues in greater detail.

Notes

1. Lawrence Levine, "The Folklore of Industrial Society," in *The Unpredictable Past*; see especially p. 295, where Levine describes the relationship between popular culture and folklore.
2. The degree to which there was a revolution in publishing in the nineteenth century has been contested, though there does seem to be a consensus that a perceptible quickening took place in these years. For a discussion of the technical developments and their role on American soil, see Lehmann-Haupt et al., *The Book in America*, especially pp. 63-98.
3. The term was coined by Raymond Williams; see *The Long Revolution* (New York: Columbia University Press, 1961).
4. For a good brief introduction to music in early American life, see Jack Larkin's chapter on the subject in *The Reshaping of Everyday Life*, pp. 232-57.
5. Lehmann-Haupt et al,., *The Book in America*, p. 7. In *The Popular Book*, Hart explains the difficulties facing the South: "The Southern colonists lived on widely separated plantations (by 1685 Virginia's population, smaller than that of a contemporary London parish, was spread over an area greater than England itself), and without cities they had no popular centers for the development of intellectual life. Lacking a cohesive pattern of schools and churches, printing houses and booksellers, a large reading public could not develop" (p. 10).
6. Lehmann-Haupt and Silver, *The Book in America,* p. 15.
7. Ibid., p. 7; Hart, *The Popular Book*, pp. 9-10.
8. Literacy rates in the colonies are very difficult to gauge, or to find consensus on, in contemporary treatments of the subject. But virtually all the authorities I have encountered—including Kenneth Lockridge, Cathy Davidson, E. Jennifer Monaghan, all of whom will be cited below—agree that literacy was relatively low outside New England prior to the Revolution.
9. Esmond Wright, *Franklin of Philadelphia* (Cambridge, MA: Harvard University Press, 1986), pp. 53-55.
10. Mott, *American Journalism*, pp. 9-12.
11. Mott, *A History of American Magazines*, p. 24; Paul Nord, "A Republican Literature: Magazine Reading and Readers in Late-Eighteetnh-Century New York" in *Reading in America*, pp. 114-39.

12. Victor Neuburg, "Chapbooks in America: Reconstructing the Popular Reading of Early America," in *Reading in America*, pp. 81-113, and esp. pp. 81-83.

13. Hart, *The Popular Book*, pp. 40-41; Neuberg, "Chapbooks in America," pp. 95, 102-4, 107.

14. Davidson, *Revolution and the Word*, pp. 23-24; Hart, *The Popular Book*, pp. 47-50. For a discussion of Weems' marketing strategies and relationship with Carey, see Zboray's chapter on the subject in his *A Fictive People*.

15. Hart, *The Popular Book*, pp. 25, 53; Davidson, *Revolution and the Word*, pp. 27-29.

16. For initials on wills as a measure of literacy, see Kenneth Lockridge, *Literacy in Colonial New England: An Enquiry into the Social Context of Literacy in the Early Modern West* (New York: W.W. Norton, 1974). E. Jennifer Monaghan contests Lockridge's findings in "Literacy Instruction and Gender in Colonial New England," in *Reading in America*, pp. 53-82. Davidson herself explores the literacy question in *Revolution and the Word*, pp. 55-79.

17. Monaghan, "Literary Instruction and Gender," pp. 62-63.

18. Ibid., pp. 55-57; Hart, *The Popular Book*, p. 47; Maris Vinovskis and Richard Bernard, "Beyond Catherine Beecher: Female Education in the Antebellum Period," *Signs* 3 (Summer 1978): 864-65.

19. Republican Motherhood is the subject of much scholarly literature. Linda Kerber, *Women of the Republic: Intellect and Ideology in Revolutionary America* (New York: W.W. Norton, 1986) offers an especially good treatment. See also Mary Beth Norton, *Liberty's Daughters: The Revolutionary Experience of American Women* (Boston: Little Brown, 1980).

    The discourse on Republicanism is also massive. One generally acknowledged authority on the subject is Gordon Wood, whose *The Creation of the American Republic, 1776-1787* (New York: Norton, 1969) and *The Radicalism of the American Revolution* (New York: Knopf, 1992) are considered definitive treatments. Sean Wilentz delineates a somewhat sharper, more communitarian vision of Republicanism in *Chants Democratic: New York City and the Rise of the American Working Class, 1788-1850* (New York: Oxford, 1984). For a very useful summary of the historiographic strands running through the dialogue on the subject, see David Paul Nord, "A Republican Literature," in *Reading in America*, pp. 115-16.

20. For an excellent summary treatment of the degree of democratization in early American education, see Davidson, *Revolution and the Word*, pp. 55-70.

21. Berkeley is quoted in Davidson, *Revolution and the Word*, p. 38.

22. M.M. Bakhtin, "Epic and Novel: Toward a Methodology for the Study of the Novel," in *The Dialogic Imagination: Four Essays by M.M. Bakhtin*, edited by Michael Holquist (1975; Austin: University of Texas Press, 1981), pp. 3-40. The discussion that follows also owes something to Bakhtin, whose influence shows up in the work of later scholars like Davidson; see, for example, *Revolution and the Word*, p. 14.

23. Frederic Jameson, "Reification and Utopia in Mass Culture," *Social Text* (Winter 1979): 130-48.

24. Hart, *The Popular Book*, pp. 28-30.

25. Ibid., pp. 53-54.

26. Nina Baym, *Novels, Readers and Reviewers: Responses to Fiction in Antebellum America* (Ithaca, NY: Cornell University Press, 1984), p. 32.

27. Hart, *The Popular Book*, pp. 17, 29.
28. Davidson, *Revolution and the Word*, p. 66.
29. Ibid., pp. 70, 131.
30. Ibid., pp. 75-77.
31. For Davidson's discussion of gothic novels, see *Revolution and the Word*, pp. 212-53, especially her reading of *Arthur Mervyn* on pp. 236-53. For a provocative analysis of Brown that emphasizes his conservatism despite some important differences in the two novels, see Jane Tompkins' discussion of *Wieland* (pp. 40-61) and *Arthur Meryvn* (pp. 62-93) in *Sensational Designs*.
32. In recent years, copyrights have come to be seen as major sources of income for their owners, often large corporations. If intellectual property rights protect writers, they can also constrain discourse for fear of lawsuits and fees.

Sources for "A Temple of the Imagination"

Charlotte Temple has been reprinted by Oxford University Press, with an introduction by Cathy N. Davidson (New York: Oxford University Press, 1986). In addition, see Davidson, "The Life and Times of Charlotte Temple: The Biography of a Book," in *Reading in America: Literature and Social History* (Baltimore, MD: The Johns Hopkins University Press, 1989); Jane Tompkins, "Susanna Rowson, Father of the American Novel," in *The (Other) American Traditions: Nineteenth Century Women Writers,* edited by Joyce Warren (New Brunswick, NJ: Rutgers University Press, 1993); Patricia L. Parker, *Susanna Rowson* (Boston: Twayne Publishers, 1986). *Charlotte Temple* and Susanna Rowson are also discussed in Davidson's *Revolution and the Word: The Rise of the Novel in America* (New York: Oxford, 1986) and by Leslie Fiedler in *Love and Death in the American Novel* (1960; New York: Dell, 1966).

2
DEMOCRATIC VISTAS

Further Reading

Though dated, Frank Luther Mott's *American Journalism: A History of News-papers in the United States Through 250 Years, 1690-1940* (New York: Macmillan, 1941) remains the standard in the field in terms of sheer comprehensiveness, as does his multivolume *History of American Magazines* (Cambridge, MA: Harvard University Press, 1938), both of which were also an important source for Chapter 1. Two shorter, more analytically nuanced works are Michael Schudson's *Discovering the News: A Social History of American Newspapers* (New York: Harper & Row, 1978) and Dan Schiller's *Objectivity and the News: The Public and the Rise of Commercial Journalism* (Philadelphia: University of Pennsylvania Press, 1985). The transformative role of the telegraph is ably discussed in Daniel J. Czitrom, *Media and the American Mind from Morse to McLuhan* (Chapel Hill: University of North Carolina Press, 1982). For more on the telegraph as well as other pivotal communications technologies of the nineteenth and twentieth centuries, see Steven Lubar, *InfoCul-*

ture: The Smithsonian Book of Information Age Inventions (Boston: Houghton Mifflin, 1993).

The best single work on antebellum theater is David Grimsted, *Melodrama Unveiled: American Theater and Culture, 1800-1850* (1968; Berkeley: University of California Press, 1987). See also Robert Toll's engaging *On with the Show: The First Century of American Show Business* (New York: Oxford University Press, 1976); Howard Taubman, *The Making of the American Theater* (New York: Coward McCann, 1965), and Carl Bode, *The Anatomy of American Popular Culture, 1840-1861* (Berkeley: University of California Press, 1959), which discusses many aspects of antebellum popular culture. For a superb discussion of the role of Shakespeare in the nineteenth-century United States, see Lawrence Levine, *Highbrow/Lowbrow: The Emergence of Cultural Hierarchy in America* (Cambridge, MA: Harvard University Press, 1988).

On regional archetypes like Davy Crockett on the American stage and in print, see Constance Rourke's now classic *American Humor: A Study of the National Character* (New York: Harcourt Brace, 1931). This subject is also ably handled from a more sharply political perspective in Alexander Saxton, *The Rise and Fall of the White Republic: Class Politics and Mass Culture in Nineteenth-Century America* (London: Verso, 1990). Saxton's book also features an extensive study of minstrel shows. Minstrelsy is also an important topic in David R. Roediger, *The Wages of Whiteness: Race and the Making of the American Working Class* (London: Verso, 1991). It is also the subject of two notable books: Robert Toll's *Blacking Up: The Minstrel Show in Nineteenth-Century America* (New York: Oxford University Press, 1974), and Eric Lott's more theory-oriented *Love and Theft: Blackface Minstrelsy and the American Working Class* (New York: Oxford University Press, 1993). Antebellum African-American culture is discussed in Lawrence Levine's highly regarded *Black Culture and Consciousness: Afro-American Folk Thought from Slavery to Freedom* (New York: Oxford University Press, 1977) and Mel Watkins, *On the Wild Side: Laughing, Lying and Signifying—The Underground Tradition of African-American Humor That Transformed American Culture, from Slavery to Richard Pryor* (New York: Simon & Schuster, 1994).

The standard work on P.T. Barnum is Neil Harris, *Humbug: The Art of P.T. Barnum* (Chicago: University of Chicago Press, 1973). See also Toll's *On with the Show*. Barnum's memoirs came out in three versions. The first was his *Life of P.T. Barnum*, published in 1855; it was followed by *Struggles and Triumphs; or, Forty Years' Recollections of P.T. Barnum* in 1869 and *Struggles and Triumphs; or, Sixty Years' Recollections of P.T. Barnum* in 1889. A combined edition was published in 1927. The memoir most readily available is an abridged version of the 1869 edition, edited by Carl Bode (New York: Penguin, 1981).

As noted in the "Further Reading" section of the last chapter, recent years have witnessed an explosion of innovative new scholarship on antebellum popular fiction and its audiences, especially fiction by women. In addition to drawing on those works, I have used a number of others, among them a series of works by Nina Baym: *Woman's Fiction: A Guide to Novels by and about Women in America, 1820-1970* (Ithaca, NY: Cornell University Press, 1978); *Novels, Readers, and Reviewers: Responses to Fiction in Antebellum Fiction* (Ithaca, NY: Cornell University Press, 1984); and a collection of essays, *Feminism and American Literary History* (New Brunswick, NJ: Rutgers University Press, 1992). See also Mary Kelley, *Private Woman, Public Stage: Literary Domesticity in Nineteenth-Century America* (New

York: Oxford University Press, 1984); Michael Denning, *Mechanic Accents: Dime Novels and Working-Class Culture in America* (London: Verso, 1987); David S. Reynolds, *Beneath the American Renaissance: The Subversive Imagination in the Age of Emerson and Melville* (Cambridge, MA: Harvard University Press, 1988); Barbara Bardes and Suzanne Gossett, *Declarations of Independence: Women and Political Power in Nineteenth-Century American Fiction* (New Brunswick, NJ: Rutgers University Press, 1990); Susan Coultrap-McQuin, *Doing Literary Business: American Women Writers in the Nineteenth Century* (Chapel Hill: University of North Carolina Press, 1990); and Richard Brodhead, *Cultures of Letters: Scenes of Reading and Writing in Nineteenth-Century America* (Chicago: University of Chicago Press, 1993). In addition, two recent essay collections usefully sample this scholarship: *The Culture of Sentiment: Race, Gender and Sentimentality in 19th Century America,* edited by Shirley Samuels (New York: Oxford University Press, 1992); and *The (Other) American Traditions: Nineteenth Century Women Writers,* edited by Joyce Warren (New Brunswick, NJ: Rutgers University Press, 1993).

On slave narratives and other African-American writings, see Marion Wilson Starling, *The Slave Narrative: Its Place in American History* (1946; Washington, DC: Howard University Press, 1988); Charles T. Davis and Henry Louis Gates, eds., *The Slave's Narrative* (New York: Oxford University Press, 1985); and Hazel Carby, *Reconstructing Womanhood: The Emergence of the Afro-American Woman Novelist* (New York: Oxford University Press, 1987).

Notes

1. For an excellent analysis of Jefferson's attitudes on race, see Ronald Takaki's chapter on the subject in *Iron Cages: Race and Culture in the Nineteenth Century* (1979; New York: Oxford University Press, 1990), pp. 36-65. Jefferson's famous quote is cited on pp. 46-47.
2. U.S. Census Bureau figures published in Bernard Bailyn, Robert Dallek, and David Donald et al., *The Great Republic: A History of the American People,* vol. I (Boston: Little, Brown, 1977), p. xxxii; James D. Hart, *A History of America's Literary Taste* (New York: Oxford University Press, 1950), p. 67; Kelley, *Private Woman, Public Stage,* pp. 12-14.
3. For a more detailed analysis of these new techniques, see Hellmut Lehmann-Haupt with Lawrence C. Wroth and Rollo G. Silver, *The Book in America,* 2nd ed. (New York: R.R. Bowker Company, 1952), pp. 145-75.
4. Mott, *American Journalism,* pp. 71, 95, 115.
5. Quoted in ibid., p. 169.
6. Political scientist Richard L. Rubin described party control of the press in the nineteenth century as "a dependent partnership." See his chapter on the subject (and the subsequent chapter on the Jacksonian period) in his *Press, Party, and Presidency* (New York: Norton, 1981), pp. 7-28; 29-54.
7. For Hamilton's role in the formation of the *Post,* see Mott, *American Journalism,* pp. 184-86.
8. Ibid., pp. 220-25.
9. Ledger cited in ibid., p. 241. Brooklyn, by the way, did not become part of greater New York until 1898.
10. Ibid., pp. 229-34.

11. Schudson, *Discovering the News*, pp. 50-57; Mott, *American Journalism*, pp. 235-39. Schudson believes the emergence of the penny press signals the emergence of a new middle class, a term he uses without much elaboration. In *Objectivity and the News*, Schiller takes Schudson to task for this omission and emphasizes the artisanal/mechanic accents of newspapers and the sense of class conflict that suffuses them. See pp. 8-10, and Schiller's chapter on the emergence of a mass press audience, pp. 12-46.

12. The reciprocal relationship between newspapers and technology is discussed in Schudson, *Discovering the News*, pp. 31-35.

13. Bennett's claim is cited in Czitrom, *Media and the American Mind*, pp. 15-16.

14. For the political accents of the penny press, see Saxton, *Rise and Fall of the White Republic*, pp. 95-108. Artisan radicalism in general, and the Workingmen's Party in particular, are central in Sean Wilenz, *Chants Democratic: New York City and the Rise of the American Working Class, 1788-1850* (New York: Oxford, 1984). For a concise essay on Workingmen's parties, see Franklin Rosemont's essay on the subject in *Working for Democracy: American Workers from the Revolution to the Present*, edited by Paul Buhle and Alan Dawley (Urbana: University of Illinois Press, 1985), pp. 11-20.

15. As his title indicates, the centrality of race to class politics is central to Saxton's *Rise and Fall of the White Republic*, as well as to Roediger in *Wages of Whiteness*. Both works were important in shaping my understanding of this period, although as my subsequent discussion will indicate, I think both authors underestimate some significant abolitionist currents running through some antebellum working-class movements, as well as the morally and politically textured writing of women—and, ironically, African Americans themselves—in shaping the terms of the debate. For discussion of the Calhoun-Walsh axis, see Wilenz, *Chants Democratic*, pp. 327-35. While questionable in other ways, Arthur M. Schlesinger, Jr., *The Age of Jackson* (Boston: Little, Brown, 1945) offers a reasonable treatment of these strange bedfellows on pp. 406-10.

16. Alessandra Lorini, "Public Rituals, Race Ideology and the Transformation of Urban Culture: The Making of the New York African-American Community, 1825-1918," Ph.D. diss., Columbia University, New York, 1991, pp. 17-35.

17. Mott, *American Journalism*, pp. 283-85; 318-19. For those interested in an exhaustive survey of the subject, see Mott's *History of American Magazines*. Mott also authored a study of fiction, *Golden Multitudes: The History of Best Sellers in the United States* (New York: Macmillan, 1947).

18. Taubman, *Making of the American Theater*, pp. 27-29, 51; Grimsted, *Melodrama Unveiled*, p. 22.

19. Toll, *On with the Show*, pp. 3-4; Carl Bode, *Anatomy of American Popular Culture*, pp. 19-37; Grimsted, *Melodrama Unveiled*, p. 99.

20. Toll, *On with the Show*, pp. 41-45.

21. For a discussion of the role of opera in popular culture, see Levine, *Highbrow/Lowbrow*, pp. 85-104.

22. For particularly good descriptions of Bowery B'hoys and Gals, their relations with others, and their place in urban New York, see Christine Stansell, *City of Women: Sex and Class in New York, 1789-1860* (1982; Urbana: University of Illinois Press, 1987), passim.

23. Maine farmer quoted in Grimsted, *Melodrama Unveiled*, p. 52.

24. Ibid., p. 53. See also Robert C. Allen, *Horrible Prettiness: Burlesque and American Culture* (Chapel Hill: University of North Carolina Press, 1991), pp. 51-61. Although the focus of Allen's book is the late nineteenth and early twentieth centuries, his chapter on the American theater before the advent of burlesque is useful.

25. The emergence of cultural hierarchy is the major theme of Levine's *Highbrow/Lowbrow*. See especially Chapter 2, "The Sacralization of Culture," pp. 83-168.

26. Grimsted, *Melodrama Unveiled*, pp. 62, 85.

27. Taubman, *Making of the American Theater*, pp. 71, 75-76; Grimsted, *Melodrama Unveiled*, p. 85. For more extended treatments of Wright, Cushman, and Mowatt, see their entries in *Notable American Women*, edited by Edward T. James (Cambridge, MA: Harvard University Press, 1971). See also Celia Morris, *Fanny Wright: Rebel in America* (1984; Urbana: University of Illinois Press, 1992).

28. Saxton, *Rise and Fall of the White Republic*, p. 114.

29. Levine, *Highbrow/Lowbrow*, pp. 16-19. The first chapter of Levine's book is a fascinating study of Shakespeare in the antebellum United States.

30. Ibid., pp. 44-45; Grimsted, *Melodrama Unveiled*, pp. 112-22, 241.

31. Saxton, *Rise and Fall of the White Republic*, pp. 81, 117.

32. William Dunlap, *The Archers; or the Mountaineers of Switzerland*, quoted in *Melodrama Unveiled*, p. 184. Grimsted is one of a number of writers who have noted the power of comedy as a form of social commentary, though few make the case with the same degree of concreteness.

33. Ibid., pp. 182-83.

34. Grimsted, *Melodrama Unveiled*, pp. 215-18. The "Bad man!" line comes from James Croswell, *A New World Planted* (1802).

35. Toll, *On with the Show*, pp. 17-18; Grimsted, *Melodrama Unveiled*, pp. 215-18. For an analysis of *Nick of the Woods*, see Takaki, *Iron Cages*, pp. 84-92.

36. Roediger, *Wages of Whiteness*, p. 24.

37. Grimsted, *Melodrama Unveiled*, pp. 190-91.

38. Toll, *Blacking Up*, pp. 70-71.

39. For Shakespeare parodies, see Levine, *Highbrow/Lowbrow*, pp. 13-16. Roediger emphasizes the masculine milieu of minstrelsy in his chapter on the subject in *Wages of Whiteness*, pp. 115-31.

40. Toll, *On with the Show*, p. 57; Grimsted, *Melodrama Unveiled*, p. 99.

41. The alliance of minstrels (and other creators of popular culture) with the Democratic Party is central to Saxton's *Rise and Fall of the White Republic*; see especially p. 165. For the intensification of racism in minstrelsy, see Toll, *Blacking Up*, pp. 87-97.

42. Toll, *Blacking Up*, pp. 45-47. For a description of the variety and vitality of black culture, see Lawrence Levine's magnificent *Black Culture and Consciousness: Afro-American Folk Thought from Slavery to Freedom* (New York: Oxford Unversity Press, 1977). For the ambivalent appeal of black culture to Irish Americans, see Roediger, *Wages of Whiteness*, pp. 150-56.

43. For white-black minstrel mixing, see Toll, *Blacking Up*, pp. 42-45. Levine notes the absorption of resistant minstrel song by African Americans in *Black Culture and Consciousness*, pp. 192-95.

44. Barnum quoted in Toll, *On with the Show*, p. 27.

45. For a brief description of medicine shows, see Don B. Wilmeth's essay on "Stage Entertainment" in *The Handbook of American Popular Culture*, edited by M. Thomas Inge (Westport, CT: Greenwood Press, 1978), pp. 304.

46. An autopsy after Heth's death led doctors to conclude that she could only have been half as old as she claimed to be, though her former owner continued to claim she was alive and living in Connecticut. He even convinced James Gordon Bennett of the *Herald* to run a story on it; it was later retracted, as was another story that Barnum had concocted Heth's claims. See Harris, *Humbug*, pp. 25-26.

47. Barnum quoted in Harris, *Humbug*, pp. 54-5. This quote also appears on p. 112 of Bode's edition of *Struggles and Triumphs*.

48. Mott, *American Journalism*, pp. 225-26; Harris, *Humbug*, pp. 68-70.

49. On the role of the confidence man among the ranks of the upwardly mobile, see Karen Halttunen's highly regarded *Confidence Men and Painted Women: A Study of Middle-Class Cuture in America, 1830-1870* (New Haven, CT: Yale University Press, 1982). Neil Harris calls public interest in Barnum's kind of manipulation the "operational aesthetic." See his description on p. 57, and his chapter on the subject, in *Humbug*, pp. 61-89.

50. For a discussion of the role of Brer Rabbit in slave tales, see Levine, *Black Culture and Consciousness*, pp. 121-33, 370-75.

51. For a discussion of Smith's Jack Downing and selections of his work, see Walter Blair, *Native American Humor* (1937; New York: Harper & Row, 1960). Constance Rourke also analyzes the Downing letters in *American Humor*, pp. 23-27.

52. David Crockett, *A Narrative of the Life of David Crockett by Himself* (1834; Lincoln: Bison/University of Nebraska Press, 1987), p. 8. Crockett's maxim appears in copies of the title page and advertisements included in this edition; it also appears in modified form in the text itself (p. 13). Paul Andew Hutton's introduction is a good source of bibliographic and background information on Crockett. Constance Rourke is also the author of a biography, *Davy Crockett* (New York: Harcourt Brace, 1934).

53. Quoted by Hutton in *Narrative of the Life of David Crockett*, p. xvi.

54. Crockett almanacs are ably analyzed in David Reynolds, *Beneath the American Renaissance*, pp. 441-42, 450-53. For the significance of John Henry to the African-American community, see Levine, *Black Culture and Consciousness*, pp. 420-27. An anonymous portrait of Sal Fink is included in Blair, *Native American Humor*, pp. 284-85.

55. Reynolds, *Beneath the American Renaissance*, p. 451.

56. Scholarship on antebellum reform is enormous. For one good survey, see Ronald Walters, *American Reformers, 1815-1865* (New York: Hill & Wang, 1978). For a discussion of *The Drunkard*, see Bode, *Anatomy of American Popular Culture*, pp. 5-7.

57. For a broad, contextual survey of the Awakenings in American life, see William G. McGloughlin, *Revivals, Reawakenings and Reform* (Chicago: University of Chicago Press, 1969) and Lewis Perry, *Intellectual Life in America* (Chicago: University of Chicago Press, 1989). For the cultural life of revivals, see Dickson D. Bruce, Jr., *And They All Sang Hallelujah: Plain-Folk Camp-Meeting Religion, 1800-1845* (Knoxville: University of Tennessee Press, 1974) and

Whitney R. Cross, *The Burnt-Over District: The Social and Intellectual History of an Enthusiastic Religion in Western New York, 1800-1850* (Ithaca, NY: Cornell University Press, 1950).

58. For a good brief survey of these movements, see Ronald Walters, *American Reformers 1815-1860* (New York: Hill & Wang, 1978). See also John L. Thomas's highly regarded essay "Romantic Reform in America" in *Antebellum Reform*, edited by David Brion Davis (New York: Harper & Row, 1967), pp. 153-76 (the essay originally appeared in the Winter 1965 issue of *American Quarterly*).

59. Bode devotes a chapter to the American Tract Society in *Anatomy of Popular Culture*, pp. 132-48. Halttunen's *Confidence Men and Painted Women* focuses on middle-class self-help literature and other kinds of manuals.

60. Mott, *A History of American Magazines,* pp. 356-63. For discussions of Bonner and Fern, see Joyce Warren, *Fanny Fern: An Independent Woman* (New Brunswick, NJ: Rutgers University Press, 1992) and Kelley, *Private Woman, Public Stage.*

61. Michael Denning, *Mechanic Accents: Dime Novels and Working-Class Culture in America* (London: Verso, 1987). The relationship between reform literature and sensation fiction is extensively explored in Reynolds, *Beneath the American Renaissance*; see esp. pp. 169-224.

62. For discussions of Lippard, see Bode, *Anatomy of American Popular Culture*, pp. 162-68; Reynolds, *Beneath the American Renaissance*, pp. 204. Lippard is the focus of one chapter of Denning's *Mechanic Accents*; see pp. 85-117. The most sustained analysis of his career is Reynolds, *George Lippard* (Boston: Twayne, 1982). Reynolds also edited a collection of Lippard's work, *George Lippard, Prophet of Protest: Writings of an American Radical, 1822-1854* (New York: Peter Lang, 1986).

63. On the erotic dimensions of popular fiction and its relation to reform literature and artisanal radicalism, see Reynolds, *Beneath the American Renaissance*, pp. 54-91, 211-24.

64. For discussions of Southworth, see Coultrap-McQuin, *Doing Literary Business*, pp. 49-78 (the description of Southworth as "queen" appears on p. 51); Baym, *Woman's Fiction*, pp. 110-39. Southworth is also discussed throughout Kelley's *Private Woman, Public Stage*. Denning emphasizes Southworth's working-class audience in *Mechanic Accents* (p. 188), where he also notes the post-Civil War direction of dime fiction about women.

65. Ronald Zboray, *A Fictive People: Antebellum Economic Development and the American Reading Public* (New York: Oxford University Press, 1993), pp. 65-67.

66. For the role of Scott and the varieties of plantation fiction, see William Taylor's now classic *Cavalier and Yankee: The Old South and the American National Character* (New York: Doubleday, 1961). Twain is quoted in James Chandler, "The Historical Novel Goes to Hollywood: Scott, Griffith, and Film Epic Today," in *The Romantics and Us,* edited by Gene W. Ruoff (New Brunswick, NJ: Rutgers University Press, 1990), p. 247.

67. For an introduction to Irving's career, see Haskell Springer, "Washington Irving and the Knickerbocker Group," in *The Columbia Literary History of the United States*, edited by Emory Elliot (New York: Columbia University Press, 1988), pp. 229-39.

68. Good contextualized analyses of Cooper include H. Daniel Peck, "Cooper and the Writers of the Frontier," in *The Columbia Literary History of the United States*, pp. 240-61; Tompkins, *Sensational Designs*, pp. 94-121; and Leslie Fiedler, *Love and Death in the American Novel* (New York: Dell, 1960), pp. 150-205.

69. For good readings of Whitman, see Reynolds, *Beneath the American Renaissance*. Of particular note is Justin Kaplan's *Walt Whitman: A Life* (New York: Simon & Schuster, 1980). Renolds also authored a biography of Whitman (New York: Alfred A. Knopf, 1995).

70. Hawthorne's remark, which has been widely cited, can be found in Fred Lewis Pattee, *The Feminine Fifties* (New York: D. Appleton-Century Company, 1940), p. 110. Mott's comment appears in *Golden Multitudes*, p. 126. For another treatment with at least a faintly condescending air, see James D. Hart, *The Popular Book: A History of America's Literary Taste* (New York: Oxford University Press, 1950), pp. 85-124.

71. For the role of *Harper's Weekly* and other newsmagazines, see Alice Fahs, "Publishing the War," Ph.D. diss., New York University, 1993.

72. See Zboray's chapter on this subject in *A Fictive People*, pp. 156-79.

73. Baym notes the departure from the Richardsonian tradition and the hard edges in domestic novels in *Woman's Fiction*, pp. 25-30. See also Reynolds, *Beneath the American Renaissance*, pp. 349-51.

74. Reynolds, *Beneath the American Renaissance*, p. 342. For a more critical assessment of this strategy, see Ann Douglas, *The Feminization of American Culture* (1977; New York: Anchor/Doubleday, 1988).

75. For the "masculine" perogatives afforded black women (Tubman in particular), see Lyde Cullen Sizer, "Acting Her Part: Narratives of Union Women Spies," in *Divided Houses: Gender and the Civil War*, edited by Catherine Clinton and Nina Silber (York: Oxford University Press, 1992), pp. 114-33.

76. For a description and analysis of this exchange, see Lyde Cullen Sizer, "'A Revolution in Woman Herself': Northern Women Writers and the American Civil War," Ph.D. diss., Brown University, 1994.

77. Starling, *Slave Narrative*, p. 2.

78. *Maum Guinea* is structured as a series of slave reminiscences and borrows the narrative style and stories common to slave narratives. For an analysis, see Sizer, "A Revolution in Woman Herself."

79. For what many now consider the definitive biography of Stowe, see Joan D. Hendrick, *Harriet Beecher Stowe: A Life* (New York: Oxford University Press, 1994).

80. For two opposing readings of *Uncle Tom's Cabin*, see Douglas, *Feminization of American Culture*, pp. 3-13; and Tompkins, *Sensational Designs*, pp. 122-46. The critic quoted is Gerald Early. See *"The Color Purple* as Everybody's Protest Art" in *Tuxedo Junction: Essays on American Culture* (New York: Ecco Press, 1989), pp. 44-45. The Lincoln quote, which is quite famous, is cited by Carl Sandburg in *Abraham Lincoln: The War Years,* vol. III (New York: Harcourt, Brace & Company, 1939), p. 201.

81. Various stage versions of *Uncle Tom's Cabin* are discussed in Toll, *Blacking Up*, pp. 90-96, 151-55. Among those producing dramatic versions was P.T. Barnum, who featured what he called a "just and sensible" show at his dime museum in

1853 that did not "foolishly and unjustly elevate the negro above the white man in intellect and morals" (see p. 153).

82. For more on the relationship of *Uncle Tom's Cabin*, *Birth of a Nation*, and *Gone with the Wind*, see Leslie Fielder, *What Was Literature? Class Culture and Mass Society* (New York: Touchstone, 1984). These subjects are also discussed in Jim Cullen, *The Civil War in Popular Culture: A Reusable Past* (Washington, DC: Smithsonian Institution Press, 1995).

83. Mott, *American Journalism*, p. 279.

Sources for "The Astor Place Riot"

Works that discuss the Astor Place riot include David Grimsted, *Melodrama Unveiled: American Theater and Culture 1800-1850* (1968; Berkeley: University of California Press, 1987); Lawrence W. Levine, *Highbrow/Lowbrow: The Emergence of Cultural Hierarchy in America* (Cambridge, MA: Harvard University Press, 1988); Robert C. Toll, *On with the Show: The First Century of American Show Business* (New York: Oxford University Press, 1976); and Richard Moody, *The Astor Riot* (Bloomington: University of Indiana Press, 1958). For a description of the cultural life of the Bowery, see Christine Stansell, *City of Women: Sex and Class in New York 1789-1860* (1982; Urbana: University of Illinois Press, 1987). Lydia Maria Child's eyewitness description of the riot can be found in *Lydia Maria Child: Selected Letters, 1817-1880,* edited by Milton Meltzer and Patricia G. Holland (Amherst: University of Massachusetts Press, 1982).

Sources for "The Art and Life of Fanny Fern"

Fanny Fern's 1854 novel *Ruth Hall: A Domestic Tale of the Present Time* was republished in 1986 by Rutgers University Press. This excellent edition, which includes a selection of Fern's columns and bibliograpic references, also has a fine introduction by Joyce Warren. Warren is the author of *Fanny Fern: An Independent Woman* (New Brunswick, NJ: Rutgers University Press, 1992), which is likely to remain the standard work on Fern for some time to come.

Other works that discuss Fern's life and career include Mary Kelly, *Private Woman, Public Stage: Literary Domesticity in Nineteenth-Century America* (New York: Oxford University Press, 1985); Nina Baym, *Woman's Fiction, A Guide to Novels by and about Women in America, 1820-1870* (Ithaca, NY: Cornell University Press, 1978); Frank Mott, *A History of American Magazines 1850-1865* (Cambridge, MA: Harvard University Press, 1938), and "Sara Payson Willis Parton," in *Notable American Women: A Biographical Dictionary*, edited by Edward T. James (Cambridge, MA: Harvard University Press, 1971).

3

STAGES OF DEVELOPMENT

Further Reading

The emerging chasm between classes and the ambivalence of the U.S. elite vis-à-vis the mass society of the late nineteenth century have been given their most focused expression in Lawrence Levine, *Highbrow/Lowbrow: The Emergence of Cultural Hierarchy in America* (Cambridge, MA: Harvard University Press, 1988). For other works that discuss these issues, see Alan Trachtenberg, *The Incorporation of America: Culture and Society in the Gilded Age* (New York: Hill & Wang, 1982); Roy Rosenzweig, *Eight Hours for What We Will: Workers and Leisure in an Industrial City, 1870-1920* (New York: Cambridge University Press, 1983); and Kathy Peiss, *Cheap Amusements: Working Women and Leisure in Turn of the Century New York* (Philadelphia, PA: Temple University Press, 1986).

The literature on emancipation and its effects on African Americans is enormous. For one particularly highly regarded and comprehensive survey, see Leon F. Litwack, *Been in the Storm So Long: The Aftermath of Slavery* (New York: Vintage, 1980). For a general study that focusses on black women, see Jacqueline Jones, *Labor of Love, Labor of Sorrow: Black Women, Work, and the Family from Slavery to Freedom* (New York: Vintage, 1985). The synthetic character of African-American cultural life has been widely remarked upon, although the particular proportions have been disputed. Some of the works that explore this culture, in its broadest formulations, include Eugene Genovese, *Roll, Jordan, Roll: The World the Slaves Made* (New York: Vintage, 1976); Herbert G. Gutman, *The Black Family in Slavery and Freedom, 1750-1925* (New York: Vintage, 1976); John W. Blassingame, *The Slave Community: Plantation Life in the Antebellum South* (New York: Oxford University Press, 1972); Lawrence W. Levine, *Black Culture and Black Consciousness: Afro-American Folk Thought from Slavery to Freedom* (New York: Oxford University Press, 1977); and George Rawick: *From Sundown to Sunup: The Making of the Black Community* (Westport, CT: Greenwood Press, 1972). Rawick's book is part of *The American Slave: A Composite Autobiography,* a nineteen-volume collection of slave narratives and other primary sources collected by the Works Project Administration during the Roosevelt Administration.

Sources that include at least some discussion of blues and other postemancipation African-American music include LeRoi Jones (Amiri Baraka), *Blues People: Negro Music in White America* (New York: Morrow, 1963); Bernice Johnson Reagon, ed., *We'll Understand It By and By: Pioneering African-American Gospel Composers* (Washington, DC: Smithsonian Institution Press, 1992); Samuel B. Charters, *The Country Blues* (1959; New York: Da Capo, 1975); James Lincoln Collier, *The Making of Jazz: A Comprehensive History* (New York: Delta, 1978); Eric Hobsbawm, *The Jazz Scene* (1959; New York: Pantheon, 1993); Levine's *Black Culture and Consciousness;* Robert Toll, *Blacking Up: The Minstrel Show in Nineteenth-Century America* (New York: Oxford University Press, 1974); and Jeff Todd Titon, *Downhome Blues: A Musical and Cultural Analysis* (Urbana: University of Illinois Press, 1977).

All of the books on theater cited at the end of Chapter 2 were also drawn upon for this chapter. To them I would add two sources on the circus: John Culhane, *The*

American Circus: An Illustrated History (New York: Holt, 1990) and Don Wilmeth, "Circus and Outdoor Entertainment," in *The Handbook of Popular Culture*, 2nd ed., edited by M. Thomas Inge (Westport, CT: Greenwood Press, 1989).

On dime novels/Westerns, see Henry Nash Smith's now classic *Virgin Land: The American West as Symbol and Myth* (New York: Vintage, 1950). Also highly regarded is John Cawelti, *The Six-Gun Mystique* (1970; Bowling Green, OH: The Popular Press, 1984). Cawelti is also the author of an incisive study of popular fiction, *Adventure, Mystery and Romance: Formula Stories as Art and Popular Culture* (Chicago: University of Chicago Press, 1976). See also Richard Slotkin, *The Fatal Environment: The Myth of the Frontier in the Age of Industrialization* (New York: Atheneum, 1985); Michael Denning, *Mechanic Accents: Dime Novels and Working-Class Culture in America* (London: Verso, 1987); and Jane Tompkins, *West of Everything: The Inner Life of Westerns* (New York: Oxford University Press, 1993).

All of the sources on journalism cited in Chapters 1 and 2 were of continued use in this chapter. For one particularly good brief treatment of photography and chromolithography, see Steven Lubar, *InfoCulture: The Smithsonian Book of Information Age Inventions* (Boston: Houghton Mifflin, 1993).

To works on the theater cited in earlier chapters, I would add Robert C. Allen's magnificent *Horrible Prettiness: Burlesque and American Culture* (Chapel Hill: University of North Carolina Press, 1991), whose title does not quite indicate the breadth of the book, which treats other stage forms as well. Also very good on a variety of cultural forms in this period (as well as the period to be covered in the next chapter) is David Nasaw, *Going Out: The Rise and Fall of Public Amusements* (New York: Basic Books, 1993), which focuses on the reconvergence of popular culture around the turn of the century and its later refragmentation in the mid-twentieth century.

Previously cited sources on minstrelsy all discuss the entrance of African Americans to the stage, but the subject is a particular focus of Ralph Ellison, "Change the Joke and Slip the Yoke" in his essay collection *Shadow and Act* (New York: Random House, 1964), which covers a variety of aspects of black culture. See also Nathan Irvin Huggins, *Harlem Renaissance* (New York: Oxford University Press, 1971) and Mel Watkins, *On the Wild Side: Laughing, Lying and Signifying—The Underground Tradition of African-American Humor That Transformed American Culture, from Slavery to Richard Pryor* (New York: Simon & Schuster, 1994). These books pay particular attention to—and take different stances on—the opportunities and costs attendant on African-American participation in and creation of minstrelsy and popular culture in general. On burlesque, see Allen's *Horrible Prettiness* and Peter Buckley, "The Culture of 'Leg Work': The Transformation of Burlesque After the Civil War" in *The Mythmaking Frame of Mind: Social Imagination and American Culture* (Belmont, CA: Wadsworth, 1993). On concert saloons, vaudeville, and related forms, see Albert F. McLean, *American Vaudeville as Ritual* (Lexington: University of Kentucky Press, 1965); Robert W. Snyder, *The Voice of the City: Vaudeville and Popular Culture in New York* (New York: Oxford University Press, 1989); Lewis Erenberg, *Steppin' Out: New York Nightlife and the Transformation of American Culture, 1890-1930* (1981; Chicago: University of Chicago Press, 1984); and Robert C. Allen, *Vaudeville and Film: A Study in Media Interaction* (New York: Arno, 1980).

Notes

1. Levine, *Highbrow/Lowbrow*, pp. 182-85.
2. Descriptions of the Columbia Exposition can be found in Trachtenberg, *Incorporation of America*, pp. 208-34; Thomas J. Schlereth, *Victorian America: Transformations in Everyday Life* (New York: HarperCollins, 1991), pp. 160-75; John Kasson, *Amusing the Millions: Coney Island at the Turn of the Century* (New York: Hill & Wang, 1978), pp. 11-28. Douglass' description of the Exposition as a "whited sepulcher," originally quoted by W.E.B. DuBois in *The Soul of Black Folk*, is cited in Trachtenberg, *Incorporation of America*, p. 222 and in Hazel V. Carby, *Reconstructing Womanhood: The Emergence of the Afro-American Woman Novelist* (New York: Oxford University Press, 1987), p. 5. Carby includes a useful discussion of the exclusion of black women writers from the event on pp. 3-5.
3. Levine, *Black Culture*, p. 6.
4. Collier, *The Making of Jazz*, p. 19.
5. Ibid., p. 17.
6. Thomas Wentworth Higginson, *Army Life in a Black Regiment* (1869; New York: Norton, 1984), pp. 187-213. Higginson's description of spirituals is marred by unconscious condescension, but he clearly recognized the novelty and power of this music. On Northern involvement with blacks during and after the Civil War, see Willie Lee Rose, *Rehearsal of Reconstruction: The Port Royal Experiment* (New York: Vintage, 1964) and Jacqueline Jones, *Soldiers of Light and Love: Northern Teachers and Georgia Blacks, 1865-1873* (Chapel Hill: University of North Carolina Press, 1980).
7. Reagon, "Pioneering African-American Gospel Music Composers: A Smithsonian Institution Research Project," in *We'll Understand It Better By and By*, pp. 11-12. Toll notes the influence of the Jubilee Singers and other black vocal groups in *Blacking Up*, pp. 235-44.
8. Levine, *Black Culture*, pp. 166-68.
9. Quoted in ibid. p. 276. For more on Handy's role in collecting and disseminating the blues, see *Father of the Blues: W.C. Handy* (1941; New York: DaCapo Press, 1969).
10. Collier, *Making of Jazz*, p. 44. For an extended treatment of the subject, see Terry Waldo, *This Was Ragtime* (1976; New York: DaCapo, 1991).
11. Collier, *Making of Jazz*, pp. 64-65.
12. Robert C. Toll, *On with the Show: The First Century of Show Business* (New York: Oxford University Press, 1976), p. 146. For an example of how little-regarded late nineteenth-century theater is, see Howard Taubman's widely cited *Making of American Theater* (New York: Coward McCann, 1965). Taubman devotes less than 25 pages of his almost 400-page study to this period.
13. Taubman, *Making of American Theater*, pp. 104-5; Toll, *On with the Show*, pp. 149-55.
14. Toll, *On with the Show*, p. 149.
15. Ibid., pp. 155-63.
16. Ira Berlin, Joseph P. Reidy, and Leslie Rowland, eds., *Freedom: A Documentary History of Emancipation, 1861-1867*, Series II: *The Black Military Experience* (New York: Cambridge University Press, 1982), p. 733.

17. Ron Takaki, *Iron Cages: Race and Culture in 19th-Century America*, 2nd ed. (1979; New York: Oxford University Press, 1990), pp. 216-24. For representations of Asians in minstrelry, see Toll, *Blacking Up*, pp. 169-72.

18. For a discussion of *conjunto* in the context of Mexican/American music, see Manuel Peña, *The Texas-Mexican Conjunto: History of a Working-Class Music* (Austin: University of Texas Press, 1985); on the Chinese presence, see Helen Wong Jean, "Playing the Palace: A Chinese American's Recollections of Vaudeville," in *Chinese-America: History and Perspectives* (Chinese Historical Society of America, 1989), pp. 111-16.

19. See Cawelti, *Mystery, Adventure, and Romance* and *The Six-Gun Mystique*.

20. Smith, *Virgin Land*, pp. 99-100.

21. Sales figure in mentioned Sharon M. Harris, *Rebecca Harding Davis and American Realism* (Philadelphia: University of Pennsylvania Press, 1991), p. 377, n. 87; Nina Baym, *Woman's Fiction: A Guide to Novels by and about Women in America, 1820-1870* (Ithaca, NY: Cornell University Press, 1978), pp. 176, 181; Smith, *Virgin Land*, p. 103.

22. Smith, *Virgin Land*, pp. 91-94; 102-3; John Cawelti, *Mystery, Adventure, and Romance*, pp. 210-11.

23. Cawelti, *Mystery, Adenture and Romance*, pp. 211-12; Smith, *Virgin Land*, pp. 109-13, 126-35. In *Mechanic Accents,* Denning notes that Smith misses the class dimension of the Deadwood Dick novels, seeing them as a degeneration of the genre rather than a reflection of a brief confrontational moment apparent in other genres of dime novel fiction; see pp. 157-62.

24. For an excellent analysis of the ambivalence running through Alger stories and other middle-class fiction for boys, see Daniel T. Rodgers, *The Work Ethic in Industrial America, 1850-1920* (Chicago: University of Chicago Press, 1978), pp. 125-52. The observation about the typical luck of the Alger hero appears on p. 140.

25. Denning, *Mechanic Accents*, pp. 178-79, 185.

26. Ibid., pp. 50-52, 159-60.

27. Ibid., pp. 20, 73. Smith also remarks on the mass-produced quality of dime novel fiction in *Virgin Land*, p. 100.

28. For more on Bellamy and his milieu, see John L. Thomas, *Alternative America: Henry George, Edward Bellamy, Henry Demarest Lloyd and the Adversary Tradition* (Cambridge, MA: Harvard University Press, 1983).

29. For very good summaries and descriptions of realism, naturalism, and local color, see the relevant essays in Emery Elliot, ed., *The Columbia Literary History of the United States* (New York: Columbia University Press, 1988).

30. "Persons attempting to find a motive in this narrative will be prosecuted; persons attempting to find a moral in it will be banished; persons attempting to find a plot in it will be shot," reads the "Notice" at the start of the novel (1885; New York: Signet, 1987), p. 10.

31. Lubar, *InfoCulture*, p. 52.

32. Ibid., p. 58.

33. Frank Mott, *American Journalism: A History of Newspapers in the United States Through 250 Years, 1690-1940* (New York: Macmillan, 1941), p. 411.

34. Daniel Czitrom, *Media and the American Mind from Morse to McLuhan* (Chapel Hill: University of North Carolina Press, 1982), pp. 25-29; Mott, *American Journalism*, pp. 491-93.

35. Michael Schudson, *Discovering the News: A Social History of American Newspapers* (New York: Harper & Row, 1978), pp. 99-100, 103.

36. On Schurz, see Mott, *American Journalism*, p. 427; on Cahan, the *Jewish Daily Forward,* and foreign language papers, see Schudson, *Discovering the News*, pp. 97-98. See also John Bodnar, *The Transplanted: A History of Immigrants in Urban America* (Bloomington: University of Indiana Press, 1987), pp. 110-11. Bodnar's book is probably the best recent survey of American immigration.

37. Mott, *American Journalism*, pp. 411-29.

38. Information on Pulitzer was drawn from Mott, *American Journalism*, pp. 430-45, and Schudson, *Discovering the News*, pp. 91-96. For a well-regarded book-length treatment, see George Juergens, *Joseph Pulitzer and the New York World* (Princeton, NJ: Princeton University Press, 1966).

39. Mott, *American Journalism*, pp. 519-26. For a fuller treatment, see W.A. Swanberg, *Citizen Hearst* (New York: Scribners, 1961).

40. Mott, *American Journalism*, pp. 527-33; Schudson, *Discovering the News*, pp. 61-65.

41. *Recorder* and *Telegrapher* quoted in John Mack Faragher, Mari Jo Buhle, Daniel Czitrom, and Susan Armitage, *Out of Many: A History of the American People* (Englewood Cliffs, NJ: Prentice-Hall, 1994), pp. 645-46.

42. Toll, *On with the Show*, pp. 184-89.

43. Ibid., pp. 171-82.

44. On nineteenth-century attitudes toward prostitution, see Christine Stansell, *City of Women: Sex and Class in New York, 1789-1860* (Urbana: University of Illinois Press, 1982), pp. 83-101.

45. Allen, *Horrible Prettiness*, pp. 87-94.

46. Ibid., pp. 122-32.

47. Ibid., pp. 99, 132-37; Buckley, "The Culture of 'Leg Work,'" p. 122. Buckley emphasizes the degree to which the transgressions of burlesque reflected social tensions over the role of women in post-Civil War U.S. society. Howells's review, "The New Taste in Theatricals," appeared in the May 1869 *Atlantic Monthly,* p. 643.

48. Allen, *Horrible Prettiness,* pp. 148-56. Allen sees a steady decline in the subversive and artistic power of burlesque, especially in the twentieth century. In his treatment in *On with the Show*, however, Toll implicitly asserts its empowering element for star performers. See pp. 207-38.

49. For a discussion, see Toll, *On with the Show*, pp. 239-63.

50. Snyder, *Voice of the City*, pp. 12-25; Toll, *On with the Show*, pp. 267-69. I also consulted Richard Canedo's forthcoming Brown University doctoral dissertation on vaudeville. I thank Mr. Canedo for sharing his work with me.

51. Snyder, *Voice of the City*, p. 105.

52. Ibid., pp. 55-56, 109.

53. Snyder cites this statistic in a footnote on p. 198 of *Voice of the City*.

54. Ibid. pp. 44, 53; Erenberg, *Steppin' Out*, p. 195. Erenberg devotes a chapter to analyzing Tucker's persona and career; see pp. 176-205.

55. The last chapter of Snyder's *Voice of the City* is titled "Respectable Thrills," a phrase that neatly encapsulates the shifting tenor of vaudeville at the end of the century; see pp. 130-54. This shift in values is also the focus of Erenberg's *Steppin' Out*, though he seems to imply that the direction of American culture

is top-down instead of bottom-up. Kathy Peiss notes this in *Cheap Amusements*, p. 190, n. 11.

Sources for "Coney Island"

The best brief study of Coney Island is John F. Kasson's *Amusing the Million: Coney Island at the Turn of the Century* (New York: Hill and Wang, 1978). Kathy Peiss includes an excellent overview that focuses on women in *Cheap Amusements: Working Women and Leisure in Turn-of-the-Century New York* (Philadelphia, PA: Temple University Press, 1986), while David Nasaw provides a wealth of information on Coney Island in particular and amusement parks in general in *Going Out: The Rise and Fall of Public Amusements* (New York: Basic Books, 1993). Extensive references for further information can be found in Don B. Wilmeth's bibliographic essay on "Circus and Outdoor Entertainment" in *The Handbook of American Popular Culture*, 2nd ed., edited by M. Thomas Inge (Westport, CT: Greenwood Press, 1989).

Sources for "The Dark Humor of Bert Williams"

Among the books that include a discussion of Bert Williams are Robert Toll, *On with the Show: The First Century of Show Business* (New York: Oxford University Press, 1976) and *Blacking Up: Minstrel Shows in Nineteenth-Century America* (New York: Oxford University Press, 1974); Nathan Irvin Huggins, *Harlem Renaissance* (New York: Oxford University Press, 1971); Lawrence W. Levine, *Black Culture and Black Consciousness: Afro-American Folk Thought from Slavery to Freedom* (New York: Oxford University Press, 1977); Robert W. Snyder, *The Voice of the City: Vaudeville and Popular Culture in New York* (New York: Oxford University Press, 1989); Mel Watkins, *On the Wild Side: Laughing, Lying and Signifying—The Underground Tradition of African-American Humor that Transformed American Culture, from Slavery to Richard Pryor* (New York: Simon and Schuster, 1994). See also Ann Charters, *Nobody: The Story of Bert Williams* (New York: Morrow, 1970).

4
MEDIATING COMMUNITIES

Further Reading

General works on this period that focus on the commercial dimensions of popular culture include: Richard Maltby, ed., *The Passing Parade: A History of Popular Culture in the Twentieth Century* (New York: Oxford University Press, 1989); Roland Marchand, *Advertising the American Dream: Making Way for Modernity, 1920-1940* (Berkeley: University of California Press, 1985); Warren Susman, *Culture as History: The Transformation of American Society in the Twentieth Century* (New York: Pantheon, 1984); Richard Wightman Fox and T.J. Jackson

Lears, eds., *The Culture of Consumption: Critical Essays in American History, 1880-1980* (New York: Pantheon, 1983). See also Lawrence W. Levine's essays on the 1920s and 1930s in *The Unpredictable Past: Explorations in American Cultural History* (New York: Oxford University Press, 1993). For an excellent reading of consumer culture in the 1940s, see John Morton Blum, *V Was for Victory: Politics and Culture During World War II* (New York: Harcourt Brace Jovanovich, 1976).

The literature on film is enormous, and those who choose to focus on its history, theory, practice, or other aspects can take years to master one subdiscipline while remaining largely ignorant of the others. Perhaps the best single work that touches on the major elements is James Monaco's *How to Read a Film: The Art, Technology, Language, History, and Theory of Film and Media* (New York: Oxford University Press, 1977), which has been periodically updated and revised, and which includes an excellent bibliography. My discussion of the medium was also informed by a number of (generally historical) sources, including Robert Sklar's superb *Movie-Made America: A Cultural History of American Movies* (New York: Vintage, 1975), which was reissued by Vintage in an updated edition in 1995 as this book was being completed; Garth Jowett, *Film: The Democratic Art* (Boston: Focal Press, 1976); and Lary May, *Screening Out the Past: The Birth of Mass Culture and the Motion Picture Industry* (1980; Chicago: University of Chicago Press, 1983). Discussions of film are also a significant part of Robert C. Toll, *The Entertainment Machine: American Show Business in the Twentieth Century* (New York: Oxford University Press, 1982), Daniel Czitrom, *Media and the American Mind From Morse to McLuhan* (Chapel Hill: University of North Carolina Press, 1982); and Maltby's *The Passing Parade*. For an outline of film history and an extensive bibliography, see Robert Armour's essay in *The Handbook of American Popular Culture*, edited by M. Thomas Inge (Westport, CT: Greenwood Press, 1989).

The various film genres sketched in this chapter are discussed at greater length in Thomas Schatz, *The Genius of the System: Hollywood Filmmaking in the Studio Era* (New York: Pantheon, 1988) and *Hollywood Genres: Formulas, Filmmaking and the Studio System* (Philadelphia, PA: Temple University Press, 1981). See also Robert Ray, *A Certain Tendency in the Hollywood Cinema, 1930-1980* (Princeton, NJ: Princeton University Press, 1985) and Michael Wood, *America in the Movies* (1975; New York: Columbia University Press, 1989). The perspective sketched out in this chapter also owes a debt to Susman's *Culture as History* and a number of other texts in the American Studies tradition.

For a general analysis of women actors from the 1920s to the present, see Molly Haskell, *From Reverence to Rape: The Treatment of Women in Movies* (1973; Chicago: University of Chicago Press, 1987). On the history of African Americans in U.S. cinema, see Donald Bogle, *Toms, Coons, Mulattoes, Mammies & Bucks: An Interpretive History of Blacks in American Films*, (1973; rev. ed., New York: Continuum, 1989). See also Thomas Cripps, *Slow Fade to Black: The Negro in American Film, 1900-1942* (New York: Oxford University Press, 1977) and *Making Movies Black: Hollywood Filmmaking in the Civil Rights Era* (New York: Oxford University Press, 1993).

For discussions of vaudeville's decline, see Robert C. Allen, *Vaudeville and Film: A Study in Media Interaction* (New York: Arno Press, 1980); Robert W. Snyder, *The Voice of the City: Vaudeville and Popular Culture in New York* (New York: Oxford University Press, 1989); and Robert C. Toll, *On with the Show: The First Century of Show Business* (New York: Oxford University Press, 1976). See also

Robert C. Allen, *Horrible Prettiness: Burlesque and American Culture* (Chapel Hill: University of North Carolina Press, 1991).

Most of the sources used in my discussion of fiction and journalism were cited in Chapters 2 and 3. But for a concise description of the popular literary aesthetic, see John Cawelti, "The Concept of Formula in Popular Literature," *Journal of Popular Culture* 3 (1969). The pulps are ably handled in Bill Blackbeard's essay on the subject in *The Handbook of American Popular Culture*.

Standard sources on the history of radio include Erik Barnouw, *A Tower in Babel: A History of Broadcasting in the United States to 1933* (New York: Oxford University Press, 1966); Sydney W. Head, *Broadcasting in America: A Survey of Television and Radio*, 3rd ed. (Boston: Houghton Mifflin, 1972); J. Fred MacDonald, *Don't Touch That Dial: Radio Programming and American Life from 1920 to 1960* (Chicago: Nelson-Hall, 1979); Arthur Frank Wertheim, *Radio Comedy* (New York: Oxford University Press, 1979); Czitrom's *Media and the American Mind*; Susan Douglas, *Inventing American Broadcasting, 1899-1922* (Baltimore: The Johns Hopkins University Press, 1987); Robert McChesney, *Telecommunications, Mass Media, and Democracy: The Battle for Control of U.S. Broadcasting, 1928-1935* (New York: Oxford University Press, 1993); and Susan Smulyan, *Selling Radio: The Commercialization of American Broadcasting, 1920-1934* (Washington, DC: Smithsonian Institution Press, 1994).

For a very good analysis of dance halls and their role in the lives of young working-class women, see Kathy Peiss's chapter on the subject in *Cheap Amusements: Working Women and Leisure in Turn-of-the-Century New York* (Philadelphia, PA: Temple University Press, 1986), pp. 88-114. See also Peiss's "'Charity Girls' and City Pleasures: Historical Notes on Working-Class Sexuality, 1880-1920" in *Powers of Desire: The Politics of Sexuality*, edited by Ann Snitow, Christine Stansell, and Sharon Thompson (New York: Monthly Review Press, 1983). On the Castles, and middle-class dancing in general, see Lewis Ehrenberg, *Steppin' Out: New York Nightlife and the Transformation of American Culture, 1890-1930* (1981; Chicago: University of Chicago Press, 1984), pp. 158-71. For a perceptive discussion of the dance marathon craze (one that includes a good reading of the Castles), see Carol Martin, *Dance Marathons: Performing in American Culture in the 1920s and 1930s* (Jackson: University of Mississippi Press, 1994).

On the early recording industry, see James Von Schilling, "Records and the Recording Industry" in *The Handbook of American Popular Culture* and Toll, *The Entertainment Machine*. For more on African-American music, see the citations in Chapter 3. The standard source on country music is Bill Malone, *Country Music U.S.A.* (1968; rev. ed., Austin: University of Texas Press, 1985). See also Cecilia Tichi, *High Lonesome: The American Culture of Country Music* (Chapel Hill: University of North Carolina Press, 1994).

Notes

1. Edison quoted in Lary May, *Screening Out the Past*, p. 26.
2. For more elaboration on this point, see Daniel Horowitz, *The Morality of Spending: Attitudes Towards Consumer Society in America, 1875-1940* (Baltimore: The Johns Hopkins University Press, 1985).
3. Garth Jowett, *Film: The Democratic Art*, p. 37. It should be noted that the average moving picture show cost ten cents, not the proverbial nickel, and one

could see a small-time movie/vaudeville show for fifteen cents. The fact remains, however, that film was the cheapest form of mass entertainment, a major factor in its appeal to working-class audiences.

4. Maltby, *Passing Parade*, p. 37; Toll, *Entertainment Machine*, p. 18; Sklar, *Movie-Made America*, p. 19. Barton W. Currie's "The Nickel Madness" appeared in the 24 August 1905 issue of *Harper's Weekly*, p. 1246.

5. For discussion of the Progressive attitudes toward movies, see May, *Screening Out the Past*, pp. 43-59; Jowett, *Film: The Democratic Art*, pp. 74-107; and Sklar, *Movie-Made America*, pp. 29-30.

6. For an extended treatment of Jewish Americans in the film industry, see Neal Gabler, *An Empire of Their Own: How the Jews Invented Hollywood* (New York: Anchor/Doubleday, 1988).

7. Sklar, *Movie-Made America*, p. 47.

8. For a concise history of movie theaters in the United States, see Douglas Gomery, "If You've Seen One, You've Seen the Mall," in *Seeing Through Movies*, edited by Mark Crispin Miller (New York: Pantheon, 1990), pp. 49-80.

9. On Pickford and Fairbanks, see May, *Screening Out the Past*, pp. 96-146; May devotes a chapter to DeMille on pp. 199-236. On Arbuckle, see *Movie-Made America*, pp. 77-79. The terms "character" and "personality" and the social transition from one to the other is explored in Susman's *Culture as History*.

10. Toll, *Entertainment Machine*, pp. 33-35.

11. Sklar, *Movie-Made America*, pp. 161-62.

12. See Schatz's book of the same name.

13. For a thoughtful reading of *Public Enemy* and gangster films, see Jowett, "Bullets, Beer and the Hays Office: Public Enemy," in John E. O'Connor and Martin A. Jackson, eds., *American History/American Film: Interpreting the Hollywood Image*, 2nd ed. (1979; New York: Continuum, 1988), pp. 57-76.

14. On *Scar of Shame,* see Cripps, "'Race Movies' as Voices of the Black Bourgeoisie: *The Scar of Shame,"* in ibid., pp. 39-56.

15. On Selznick and his movie packaging, see Schatz's chapters on his company in *The Genius of the System*, pp. 176-98; 322-39. On MCA and its role in Universal, see pp. 463-81.

16. For a good summary of early tabloid, see Mott's chapter on the subject in *American Journalism: A History of Newspapers in the United States Through 250 Years, 1690-1940* (New York: Macmillan, 1941), pp. 666-73.

17. Jane Tompkins offers an incisive critique of Modernism's retroactive impact on the literary canon in *Sensational Designs: The Cultural Work of American Fiction, 1790-1860* (New York: Oxford University Press, 1986).

18. For more on middlebrow, see Joan Shelly Rubin, *The Making of Middlebrow Culture* (Chapel Hill: University of North Carolina Press, 1992).

19. On the decline of the dime novel, see Michael Denning, *Mechanic Accents: Dime Novels and Working-Class Culture in America* (London: Verso, 1987), pp. 201-13.

20. For a discussion of detective fiction and other genres, see John Cawelti, *Adventure, Mystery, and Romance: Formula Stories as Art and Popular Culture* (Chicago: University of Chicago Press, 1976).

21. For statistics on *Gone with the Wind*, see Jim Cullen, *The Civil War in Popular Culture: A Reusable Past* (Washington, DC: Smithsonian Institution Press, 1995), p. 67.

22. For discussions of *Uncle Tom's Cabin*, *Birth of a Nation*, and *Gone with the Wind* as part of a century-long struggle in American cultural history, see Leslie Fiedler, *What Was Literature? Class, Culture, and Mass Society* (New York: Touchstone, 1984). These works, especially *Gone with the Wind* as book and film, are also discussed in Cullen, *The Civil War in Popular Culture.*
23. On the decline of burlesque, see Allen, *Horrible Prettiness*, pp. 243-69.
24. For discussion of the evolution of the musical in general and Cohan's career in particular, see Toll, *On with the Show*, pp. 171-206.
25. Figures cited in Czitrom, *Media and the American Mind*, pp. 71, 79.
26. The phrase is Smulyan's. See *Selling Radio*, p. 13.
27. For a particularly intelligent reading of Jack Benny's show, see Margaret T. McFadden, "'America's Boyfriend Who Can't Get a Date': Gender, Race, and the Cultural Work of the Jack Benny Program, 1932-1946," *Journal of American History* 80, no. 1 (June 1993): 113-34.
28. For extended readings of some of these genres, see MacDonald, *Don't Touch That Dial.*
29. Czitrom, *Media and the American Mind*, p. 85.
30. Janice Radway, *Reading the Romance: Women, Patriarchy and Popular Literature* (Chapel Hill: University of North Carolina Press, 1984).
31. For extended readings of *Amos 'n' Andy*, see Melvin Patrick Ely, *The Adventures of Amos 'n' Andy: A Social History of an American Phenomenon* (New York: The Free Press, 1991).
32. Toll, *Entertainment Machine*, pp. 54-55; Arthur F. Wertheim, *Radio Comedy*, pp. 48-49.
33. Cited in Wertheim, *Radio Comedy*, p. 37.
34. Ibid.
35. Critic quoted in Maltby, *Passing Parade*, pp. 102-3.
36. Statistic on newspaper ownership cited in MacDonald, *Don't Touch That Dial*, p. 4.
37. Czitrom, *Media and the American Mind*, p. 86.
38. Ibid., p. 87.
39. This phenonemon has been widely commented upon, but for unusually good graphic tabulations see Maltby, *Passing Parade*, p. 70.
40. For a good basic discussion of early American music, see Jack Larkin's chapter on the subject in *The Reshaping of Everyday Life, 1790-1840* (New York: Harper & Row, 1989), pp. 232-57.
41. On Hoyt, "A Trip to Chinatown," and "After the Ball," see Toll, *On with the Show*, pp. 189-91.
42. *Nightlife* writer and *Harvard Lampoon* quoted in Nasaw, *Going Out: The Rise and Fall of Public Amusements* (New York: Basic Books, 1993), pp. 105, 113.
43. Maltby, *Passing Parade*, p. 42.
44. Statistics on phonograph production cited in Thomas Schlereth, *Victorian America: Transformations in Everyday Life 1876-1915* (New York: Harper-Collins, 1991), p. 193.
45. Schlereth, *Victorian America*, p. 193; Toll, *Entertainment Machine*, p. 47.
46. Maltby, *Passing Parade*, p. 102; Toll, *Entertainment Machine*, pp. 48, 59.
47. Quoted in Eric Hobsbawm, *The Jazz Scene* (1959; New York: Pantheon, 1993), p. 27.
48. Quoted in Maltby, *The Passing Parade*, p. 72.

49. *The Autobiography of Malcolm X* as told to Alex Haley (1965; New York: Ballantine, 1973), p. 51.

50. Malone, *Country Music U.S.A.*, p. 19.

51. Lawrence W. Levine, "The Folklore of Industrial Society: Popular Culture and Its Audiences," *American Historical Review* 97, no. 5 (December 1992): 1377. A slightly different form of this essay is included in *The Unpredictable Past*.

52. Ibid., pp. 64-68.

53. Rodgers's life and work are ably handled in Malone's chapter entitled "The First Country Singing Star." For more extensive treatment, see Nolan Porterfield, *Jimmie Rodgers: The Life and Times of America's Blue Yodeler* (Urbana: University of Illinois Press, 1979).

54. For an extended treatment of Guthrie, see Joe Klein's fine *Woody Guthrie: A Life* (1980; New York: Ballantine, 1986).

55. Ibid., pp. 141-44.

56. Malone, *Country Music U.S.A.*; Toll, *Entertainment Machine*, p. 59.

Sources for "Chaplin's Business"

Chaplin's autobiography, *My Life in Pictures* (London: Bodley Head, 1974), is a readable account of the artist's life. A more incisive perspective is provided by Theodore Huff in *Charles Chaplin* (New York: Schuman, 1951). The 1992 film *Chaplin,* directed by Richard Attenborough and with Robert Downey, Jr., in the title role, also provides an evocative introduction to the artist's world.

Sources for "Billie Holiday, The Jazz Singer"

Billie Holiday's autobiography, written with William Dufty, *Lady Sings the Blues* (1956; London: Penguin, 1992), is a classic in the literature of jazz and a vivid social document of black life in the 1930s and 1940s. See also John Chilton, *Billie's Blues: The Billie Holiday Story 1933-1959* (New York: Da Capo, 1975), and Donald Clark, *Wishing on the Moon: The Life and Times of Billie Holiday* (New York: Viking/Penguin, 1994). An erratic and fictionalized film version of *Lady Sings the Blues* (1972) stars Diana Ross as Holiday.

5
CHANNELED ENERGY

Further Reading

My sketch of television history was drawn from a number of sources, the most important of which are those by Eric Barnouw. Barnouw is the author of a three-volume history of broadcasting published by Oxford University Press: *A Tower in Babel: A History of Broadcasting in the United States to 1933* (1966); *The Golden Web: A History of Broadcasting in the United States, 1933-1953* (1968); and *The Image Empire: A History of Broadcasting in the United States from 1953* (1970). These three volumes have been usefully condensed into a one-volume history, *Tube of Plenty: The Evolution of American Broadcasting,* which was published in 1975 and revised in 1982 and 1990 (my primary source for the material in this chapter). Barnouw is essential reading for anyone interested in the history of the medium. Robert C. Toll also provides useful introductory material in *The Entertainment Machine: American Show Business in the Twentieth Century* (New York: Oxford University Press, 1982). See also Richard Maltby, ed., *The Passing Parade: A History of Popular Culture in the Twentieth Century* (New York: Oxford University Press, 1989).

On particular television genres, shows, and creators, see Horace Newcomb, ed., *Television: The Critical View,* 4th ed. (1975; New York: Oxford University Press, 1987), a pivotal collection whose contributors represent a spectrum of views on the medium. At one end is Muriel Cantor in "Audience Control" (pp. 360-61), who sees the audience as having relatively little power. At the other end is David Marc in "Beginning to Begin Again," who sees television as a fairly democratic instrument of popular will. Marc's Whitmanesque view has been developed at greater length in *Demographic Vistas: Television in American Culture* (Philadelphia: University of Pennsylvania Press, 1984), and *Comic Visions: Television Comedy and American Culture* (Boston: Unwin/Hyman, 1989). For a more sociologically based defense of the medium, see Joshua Meyrowitz, *No Sense of Place: Time Impact of Electronic Media on Social Behavior* (New York: Oxford University Press, 1989).

For expositions of television's negative effects, see Jerry Mander, *Four Arguments for the Elimination of Television* (New York: Morrow, 1977) and Neil Postman, *Amusing Ourselves to Death: Public Discourse in the Age of Show Business* (New York: Viking, 1985). Mark Crispin Miller also takes a generally skeptical view in *Boxed In: The Culture of TV* (Evanston, IL: Northwestern University Press, 1987), as does Todd Gitlin, ed., *Watching Television* (New York: Pantheon, 1986). Gitlin offers a revealing, if now somewhat dated, picture of how TV executives think in *Inside Prime Time* (New York: Pantheon, 1985). Finally, see the insightful collection of essays edited by Robert C. Allen, *Channels of Discourse, Reassembled: Television and Contemporary Criticism* (Chapel Hill: University of North Carolina Press, 1992); this is an updated edition of *Channels of Discourse,* first published in 1987.

On the role of television in family life, see Cecilia Tichi, *Electronic Hearth: Creating an American Television Culture* (New York: Oxford University Press, 1991) and Lynn Spigel, *Make Room for TV: Television and the Family Ideal in Postwar America* (Chicago: University of Chicago Press, 1992).

Sources on the "paperback revolution" of the mid-twentieth century include Kenneth C. Davis, *Two-Bit Culture: The Paperbacking of America* (Boston: Houghton Mifflin, 1984) and Thomas L. Bonn, *Undercover: An Illustrated History of American Mass Market Paperbacks* (New York: Penguin, 1982). John Tebbel has also extensively discussed the subject in his four-volume *History of Book Publishing in the United States* (New York: R.R. Bowker, 1972-81). See also the one-volume synthesis of this work, *Between Covers: The Rise and Transformation of Book Publishing in America* (New York: Oxford University Press, 1987). For recent studies of genre fiction and its complexities, see Janice Radway, *Reading the Romance: Women, Patriarchy, and Popular Literature* (Chapel Hill: University of North Carolina Press, 1987) and Jane P. Tompkins, *West of Everything: The Inner Life of Westerns* (New York: Oxford University Press, 1992). Both Radway and Tompkins recognize the political limitations and reactionary tendencies that have characterized romance novels and Westerns, but both also note the pleasures and positive uses they afford for their (highly gendered) audiences.

In addition to the sources cited on radio in Chapter 4, I would add Peter Fornatale and Joshua E. Mills, *Radio in the Television Age* (New York: The Overlook Press, 1980). On corruption in the industry, see Frederic Dannen, *Hit Men: Power Brokers and Fast Money Inside the Music Business* (New York: Times Books, 1990).

Major general histories of rock & roll include Charlie Gillett, *The Sound of the City: The Rise of Rock and Roll,* rev. ed. (1970; New York: Pantheon, 1983); Ed Ward, Geoffrey Stokes, and Ken Tucker, *Rock of Ages: The Rolling Stone History of Rock & Roll* (New York: Rolling Stone Press/Summit Books, 1986); and David P. Szatmary, *Rockin' in Time: A Social History of Rock-and-Roll,* 2nd ed. (1987; Englewood Cliffs, NJ: Prentice-Hall, 1991). See also the superb *Rolling Stone Illustrated History of Rock & Roll,* a revised and updated collection of essays edited by Anthony DeCurtis and James Henke with Holly George-Warren (1976; New York: Random House, 1992). The best book on rap is Tricia Rose, *Black Noise: Rap Music and Black Culture in Contemporary America* (Hanover, NH: Wesleyan/University of New England Press, 1994); its counterpart for country is Bill Malone, *Country Music U.S.A.*, rev. ed. (1968; Austin: University of Texas Press, 1985).

Notes

1. For an insightful reading of the film and the uneasiness it reflected, see Martin A. Jackson, "The Uncertain Peace: *The Best Years of Our Lives,"* in *American History/American Film: Interpreting the Hollywood Image,* 2nd ed. (1979; New York: Continuum, 1988), pp. 147-65.
2. Robert Sklar, *Movie-Made America: A Cultural History of American Movies* (New York: Vintage, 1975), p. 269.
3. Ibid. pp. 267-68. This comment comes at the end of Sklar's chapter on the Red Scare and gives a larger sense of crisis in Hollywood during the late 1940s.
4. Ibid., p. 272.
5. The 85 percent figure cited in Barnouw, *Tube of Plenty,* p. 198; the 98 percent figure quoted in Marc, *Demographic Vistas,* p. 2.
6. For a discussion of Minow's comment and its context, see Barnouw, *Tube of Plenty,* pp. 299-308.
7. Ibid., pp. 48-49, 77-78, 84.
8. For a discussion of Armstrong, Sarnoff, and their relationship to each other, see Tom Lewis, *Empire of the Air: The Men Who Made Radio* (New York: HarperCollins, 1991).
9. Barnouw, *Tube of Plenty,* pp. 68-77.
10. Ibid, pp. 99-100, 110-111.
11. Ibid., p. 132. Furthermore, with rumors of a coming report on the bad effects of smoking, doctors could be shown only in the "most commendable light." The industry was nervous about antagonizing a powerful constituency.
12. Ibid., pp. 117-30.
13. Doctor cited in Robert S. Kelly, "Television," in *The Handbook of American Popular Culture,* edited by M. Thomas Inge (Westport, CT: Greenwood Press, 1978), p. 324.
14. These points are central to Meyrowitz, *No Sense of Place.*
15. Barnow, *Tube of Plenty,* p. 114.

16. Figures cited in Toll, *Entertainment Machine*, pp. 60-61.
17. For a discussion of these issues, see Tichi, *Electronic Hearth*.
18. Toll includes a useful chapter on the Western in movies and television in *Entertainment Machine*, pp. 75-99. Statistics on numbers of Westerns appears on p. 90.
19. Robert C. Allen, "*The Guiding Light:* Soap Opera as Economic Product and Cultural Document" in Newcomb, ed., *Television*, pp. 141-63; this essay also appears in John O'Connor, ed., *American History/American Television* (New York: Unger, 1983). See also Ruth Rosen, "Search for Yesterday," in Gitlin, ed., *Watching Television*.
20. Bernard Timberg, "The Rhetoric of the Camera in Television Soap Opera," in Newcomb, ed., *Television*, pp. 164-78.
21. On the possible decline of soaps, see Dana Kennedy, "Soaps on the Ropes," *Entertainment Weekly, 29* October 1993, pp. 37-38 (the 40 percent viewership figure, which does not include those who tape shows on videocassette recorders for later viewing, appears on p. 38).
22. Marc, *Demographic Vistas*, pp. 16-17; "Beginning to Begin Again," pp. 337-38.
23. *Demographic Vistas*, p. 169; "Beginning to Begin Again," p. 359.
24. For intelligent readings of these and other shows, see George Lipsitz's chapters on television in *Time Passages: Collective Memory and American Popular Culture* (Minneapolis: University of Minnesota Press, 1990).
25. Ken Auletta, *Three Blind Mice: How the TV Networks Lost Their Way* (New York: Vintage, 1992), p. 234.
26. Barnouw, *Tube of Plenty*, pp. 454-55.
27. For excellent discussions of these shows, see Marc's chapter, "The Sitcom at Literate Peak: Post-Vietnam Refinements of Mass Consciousness," in *Comic Visions*, pp. 157-206. (Paul Buhle collaborated on the *M*A*S*H* material.) See also Horace Newcomb, *TV: The Most Popular Art* (New York: Anchor, 1974).
28. "From Beulah to Oprah," *New York Times,* 15 January 1993, p. C1.
29. Barnouw, *Tube of Plenty*, p. 398. Black issues and characters were also portrayed on a number of other PBS series, including *Black Journal* and *NET Playhouse.*
30. Sklar, *Movie-Made America*, p. 377.
31. Ibid., p. 285.
32. Barnouw, *Tube of Plenty*, pp. 193-95.
33. Ibid., pp. 197-98.
34. For discussions of Hitchcock and Selznick, and Hitchcock's work as an independent, see Thomas Schatz, *The Genius of the System: Hollywood Filmmaking in the Studio Era* (New York: Pantheon, 1988), esp. pp. 381-407, 482-92.
35. Cited in Sklar, *Movie-Made America*, p. 299.
36. Figures cited in Davis, *Two-Bit Culture*, pp. 63, 79, 146.
37. Ibid., pp. 43, 65.
38. Ibid., p. 118.
39. Radway, *Reading the Romance*, p. 40.
40. Gathings quoted in Davis, *Two-Bit Culture*, p. 220.
41. Ibid., p. 179.
42. Ibid., p. 333.
43. Ibid., p. 7.

44. For one account of life on the radio frontier, see the memoir of Jim Ladd, disc jockey for the Los Angeles radio station KAOS, *Radio Waves: Life and Revolution on the FM Dial* (New York: St. Martin's Press, 1991).

45. James T. Patterson, *America in the Twentieth Century: A History* (San Diego: Harcourt Brace, 1983), p. 291.

46. For more on bluegrass, see Neil V. Rosenberg, *Bluegrass: A History* (Urbana: University of Illinois Press, 1985). Malone also includes a useful chapter on the subject in *Country Music U.S.A.*

47. Malone, *Country Music U.S.A.*, p. 226.

48. Ward, *Rock of Ages*, p. 47. The album was *The Voice of Frank Sinatra.*

49. Ibid., pp. 65-66.

50. Dave Marsh, *Glory Days: Bruce Springsteen in the 1980s* (New York: Pantheon, 1987), p. 90.

51. Ward, *Rock of Ages,* p. 77.

52. There are a number of biographies of Presley. By far the best is Peter Guralnick, *Last Train to Memphis: The Rise and Fall of Elvis Presley* (Boston: Little, Brown, 1994), one of two planned volumes.

53. Carroll quoted in Fornatale and Mills, *Radio in the Television Age,* p. 42; poster cited in Steven Lubar, *InfoCulture: The Smithsonian Book of Information Age Inventions* (Boston: Houghton Mifflin, 1993), p. 232. Descriptions of Freed include his entry in Jon Pareles and Patricia Romanowski, eds., *The Rolling Stone Encyclopedia of Rock 'n' Roll* (New York: Summit Books, 1983), p. 205. This book is an excellent reference source. For more on Freed and the payola scandal—and an exposé of the ongoing problems payola poses in the record industry—see Dannen, *Hit Men.*

54. For an investigation of the Nixon administration's efforts to hamper Lennon, see Jon Weiner, "John Lennon versus the FBI," in *Professors, Politics, and Pop* (London: Verso, 1991). Weiner is also the author of *Come Together: John Lennon in His Time* (New York: Random House, 1984).

55. For an excellent reading of disco and its place in 1970s life, see Tom Smucker's essay in *The Rolling Stone Illustrated History of Rock & Roll,* pp. 561-72. See also Richard Dyer, "In Defense of Disco," in *On Record: Rock, Pop and the Written Word,* edited by Simon Firth and Andrew Goodwin (New York: Pantheon, 1990), pp. 410-18.

56. For a definitive account of the rise and fall of punk, see Jon Savage, *England's Dreaming: Anarchy, the Sex Pistols, Punk Rock and Beyond* (New York: St. Martin's Press, 1992). For an insightful study connecting punk to other antiauthoritarian cultures, see Greil Marcus, *Lipstick Traces: A Secret History of the Twentieth Century* (Cambridge, MA: Harvard University Press, 1989).

Sources for "A Bunker Mentality"

Donna McCrohan, *Archie & Edith, Mike & Gloria: The Tumultuous History of All in the Family* (New York: Workman, 1987) is an excellent compendium. See also Horace Newcomb, *TV: The Most Popular Art* (New York: Anchor, 1974) and David Marc, *Comic Visions: Television Comedy and American Culture* (Boston: Unwin/Hyman, 1989) for extended discussions of the show.

Sources for "The Integrated Sound of Los Lobos"

For an excellent reading of the musical culture from which Los Lobos sprang, see George Lipsitz, "Cruising Around the Historical Bloc: Postmodernism and Popular Music in East Los Angeles," in *Time Passages: Collective Memory and American Popular Culture* (Minneapolis: University of Minnesota Press, 1990).

6
ELECTRONIC FRONTIERS

Further Reading

Because many of the developments discussed in this chapter are ongoing, much of the literature regarding them is fragmented, complex, or quickly obsolete. I drew on Ken Auletta, *Three Blind Mice: How the TV Networks Lost Their Way* (New York: Vintage, 1992). Though already dated, Auletta's book is the definitive study of television in the late 1980s and contains a wealth of useful information about how the television industry continues to work. See also George Gilder's neoconservative manifesto, *Life After Television: The Coming Transformation of Media and American Life* (New York: Norton, 1994).

For the discussion of media technology, I relied on Steve Lubar, *InfoCulture: The Smithsonian Book of Information Age Inventions* (Boston: Houghton Mifflin, 1993). I also referred to Howard Rheingold, *Virtual Reality* (New York: Summit, 1991) and Andrew Ross, *Strange Weather: Culture, Science, and the Limits of Technology* (London: Verso, 1991).

Notes

1. For a description of the rise of C-Span and its innovations, see James Lardner, "The Anti-Network," *The New Yorker,* 14 March 1994, pp. 48-55.
2. Auletta, *Three Blind Mice,* pp. 24-27.
3. Ibid., p. 18.
4. "The age of tape" is a variation on "the age of the cassette," a term historian Paul Buhle has used to describe the 1970s and 1980s. See his introduction to the edited collection of essays, *Popular Culture in America* (Minneapolis: University of Minnesota Press, 1987), p. x. I favor "tape" here because I'm covering a slightly broader period of time and because some machinery described in the following section (e.g., reel-to-reel tape recorders) doesn't actually use cassettes.
5. Lubar, *InfoCulture,* p. 266.
6. Ibid., p. 270.
7. Ibid., pp. 270-71.
8. Valenti quoted in Erik Barnouw, *Tube of Plenty: The Evolution of American Broadcasting* (New York: Oxford University Press, 1990), p. 502.
9. Lubar, *InfoCulture,* p. 270.

10. Ibid., p. 343.
11. Statistics on video games taken from ibid., pp. 274-75.
12. O'Rourke quoted in ibid., p. 278.
13. John Fiske, *Understanding Popular Culture* (Boston: Unwin Hyman, 1989), p. 139.
14. Publicist quoted in Barnouw, *Tube of Plenty,* p. 499.
15. Auletta, *Three Blind Mice,* pp. 223-24.
16. Lubar, *InfoCulture,* p. 373.
17. For an elaboration of these metaphors and their implications, see "Just a Dataway," *The New Yorker,* 16 May 1994, pp. 6-8.

Sources for "The Mixed Media of MTV"

Some of the most important writings on MTV are in the form of scholarly articles. Pat Aufderheide's "Music Videos: The Look of Sound" in *Watching Television,* edited by Todd Gitlin (New York: Pantheon, 1986) is an incisive, though by now somewhat dated, analysis of music video, while Simon Frith's "Video Pop: Picking Up the Pieces" in *Facing the Music,* edited by Simon Frith (New York: Pantheon, 1989) is an important article by the most influential British rock critic and sociologist (both books are part of Pantheon's Guides to Popular Culture). Frith is also the author of "Making Sense of Video: Pop into the Nineties" in *Music for Pleasure* (London: Routledge, 1988), which looks at video's role in the music industry and discusses MTV specifically. Finally, Dan Rubey's "Voguing at the Carnival: Desire and Pleasure on MTV," *South Atlantic Quarterly* 90, no. 4 (December 1991): 870-906 offers a postmodern scholarly reading of music video that emphasizes the degree to which MTV represents a new kind of literacy, one that offers forms of expression to counter those of the dominant culture. For a narrative chronicle of MTV, see Jane and Michael Stern's brief essay on the subject in their *Encyclopedia of Pop Culture* (New York: Pantheon, 1992); see also Ken Tucker's chapter "Rock in the Video Age" in Ed Ward, Geoffrey Stokes, and Ken Tucker, *Rock of Ages: The Rolling Stone History of Rock & Roll* (New York: Rolling Stone Press/Summit Books, 1986).

Index